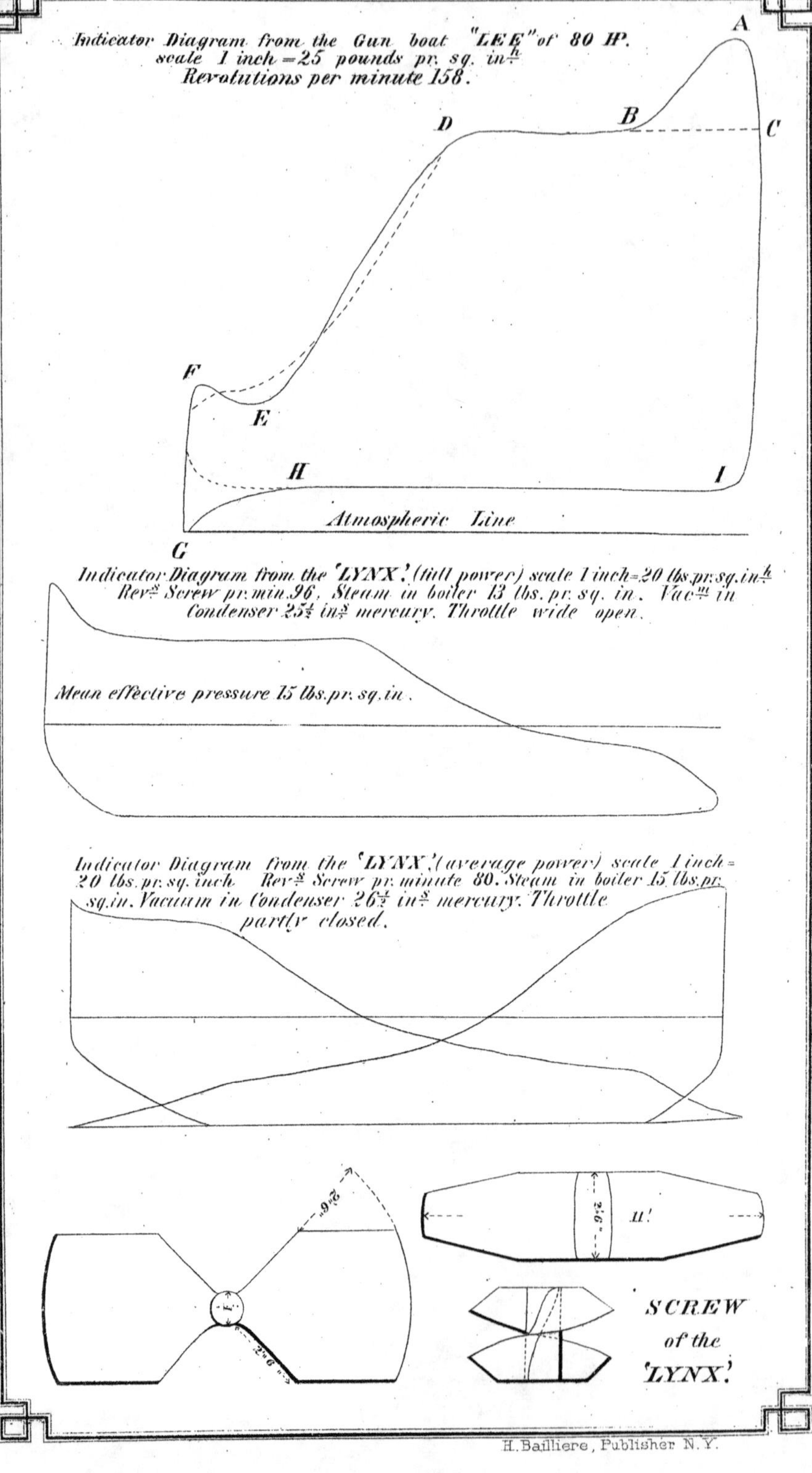

H. Bailliere, Publisher N.Y.

ENGINEERING PRECEDENTS

FOR

STEAM MACHINERY;

EMBRACING THE

PERFORMANCES OF STEAMSHIPS,

EXPERIMENTS

WITH

PROPELLING INSTRUMENTS, CONDENSERS, BOILERS, ETC.,

ACCOMPANIED BY ANALYSES OF THE SAME;

THE WHOLE BEING ORIGINAL MATTER
AND ARRANGED IN THE MOST PRACTICAL AND USEFUL MANNER

FOR ENGINEERS.

BY B. F. ISHERWOOD,
CHIEF ENGINEER U. S. NAVY.

NEW YORK:
H. BAILLIÈRE, 290 BROADWAY.
LONDON: H. BAILLIÈRE, 219 REGENT STREET.
PARIS: J. B. BAILLIÈRE ET FILS, RUE HAUTEFEUILLE.
MADRID: C. BAILLY-BAILLIÈRE, CALLE DEL PRINCIPE.

1858.

W. H. Tinson, Printer and Stereotyper, 43 & 45 Centre St., N. Y.

CONTENTS.

BRITISH GUN-BOATS IN CHINA.

BRITISH GUN-BOATS IN CHINA.

In the course of a late cruise on the southern and eastern coasts of Asia, I made many examinations of the Gun-boats employed by the British in the capture of Canton, and in other hostilities against the Chinese during the years 1857 and 1858. These Gun-boats were some of those constructed in 1856, by the Admiralty, for a projected attack upon the fortifications of Cronstadt ; as this attack was not made, their adaptation for such a purpose was not tested ; but those sent to China proved of indispensable service in the military operations on that coast, and fully established the great value of this description of vessel for littoral warfare. By the courtesy of their engineers, I examined them both in dock and afloat ; took the dimensions of their hulls and machinery, inspected their log-books, obtained many indicator diagrams from their engines, and received a candid account of their performance and general efficiency, in the various circumstances under which they had been tried.

These Gun-boats were of three classes, and were known as gun-boats of 40, 60, and 80 nominal horses power. The 60 horses power class was the original type, and the other two classes were merely variations on it. The hulls were of wood, plainly finished, and did not possess more than the usual strength given to naval steamers of their tonnage. The 40 horses power class was rigged as two-masted fore-and-aft schooners ; the 60 horses power class was rigged as three-masted fore-and-aft schooners ; the 80 horses power class was rigged as three-masted fore-topsail schooners.

A light jib-boom was carried, but the bows of all were without either cut-water or bowsprit, in order to permit the forward pivot gun to stand over the line of the keel and fire directly ahead. The hulls of all had the same beam, namely, 22 feet; but they differed in length, depth, and draught of water; those of the 40 horses power class were 109 feet 10 inches long, those of the 60 horses power class were 100 feet long, and those of the 80 horses power class were 125 feet long between perpendiculars. The water-lines of the 40 and 60 horses power classes have much fullness, the floors have little dead-rise, and the bilges are but slightly rounded. The water-lines of the 80 horses power class are sharper, the bilges better rounded, and there is more dead-rise to the floor. The load draught of water of the 40 horses power class is 6 feet; of the 60 horses power class, 7½ feet; and of the 80 horses power class, 8¼ feet.

The armament of the 40 and 60 horses power classes was the same, namely, one 8 inch shell gun of 95 cwt. (sometimes a long solid 32-pounder was substituted), pivoted on the bow; one 10 inch shell gun (sometimes an 8 inch shell gun was substituted), pivoted amidships; and two 24-pounder brass howitzers aft. The 40 horses power class was orignally intended to carry only one 10 inch shell gun. The armament of the 80 horses power class was two brass 24-pounders aft, two brass 24-pounders forward, one 10 inch shell gun pivoted amidships. When the battery was fired in the broadside direction, the vessel heeled over greatly beneath the recoil, although fitted with projecting rolling-plank on the bilges.

Each Gun-boat was officered by a lieutenant commanding, a mate, and two engineers. The crew consisted of thirty-five men. The quarters for both officers and crew were very small, and the vessels were exceedingly uncomfortable. Of course, the 80 horses power class, being the largest and fastest vessels, was decided to be the best of the three classes. The hulls of all these classes were very deficient in stability, most of them carrying, for two-thirds their length, a plank 18 or 24 inches wide projecting from their bilges at an angle of about 45 degrees with the horizon, for the purpose of lessening their excessive rolling under the recoil of their guns, as well as from the oscillation of the waves. None of the Gun-boats carried their battery at sea, their guns being transported by larger vessels. The 40 and 60 horses power classes were towed from England to China by large steamers ; the 80 horses power class sailed the distance with their screws hoisted out of water, and are said to have proved themselves good sea-boats. All the Gun-boats carried but four days' water in tank, depending entirely upon their distilling apparatus for their daily supply. The least possible quantity of provisions was carried, and the coal in bunker was limited to three and a half or four days' steaming, both on account of deficiency of space and to reduce the vessel's draught of water. The smoke pipes were hinged, in order to be laid upon the deck when the vessel was under sail alone.

The machinery of the 80 horses power class was constructed by Maudslay ; the machinery of half the 60 horses power class was also constructed by Maudslay, and that of the remaining half by Penn, who used his trunk system ; the machinery of half the 40 horses power class was constructed by Maudslay, and that of the remaining half by Penn; both builders using the same system and same dimensions. The 80 and 60 horses power classes were fitted with two engines ; the 40 horses power class had only one engine. All the engines were non-condensing, direct acting, and horizontal; and when two were used, both were placed on the same side of the keel. There was no separate expansion valve, but the steam was cut-off by lap on the steam valve, and the link motion.

The boilers, which were three in number for the 80 and 60 horses power classes, and two in number for the 40 horses power class, were all of the same type. They had cylindrical shells with flat ends ; the farther smoke connection, or uptake, was of thin iron, bolted to the shell, but not composing part of it. In the near end of each boiler was an inner cylinder of 26 inches diameter, the upper half of which was the furnace and the lower half the ash-pit. The principal heating furnace was composed of iron tubes, lying horizontally, in the same direction as the furnaces and immediately behind them ; the upper row of flues was on the same level with the tops of the furnaces. Between the furnace and near tube plate was a brick bridge 9 inches wide. The draught of the boiler depended entirely on the blast produced in the chimney by the exhaust steam from the engine ; the natural draught was so very sluggish that about four hours were required to raise steam from cold water with Welsh coal. The blast-pipe had three nozzles of different diameters, to be used as more or less steam was required, and the back pressure against the pistons, due to them and other causes, varied from 3 to 6 pounds per square inch above the atmosphere, according to the consumption of coal per hour. The farther smoke connection, or uptake, could be swept of its ashes instantaneously and very completely by a steam jet of 2 inches diameter, which drove them out of the top of the chimney ; though when this operation was performed it was necessary, for an obvious reason, to bring the wind abeam. The maximum steam pressure these boilers were intended to be worked at, was 60 pounds per square inch above the atmosphere, but the usual average was 40 pounds. At the chimney end of the boiler there was a passage with a hatch over it ; the passage was 3 feet wide to give room for sweeping the flues. A passage 21 inches wide extended also along both sides the boilers. The coal was principally stowed on both sides the engines and boilers, extending somewhat over them, and serving as a protection against shot ; the remaining portion was stowed forward of the bulkhead. The whole of the machinery, in all the vessels, lies below the water line, and the length it occupies between bulkheads is about 32 feet.

All the Gun-boats are propelled by two-bladed true screws, which are fixed with the 40 and 60 horses power classes, but hoist up with the 80 horses power class. The screw and engine shafts can be disconnected by unbolting a pair of discs ; this, however, is a slow process, and when it is desired to drag the screw revolving, the connecting-rods of the two engines are unkeyed from their crank-pins.

I will now give the dimensions of the hull and machinery of each class in detail, together with its performance.

60 Horses Power Class.

This class was the original type of Gun-boat, and the object had in view when constructing it, was to produce a vessel that could support two guns of large calibre for battering at point blank range a formidable fortress, and at the same time offer a target of the smallest possible size to the enemy. For this purpose, the vessels were to be of very small dimensions with pretty full water lines, to be low on the water, and to have so light a draught as to be able to run close in shore; as they were to receive the fire of the heaviest hostile ordnance, their machinery was to be protected by being placed below the water line, and behind the shelter of the coal-bunkers. Their steam power was to be what was necessary to carry them rapidly in and out of action, and for prompt manœuvering against wind and current. As these vessels were constructed for the sole purpose of attacking Cronstadt, and were expected to be destroyed in that service (for both officers and crews were to be volunteers), excellence of model, kind of machinery, economical application of the power, capacity to perform sea voyages of reasonable length, etc., were quite secondary considerations—very different from what they would have been, had the vessels been destined for general instead of such special service. The great considerations were, small size hull, large size ordnance—the machinery being simply that which would weigh the least, cost the least, occupy the least space, and yet be sufficient for working the vessels quickly even against the current and wind, on the few occasions it was expected to use them. The accommodations for officers and crew, and the quantity of coal and stores carried, were, for the same reason, unimportant matters. The cannon, stores, coal, etc., were to be carried to the scene of action by large screw steamers, from which the Gun-boats were to be fitted out, and sent in as bull-dogs to bait a bear. As a necessary consequence of this programme, the hulls were made with tolerably full water-lines, to give strength and displacement; the spars were made very small, and the machinery adopted was a light non-condensing engine, working at a high rotatory speed, with a steam pressure of from 50 to 60 pounds per square inch above the atmosphere, and following for two-thirds the stroke of piston. The boilers were tubular, with circular shells—simplicity, fewness of parts, and readiness of access for quick and easy repair, being the governing objects. Only 28 tons of coal were carried in the bunkers, very little water was taken in the tanks, the distilling apparatus being depended on for the daily supply; provisions and stores were also restricted to the least quantity; and then the officers and crew, limited to the fewest number, were thrust into what little space remained.

It has already been stated that the machinery of half the vessels of this class was constructed by Maudslay, and of the other half by Penn. The total weight of Maudslay's machinery including spare pieces and the water in the boilers, was 32½ tons. The dimensions of the hull will be given first, and then the dimensions of the machinery by each builder, and the performance of the vessel with it.

Dimensions of the Hull.

Length over all,	106 feet.		
Length between perpendiculars,	100 "		
Breadth of beam, extreme,	22 "		
" " molded,	21 "	2 inches.	
Depth of hold,	7 "	10 "	
Draught of water, with half coal and provisions out, Forward,	6 "	9 "	
Mean,	6 "	10½ "	
Aft,	7 "	0 "	
Deep load draft aft,	7 "	6 "	

Greatest immersed transverse section at 6 ft. 10½ ins., mean draught of water, 130 square feet.

Maudslay's Machinery.

Dimensions of the Engines.

Number of cylinders,...............	2
Diameter of the cylinders, ...	15½ inches.
Stroke of the pistons, ...	18 "
Space displacement of both pistons per stroke, ...	3.931 cubic feet.
Diameter of piston rod,.............	2 inches.
Stroke of steam valve, ...	4½ "
Lap " "	1¼ "
Area of steam port (1½ by 10 inches),.	15 square ins.
Area of exhaust port (2½ by 10 inches),	25 "
Diameter of main shaft, ...	5½ inches.
Weight of engines,.................	8 tons 14 cwt.

Dimensions of the Boilers.

Number of boilers,.................	3
Length of the cylindrical shell of the boiler,.........................	15 ft. 4 ins.
Length of the cylindrical shell of the boiler and the uptake,............	17 ft. 4 ins.
Diameter of the cylindrical shell of the boiler,.........................	4 feet.
Number of furnaces in each boiler,....	1
Breadth of grates in each furnace,....	26 inches.
Length " " "	4 ft. 6 ins.
Total grate surface in the three boilers,	29.25 square ft.
Number of iron tubes in each boiler, ..	82
Internal diameter of tubes, ...	2 inches.
Length of tubes, ...	8 feet.
Weight of each tube,................	25 lbs.
Tube surface in the three boilers,	1,030 square ft.
Heating surface other than tubes in the three boilers,..........	110 "
Total heating surface in the three boilers,	1,140 square ft.

Cross area of all the tubes,.......... 5.367 square ft.
Height of chimney above the grates, ... 24 feet.
Diameter of the chimney,........... 2 "
Weight of the three boilers complete, .. 13 tons 1 cwt.
Weight of water in the three boilers, .. 9 tons.

Dimensions of the Screw.

Diameter of the screw, ... 6 feet.
" " hub,................ 10 inches.
Pitch of the screw, ... 8 feet.
Length of the screw in the direction of its axis,......................... 16 inches.
Number of blades,.................. 2
Fraction used of the pitch,........... $\frac{1}{3}$
Area of the blades projected on a plane at right angles to axis, ... 9.243 square ft.
Helicoidal area of the blades,......... 11.270 "
Mean angle of the helicoidal surface, in function of its propelling efficiency,.. 28° .. 52′
Weight of the screw,.. 7 cwt. 2 qrs., or 840 lbs.

Performance with Maudslay's Machinery.

The following is the maximum performance in smooth water uninfluenced by wind or current :

Speed of the vessel per hour in knots of 6,086 feet, ... 8.38
Number of double strokes of piston and revolutions of the screw made per minute,..... 154
Slip of the screw in per centums of its speed,.. 31
Mean gross effective pressure on pistons in pounds per square inch, by Indicator,...... 40
Gross horses power developed, by the Indicator, 207.82
Calculated thrust of the screw in pounds,....4,552
Throttle,............................Wide open.

Steam cut-off at from commencement of stroke,	$\frac{2}{3}$
Back pressure against pistons above the atmosphere in pounds per square inch,..........	6
Steam pressure in boilers in pounds per square inch above the atmosphere,..............	55
Pounds of steam passed through the cylinders per minute, inclusive of quantity comprised between valves and pistons,..............	127.59

Distribution of the Power during the above Performance.

The following distribution of the power considers, that from the gross power developed by the engine, the power required to work the engines and shafting *per se* must be deducted, and that the remainder is the net power applied to the screw shaft. Of this net power, 7½ per centum, as determined by the experiments of Morin, is first absorbed by the friction of the load, which is an additional friction to the friction of the engine *per se*, and is directly as the load or pressure under which the engine works. Deducting this 7½ per centum from the net power, we have a remainder, part of which is absorbed in overcoming the cohesive resistance of the water to the screw surface—that is to say, the resistance which the water opposes to separation by the passage of the screw blades through it in their helical paths; this is sometimes, but erroneously called the "friction of the water on the screw blades;" it is in the direct ratio of the surface and as the square of the velocity. From collating a number of experiments, I find it to be 0.45 pound per square foot of surface, moving with a velocity of 10 feet per second; and I have calculated this loss of labor, from this data. After deducting the power required to overcome the cohesive resistance of the water to the screw surface, the remainder is divided between the power expended in the slip of the screw and in the propulsion of the vessel, and in the ratio of the speed of the slip to the speed of the vessel. The same method of calculation has been adopted for every case, and the results are therefore strictly comparable.

Proceeding, then, with the Distribution of the Power during

the above performance, and taking the pressure required to work the engines and shafting *per se* at $2\frac{1}{2}$ pounds per square inch of pistons, the power thus absorbed will be 12.99 horses.

Deducting from the total power of 207.82 horses developed by the engines this power of 12.99 horses, there remains the power of 194.83 horses applied to the shaft, of which $7\frac{1}{2}$ per centum, or 14.61 horses, is absorbed by the friction of the load.

The power required to overcome the cohesive resistance of the water to the screw surface, calculated as above set forth, is 10.31 horses.

Deducting now from the power of 194.83 horses applied to the screw shaft the powers 14.61 horses absorbed by the friction of the load, and 10.31 horses required to overcome the cohesive resistance of the water to the screw surface, there remains 169.71 horses power for the slip of the screw and the propulsion of the vessel. The slip being 31 per centum will amount to 52.67 horses power, leaving for the propulsion of the vessel 117.24 horses power.

Collecting the foregoing, we have the following distribution of the power during the performance with the Maudslay machinery, namely :

	Horses.		Per Centum.
Gross indicator power developed by the engines	207.82		
Power required to work the engines and shafting *per se*	12.99		
Net power applied to the screw shaft	194.83	or	100.00
Power absorbed by the friction of the load,	14.61	"	7.50
Power expended in overcoming the cohesive resistance of water to the screw blades,	10.31	"	5.29
Power expended in the slip of the screw,	52.67	"	27.03
Power expended in the propulsion of the vessel,	117.24	"	60.18
Totals,	194.83	or	100.00

Penn's Machinery.

Dimensions of the Engines.

Number of cylinders, ...	2
Diameter of the cylinders, ...	21 inches.
Diameter of the trunks, ...	11 "
Diameter of a plain cylinder whose area is equal to the annular area between cylinder and trunk, ...	17.888 inches.
Stroke of the pistons, ...	12 "
Space displacement of both pistons per stroke, ...	3.491 cubic feet.
Stroke of steam valve, ...	5 inches.
Lap " "	1½ "
Area of steam port (2 by 9 inches), ...	18 square inches.
" exhaust port (3¼ by 9 inches)....	29½ "
Diameter of main shaft................	5½ inches.

Dimensions of the Boilers.

Number of boilers, ...	3
Length of the cylindrical shell of the boiler,	14 feet.
Length of the cylindrical shell of the boiler and the uptake, ...	16 "
Diameter of the cylindrical shell of the boiler, ...	4 "
Number of furnaces in each boiler, ...	1
Breadth of grates in each furnace, ...	26 inches.
Length " " "	4 feet 6 inches.
Total grate surface in the three boilers...	29.25 square feet.
Number of tubes in each boiler, ...	96
Internal diameter of tubes, ...	1½ inches.
Length of tubes, ...	6 feet 8 inches.
Tube surface in the three boilers, ...	754 square feet.
Heating surface other than tubes in the three boilers, ...	110 "
Total heating surface in the three boilers,	864 "

Cross area of all the tubes,	3.514 sq. feet.
Height of chimney above the grates,	24 feet.
Diameter of the chimney,	2 "

Dimensions of the Screw.

Diameter of the Screw,	6 feet.
" " hub,	10 inches.
Pitch of the screw,	6 feet.
Length of the screw in the direction of its axis	9 inches.
Number of blades,	2
Fraction used of the pitch,	$\frac{1}{4}$th.
Area of the blades projected on a plane at right angles to axis,	6.918 sq. feet.
Helicoidal area of the blades	7.748 "
Mean angle of the helicoidal surface in function of its propelling efficiency,	21° .. $50\frac{1}{2}'$

Performance with Penn's Machinery.

The following is the maximum performance in smooth water uninfluenced by wind or current.

Speed of the vessel per hour in knots of 6086 feet,	8.26
Number of double strokes of piston and revolutions of the screw made per minute,	185
Slip of the screw in per centums of its speed,	$24\frac{1}{2}$
Mean gross effective pressure on pistons in pounds per square inch, by Indicator,	32.96
Gross horses power developed by the engines, by Indicator,	185.73
Throttle,	Wide open.
Steam cut-off at from commencement of stroke,	$\frac{2}{3}$ds.
Back pressure against pistons above the atmosphere in pounds per square inch,	6
Steam pressure in boilers in pounds per square inch above the atmosphere,	48

Pounds of steam passed through the cylinders per minute, inclusive of quantity comprised between valves and pistons,.................................. 127.74

Distribution of the Power during the above Performance.

Taking the pressure required to work the engines and shafting, *per se*, at 2½ pounds per square inch of pistons, and making the calculations precisely in the same manner as before, we have the following for the Distribution of the Power during the performance with the Penn machinery; namely :—

	Horses.	Per Centum.
Gross Indicator power developed by the engines, ...	185.73	
Power required to work the engine and shafting *per se*, ...	14.09	
Net power applied to the screw shaft,...	171.64	or 100.00
Power absorbed by the friction of the load,	12.87	7.50
Power expended in overcoming the cohesive resistance of the water to the screw blades, ...	10.03	5.84
Power expended in the slip of the screw,..	36.44	21.23
Power expended in the propulsion of the vessel, ...	112.30	65.43
Totals,..........	171.64	or 100.00

Comparison of the Performances with Maudslay's and with Penn's machinery.

The Boilers in both cases were equivalent, their type, and the number of their furnaces were the same, and although they differed in the dimensions of their tubes, which with Penn's machinery presented less surface and less cross area or calorimeter than with Maudslay's, yet as their draught was produced by an artificial blast in the chimney, whatever quantity of coal per unit of time could be burned in one case, could be burned in the other, and with about equal evaporative effect, as we perceive from the experimental results. We may therefore assume, that the weights of steam passed through the cylinders per unit of time, correctly represent the weights of coal consumed to obtain them. The point of cutting off the steam and the back pressure against the piston was the same in both cases, and as the weight of steam used governs the number of revolutions that it is possible for the screw to make, therefore, under such circumstances, equal weights of steam in the two cases will give accurately the *comparative* number of revolutions that it is possible the screws could make, and by consequence the comparative speeds of the vessel.

It will be observed, that in both cases equal weights of steam or fuel were used, while the resulting speeds were 8.38 knots per hour with Maudslay's machinery, and 8.26 knots with Penn's. We will now determine the relative quantities of steam or fuel required to give the vessel with Penn's machinery the same speed given with Maudslay's. To produce this equality of speed, the number of revolutions made by Penn's screw must be increased in the ratio of 8.26 to 8.38, when instead of 185 per minute it will become (8.26 : 185 : : 8.38 :) 187.69 ; to make which the mean gross effective pressure of 32.96 pounds per square inch must be inceased in the following manner, namely :—First deduct from it the pressure of 2½ pounds per square inch required to work the engines *per se*, then increase the remainder in the ratio of the square of the numbers (185. and 187.69) of revolutions made in equal time, and add, finally, the pressure of 2½ pounds per square inch which was at first deducted ; the sum will be the gross mean effective pressure in pounds per square inch of pistons required to make 187.69 revolutions of the screw per minute. The mean gross effective pressure required to make 185 revolutions per minute is 32.96 pounds per square inch, and deducting from it 2½ pounds there remain 30.46 pounds, which increased in the ratio of 185^2 to 187.69^2 becomes 31.34 pounds, adding to which 2½ pounds, we have, finally, 33.84 pounds for the pressure per square inch of pistons required to make 187.69 revolutions of the screw per minute. The quantity of steam used per minute to produce this pressure will be 131.51 pounds, and as there were used for Maudslay's machinery 127.59 pounds, we have finally ; that for a speed of vessel of 8.38 knots per hour, the fuel with Maudslay's and with Penn's machinery will compare as 127.59 to 131.51, or $(\frac{131.51-127.59\times100}{127.59}=)$ 3 per centum more will be required with Penn's than with Maudslay's machinery.

If, however, the comparison be made by taking the respective powers developed by the engines as the measure of the cost, and the cubes of the speeds of the vessel as the measure of the useful effects produced, we shall obtain a very different result ; because the weight of fuel consumed does not measure *pro rata* the power it produces. And this results from the facts, that while the mean effective pressure on the pistons per square inch differed much, the back pressures and friction pressures remained constant, and were consequently a higher per centage of the total or whole mean pressure used, reckoning from zero, in the case of the lower mean effective pressure than in the case of the higher. The mean effective pressure with Maudslay's machinery was $(40-2\frac{1}{2}=)$ $37\frac{1}{2}$ pounds per square inch, adding to which the pressure of $2\frac{1}{2}$ pounds required to work the engines *per se*, and the back pressure composed of the atmospheric (14.7 pounds) and of that due to the blast and steam passages (6 pounds), we have a total mean pressure reckoning from zero of $(37.5+2.5+14.7+6.0=)$ 60.7 pounds per square inch, of which the pressure usefully applied was $(\frac{37.5\times100}{60.7}=)$ 61.78 per centum. With Penn's machinery, the mean effective pressure was $(32.96-2.50=)$ 30.46 pounds per square inch, adding to which the pressure required to work the engines *per se*, and the back pressure composed of the atmospheric (14.7 pounds) and of that due to the blast and steam passages (6 pounds), we have a total mean pressure reckoning from zero of $(30.46+2.50+14.70+6.00=)$ 53.66 pounds per square inch, of which the pressure usefully applied was only 56.76 per centum instead of the 61.78 per centum as before with Maudslay's machinery. This difference is due entirely to the *pressures* employed, and is purely a question of capacity of cylinder ; for if Penn had used a cylinder of as much less capacity than the one he did use as the mean pressure in it was less than the mean pressure in Maudslay's cylinder, this difference would entirely disappear and without affecting the power developed by the engine ; for the same quantity of steam being passed through the cylinders in both cases in equal times, the resulting powers would be the same, because the products of the space displacement of the piston per stroke and the pressure on it would in both cases be the same.

Independently too, of the loss of fuel due to the relation of the pressures, there was more steam lost in the clearance and valve passages of Penn's cylinder, owing to their greater bulk in proportion to the bulk of space displaced by its piston per stroke, than with Maudslay's cylinder. Also, the quantity of steam consumed in working the engines *per se*, was greater with Penn's than with Maudslay's ; because the *pressure* for this purpose being for both the same $2\frac{1}{2}$ pounds per square inch, the quantity of steam thus used would be as much greater with Penn's engine than with Maudslay's, as the product of the space displacement per stroke and the number of double strokes made per minute by he pistons of the former exceeded the similar product with the latter ; that is to say, the respective quantities of steam consumed in working the engines *per se*, was in the ratio of ($3.491 \times 185 =$) 645.835 for Penn's to ($3.931 \times 154 =$) 605.374 for Maudslay's.

Having thus ascertained the relative economical efficiencies of Maudslay's and Penn's machinery considered as a whole, in rapport of fuel, and discovered the causes of the differences ; there remains to ascertain the relative economical efficiencies in function of the net power applied to the screw shaft ; that is, of the power which remains after deducting from the gross horses power developed by the engines, the power required to work them *per se*. For this purpose, these net powers will be taken as the measure of the cost, and the cubes of the respective speeds of vessel as the measure of the useful effects produced; and the results will be as follows, namely :

Net horses power applied to the screw shaft.	SPEEDS OF VESSEL IN KNOTS PER HOUR.	Relative economical efficiencies of the screw.
	MAUDSLAY.	
194.83 or 1.13511	8.38 or 1.01453, and $1.01453^3=1.04422$, and $\frac{1.04422}{1.13511}=$	0.91993
	PENN.	
171.64 or 1.00000	8.26 or 1.00000, and $1.00000^3=1.00000$, and $\frac{1.00000}{1.00000}=$	1.00000

Hence we see, that the application of the *power* by Penn's *screw* was better than by Maudslay's in the ratio of 1.00000 to 0.91993, or say 8 per centum ; thus reversing the result given when the comparison was made in rapport of *fuel*, in which case Maudlay's *machinery as a whole* gave an economical efficiency 3 per centum greater than Penn's.

Of the net power applied to the screw shaft in Maudslay's machinery, there was uselessly expended by the screw in overcoming the cohesive resistance of the water to its passage 5.29 per centum ; with Penn's screw, this useless expenditure of power was 5.84 per centum, or sensibly the same ; but the loss of useful effect by the slip of the screw, which, with Maudslay's, amounted to 27.03 per centum of the net power applied to the shaft, was, with Penn's, only 21.23 per centum.

It must here be remarked that the foregoing comparison has been made for steaming in smooth water and a calm ; if, however, the resistance to the propelling effort of the screw be increased by a rough sea, a head wind, or by towing another vessel, the slips of the two screws would be increased in the ratio of that increased resistance ; for example : suppose that from either of the causes mentioned, the resistance to the propelling effort of the screw be increased one-third—a common case when steaming against a moderate head breeze and swell—then the 31 per centum slip of Maudslay's screw would become ($31\times1\frac{1}{3}=$) $41\frac{1}{3}$ per centum, while the $24\frac{1}{2}$ per centum slip of Penn's screw would become only ($24\frac{1}{2}\times1\frac{1}{3}=$) $32\frac{2}{3}$ per centum ;

and Penn's machinery, owing to the better proportions of its screw, would become decisively superior to Maudslay's whichever way the calculation was made, either by fuel, gross, or net powers expended. The relative economical efficiencies of two screws as determined by a trial in smooth water and a calm, may be either exaggerated or reversed by a trial at sea under the conditions of wind and wave usually found there.

The 60 horses power class of vessels will steam steadily at sea in good weather, with an average speed of 6¾ knots per hour, cutting off by lap and the link motion at half stroke, and consuming 8 tons of Welsh coal per 24 hours; at which rate they carry just 3½ days' supply of coal in their bunkers, and make a voyage of 567 nautical miles.

40 Horses Power Class.

The draught of water of the 60 horses power class Gun-boats being found too great for certain descriptions of service, such as where oared boats had to be pursued close in shore and up shallow streams; it was determined to build a class of the least possible draught of water, and to that end all other considerations were to be sacrificed. The battery was to be reduced to a single 10 inch pivot shell gun; the spars to two jury-masts with fore and aft sail, and a very light jib-boom; and the machinery to a single engine of 40 nominal horses power supplied with steam from two boilers only, the bunkers stowing but 22 tons of coal. The hull, to gain the necessary additional displacement for lightening the draught, was made 9 feet ten inches longer between perpendiculars than the hull of the 60 horses power class; the depth of hold was also lessened, but the same beam was preserved. The original intention was so far departed from, however, as regards battery, as to increase it to the same as the 60 horses power class. The 40 horses power class, owing to the enormous slip of its screw and consequent great waste of its power, possessed but little speed; and the comfort of the persons embarked was of course much less than on board the other classes ; it has naturally been condemned as the worst of the Gun-boat species, as indeed it is for all service where the other classes can be employed ; but its draught of water is much less, and it can penetrate where they cannot.

Dimensions of the Hull.

Length over all, ...	116 feet.
Length between perpendiculars, ...	109 feet 10 inches.
Breadth of beam, extreme, ...	22 feet.
Mean draught of water with half coal and provisions out, ...	5 feet 3 inches.
Deep load draught of water. Forward, .	5 " 6 "
Mean, ...	5 " 9 "
Aft, ...	6 " 0 "
Greatest immersed transverse section at 5 feet 3 inches mean draught of water, ...	95 square feet.

Dimensions of the Engine.

Number of cylinders, ...	1
Diameter of the cylinder, ...	21 inches.
Stroke of the piston, ...	12 "
Space *displacement* of the piston per stroke,	2.405 cubic feet.
Diameter of piston rod, ...	2¾ inches.
Diameter of main shaft, ...	5½ "

Dimensions of the Boilers.

Number of boilers, ...	2
Length of the cylindrical shell of the boiler,	14 feet.
Length of the cylindrical shell of the boiler and the uptake, ...	16 "
Diameter of the cylindrical shell of the boiler, ...	4 "
Number of furnaces in each boiler, ...	1

Breadth of grates in each furnace,.......	26 inches.
Length " " "	4 feet 6 inches.
Total grate surface in the two boilers,....	19.50 sq. feet.
Number of tubes in each boiler,.........	96
Internal diameter of tubes,.............	1½ inch.
Length of tubes,.....................	6 feet 8 inches.
Tube surface in the two boilers,.........	503 square feet.
Heating surface other than tubes in the two boilers,......................	73 "
Total heating surface in the two boilers,..	576 "
Cross area of all the tubes,.............	2.342 "
Height of chimney above the grates,.....	22 feet.
Diameter of the chimney,..............	2 feet 9 inches.

Dimensions of the Screw.

Diameter of the screw,................	4 feet 9 inches.
" " hub,................	9 inches.
Pitch of the screw,...................	6 feet.
Length of the screw in the direction of its axis............................	9 inches.
Number of blades,....................	2
Fraction used of the pitch,.............	¼th.
Mean angle of the helicoidal surface in function of its propelling efficiency,.....	26° 52′
Area of the blades projected on a plane at right angles to axis,................	4.320 sq. feet.
Helicoidal area of the blades,...........	5.111 "

Performance.

The following is the maximum performance in smooth water uninfluenced by wind or current :

Mean draught of vessel,...............	5 feet 9 inches.
Speed of the vessel per hour in knots of 6,086 feet........................	6.2

Number of double strokes of piston and revolutions of the screw made per minute,	210
Slip of the screw in per centum of its speed, ...	50
Mean gross effective pressure on pistons in pounds per square inch, by indicator,...	27.4
Gross horses power developed by the engines, by indicator, ...	119.71
Throttle,............................	Wide open,
Steam cut-off at from commencement of stroke,............................	$\frac{2}{3}$ds.
Back pressure against pistons above the atmosphere in pounds per square inch, .	6
Steam pressure in boilers in pounds per square inch above the atmosphere,.....	44
Pounds of steam passed through the cylinders per minute,......................	85
Calculated thrust of the screw in pounds,.	2,492

Distribution of the Power during the above Performance.

Taking the pressure required to work the engines and shafting *per se* at 2½ pounds per square inch of pistons, and making the calculations in precisely the same manner as before, we have the following for the distribution of the power during the performance of the 40 horses power class, namely :

	HORSES.	PER CENTUM.
Gross indicator power developed by the engines, ...	119.71	
Power required to work the engines and shafting *per se*, ...	10.93	
Net power applied to the screw shaft,....	108.78 or	100.00

Power absorbed by the friction of the load,	8.1	or	7.50
Power expended in overcoming the cohesive resistance of the water to the screw blades, ...	5.62	"	5.16
Power expended in the slip of the screw,..	47.50	or	43.67
Power expended in the propulsion of the vessel,...........................	47.50	"	43.67
Totals, ...	108.78	"	100.00

80 Horses Power Class.

It was finally determined to construct a superior class of Gun-boats which, while preserving the same beam as the others, should differ from them by having much sharper water lines, greater length and depth of hull, and greater draught of water. The Gun-boats of this class were to be propelled by engines whose power should exceed that of the other classes in a higher ratio than the increased resistance of hull, in order to secure a higher speed. Their screws were to hoist up, so that the vessel could make long voyages under sail alone ; for which purpose they were rigged as three masted fore-topsail schooners, with much more canvas in proportion than the other classes ; but they were so deficient in stability as to require a plank of 18 or 24 inches width, and extending along about two-thirds the length of the hull, to be projected from just above the turn of the bilge at an angle of 45 degrees from the horizon, to check their excessive rolling in a sea-way, and from the reaction of their battery when fired in broadside. There were but four Gun-boats of this class, namely : the "Algerine," the "Slaney," the "Lee," and the "Lieven." They made the voyage from England to China under sail alone, with their screws hoisted up, but without their ordnance on board, which was sent out in larger vessels. In this condition they were reported to be good sea boats and fast sailers. They carry 50 tons of coal in their bunkers. This class of Gun-boats were much praised for their good qualities, and gave entire satisfaction.

Dimensions of the Hull.

Length over all,	132 feet.
Length between perpendiculars,	125 "
Breadth of beam, extreme,	22 "
Draught of water with half coal and provisions out, — Forward,	7 feet 6 inches.
Mean,	7 " 9 "
Aft,	8 " 0 "
Deep load draught,	8 " 3 "
Greatest immersed transverse section at 7 feet 9 inches mean draught,	142 square feet.

Dimensions of the Engines.

Number of cylinders,	2
Diameter of the cylinders,	18 inches.
Stroke of the pistons,	18 "
Space displacement of both pistons per stroke,	5.301 cub. feet
Diameter of piston rod,	$2\frac{1}{4}$ inches.
Diameter of main shaft,	$5\frac{1}{2}$ "

Dimensions of the Boilers.

Number of boilers,	3
Length of the cylindrical shell of the boiler,	16 feet 2 inches.
Length of the cylindrical shell of the boiler and the uptake,	17 " 6 "
Diameter of the cylindrical shell of the boiler,	4 " 6 "
Number of furnaces in each boiler,	1
Breadth of grates in each boiler,	30 inches.
Length of grates in each furnace,	5 feet.
Total grate surface in the three boilers,	39.50 sq. feet.
Number of tubes in each boiler,	109
Internal diameter of tubes,	2 inches.

Length of Tubes,	8 feet 1½ inch.
Tube surface in the three boilers,	1,391 square feet.
Heating surface other than tubes in the three boilers,	142 "
Total heating surface in the three boilers,	1,533 "
Cross area of all the tubes	7.134 "
Height of chimney above the grates,	25 feet.
Diameter of the chimney,	30 inches.

Dimensions of the Screw.

Diameter of the screw,	6 feet 6 inches.
Diameter of the hub,	7 inches.
Pitch of the screw,	8 feet.
Length of the screw in the direction of its axis,	16 inches.
Number of blades,	2
Fraction used of the pitch,	⅓d.
Mean angle of the helicoidal surface in function of its propelling efficiency,	26° 16′
Area of the blades projected on a plane at right angles to axis,	10.794 sq. feet.
Helicoidal area of the blades,	13.247 "

Performance.

The following is the performance in smooth water, uninfluenced by wind or current:

Mean draught of vessel,	7 feet 9 inches.
Speed of the vessel per hour in knots of 6,086 feet,	9.27
Number of double strokes of piston and revolutions of the screw made per minute,	161
Slip of the screw in per centum of its speed,	27
Mean gross effective pressure on pistons in pounds per square inch, by indicator,	42.8

Gross horses power developed by the engines, by indicator, ...	316.35
Throttle, ...	Wide open.
Steam cut-off at from commencement of stroke, ...	$\frac{5}{8}$ths.
Back pressure against pistons above the atmosphere, in pounds per square inch, .	6
Steam pressure in boilers in pounds per square inch above the atmosphere,.....	60
Pounds of steam passed through the cylinders per minute,....................	169.42
Calculated thrust of the screw in pounds,.	6,570

Distribution of the Power during the above Performance.

Taking the pressure required to work the engines and shafting *per se* at 2½ pounds per square inch of pistons, and making the calculations in precisely the same manner as before, we have the following for the distribution of the power during the performance of the 80 horses power class, namely :

	Horses.		Per Centum.
Gross Indicator power developed by the engines, ...	316.35		
Power required to work the engines and shafting *per se*,....................	18.33		
Net power applied to the screw shaft,...	298.02	or	100.00
Power absorbed by the friction of the load,......................... ..	22.35	"	7.50
Power expended in overcoming the cohesive resistance of the water to the screw blades,..........................	19.24	"	6.46
Power expended in the slip of the screw,	69.24	"	23.23
Power expended in the propulsion of the vessel, ...	187.19	"	62.81
Totals, ...	298.02	or	100.00

The average performance when steaming steadily at sea in good weather is as follows ; namely—

Consumption of Welsh coal, in tons, per 24 hours,..	12
Speed of the vessel per hour, in knots of 6,086 feet,..	$7\frac{3}{4}$
Number of double strokes of engines, piston and revolutions of the screw made per minute,...........	130
Steam cut-off at by lap and link motion, from commencement of stroke of piston,................	$\frac{1}{2}$

At the above rate of steaming, the bunkers carry four days' supply of coal, and the vessel can make with it a voyage of 746 nautical miles.

The Machinery of the Gun-boats, though well made, and by the best builders, was constantly out of order. Both Boilers and Engines gave continual trouble ; the first from the use of high pressure steam and sea water ; the last from the high rotatory velocity employed. In fact, the rotary speed of the Engines was so great that it was impossible to keep them in order. During the hostilities at and around Canton, the English established a shop on shore at Hongkong for repairing ; they also had at the same place the floating workshop "Volcano," sent out from England completely fitted up with tools and power for doing a large amount of casting, forging and finishing ; and both these establishments were kept constantly employed on the Gun-boats, there being, out of about fifteen, usually a couple undergoing repair ; in fact the repairs upon them were enormous. For economy of fuel, durability, and reliability as war vessels for constant use, the machinery of these Gun-boats cannot be recommended, however well adapted to the momentary purpose for which they were constructed.

In the following Table will be found a Résumé of the principal facts concerning these Gun-boats that are of interest to the Engineer ; and as the battery of all was about the same, a simple inspection will show the relative efficiency of the different Classes carrying the same armament at different speeds with different draughts of water, and the relative cost of the same in power and fuel.

RESUME of the Dimensions of the Hulls and Screws of the Different Classes Gun-boats; and of the Results obtained in Rapport of Speed, Power, Distribution of the Power, and Economical application of the same.

CLASS.	Maximum speed per hour in smooth water uninfluenced by wind or current; in knots of 6,086 feet,...........	DIMENSIONS OF THE HULLS.					POWER. ABSOLUTE QUANTITIES.					POWER. RELATIVE ECONOMICAL EFFICIENCIES.			POWER. DISTRIBUTION OF THE NET POWER APPLIED TO THE SCREW SHAFT; IN PER CENTUM.				SCREWS.	SCREWS. DIMENSIONS.					
		Length between perpendiculars; in feet,........	Extreme breadth; in feet,.....................	Mean draught of water; in feet, ...	Greatest immersed transverse section; in square feet, ...	Relative resistances of the Hulls,...............	Mean gross effective pressure on Piston; in pounds per square inch, ...	Mean back pressure (including atmosphere) against Piston; in pounds per square inch,	Gross horses power developed by the Engines; per Indicator,..................	Net horses power applied to the screw shaft; per Indicator,...	Pounds of Steam passed through the Cylinders per minute (representing Fuel),.....	In Rapport of gross horses power developed by the engines,.........................	In Rapport of Net horses power applied to the screw shaft, ...	In Rapport of weight of steam consumed,..	In overcoming the Friction of the Load,...	In overcoming the cohesive resistance of the water to the passage of the screw surface,.....................................	In the Slip of the Screw,...................	In the Propulsion of the Vessel,...........	Slip of the Screws in per centum of their speeds,..	Diameter; in feet......................	Pitch; in feet,........................	Fraction used of the Pitch,...............	Helicoidal area; in square feet, ...	Projected area in square feet, on a plane at right angles to axis,...................	Mean angle of the Helicoidal surface with the plane of the diameter, in function of surface and of its propelling efficiency,..
60 Horses Power (Maudslay's Machinery), ..	8.38	100	22	6.875	130	1.000	40.00	20.7	207.82	194.83	127.59	0.93315	0.91993	1.04536	7.50	5.29	27.03	60.18	31.0	6	8	⅓	11.270	9.243	28° .. 52′
Ditto, (Penn's Machinery),......	8.26	100	22	6.875	130	1.000	32.96	20.7	185.73	171.64	127.74	1.00000	1.00000	1.00000	7.50	5.84	21.23	65.43	24.5	6	6	¼	7.748	6.918	22° .. 50½′
40 Horses Power, ...	6.20	109⅝	22	5.250	95	1.000	27.40	20.7	119.71	108.78	85.00	0.65611	0.667262	0.63553	7.50	5.16	43.67	43.67	50.0	4¾	6	¼	5.111	4.320	26° .. 52′
80 Horses Power,.....	9.27	125	22	7.750	142	1.179	42.80	20.7	316.35	298.02	169.42	0.97847	0.95987	1.25661	7.50	6.46	23.23	62.81	27.0	6½	8	⅓	13.247	10.794	26° .. 16′

To face page 30.

The calculations of the "Relative Economical Efficiencies" have been made by taking the product of the cubes of the speeds and the "Relative Resistances of the Hull" for the measure of the effects produced, and, respectively, the "Gross Horses power developed by the Engines," the "Net Horses power applied to the Screw Shaft," and the "Weight of Steam consumed" in equal times, for the measure of the costs. The higher the numbers, the greater the efficiency they express.

In the case of "Weight of Steam consumed," though it will not—owing to certain considerations connected with the working of the engine, and the back pressure on its steam piston—require weights in the ratio of the cubes of the speed to raise a lower speed to a higher one, as is the ratio with *power*, yet, as the resistance of the same vessel is as the square of its speed, and as the weight of the steam consumed in each case was the maximum the boilers could furnish, it is fair to compare its effect with the cube of the speed it produced.

In fact, the weight of steam, *cæteris paribus*, required to propel a vessel at different speeds, is *always* in a much lower ratio than the cubes of the speeds. The actual ratio is variable, as it is the resultant of several variable elements ; it depends on the ratio of the back pressure plus the pressure required to work the engines *per se* to the total mean gross pressure on the piston, reckoning from zero, and on the relative excellence of the application of the power by the screw. And it frequently happens, as we perceive in the annexed Table, that the relative economical efficiency "In Rapport of weight of Steam consumed" is so far from being the same as "In Rapport of Net Horses Power applied to the Screw shaft," that it may be greatly the reverse. And in this connection the Table makes very apparent the advantage of employing a high "Mean gross effective pressure," because the "Back pressure" with all the different Classes of Gun-boats being the same, it is found that, in three out of the four cases, the efficiency "In Rapport of weight of Steam consumed" is greater with the higher "Mean gross effective pressure on piston" than with the lower, and that the efficiency in rapport of power is thereby reversed, notwithstanding that the lower is applied by a screw of better proportions. In the fourth case, where the proportions of the screw were most defective, and where the mean gross effective pressure was also the lowest, the relative economical efficiency in rapport of steam or fuel consumed is lower than in rapport of power.

The "Relative Economical Efficiencies" in the case of *Powers* result entirely from their application by the Screws; consequently those columns express also, the relative excellence of the screws as transmitters usefully of the power applied to them. Now the losses of useful effect by the screw are the powers expended in its slip and in overcoming the cohesive resistance of the water to the movement of the helicoidal surface; the latter, it will be observed, is nearly the same with all; hence, we are to consider the difference in the economical efficiencies in rapport of power as resulting almost wholly from the difference of *slip*, the less slip giving the higher efficiency.

Under the head of "Relative Resistances of the Hulls," it will be seen that, although those of the 60 and 40 Horses Power Classes differed in length and in draught of water, yet their resistance was the same, the additional length being compensated by the less draught. The 80 Horses Power Class, though 25 per centum longer than the 60 Horses Power and drawing nearly 13 per centum more water, had only 18 per centum more resistance.

The relative resistances of the hulls are determined from their speeds and from the horses power expended in their propulsion at those speeds, as found under the head of "Distribution of the Power." For it is obvious, that any speed being assumed for all, and the horses power usefully expended in the propulsion of the simple hulls at the different experimental speeds being increased or diminished in the ratio of the cubes of those speeds to the cube of the assumed speed, the different powers thus obtained will express directly the different resistances of the respective hulls.

INDICATOR DIAGRAM.

THE Indicator Diagram, Fig. 7, from the Gun-boat "LEE," of 80 nominal horses power, shows the general distribution of the pressure for all the Gun-boats, and strikingly exhibits the irregularities that occur from high speeds. It will be observed that the valve opens both steam and exhaust ports at about the end of the stroke, the expansion curve following nearly to the end of the stroke before the exhaust takes place, and the cushioning at the opposite extremity being hardly perceptible. The reader must bear in mind that the engine piston is making 158 double strokes of 18 inches each per minute, and that there is a very considerable steam pressure upon the sensitive spring of the Indicator piston. In the boiler this pressure was 60 pounds per square inch, and in the cylinder 55 pounds per square inch above the atmosphere.

The first irregularity occurs at A and is caused by the momentum of the moving parts of the Indicator suddenly thrown up by a pressure of 55 pounds per square inch, and the slope of the line from A to B is the resultant of the rapid travel of the steam piston while the Indicator piston is rebounding from A. There is no pressure in the cylinder answering to this slope, the true pressure is simply as shown by the dotted line from B to C. From B to D the pressure remains uniform, and at D the steam port is closed by the lap of the valve and expansion commences. From the point D, where the steam piston has its maximum velocity (about 900 feet per minute) the pressure falls more rapidly than the Indicator piston follows, and the result is, that the momentum of the latter carries it below the proper level, just as it previously carried it above, and the pencil descends to E, whence it rebounds, and the resultant of its vertical and longitudinal movement produces the slope line EF. At F the exhaust suddenly takes place, and again the momentum of the Indicator piston becomes apparent in its descent to G—too low—whence it rebounds to H, and follows thence parallel to the atmospheric line to I, where the steam is again admitted.

The true Indicator diagram is shown by the dotted lines; the divergencies from it of the diagram, as actually taken by the Indicator, are referable solely to the momentum of the moving parts of the Indicator combined with the great velocity of the steam piston.

BRITISH DISPATCH SCREW STEAMER

"L Y N X."

BRITISH DISPATCH SCREW STEAMER
"LYNX."

THE "LYNX" is one of the 3d class Dispatch vessels built about 1854 by the British Admiralty, and employed as Tenders for small squadrons of sailing ships, and particularly for the suppression of the slave trade on the western coast of Africa, in the Mozambique Channel, and among the West India islands. In such service they have proved eminently useful. The "LYNX" was at Simon's Bay, South Africa, in July, 1858, where the writer saw her and obtained from her Chief Engineer the following information.

She was originally intended to have very high speed and to be employed in the Russian war. Her boilers, which were very large, were of two kinds ; one was low, lying wholly beneath the water line and was the only one to be used in battle ; the other, much higher, rose above the water line and was to be used together with the low boiler when high speed was required in carrying dispatches, etc. With this arrangement the machinery occupied so much room that but very little fuel could be carried after the military portion of the vessel was provided for ; and when the "LYNX" was to be employed on distant service, it was found necessary to remove the high boiler and use the space vacated for the stowage of coal. With this additional room the bunkers contain 69 tons, which is sufficient for only $6\frac{1}{4}$ days' average steaming at sea. It is stowed along the sides and over the top of the boiler. Ten days' supply of water is carried in tanks, and the distilling apparatus is depended on for the rest.

The vessel has a light barque rig, the screw hoists up through a well in the usual manner, and the steam power is very sparingly used—never except in cases of emergency, as pursuing slavers, entering or leaving port with dispatches against a head wind, etc. ; but the passage between ports is *always* made under canvas alone in the same manner as an ordinary sailing vessel.

The original war battery consisted of two 68-pounders mounted on pivots amidships between the fore and main masts, and two brass 24-pounder howitzers. The present battery is one 32-pounder amidship on pivot and four brass 24-pounder howitzers in broadside.

The present personnel consists of 65 souls ; the officers are a Lieutenant commanding, two Mates, a 2d Master, a Master's Assistant, an Assistant Surgeon, an Assistant Paymaster, a Gunner, and three Assistant Engineers, the Senior acting as Chief. The two Mates, the 2d Master, and the Master's Assistant are watch officers.

The hull is of wood and has very sharp water lines and much dead rise to the floor ; it rolls so much at sea and heels over so much under fire as to require horizontally projecting planks along the bilges to check the movement.

The vibratory movement of the stern is excessive when the engines are working, so much so that it is impossible to write on board ; and this movement is the most violent when the screw is making between 50 and 70 revolutions per minute; below and above these numbers it is not so great.

The boiler is altogether too small to properly supply the engine with steam and its draught is sluggish ; it is, in fact, only half enough boiler, the other half having been removed. In order to burn 11 tons of coal per 24 hours the draught has to be increased by a strong steam jet in the chimney, under which circumstances 23½ per centum of the cylinders can be filled with steam of 12 pounds initial pressure, the boiler pressure being 15 pounds, and the number of double strokes of piston made per minute 80. This is the maximum that can be constantly maintained, though steam enough can be generated for a short time, under favorable circumstances, to carry the revolutions of the screw up to 96 per minute.

Dimensions of the Hull.

Length between perpendiculars,		165 feet.
Extreme beam,		26 feet.
Deep load draught	Forward,	11 feet.
	Mean,	11½ feet.
	Aft,	12 feet.
Greatest immersed transverse section,		238 sq. feet.
Resistance of the hull at a speed of 8.4 knots per hour, calculated from the power propelling it,		6,799 pounds.

Dimensions of the Engines.

Two direct acting Trunk engines by PENN. The steam valve is a packed slide and cuts off the steam by lap and the link motion. There is no separate cut-off valve.

Diameter of the cylinders,	39 inches.
Diameter of the Trunks,	17 inches.
Diameter of a plain cylinder of equal area,	$35\frac{1}{10}$ inches.
Area of one piston,	967.61 sq. inches.
Stroke of pistons,	20 inches.
Space displacement of both pistons per stroke,	22.40 cubic feet.

Dimensions of the Boiler.

There is one tubular boiler with furnaces at both ends; it is fired from two fire rooms, one forward and the other abaft the boiler. The tubes, instead of being placed above, are on the same level with the furnaces, and the whole boiler is below the water line. There are two furnaces at each end of the boiler, and the tubes are returned by their sides and between them. The smoke chimney is placed at the forward end of the boiler, and the after furnaces discharge into it through a narrow passage or deep flue lying between their tube boxes. The shell of the boiler has partitions in the water part, but the steam room is one space. The partitions are necessary in so wide a boiler athwartship for a sea-going vessel on account of the heeling over under canvas, and the excessive rolling.

The tubes are put in with ferrules, and the boiler requires the constant use of a strong steam jet in the chimney to supply the engines.

Total number of furnaces,	4
Width of the fire grates,	2 feet 6 inches.
Length of the fire grates,	6 " 3 "
Total area of fire grate surface,	62½ square feet.
Total number of tubes,	288
Internal diameter of the tubes,	2¼ inches.
Length of the tubes,	6 feet 6 inches.
Total area of tube surface,	1,225 square feet.
Total cross area of tubes inside of ferrules,	6.28 "

Dimensions of the Screw.

One true screw of brass of the outline of blade shown in Fig. 4, which exhibits an end view of it. It is cut to this shape to render it narrow enough to hoist up through the well. At the deep load draught of water, the apex of the upper blade, when vertical, projects 6 inches above the water line.

Diameter of the screw,	11 feet.
Diameter of the hub,	1 foot.
Pitch,	9 feet 8 inches.
Length of the screw in the direction of the axis,	2 " 5 "
Number of blades,	2
Mean fraction used of the pitch in function of area and propelling efficiency,	0.415
Projected area of the blades on a plane at right angles to axis,	36.50 sq. feet.

Helicoidal area of the blades,........... 44.70 sq. feet.
Mean angle of the blades from the plane of rotation and in function of area and propelling efficiency,................... $25\frac{1}{2}°$

§ *Performance in Smooth Water.*

The following is the maximum performance in smooth water, uninfluenced by wind or current, at a measured mile, the vessel being at her deep load draught:

Speed of the vessel per hour in geographical miles of 6,086 feet, ... 8.4
Number of double strokes of engines' pistons and of revolutions of the screw made per minute,........................ 96
Slip of the screw in per centum of its speed, 8.19
Mean gross effective pressure on the pistons in pounds per square inch; by Indicator, 15
Gross horses power developed; by Indicator, 281.49
Steam pressure in boiler in pounds per square inch above atmosphere,........ 13
Steam cut-off at from commencement of stroke of piston,.................... 0.47
Vacuum in condensers per gauge in inches of mercury,........................ $25\frac{1}{2}$
Calculated thrust of the screw,.........6,799 pounds.

Distribution of the Power during the above Performance.

Taking the pressure required to work the engines *per se* at $1\frac{1}{2}$ pound per square inch of pistons, the power thus absorbed will amount to 28.15 horses, which deducted from the 281.49 gross horses power developed by the engines, leaves 253.34 horses power applied to the screw shaft.

Of this 253.34 horses power, $7\frac{1}{2}$ per centum or 19.00 horses power, was expended in overcoming the friction of the load.

The power required to overcome the cohesive resistance of the water to the passage of the screw surface through it, calculated for a value of 0.45 pound per square foot of helicoidal surface, moving in its helical path with a velocity of 10 feet per second, and modified in the ratio of the square of the velocity, amounts to 43.13 horses power.

Deducting from the power of 253.34 horses applied to the screw shaft, the powers 19.00 and 43.13 horses expended in overcoming the friction of the load and the cohesive resistance of the water, there remains 191.21 horses power, of which 8.19 per centum, or 15.66 horses power, was expended in the slip of the screw, leaving the remaining 175.55 horses power applied to the propulsion of the hull.

Collecting the foregoing, we have the following distribution of the power, namely :

	Horses.		Per Centum.
Gross power developed by the engines, . . .	281.49		
Power expended in working the engines *per se*, . . .	28.15		
Net power applied to the screw shaft, ...	253.34	or	100.00
Power expended in overcoming the friction of the load, . . .	19.00	"	7.50
Power expended in overcoming the cohesive resistance of the water to the screw surface, . . .	43.13	"	17.02
Power expended in the slip of the screw, . .	15.66	"	6.18
Power expended in the propulsion of the hull,	175.55	"	69.30
Totals, . . .	253.34	or	100.00

In observing the above "Distribution of the Power," the first thing that strikes us is the excessive loss of useful effect from the cohesive resistance of the water to the screw surface, which amounts to 17.02 per centum of the "net power applied to the screw shaft," while the loss by slip is only 6.18 per centum. In general, it will be found, that as one of these losses is decreased, the other must necessarily increase, but not in any fixed ratio, as it depends entirely on the proportions of the screw. The most advantageous method of reducing the *sum* of these losses, when the slip, as in the present case, is small, is to reduce the fraction used of the pitch; that is to say, to reduce the length of the screw; for, *ceteris paribus*, a reduction of one-half in the length of the screw increases its slip only one-seventh, while it decreases the loss from the cohesive resistance of the water one-half. In the case of the "LYNX," the sum of the losses by the screw are (17.02+6.10=) 23.02 per centum of the net power, the fraction of pitch used being 0.415. Suppose, now, this fraction reduced to 0.200, then the slip would be increased from 8.19 per centum of its speed to 9.43 per centum, and its loss of useful effect would, instead of 6.18 per centum of the net power, be 7.11 per centum, while the loss from the cohesive resistance of the water would fall from 17.02 to 8.53 per centum of the net power, including the effect due to the greater velocity of rotation to give the same speed of vessel. Hence, with this simple modification, the sum of the losses by the screw instead of being 23.20 per centum as before, would only be (7.11+8 53=) 15.64 per centum, leaving (23.20−15.64=) 7.56 per centum additionally to be applied usefully to the propulsion of the vessel. The screw is then very faulty in employing too large (0.415) a fraction of its pitch.

The above results are strictly true as regards the "Distribution of the *Net Power*;" but as regards the fuel or steam consumed, a slight reduction must be made for the greater power absorbed in working the engines *per se*, when the slip of the screw is greater; because the *pressure* required for this purpose being constant (1½ pounds per square inch), the *power* will be in the direct ratio of the number of double strokes of engine piston made in equal times, and with greater slip more double strokes must be made to give the vessel equal speed. In the case of the "LYNX," the proposed modification of the screw would increase the number of double strokes of piston from 96 to 99.84 per minute, and the power thus absorbed from 28.15 to 29.27 horses, the difference being only 1.12 horse power.

§ *Performance at Sea.*

The following is the average performance that can be maintained at sea with full steam power, unassisted by sail, and under the ordinary conditions of practice:

Speed of the vessel per hour in geographical miles of 6,086 feet, ...	6.4
Number of double strokes of engine's pistons and of revolutions of the screw made per minute, ...	80
Slip of the screw in per centum of its speed,	12.28
Mean gross effective pressure in pounds per square inch of pistons ; by Indicator, ...	12.4
Gross horses power developed by the engines; by Indicator, ...	193.97
Steam pressure in boiler in pounds per square inch above atmosphere, ...	15
Steam cut-off at from commencement of stroke of piston, ...	0.235
Vacuum in the condensers in inches of mercury, ...	$26\frac{1}{2}$
Consumption of best Welsh steam coal in tons per 24 hours, ...	11

Making the calculations as before, we have the following:

Distribution of the Power during the above Performance.

	Horses.		Per Centum.
Gross power developed by the engines, ...	193.97		
Power expended in working the engines *per se*, ...	23.46		
Net power applied to the screw shaft, ...	170.51	or	100.00
Power expended in overcoming the friction of the load, ...	12.79	"	7.50

Power expended in overcoming the cohesive resistance of the water to the screw surface,	24.96	or	14.64
Power expended in the slip of the screw,	16.30	"	9.56
Power expended in the propulsion of the hull,	116.46	"	68.30
Totals,	170.51	or	100.00

§ *Indicator Diagrams.*

Figs. 2 and 3 are diagrams taken by the indicator from the cylinders; they show the distribution of the pressure by the steam valve cutting off by lap and the link motion. There is no separate expansion valve, it will be remembered, and the lap was originally intended to cut off at $\frac{5}{8}$ths the stroke from the commencement. After the removal of one boiler it was found necessary to increase the lap in order to cut off shorter, and to modify the exhaust side of the valve proportionally. This was done by pinning on pieces and chipping the exhaust, and it was not till after much experimenting and altering that the valve was made to give the excellent diagrams shown in the figs. It is evident that with such a good distribution of the pressure and cutting off so short as 23½ per centum of the stroke from the commencement, there is no necessity for a separate expansion valve. In fig. 3 the cushioning commences when the piston is within one-sixth of its stroke from the end, which just suffices to fill the clearance and steam ports with compressed steam of boiler pressure ready for the return stroke. The exhaust commences to open also when the piston is one-sixth of its stroke from the end, which, at the high rotatory speed employed appears to be about the proper distance to allow the emptying of the cylinder for the return stroke, so that the latter may begin with a maximum exhaustion on the vacuum side. When the steam follows farther, as in fig. 2, both the cushioning and the exhaust begin much later.

SCREW STEAMSHIPS

"SYDNEY," "IRELAND," "SCOTLAND."

SCREW STEAMSHIPS

"SYDNEY," "IRELAND," "SCOTLAND."

---

§ During the year 1858 there arrived at Hongkong, China, three screw steam vessels, employed as transports for troops by the British government. They were the "Sydney," the "Ireland," and the "Scotland." The first two were built for postal service between England, South Africa, and India: the last was for service between England and Australia. The hulls of these vessels were of iron; they were built on the Clyde, and had the same lines, and were of the same dimensions; their machinery, however, was by different builders, and of different types and dimensions. The "Sydney" was lightly rigged as a barque; the other two were full ship-rigged, and intended to go under sail alone with their screws hoisted out of the water, when the wind was favorable; in fact, their steam power was strictly auxiliary: the "Sydney," on the contrary, was a full powered steamer, and her screw did not hoist up.

In the following pages there will first be given the dimensions of the hull, and afterwards, separately, the dimensions of the machinery of each vessel, and her maximum performance with it in smooth water uninfluenced by wind or current, and her average performance at sea with full steam power, unassisted by sail, and under the conditions of ordinary practice. The date, which will be found to be strictly comparable, was obtained by the writer from the Chief Engineers of the vessels, and from an examination of their log-books. The information thus obtained is valuable, not only as Engineering Precedents, but as showing the results attained from the same hull, by the employment of machinery of widely different type and power, and of propelling instruments of very different proportions.

§ Appended to each "Performance" is a "Distribution of the Power" exerted. In determining this power the following method was adopted, namely:—The experimental indicated gross horses power obtained from the Engineers was analyzed, and the portion of it "expended in the propulsion of the hull" was determined in the case of each vessel; and as the hulls were precisely alike, this power must be the same, *cæteris paribus*, for equal speed with all three vessels, hence this power in the three cases was found for an assumed speed of vessel (9 knots per hour) from the experimental power by increasing or diminishing it in the ratio of the cube of the experimental speed to the cube of 9 knots per hour, and the *mean* was taken for the true power "expended in the propulsion of the hull" at 9 knots, from which, in the same ratio this propelling power was found for the experimental speed in the case of each vessel. The per centum of slip being given, the power expended in it is easily calculated from the power expended in propelling the vessel, being simply in the ratio of the speed of the slip to the speed of the vessel. The power "required to work the engines *per se*" is calculated in the case of the geared engines of the "SYDNEY" for a piston pressure of 1¾ pound per square inch; and in the cases of the other two vessels with direct acting engines, for a piston pressure of 1½ pound per square inch. The "power required to overcome the cohesive resistance of the water to the screw surface" has been calculated in precisely the same manner in all three cases, namely, in the ratio of the squares of the helical speeds of the screw surface and for a value of 0.45 pounds per square foot of surface moving with a velocity of 10 feet per second. The "power absorbed by the friction of the load" is proportional in all three cases, and is taken at 7½ per centum of the "net power applied to the shaft," according to the experiments of MORIN. Having thus determined all these portions of power required, their sum will be the " gross horses power developed by the engines," which thus synthetically obtained differs but very slightly from the experimental gross horses powers, and has the advantage of being strictly comparable for the three vessels.

In the case of the performance at sea under the conditions of ordinary practice, the results are also strictly comparative, the resistance of the hull and the slip of the screw being taken in each case at one half more than in smooth water uninfluenced by wind or current; such an increase being the average resulting from the usually found roughness of the sea, and from the influence of the wind which is generally ahead when the vessel is under steam alone.

The performance given as the average at sea, it will be observed, is the highest that can be sustained, and is what results from using all the steam the boilers can be made to generate.

Dimensions of the Hull.

Length on keel,	209 feet.
Length between perpendiculars,	217 "
Length over all,	230 "
Breadth of beam, extreme,	33 "
Light draught of water { Forward,	13 "
Light draught of water { Mean,	15 "
Deep load draught,	18¾ "
Mean draught of water,	16⅜ "
Greatest immersed transverse section at 16⅜ feet mean draught,	450 sq. feet.

The water lines fore and aft were very sharp. The resistance of the hull at a speed of 10 geographical miles per hour is 17,740 pounds ; that is to say, this would be the thrust of the screw propelling the hull normally at that speed.

"SYDNEY."

§ *Dimensions of the Engines.*

Two condensing, geared engines with vertical cylinders on the same side of the keel and walking beams overhead. They have an independent expansion valve adapted for three grades of cutting-off, but it is rarely used ; the steam slide valve cuts off by lap at $\frac{6}{10}$ths the stroke of piston from the commencement. The pistons make one double stroke for every $2\frac{1}{4}$ revolutions of the screw. The machinery was built by Tulloch and Denny, Dumbarton.

Diameter of cylinders, ...	66 inches.
Stroke of pistons, ...	$4\frac{1}{2}$ feet.
Space displacement of both pistons per stroke, ...	213.822 cubic feet.
Diameter of screw shaft, ...	11 inches.

Dimensions of the Gearing.

The teeth of the cog-wheels are arranged in four parallel rows in steps ; that is, the teeth of each row are slightly in advance of those of the preceding row.

Width of each row of teeth on the face of the wheel, ...	8 inches.
Pitch of the teeth, ...	4 "
Multiple of gearing, ...	$2\frac{1}{4}$.

Dimensions of the Screw.

The screw is of cast iron, has an expanding pitch fore and aft, and does not hoist up.

Diameter of the screw, ...	14 feet.
Diameter of the hub, ...	21 inches.
Initial pitch, ...	18 feet.

Mean pitch (from which the slip is calculated), ...	18¾ feet.
Final pitch, ...	19½ "
Number of blades, ...	2
Length of the screw in the direction of its axis, ...	1 foot 10½ inches.
Fraction used of the pitch, ...	⅕
Area of the blades projected on a plane at right angles to their axis, ...	30.307 square feet.
Helicoidal area of the blades, ...	37.180 " "
Mean angle of the screw surface from the plane of rotation in function of area and propelling efficiency, ...	28° 14½′

Dimensions of the Boilers.

Two boilers with furnaces at each end and tubes returned above them. There is a fore and aft passage-way between the boilers. The chimney, into which all the furnaces discharge, is placed at the centre of the length of the boilers and immediately over the passage way. After the heated gases have traversed the tubes, they are led back to the chimney through a narrow deep flue lying side by side with the tubes. The furnaces are of two different widths, and have two different numbers of tubes correspondingly.

Total number of furnaces, ...	12
Width of the fire grate in eight of the twelve furnaces, ...	2½ feet.
Width of the fire grate in the remaining four furnaces, ...	3 "
Length of the fire grates in all the furnaces, ...	7 "
Total fire grate surface, ...	224 square feet
Number of tubes to each of the 2½ feet wide furnaces, ...	66
Number of tubes to each of the 3 feet wide furnaces, ...	88

Total number of tubes, ... 880.
Internal diameter of tubes, ... $3\frac{1}{4}$ inches.
Length of the tubes, ... $6\frac{1}{2}$ feet.
Total surface in the tubes, ... 4866.77 square feet.
Cross area of all the tabes, ... 50.70 " "

§ *Performance in Smooth Water.*

The following is the maximum performance at a measured mile in smooth water uninfluenced by wind or current:

Mean draught of water of the vessel in feet,	$16\frac{3}{8}$
Speed of the vessel per hour in knots of 6,086 feet,..........................	10.574
Number of double strokes of engines' pistons made per minute, ...	$29\frac{1}{4}$
Number of revolutions made by the screw per minute, ...	65.8125
Slip of the screw in per centum of its speed (calculated for $18\frac{3}{4}$ feet pitch),........	13.08
Mean gross effective pressure on pistons in pounds per square inch; by Indicator,...	17.11
Gross horses power developed by the engines,.............................	933.91

Distribution of the Power during the above Performance.

	Horses.	Per Centum.
Gross power developed by the engines,.	933.91	
Power required to work the engines and gearing *per se* ($1\frac{3}{4}$ lb. pr. sq. in.),.....	95.53	
Net power applied to the screw shaft, ..	838.38	or 100.00

Power absorbed by the friction of the load (7½ per centum of the net power),	62.88	7.50
Power required to overcome the cohesive resistance of the water to the screw surface,	33.82	4.03
Power expended in the slip of the screw,	97.01	11.57
Power expended in the propulsion of the hull,	644.67	76.90
Totals,	838.38	100.00

§ *Performance at Sea.*

The following is the average performance that can be sustained at sea with full steam power, unassisted by sail, and under the conditions of ordinary practice. The bunkers stow 500 tons of coal, sufficient for 12½ days' average steaming and a voyage of 2,600 miles.

Speed of the vessel per hour in knots of 6,086 feet,	8.69
Number of double strokes of engines' pistons made per minute,	26
Number of revolutions made by the screw per minute,	58½
Slip of the screw in per centum of its speed (calculated for 18¾ feet pitch),	19.62
Mean gross effective pressure on pistons in pounds per square inch,	17.23
Gross horses power developed by the engines,	835.97
Steam pressure in boilers in pounds per square inch above atmosphere,	9
Steam cut-off in cylinders from commencement of stroke,	$\frac{6}{10}$ths.
Consumption of Welsh coal per 24 hours, in tons of 2,240 pounds,	40

Distribution of the Power during the above Performance.

	Horses.		Per Centum.
Gross power developed by the engines,..	835.97		
Power required to work the engines and gearing *per se* (1¾ lb. pr. sq. in.),.....	88.71		
Net power applied to the screw shaft, ..	747.26	or	100.00
Power absorbed by the friction of the load (7½ per centum of the net power),	56.04	"	7.50
Power required to overcome the cohesive resistance of the water to the screw surface, ...	23.75	"	3.18
Power expended in the slip of the screw,	130.96	"	17.52
Power expended in the propulsion of the hull, ...	536.51	"	71.80
Totals,........	747.26	or	100.00

"IRELAND."

§ *Dimensions of the Engines.*

The engines were built by Thomas Richardson & Sons, Hartlepool Iron Works, near Newcastle, and consist of three direct acting, half trunk, condensing cylinders placed vertically on pillars over the shaft, and acting on cranks that make angles of 120° with each other. The half trunk extends downward from the lower side of the piston, while from the upper side a hollow piston rod of 4 inches outside diameter works through a stuffing box in the top of the cylinder; the object of making this piston rod hollow is to lubricate through it the pin in the half trunk to which the connecting rod is attached. The cylinder valves are worked by a separate shaft, taking its motion from the engine shaft by means of two spur wheels of equal diameter. The link motion is not employed, but backing is effected by reversing the eccentric by hand on the valve shaft. Two of the cylinders are 36 inches in diameter, and have half trunks 17 inches in diameter; the third cylinder is $36\frac{1}{2}$ inches in diameter, and has a half trunk $17\frac{1}{2}$ inches in diameter. The steam in the cylinders is cut off by lap at $\frac{6}{10}$ths the stroke of piston from the commencement, and there is no independent expansion valve. If the areas of the half trunks and hollow piston rods be deducted, the engines will be equivalent to three plain cylinders of the following dimensions, namely:

Diameter of the cylinders,	33.862 inches.
Area of each cylinder,	900.59 sq. inches.
Stroke of the pistons,	3 feet 10 inches.
Space displacement of the three pistons per stroke,	71.922 cubic feet.
Diameter of the main shaft,	9 inches.

Dimensions of the Screw.

The screw is of cast iron; it has a uniform pitch, and hoists out of water.

Diameter of the screw,	$12\frac{1}{3}$ feet.
Pitch,	21 "
Number of blades,	2
Length of the screw in the direction of its axis,	$3\frac{1}{2}$ feet.
Fraction used of the pitch,	$\frac{1}{3}$
Area of the blades projected on a plane at right angles to their axis,	39.560 sq. feet.
Helicoidal area of the screw,	55.220 "
Mean angle of the screw surface from the plane of rotation in function of area and propelling efficiency,	34° 20′

Dimensions of the Boilers.

Two boilers with tubes returned above the furnaces.

Total number of furnaces, ...	6
Width of fire grates, ...	2¾ feet.
Length of fire grates, ...	6½ "
Total fire grate surface, ...	107.25 sq. feet.
Total number of tubes, ...	420
Internal diameter of tubes, ...	3 inches.
Length of tubes, ...	6½ feet.
Total heating surface in the tubes, ...	2,144.14 sq. feet.
Cross area of all the tubes, ...	20.58 "

Performance in Smooth Water.

The following is the maximum performance at a measured mile in smooth water, uninfluenced by wind or current:

Mean draught of water of the vessel in feet, ...	16⅝
Speed of the vessel per hour in knots of 6,086 feet, ...	8.50
Number of double strokes of engines' pistons and of revolutions of the screw made per minute, ...	52
Slip of the screw in per centum of its speed, ...	21.05
Mean gross effective pressure on pistons in pounds per square inch; by Indicator, .	16.27
Gross horses power developed by the engines, ...	530.98

Distribution of the Power during the above Performance.

	HORSES.		PER CENTUM.
Gross power developed by the engines,...	530.98		
Power required to work the engines *per se* (1½ pounds per square inch),.........	48.96		
Net power applied to the screw shaft,.....	482.02	or	100.00
Power absorbed by the friction of the load (7½ per centum of the net power),.....	36.15	"	7.50
Power required to overcome the cohesive resistance of the water to the screw surface, ...	21.70	"	4.50
Power expended in the slip of the screw,..	89.28	"	18.52
Power expended in the propulsion of the hull, ...	334.89	"	69.48
Totals, ...	482.02	or	100.00

§ *Performance at Sea.*

The following is the average performance that can be sustained at sea with full steam power, unassisted by sail, and under the conditions of ordinary practice. The bunkers stow 150 tons of coal, sufficient for 7½ days' average steaming, and a voyage of 1,200 miles.

Speed of the vessel per hour in knots of 6,086 feet,........................	6.66
Number of double strokes of engines' pistons and of revolutions of the screw made per minute,.......................	47
Slip of the screw in per centum of its speed,...........................	31.55
Mean gross effective pressure on pistons in pounds per square inch,..............	14.99

Gross horses power developed by the engines,	442.23
Steam pressure in boilers in pounds per square inch above atmosphere,	8
Steam cut-off at in cylinders from commencement of stroke,	$\frac{6}{10}$
Consumption of Welsh coal per 24 hours in tons of 2,240 pounds,	20

Distribution of the Power during the above Performance.

	Horses.		Per Centum.
Gross power developed by the engines,	442.23		
Power required to work the engines *per se* ($1\frac{1}{2}$ pound per square inch),	44.25		
Net power applied to the screw shaft,	397.98	or	100.00
Power absorbed by the friction of the load ($7\frac{1}{2}$ per centum of the net power),	29.85	"	7.50
Power required to overcome the cohesive resistance of the water to the screw surface,	16.02	"	4.03
Power expended in the slip of the screw,	111.09	"	27.91
Power expended in the propulsion of the hull,	241.02	"	60.56
Totals,	397.98	or	100.00

"SCOTLAND."

§ *Dimensions of the Engines.*

Two condensing, direct acting, half trunk engines with the cylinders placed vertically over the shaft, and acting on cranks at right angles to each other. The half trunk extends downward from the lower side of the piston, while from its upper side a hollow piston rod of 4 inches outside diameter works through a stuffing box in the top of the cylinder ; the lubrication of the pin in the half trunk, to which the connecting rod is attached, is done through this hollow piston rod, which serves also as a guide to the piston. There is no separate expansion valve, but the steam is cut off by lap at $\frac{6}{10}$ths the stroke of the piston from the commencement. The diameter of the cylinders is 43 inches—o the trunks 22 inches ; if the areas of the hollow piston rod and half trunk be deducted, the engines will be equivalent to two plain cylinders of the following dimensions, namely :

Diameter of the cylinders,	39.987 inches.
Area of each cylinder,	1,255.85 sq. inches.
Stroke of the pistons,	$3\frac{1}{2}$ feet.
Space displacement of both pistons per stroke,	61.048 cubic ft.

Dimensions of the Screw.

The screw is of cast iron, has a uniform pitch, and hoists out of water.

Diameter of the screw,	$13\frac{1}{2}$ feet.
Pitch,	$17\frac{1}{2}$ "
Number of blades,	2
Length of screw in direction of axis	2 feet $2\frac{1}{4}$ inches.
Fraction used of the pitch,	$\frac{1}{4}$
Area of the blades projected on a plane at right angles to their axis,	35.589 sq. feet.
Helicoidal area of the blades,	44.210 "
Mean angle of the screw surface from the plane of rotation in function of area and propelling efficiency,	27° 28′

Dimensions of the Boilers.

One boiler with tubes returned above the furnaces.

Total number of furnaces,	6
Width of fire grates,	$2\frac{1}{2}$ feet.

Length of fire grates,	7 feet.
Total fire grate surface,	105.00 sq. feet.
Total number of tubes,	360
Internal diameter of tubes,	$2\frac{3}{4}$ inches.
Length of tubes,	7 feet.
Total surface in the tubes,	2,474.01 sq. feet.
Cross area of all the tubes,	27.61 "

Performance in Smooth Water.

The following is the maximum performance at a measured mile in smooth water, uninfluenced by wind or current:

Mean draught of water of the vessel in feet,	$16\frac{5}{8}$
Speed of the vessel per hour in knots of 6,086 feet,	8.738
Number of double strokes of engines' pistons and of revolutions of the screw made per minute,	59
Slip of the screw in per centum of its speed,	14.16
Mean gross effective pressure on pistons in pounds per square inch; by Indicator,	16.99
Gross horses power developed by the engines,	532.67

Distribution of the Power during the above Performance.

	Horses.	Per Centum.
Gross power developed by the engines,	532.67	
Power required to work the engines *per se* ($1\frac{1}{2}$ pound per square inch),	47.15	
Net power applied to the shaft,	485.52 or	100.00

Power absorbed by the friction of the load ($7\frac{1}{2}$ per centum of the net power),.....	36.41	or	7.50
Power required to overcome the cohesive resistance of the water to the screw surface, ...	25.29	"	5.21
Power expended in the slip of the screw,	60.01	"	12.36
Power expended in the propulsion of the hull, ...	363.81	"	74.93
Totals,.........................	485.52	or	100.00

§ *Performance at Sea.*

The following is the average performance that can be sustained at sea with full steam power, unassisted by sail, and under the conditions of ordinary practice. The bunkers stow 180 tons of coal, sufficient for 9 days' average steaming, and a voyage of 1,500 miles.

Speed of the vessel per hour in knots of 6,086 feet, ...	6.93
Number of double strokes of engines' pistons and of revolutions of the screw made per minute,.......................	51
Slip of the screw in per centums of its speed, ...	$21\frac{1}{4}$
Mean gross effective pressure on pistons in pounds per square inch,..............	15.90
Gross horses power developed by the engines, ...	432.09
Steam pressure in boiler in pounds per square inch above atmosphere,........	11
Steam cut-off at in cylinders from commencement of stroke,................	$\frac{6}{10}$ths.
Consumption of Welsh coal per 24 hours in tons of 2,240 pounds, ...	20

Distribution of the Power during the above Performance.

	Horses.		Per Centum.
Gross power developed by the engines, ...	432.09		
Power required to work the engines *per se* (1½ pounds per square inch), ...	40.75		
Net power applied to the shaft, ...	391.34	or	100.00
Power absorbed by the friction of the load (7½ per centum of the net power,)	29.35	"	7.50
Power required to overcome the cohesive resistance of the water to the screw surface, ...	16.33	"	4.17
Power expended in the slip of the screw,	73.45	"	18.77
Power expended in the propulsion of the hull, ...	272.21	"	69.56
Totals, ...	391.34	or	100.00

§ *Relative economical efficiencies of the Screws of the three Vessels.*

It will be observed, that in the cases just discussed of the three vessels, the same hull was propelled by screws of very different dimensions which distributed the power in very different proportions ; and as, if we make the comparison by the *net* powers applied to the screw shaft, we shall have eliminated the influence of the more or less friction resistance of the engines *per se ;* any difference that may be found in the economical performances of the vessels, will be due entirely to the screws. There remains, then, to determine the relative economical efficiencies of these screws in function of the net powers applied to their shafts. In making this comparison, the net powers will be taken as the measure of the costs, and the cubes of the speeds of the vessels will be taken as the measure of the effects produced:—the quotients arising from the respective divisions of the latter by the former quantities, will show the relative economical efficiencies,—the higher numbers denoting a corresponding higher efficieacy. As this relative efficiency is not the same when performing in smooth water and at sea, it has been determinnd in the following Tables for both cases. In these Tables will also be found the slips of the screws in per centum of their speeds, and the losses of labor by the screws in per centum of the net powers applied to their shafts. Also, the per centum of these net powers utilized in the propulsion of the hull.

In Smooth Water.

NAME OF VESSEL.	Speed of the Vessel per hour, in knots of 6,086 feet.	Net powers applied to the Screw Shaft, in Horses.	Relative economical efficiencies of the Screws.	Slip of the Screws, in per centum of their speed.	LOSSES OF LABOR BY THE SCREWS IN PER CENTUM OF THE NET POWERS APPLIED TO THEIR SHAFTS.			Per centum of the net power utilized by the screws in propelling the vessel.
					Slip.	Cohesive resistance of the water.	Total losses by the Screws.	
SYDNEY,....	10.574	838.38	1.1063	13.08	11.57	4.03	15.60	76.90
IRELAND,...	8.500	482.02	1.0000	21.05	18.52	4.50	23.02	69.48
SCOTLAND,..	8.733	435.52	1.0735	14.16	12.36	5.21	17.57	74.93

At Sea.

NAME OF VESSEL.	Speed of the Vessel per hour, in knots of 6,086 feet.	Net powers applied to the Screw Shaft, in Horses.	Relative economical efficiencies of the Screws.	Slip of the Screws, in per centum of their speed.	LOSSES OF LABOR BY THE SCREWS IN PER CENTUM OF THE NET POWERS APPLIED TO THEIR SHAFTS.			Per centum of the net power utilized by the screws in propelling the vessel.
					Slip.	Cohesive resistance of the water.	Total losses by the Screws.	
SYDNEY,....	8.69	747.23	1.1837	19.62	17.52	3.18	20.70	71.80
IRELAND,...	6.66	397.93	1.0000	31.55	27.91	4.03	31.94	60.56
SCOTLAND,..	6.93	391.34	1.1460	21.25	18.77	4.17	22.94	69.56

An examination of the above tables shows, that the screw of the "SYDNEY" gave the highest results both "in smooth water" and "at sea," but higher at sea than in smooth water, being nearly $10\frac{7}{10}$ per centum more economical than the screw of the "IRELAND" in smooth water, and $18\frac{3}{8}$ per centum more economical at sea.

Next in efficiency is the screw of the "SCOTLAND," which is nearly 8 per centum more economical in smooth water than the screw of the "IRELAND," and $14\frac{6}{10}$ per centum more economical at sea.

Looking at the column of "Slips of the screws in per centum of their speed," we remark, that these slips stand inversely in the same order as the economical efficiencies of their screws, the screw of least slip having the greatest economical efficiency;—and as the effect of the sea under equal conditions is to *proportionally* increase these slips,—that is, to increase them by equal per centages of themselves,—the *positive* losses by them become *disproportionately* greater; consequently, we find that, at sea, the efficiencies of those screws which have the least slip is relatively greater than in smooth water.

The losses of labor due to overcoming the "cohesive resistance of the water" to the screw surface, does not vary much with the different screws; the greatest difference amounts to but $1\frac{1}{5}$ per centum of the net power. Even in this respect, however, the screw of the "SYDNEY" is still the most efficient.

We arrive then at these results—that as the loss of labor due to the power expended in overcoming the cohesive resistance of the water by the screw surface, is nearly the same with all three screws, the difference in their economical efficiency is due nearly entirely to the difference of their slips, which is their only remaining loss of labor; and that the screws of least slip have the greatest economical efficiency.

It is worthy of remark, that the screw of the "SYDNEY," which gives the highest result, has the greatest diameter, the least fraction of pitch, and an expanding pitch whose mean is but little greater than the least pitch of the other screws; while the screw of the "IRELAND," which gives the lowest result, has the least diameter, the greatest fraction of pitch, and the greatest pitch : its pitch is uniform.

To still better appreciate the influence of the different proportions used of the screws, their governing dimensions have been grouped in the following Table, where will also be found the number, proportionally, of revolutions required to be made by them in equal times to give the vessel the same speed in smooth water ; their normal slips, and the power value, proportionally, of the resistances opposed by the cohesion of the water to the passage through it of the helicoidal surfaces for the same speed of vessel.

NAME OF VESSEL.	Diameter of the Screw, in feet.	Pitch of the Screw, in feet.	Fraction used of the Pitch.	Helicoidal Area of the Screw, in square feet.	Mean Angle from the Plane of Rotation of the Helicoidal Surface in Function of Area and Propelling Efficiency.	Slip of the Screws in per centum of their speed.	Proportional number of revolutions of the Screw, required to propel the vessel at equal speed.	Proportional Power value of the cohesive resistance of the Water to the screw surface for equal speed of vessel.
SYDNEY,...	14	18¾	$\frac{1}{5}$	37.18	28° .. 14½′	13.08	1.0173	1.0000
IRELAND,..	12⅓	21	$\frac{1}{3}$	55.22	34° .. 20′	21.05	1.0000	1.2352
SCOTLAND,	13½	17½	$\frac{1}{4}$	44.21	27° .. 28′	14.16	1.1037	1.3253

From this Table it appears that the screw of the "SYDNEY" has not only the least loss of useful effect from slip, but also the least loss from the cohesive resistance of the water to its passage.

§ The following Table exhibits the Dynamical relation between the screws in complex function of their elements, and the space displacement of the pistons per stroke and the mean effective pressure on them in pounds per square inch after deducting the pressure required to work the engines *per se.* It shows also with the same vessel, the resulting development of power and speed obtained.

NAME OF VESSEL.	Space displacement of Piston per stroke, in cubic feet.	Mean effective pressure, in pounds per square inch, after deducting pressure required to work the engines *per se*.	Multiple of Gearing.	PITCH OF THE SCREWS.		REVOLUTIONS OF THE SCREWS PER MINUTE.		Speed of the Vessel per hour, in knots of 6,086 feet.	Relative Economical Efficiencies of the Screws, in the application of the Power.
				In feet.	Proportionally.	Number.	Proportionally.		
SYDNEY,...	213.822	15.36	2¼	18¾	1.0714	65.8125	1.2656	10.574	1.1837
IRELAND,..	71.922	14.77	Direct.	21	1.2000	52.	1.0000	8.500	1.0000
SCOTLAND,	61.048	15.49	Direct.	17½	1.0000	59.	1.1346	8.738	1.1460

BRITISH WAR SCREW STEAMSHIP

"CONFLICT."

BRITISH WAR SCREW STEAMSHIP

"CONFLICT."

§ The "Conflict" is a war screw steamship belonging to the British Navy. At different times different screws have been applied to her, and the trials with them having all been made at sensibly the same draught of water and at a measured mile, the results are fairly comparable. I have collected these experiments, but before discussing them it is convenient to give the dimensions of the Hull and Engines, viz. :

Hull.

Length between perpendiculars,	192 feet 6 inches.
Breadth, extreme,	34 feet 4 inches.
Mean draught of water during the trials,	14 feet 6 inches.
Constructor's deep load draught of water,	15 feet 9 inches.
Greatest immersed transverse section at 14½ feet draught,	402 square feet.
Displacement at 14½ feet draught of water,	1,443 tons.
Displacement at 14½ feet draught per inch of draught,	12.33 tons.
Ratio of displacement to circumscribing parallelopipedon,	0.576

Ratio of area of load water line to circumscribing parallelogram, ... 0.782
Ratio of greatest immersed transverse section to circumscribing parallelogram,........ 0.880
Resistance of the hull at a speed of 9 geographical miles per hour, ... 16,360 pounds.

Engines.

Four horizontal, condensing, direct acting engines ; the pistons making one double stroke to each revolution of the screw.

Diameter of the cylinders, ... 46 inches.
Stroke of pistons, ... 2 feet.
Space displacement of the *four* pistons per stroke,............................ 92.33 cubic feet.

§ *Experimental Screws.*

The screws experimented with were five in number, viz. :—a common screw of uniform length from hub to periphery; a common screw with the corners of the blades rounded off; the same with the hub and central portion of the blades inclosed in a globe of 35.2 per centum the diameter of the screw, according to Griffith's arrangement ; a common screw with its surface arranged to correspond with the surface of Sir THOMAS MITCHELL'S Boomerang propeller; and finally the Boomerang propeller of Sir THOMAS MITCHELL. All these screws had a uniform pitch, were two bladed, and 13½ feet diameter.

It is to be regretted that the Indicator power was not obtained in all the trials, but the determination of the principal points of interest in the cases intended for direct comparison, can be correctly inferred from the slips of the screws alone, the close approximation of the dimensions of the screws directly compared making the power required to overcome the cohesive resistance of the water by their blades about equal.

The problems solved by these experiments are, 1st :—The increase of slip due to the rounding off of the corners of the blades of the screw. 2d :—The increase of slip due to inclosing the hub and central portions of the blades in a globe of 35.2 per centum of the diameter of the screw. 3d :—The difference of slip due to the difference between an arrangement of the same area of the same helicoidal surface in the form of the common screw and in the form of MITCHELL'S Boomerang propeller.

The common screws I shall designate respectively as screws A, B, C, D and E ; their data and results, as well as those of the Boomerang propeller, will be given separately, and are as follows, viz. :

§ Experiment with Screw A.

Screw A is a common screw of uniform length from hub to periphery and of unform pitch ; it has the following dimensions, viz. :

Diameter of the screw,.............	13 feet 6 inches.
Number of blades, ...	2
Pitch,...........................	16 feet 6 inches.
Length of the screw in the direction of the axis, ...	2 feet 9 inches.
Fraction used of the pitch..........	$\frac{1}{6}$d.
Projected area of the blades on a plane at right angles to axis,......	47.450 square feet.
Helicoidal area of the blades,........	57.653 " "
Mean angle of the screw surface from its plane of rotation, in function of its area and propelling efficiency,..	26° 7′

With this screw the following results were obtained at the measured mile at the Nore, November 7th, 1848, viz. :

Speed of the vessel per hour in geographical miles of 6,086 feet,..........................	9.289
Number of double strokes of engines' pistons and revolutions of the screw made per minute, ...	68
Slip of the screw in per centum of its speed,....	16.02

Mean gross effective pressure on pistons in pounds per square inch; by Indicator,..............	14.19
Gross horses power developed by the engines,...	777.50

Distribution of the Power with Screw A.

The pressure required to work the engine *per se*, being taken at 1½ pound per square inch of pistons, amounts to 82.19 horses power, which deducted from the total horses power 777.50 developed by the engines, leaves 695.31 horses power applied to the screw shaft.

Of the power 695.31 horses applied to the screw shaft, 7½ per centum or 52.15 horses power were absorbed in the friction of the load, which being deducted leaves 643.16 horses power.

The power expended in overcoming the cohesive resistance of the water by the screw blades, calculated in the ratio of the square of the velocity and for a value of 0.45 pound avoirdupois per square foot of screw surface moving in its helical path with a speed of 10 feet per second, amounts to 55.99 horses power, which deducted from the 643.16 horses power, leaves 587.17 horses power expended in the slip of the screw and in the propulsion of the vessel.

Of these 587.17 horses power, 16.02 per centum or 94.06 horses power were expended in the slip of the screw, leaving 493.11 horses power expended in the propulsion of the simple hull.

Collecting the foregoing we have the following distribution of the power, viz.:

	Horses Power.	Per Centum.
Gross horses power developed by the engines,..........................	777.50	
Power required to work the engines *per se*,..........................	82.19	
Power applied to the screw shaft,......	695.31 or	100.00

Power expended in overcoming the friction of the load, ...	52.15	or	7.50
Power expended in overcoming the cohesive resistance of the water by the screw blades, ...	55.99	"	8.05
Power expended in the slip of the screw,	94.06	"	13.53
Power expended in the propulsion of the simple hull, ...	493.11	"	70.92
Totals, ...	695.31	or	100.00

§ *Experiment with Screw B.*

Screw B is a common screw, but instead of being of uniform length from hub to periphery, each corner of the blades was cut off 18 inches, thus operating a considerable reduction of the surface at the periphery where it has the greatest propelling effect. This screw has the following dimensions, viz. :

Diameter of the screw, ...	13 feet 6 inches.
Number of blades, ...	2
Pitch, ...	15 feet 2 inches.
Length (extreme) of the screw in the direction of the axis, ...	2.528 feet.
Mean fraction used of the pitch in function of surface and efficiency of the same, ...	0.30
Projected area of the blades on a plane at right angles to axis, ...	43.52 square feet.
Helicoidal area of the blades, ...	50.00 " "

With this screw the following results were obtained, viz. :

Speed of the vessel per hour in geographical miles of 6,086 feet, ...	9.424
Number of double strokes of engines' pistons and revolutions made by the screw per minute, ...	$75\frac{3}{4}$

Slip of the screw in per centum of its speed, ... 16.81
Mean gross effective pressure in pounds per square inch of pistons, ... 13.3
Gross horses power developed by the engines, ... 812

Distribution of the Power with Screw B.

The power required to work the engines *per se*, calculated as for screw A, amounts to 91.58 horses, leaving 720.42 horses applied to the shaft.

Of these 720.42 horses power, 7½ per centum or 54.03 horses power were absorbed by the friction of the load.

The power required to overcome the cohesive resistance of the water by the screw blades, calculated as for screw A, amounts to 65.13 horses.

Deducting the above two quantities from the power applied to the shaft, there remains 601.26 horses power, of which 16.81 per centum or 101.07 horses power was expended in the slip of the screw, leaving the remainder 500.19 horses power for the power propelling the simple hull.

If the power expended in propelling the vessel with screw B, were in exact rapport with the power propelling the simple vessel with screw A, calculating for the differences of speed in the two cases, in the ratio of the cubes of the speeds, it would be 514.85 horses power instead of the above determination of 500.19 horses power.

Collecting the foregoing, we have the following distribution of the power, viz.:

	Horses Power.		Per Centum.
Gross horses power developed by the engines, ...	812.00		
Power required to work the engines *per se*, ...	91.58		
Power applied to the screw shaft, ...	720.42	or	100.00

Power expended in overcoming the friction of the load, ...	54.03	or	7.50
Power expended in overcoming the cohesion of the water by the screw blades, ...	65.14	"	9.04
Power expended in the slip of the screw, ...	101.07	"	14.03
Power expended in the propulsion of the simple hull, ...	500.19	"	69.43
Totals, ...	720.42	or	100.00

The slip of screw B, to be in exact rapport with slip of screw A, should be 15.04 per centum instead of 16.81 ; this difference is due to errors of data, to which cause also must be ascribed the difference between 514.85 and 500.19 horses power required to propel the simple hull at equal speeds.

§ *Experiment with Screw C.*

Screw B was altered into screw C by inclosing its hub and the central portion of its blades in a wooden globe of 4¾ feet diameter, according to GRIFFITH's arrangement. In this case the diameter of the globe was 35.2 per centum of the diameter of the screw, and it reduced the helicoidal area of the latter to 43.00 square feet, and the projected area on a plane at right angles to axis to 38.80 square feet. The fraction of the pitch used in function of surface and efficiency of the same, was reduced to 0.29 from the same cause.

The following are the results obtained from screw C, viz. :

Speed of the vessel per hour in geographical miles of 6,086 feet, ...	9.425
Number of double strokes of engines' pistons and revolutions of the screw made per minute, ...	77
Slip of the screw in per centum of its speed, ...	18.15

Mean gross effective pressure on pistons in pounds per square inch (by calculation), ... 13.475

Gross horses power developed by the engines (by calculation), ... 836.05

The slip of screw C' to have been in exact rapport with slip of screw B, should be 17.67 per centum instead of 18.15 per centum; and to have been in exact rapport with the slip of screw A, it should be 15.82 per centum instead of 18.15 per centum.

Distribution of the Power with Screw C.

The power developed by the engines with screw C will be deduced by calculation from the power developed by the engines with screw B, and in the following manner, viz.:

The speed of the vessel being the same with both screws B and C, the power required to propel the simple hull will be the same, viz., 500.19 horses.

The power expended in the slip of the screw will be to the power expended in propelling the simple hull, as the speed of the slip is to the speed of the vessel, viz., in the ratio of 18.15 to (100.00−18.15=) 81.85; consequently as 81.85 : 500.19 : : 18.15 to 110.91 horses, the power expended in the slip of screw C.

The power required to overcome the cohesive resistance of the water by the screw blades and by the central globe, is by calculation 76.23 horses.

The sum of the three preceding quantities amounts to 687.33 horses, and the friction of the load will be such a quantity as added to this will be 7½ per centum of the entire aggregate. This quantity is 55.65 horses power, which added to the 687.33 horses power, makes a total of 742.98 horses power applied to the shaft.

The power required to work the engine *per se*, calculated as before, is 93.07 horses, which added to the above 742.98 horses power, makes a total gross power developed by the engines of 836.05 horses.

Collecting the foregoing, we have the following distribution of the power, viz.:

	HORSES POWER.		PER CENTUM.
Gross horses power developed by the engines, ...	836.05		
Power required to work the engines *per se*, ...	93.07		
Power applied to the screw shaft, ...	742.98	or	100.00
Power expended in overcoming the friction of the load, ...	55.65	or	7.50
Power expended in overcoming the cohesion of the water by the screw blades, etc.	76.23	"	10.27
Power expended in the slip of the screw,	110.91	"	14.90
Power expended in the propulsion of the simple hull, ...	500.19	"	67.33
Totals, ...	742.98	or	100.00

§ *Experiment with Screw D.*

Screw D was a common screw of uniform length from hub to periphery, and it had the following dimensions, viz:

Diameter of the screw, ...	13 feet 6 inches.
Number of blades, ...	2
Pitch, ...	19.885 feet.
Length of the screw in the direction of its axis, ...	2.486 "
Fraction used of the pitch, ...	0.25
Projected area of the blades on a plane at right angles to axis, ...	35.587 sq. feet.
Helicoidal area of the blades, ...	46.540 "
Mean angle of the screw surface from its plane of rotation in function of its area and propelling efficiency, ...	30° 34½′

With this screw the following results were obtained, viz.:

Speed of the vessel per hour in geographical miles of 6,086 feet, ...	9.6
Number of double strokes of engines' pistons and revolutions of the screw made per minute,.........................	62
Slip of the screw in per centums of its speed,.............................	21.01
Mean gross effective pressure in pounds per square inch of pistons (by calculation),	17.25
Gross horses power developed by the engines (by calculation), ...	861.92

The slip of screw D to be in exact rapport with the slip of screw A, should be 20.40 instead of 21.01 per centum.

The calculation of the power developed by the engines with screw D (not having been obtained by indicator), will be made from the power developed with screw A, and in the following manner, viz.:

Distribution of the Power with Screw D.

The power required to work the engines *per se*, taken as before at $1\frac{1}{2}$ pound per square inch of pistons, amounts to 74.94 horses.

The power required to propel the simple hull under the same conditions, will be in the ratio of the cubes of the speeds. The speed of the vessel with screw A was 9.289 miles per hour, with a power of 493.11 horses, and as the speed with screw D was 9.600 miles per hour, the power will be (9.289^3 : 493.11 : : 9.600^3 :) 544.39 horses.

And as the power expended in the slip of the screw, is to the power expended in the propulsion of the vessel, as the speed of the former is to the speed of the latter, and as the slip is 21.01 per centum, the speed of the vessel will be expressed relatively by (100.00—21.01=) 78.99; and as 78.99 : 544.39 : : 21.01 : 144.80 horses, the power expended on the slip of the screw.

The power expended in overcoming the cohesive resistance of the water by the screw blades, calculated in the ratio of the square of the velocity, and for a value of 0.45 pound avoirdupois per square foot of screw surface, moving in its helical path with a speed of 10 feet per second, amounts to 38.77 horses.

Adding together the powers expended in propelling the simple vessel, 544.39 horses; in the slip of the screw 144.80 horses, and in overcoming the cohesive resistance of the water by the screw blades 38.77 horses; we have an aggregate of 727.96 horses power, $7\frac{1}{2}$ per centum of which, including itself, amounts to 59.02 horses power, which is the friction of the load.

Adding to the 727.96 horses power, the power 59.02 horses absorbed by the friction of the load, and the power 74.94 horses absorbed by the friction, etc., of the engines *per se*, we have for the total power developed by the engines 861.92 horses.

Collecting the foregoing, we have the following distribution of the power.

	Horses Power.		Per Centum.
Gross horses power developed by the engines,	861.92		
Power required to work the engines *per se*,	74.94		
Power applied to the screw shaft	786.98	or	100.00
Power expended in overcoming the friction of the load,	59.02	"	7.50
Power expended in overcoming the cohesive resistance of the water by the screw blades,	38.77	"	4.93
Power expended in the slip of the screw,	144.80	"	18.40
Power expended in the propulsion of the simple hull,	544.39	"	69.17
Totals,	786.98	or	100.00

The gross power, 861.92 horses, corresponds to a mean gross effective pressure of 17.253 pounds per square inch of pistons.

6

§ *Experiment with Screw E.*

Screw E was formed from screw D by reducing its helicoidal surface to 27.837 square feet, in such a manner as not only to make it equal in projected area, but to give it the same outline of blade as the Boomerang propeller of Sir Thomas Mitchell, against which it was to be tried. Screw E had the following dimensions, viz.:

Diameter of the screw, ...	13 feet 6 inches.
" " hub, ...	2 "
Number of blades, ...	2
Pitch, ...	19.885 feet.
Length (extreme) of the screw in the direction of the axis, ...	2.000 "
Mean fraction used of the pitch in function of surface and efficiency of the same, ...	0.118
Projected area of the blades on a plane at right angles to axis, ...	21.056 sq. feet.
Helicoidal area of the blades, ...	27.837 "

With this screw the following (which are the means of three double courses run) results were obtained, except the piston pressure and horses power developed by the engines, which are derived by calculation as in the case of screw D and others; the indicated power not having been given.

Speed of the vessel per hour in geographical miles of 6,086 feet, ...	9.524
Number of double strokes of engines' pistons and revolutions of the screw made per minute, ...	65.875
Slip of the screw in per centum of its speed, ...	26.25
Mean gross effective pressure in pounds per square inch of pistons (by calculation), .	16.22

Gross horses power developed by the engines (by calculation), ... 860.98

Distribution of the Power with Screw E.

The power required to work the engines *per se*, calculated as for screw A, amounts to 79.62 horses, leaving 781.36 horses applied to the shaft.

Of these 781.36 horses power, 7½ per centum or 58.60 horses power were absorbed by the friction of the load.

The power expended in overcoming the cohesive resistance of the water by the screw blades, calculated in the ratio of the square of the velocity, and for a value of 0.45 pound avoirdupois per square foot of screw surface, moving in its helical path with a speed of 10 feet per second, amounts to 22.73 horses.

The power required to propel the simple hull, calculated from the power required with screw B in the ratio of the cubes of the speeds, amounts to 516.27 horses.

The power expended in the slip of the screw, deduced from the power expended in propelling the simple hull, in the direct ratio of the speeds of the slip and of the vessel, amounts to 183.76 horses.

Collecting the foregoing, we have the following distribution of the power, viz. :

	HORSES POWER.	PER CENTUM.
Gross horses power developed by the engines, ...	860.98	
Power required to work the engines *per se*, ...	79.62	
Power applied to the screw shaft,....	781.36	or 100.00

Power expended in overcoming the friction of the load,..............	58.60	or	7.50
Power expended in overcoming the cohesive resistance of the water by the screw blades, ...	22.73	"	2.91
Power expended in the slip of the screw,	183.76	"	23.52
Power expended in the propulsion of the simple vessel,................	516.27	"	66.07
Totals,........	781.36	or	100.00

§ *The Boomerang Propeller.*

This propeller, which is a true screw with its two blades inclined to the axis in opposite directions, derives its name from an offensive missile called the Boomerang, used by the Australian savages. In their hands it is an instrument of hard wood, thin, with sharp edges and helicoidal surfaces, and flexed into a reversed curve in the direction of its greatest length. To form a good idea of it, take a long, narrow, rectangular strip of tolerably stiff paper, and holding one extremity in each hand, twist them till they make angles with each other ; the warped surface connecting the extremities, will be a helicoid and will have a greater or less pitch as the angle made by the extremities is greater or less ; finally, flex the paper into a reversed curve in the direction of its greatest length. When the Boomerang is to be hurled, the savage grasps it at the middle or axis, and giving it a whirling or rotatory motion, projects it at the object. It thus becomes a missile *screwing* its way through the air, whose direct resistance it thus avoids to a very great extent ; the sharp advancing edge also assists this effect, and the Boomerang strikes its object with greater force than any other missile of equal weight and superficies thrown with the same initial velocity. The rotatory motion which is imparted to it before projection, also enables it to be thrown with great accuracy, for whatever direction it has when it leaves the hand it will retain, owing to the constant balance maintained by the rapid rotation of the particles around the axis ; this effect is precisely the same that is attained by the grooving of the rifle. The sharp advancing edge is not only useful as diminishing the resistance to the air, but is advantageous in inflicting a greater injury on a living object. It is thus apparent, that a Boomerang in a vigorous and practised hand may prove a very formidable missile ; but it cannot be argued therefrom that it will be a superior propeller for a vessel. When so applied, it is in fact a two bladed true screw, with one blade inclined forward and the other inclined backward, and it will produce exactly the same propulsive effect as a common screw of the same diameter, number of blades, pitch and projected surface ; but it will be economically less efficient than the common screw, from the fact, that owing to the inclination of the blades towards the axis, the helicoidal surface will be greater in the ratio of the hypothenuse to the perpendicular of the right angled triangle made by the blades with the axis, and consequently, the power expended in overcoming the cohesive resistance of the water by the blades, will be proportionally greater. The only peculiarity that distinguishes the Boomerang from the common two bladed screw, lies in the fact that one blade is inclined forward and the other aft, thus making an acute and an obtuse angle with the axis, instead of standing at right angles to it. By this arrangement the water is pressed by one blade towards the axis and by the other blade from the axis ; now it is evident that if anything is to be gained by inclining the blades, both blades should be inclined in the same direction, for if equally inclined in opposite directions, as with the Boomerang, the gain by one, if there be any, will be balanced by the corresponding loss from the other. In fact, however, the inclination of the blades fore and aft produces no other effect than the serious practical inconvenience of requiring a much longer screw to obtain equal propulsive efficiency ; and of course, requiring a proportionally longer opening in the dead wood of the vessel.

The dimensions of the Boomerang propeller applied to the "CONFLICT," and tried against the common screw E of similar outline of blade and equal projected surface, were as follows, viz.:

Diameter, ...	13 feet 6 inches.
" of the hub, ...	2 feet.
Number of blades, ...	2
Pitch, ...	20 feet.
Length (extreme) in the direction of the axis, ...	4 feet.
Mean fraction used of the pitch in function of surface and efficiency of the same, ...	0.118
Projected area of the blades on a line at right angles to axis, ...	21.056 square feet.
Helicoidal area of the blades, ...	30.916 " "

With this propeller the following results were obtained—excepting the piston pressure and power developed by the engines, which were derived by calculation as in the case of screw E—they are the means of three double courses run:

Speed of the vessel per hour in geographical miles of 6,086 feet, ...	9.724
Number of double strokes of engines' pistons and revolutions of the screw made per minute, ...	66.688
Slip of the screw in per centum of its speed, ...	26.05
Mean gross effective pressure in pounds per square inch of pistons (by calculation), ...	16.99
Gross horses power developed by the engines (by calculation), ...	912.96

Distribution of the Power with the Boomerang Propeller.

The power required to work the engines *per se*, taken as before at $1\frac{1}{2}$ pound per square inch of pistons, amounts to 80.61 horses.

The power required to propel the simple vessel under the same conditions, will be in the ratio of the cubes of the speeds. The speed of the vessel with screw B was 9.424 miles per hour with a power of 500.19 horses, and as the speed with the Boomerang was 9.724 miles per hour, the power will be ($9.424^3 : 500.19 : : 9.724^3$:) 549.46 horses.

And as the power expended in the slip of the screw, is to the power expended in the propulsion of the vessel, as the speed of the former is to the speed of the latter, and as the slip is 26.05 per centum, the speed of the vessel will be expressed relatively by (100.00−26.05=) 73.95 ; and as 73.95 : 549.46 : : 26.05 : 193.56 horses, the power expended on the slip of the screw.

The power expended in overcoming the cohesive resistance of the water by the screw blades, calculated in the ratio of the square of the velocity, and for a value of 0.45 pound avoirdupois per square foot of screw surface moving in its helical path with a speed of 10 feet per second, amounts to 26.91 horses.

Adding together the powers expended in propelling the simple vessel 549.46 horses ; in the slip of the screw 193.56 horses ; and in overcoming the cohesive resistance of the water by the screw blades 26.91 horses ; we have an aggregate of 769.93 horses power, 7½ per centum of which including itself, amounts to 62.42 horses power, which is the friction of the load.

Adding to the 769.93 horses power, the power 62.42 horses absorbed by the friction of the load, and the power 80.61 horses absorbed by the friction of the engines *per se*, we have for the total power developed by the engines 912.96 horses.

Collecting the foregoing, we have the following distribution of the power, viz. :

	Horses Power.	Per Centum.
Gross horses power developed by the engines, ...	912.96	
Power required to work the engines *per se*,	80.61	
Power applied to the screw shaft, ...	832.35	or 100.00

Power expended in overcoming the friction of the load, ...	62.42 or	7.50
Power expended in overcoming the cohesive resistance of the water by the screw blades, ...	26.91 "	3.23
Power expended in the slip of the screw, ..	193.56 "	23.26
Power expended in the propulsion of the vessel, ...	549.46 "	66.01
Totals, ...	832.35 or	100.00

The gross power 912.96 horses, corresponds to a mean gross effective pressure of 16.99 pounds per square inch of pistons.

§ Explanation of the annexed Table containing a Summary of the Experimental Results.

In the preceding pages, the Experiments with the different Screws applied to the "Conflict," have been discussed in strict accordance with the observed data, which is remarkably correct, the deviations from truth being so slight as to occasion no error of sufficient importance to be of practical consequence; nevertheless, in order to appreciate with precision the relative economical efficiencies of these screws and to exactly distribute the power used with them, I have grouped them in the annexed Table, where will be found both the observed data and its rectification by calculation, together with an exact distribution of the power in the different cases for a uniform speed of vessel of 9 knots per hour. These rectified results being all obtained by the same process and for the same values, are strictly comparable, and determine perfectly the relative efficiencies of the screws, and the causes of the same.

Columns 1, 2, 3, 4, 5, 6 and 7, contain the dimensions of the screws, from which it will be seen that the experiments embraced variations in their pitch, in the fraction used of the pitch, in the outline of the blades and in their inclination to the axis;

also the substitution of a large globe for the hub and central portions of the blades. These columns in connection with the foot notes sufficiently explain themselves. The fractions used of the pitch in Column 5, are what are due to the surface and efficiency of the same, calculated as the square of the distance of the surface from the axis.

Columns 8, 9 and 10, give, respectively, the *observed* number of revolutions made by the screws per minute, their slips in per centum of their speed, and the speed of the vessel per hour. Column 11 contains the slips of column 9 rectified in accordance with the pitches and fractions used of the pitch; the mean of all the experiments being taken for the standard or starting point, from which the several rectified slips are deduced from a logarithmic curve. Column 12 contains the *true* experimental speeds of the vessel, derived from the rectified slips of Column 11 and the observed revolutions of the screws in Column 8, which are assumed to be correct as they were taken by a Counter worked by the engine.

Columns 13, 14 and 15, contain, respectively, the observed number of double strokes of engines' pistons made per minute; the mean gross effective pressure by indicator in pounds per square inch of pistons; and the gross horses power developed by the engines. This data, it is to be regretted, was only ascertained in the cases of screws A and B, and from their mean has been deduced the power 452.57 horses required to propel the simple vessel at the speed of 9 knots per hour, as contained in Column 27. Columns 16 and 17 contain, respectively, the mean gross effective pressure in pounds per square inch of pistons, and the gross horses power developed by the engines for the true experimental speeds of vessel contained in Column 12; these quantities have been calculated from the contents of Columns 22 to 27 both inclusive, on the hypothesis that the resistance of the vessel varied as the square of its velocity, and the power required to work the engines *per se* directly as the number of double strokes of piston made in equal times.

Columns 18 and 19 contain the number of revolutions of the screws and of double strokes of engines' pistons required to be made in equal times to give the vessel a speed of 9 knots per hour ; the columns are calculated for the rectified slips in Column 11.

Columns 20 and 21 contain, respectively, the mean effective gross pressure on the pistons in pounds per square inch, and the gross horses power developed by the engines required for a speed of vessel of 9 knots per hour, and for the number of revolutions of the screws and double strokes of engines' pistons contained in Columns 18 and 19. These pressures and powers are calculated from Columns 22 to 27 both inclusive.

Columns 22, 23, 24, 25, 26 and 27, contain the distribution of the total horses power required to propel the vessel with the different screws at the uniform speed of 9 knots per hour, and with the rectified slips of the screws as given in Column 11. Column 22 contains the horses power required to work the engines *per se* at the number of double strokes of pistons given in Column 19 and for the pressure of 1½ pound per square inch of pistons. Column 25 contains the horses power required to overcome the cohesion of the water by the screw blades ; calculated for the number of revolutions of the screw in Column 18, and in the ratio of the square of the velocity of the helicoidal surfaces in their helical paths, for a value of 0.45 pound per square foot of surface and a velocity of 10 feet per second. Column 27 contains the horses powers required to propel the simple hull at the speed of 9 knots per hour ; this power is derived from the means of the indicated powers in Columns 14 and 15 for the two experimental speeds of vessel given in Column 12 and on the supposition that the resistance of the vessel varied as the square of its velocity. Column 26 contains the horses powers expended in the slips of the screws, deduced from Column 27 for the true slips in Column 11, in the ratio of the speeds of the screws to the speeds of the vessel. Column 24 contains the horses powers required to overcome the friction of the load. They are 7½ per centum of the sum of Columns 25, 26 and 27, including themselves. Column 23 contains the horses powers applied to the screw shaft: they are the sum of Columns 24, 25, 26 and 27. Column 24 is 7½ per centum of Column 23. Column 21 is the sum of the Columns from 22 to 27 both inclusive.

TABLE containing a Summary of the Experimental Results obtained from the Different Screws applied to H. B. M.'s Steamer "CONFLICT," with a Rectification of these Results, and an Analysis of them exhibiting the Distribution of the Power in each case, and the Relative Efficiencies of the Screws in function of the Gross and Net Powers applied.

DESIGNATION OF THE SCREW	DIMENSIONS OF THE SCREWS.						
	Diameter, in feet.	Number of Blades.	Pitch, in feet.	Length in direction of Axis, in feet.	Fraction used of the Pitch.	Helicoidal area, in square feet.	Projected area on a plane at right angles to axis, in square feet.
No. of Col'n,.....	1	2	3	4	5	6	7
A*	13.5	2	16.500	2.750	0.333	57.653	47.450
B**	"	"	15.167	2.528	0.300	50.000	43.520
C†	"	"	15.167	2.528	0.290	43.000	38.800
D‡	"	"	19.885	2.486	0.250	46.540	35.587
E‖	"	"	19.885	2.000	0.118	27.837	21.056
Boomerang ¶	"	"	20.000	4.000	0.118	30.916	21.056

DESIGNATION OF THE SCREW	SLIPS OF THE SCREWS AND SPEEDS OF VESSEL.					POWERS OF THE ENGINES.				
	OBSERVED.			CALCULATED.		OBSERVED.			CALCULATED.	
	Number of Revolutions made by the Screw per minute.	Slips of the Screws in per centum of their speed, as ascertained by Experiment.	Speed of the vessel per hour, in knots of 6,086 feet, as ascertained experimentally.	Slips of the Screws in per centum of their speed, as rectified.	Speed of the vessel per hour, in knots of 6,086 feet, calculated from the rectified slips.	Number of double strokes of Pistons made per minute.	Mean effective gross pressure on Pistons, in pounds per square inch, by Indicator.	Horses Power developed by Engines, by Indicator.	Mean effective gross pressure on Pistons, in pounds per square inch, by Calculation.	Horses Power developed by Engines, by Calculation.
No. of Col'n,.....	8	9	10	11	12	13	14	15	16	17
A*	68.000	16.02	9.289	17.59	9.116	68.000	14.19	777.50	13.86	759.52
B**	75.750	16.81	9.424	16.50	9.458	75.750	13.30	812.00	13.19	805.50
C†	77.000	18.15	9.425	17.38	9.512	77.000	—	—	14.10	874.78
D‡	62.000	21.01	9.600	22.41	9.430	62.000	—	—	16.87	842.67
E‖	65.875	26.25	9.524	25.90	9.570	65.875	—	—	16.92	898.05
Boomerang ¶	66.688	26.05	9.724	26.05	9.724	66.688	—	—	17.57	944.22

DESIGNATION OF THE SCREW	TO GIVE THE VESSEL A SPEED OF 9 KNOTS PER HOUR.									
	TOTAL ENGINE POWERS.				DISTRIBUTION OF THE TOTAL ENGINE POWERS. IN HORSES POWERS.					
	Number of Revolutions made by the Screws per minute.	Number of double strokes of Engines' Pistons made per minute.	Mean effective gross pressure on Pistons, in pounds per square inch.	Gross Horses Power developed by Engines.	Working the Engines, *per se.*	Remaining after deducting the power required to work the Engines, *per se.*	Overcoming the Friction of the Load.	Required to overcome the Cohesion of the Water by the Screw blades.	Slip of the Screws.	Propelling the Vessel.
No. of Col'n,.....	18	19	20	21	22	23	24	25	26	27
A*	67.12	67.12	13.55	733.04	81.13	651.91	48.89	53.85	96.60	452.57
B**	72.09	72.09	12.61	732.58	87.13	645.45	48.40	55.05	89.43	452.57
C†	72.85	72.85	12.78	750.01	88.05	661.96	49.64	64.55	95.20	452.57
D‡	59.17	59.17	15.49	738.53	71.52	667.01	50.02	33.71	130.71	452.57
E‖	61.95	61.95	15.14	755.59	74.88	680.71	51.05	18.90	158.19	452.57
Boomerang ¶	61.72	61.72	15.27	759.35	74.60	684.75	51.36	21.40	159.42	452.57

DESIGNATION OF THE SCREW	IN PER CENTUM OF THE POWER REMAINING AFTER DEDUCTING WHAT IS REQUIRED TO WORK THE ENGINES.				RELATIVE ECONOMICAL EFFICIENCIES OF THE SCREWS.	
	Overcoming the Friction of the Load.	Required to overcome the Cohesion of the Water by the Screw blades.	Slips of the Screws.	Propelling the Vessel.	Powers proportionably, which remain after deducting the power required to work the Engines, *per se.*	Gross Powers proportionably, developed by Engines.
No. of Col'n,.....	28	29	30	31	32	33
A*	7.50	8.26	14.82	69.42	1.0100	1.0007
B**	7.50	8.53	13.85	70.12	1.0000	1.0000
C†	7.50	9.75	14.38	68.37	1.0256	1.0238
D‡	7.50	5.05	19.60	67.85	1.0334	1.0081
E‖	7.50	2.78	23.24	66.48	1.0546	1.0314
Boomerang ¶	7.50	3.12	23.28	66.10	1.0609	1.0366

* Screw A is a common screw of uniform pitch and length from hub to periphery.

** Screw B is a common screw of uniform pitch and length from hub to periphery, except that the corner of the blades are rounded off on a radius of 18 inches.

† Screw C is screw B with the hub and central portions of the blades inclosed in a globe of 4.75 feet diameter, according to Griffith's arrangement.

‡ Screw D is a common screw of uniform pitch and length from hub to periphery.

‖ Screw E is screw D with its surface reduced in such a manner as to make it equal to in projected area, and to give it the same outline of blade, as the Boomerang.

¶ Boomerang propeller of Sir Thomas Mitchell; the surface of the blades a true helicoid; one blade inclined forward, the other aft; the blades have an irregular outline.

To face page 91.

Columns 28, 29, 30 and 31, contain the quantities in Columns 24, 25, 26 and 27, expressed in per centum of Column 23 ; they consequently show proportionably the distribution of the power applied to the screw shaft.

Columns 32 and 33 contain the relative economical efficiencies of the screws. Column 32 expresses this relation in proportion to the net powers applied to the screw shaft, which are given in Column 23. Column 33 expresses this same relation in proportion to the gross powers developed by the engines, which are given in Column 21. The difference between Columns 32 and 33, is caused by the fact, that the net power applied to the shaft is, for the same screw, in the ratio of the cubes of the speed of the vessel ; while the gross power is composed of this net power and the power required to work the engines *per se*, which latter power is only in the direct ratio of the speed of the vessel. The higher the numbers in Columns 32 and 33 the less is the economical efficiency.

It is believed that the annexed Table is so complete in itself as to need no further explanation.

§ *Discussion of Results of the Experiments.*

In examining the foregoing Table of Experimental Results, our notice is first arrested by the slight difference in the economical efficiencies of the screws, although the latter offer considerable diversity of form and dimensions; the lowest efficiency, measured by the power applied to the screw shaft, being only 6 per centum less than the highest. On closer examination, we find this to result from the facts that the loss of useful effect by the screws is composed of the sum of the powers expended on the slip and required to overcome the cohesive resistance of the water by the blades; and that we cannot diminish one without increasing the other. Hence we find, that within moderate limits, the economical efficiency remains nearly the same, although the slip may vary considerably, as well as the power required to overcome the cohesive resistance of the water, the one increasing as the other diminishes. With the screws applied to the "CONFLICT," the slips varied from 16.50 to 26.05 per centum, and the power expended in overcoming the cohesive resistance of the water to the blades varied from 2.78 to 9.75 per centum of the power applied to the screw shaft; yet, as above stated, the extreme variation in economical efficiency among their screws was only 6 per centum, measured by the net power applied to the shaft, and if measured by the gross power developed by the engines, it falls to $3\frac{7}{10}$ per centum; and were it to be measured by the *total* quantities of steam used in the different cases (including the waste in the cylinder nozzles and clearance), which correctly represents the quantities of fuel expended, this variation would be reduced still lower, and in fact, in some of the cases, the relative economical efficiencies would be actually reversed, because the screws giving the lower results in the Table being of greater pitch, make fewer revolutions to propel the vessel a given distance, and consequently waste less steam in the cylinder nozzles and clearances which have not to be filled so often. These remarks, however, only apply when the screws are propelling the normal resistance of the vessel, that is to say, when the latter is uninfluenced by head winds or seas or having a vessel in tow. In such cases, an entirely different scale of relative economical efficiencies will result, owing to the facts: That with a considerable increase of the normal resistance of the vessel, the number of revolutions made by the screw in a given time will, with equal steam pressure, remain nearly the same, and consequently, the loss of useful effect by the power required to overcome the cohesive resistance of the water by the screw blades, will remain nearly as before ; not so, however, with the loss of useful effect by the slip which increases in the direct ratio of the resistance ; and if we suppose the normal resistance of the vessel to be increased by a moderate head wind and sea 50 per centum—an ordinary case in practice—then the slips of the screw will be increased one-half also, and a slip that with the normal resistance was only 16 per centum, will become 24 per centum, while a slip of 26 per centum will become 39 per centum, the increased difference of the slips being 5 per centum, which is unaccompanied by anything at all approaching proportional decrease in the power required to overcome the cohesive resistance of the water by the screw blades ; consequently, nearly the whole of this additional 5 per centum of slip tells against the screw of greater slip, and becomes more and more exaggerated as the normal resistance of the vessel is more and more increased. Hence, it will be found that the relative economical efficencies of screws experimented with in smooth water and uninfluenced by wind, are by no means the measure of their economical efficiencies at sea, struggling against the vicissitudes of weather and an average increase of the normal resistance of the vessel from one-third to one-half, according to its size. This important consideration has too frequently, if not always, been overlooked in proportioning screws for marine propulsion ; for which purpose the screw of least slip in smooth water is, in general, the most efficient. But with screws of equal diameter, a marked reduction of slip can only be obtained by lessening the pitch, which involves a greater speed of engine for equal speeds of vessel, and this is a very serious practical inconvenience, especially with large engines, as regards their durability and certainty of action. Some reduction of slip can, it is true, be obtained by employing a greater fraction of the pitch, but this involves, if carried beyond four-tenths even in extreme cases, a disproportionately increased loss by the power required to overcome the cohesive resistance of the water; it also involves the no less serious practical inconvenience of increased length and weight of screw.

Under the conditions of the Experiments, the screw giving the highest economical result was screw B, which had the least slip, namely, 16.50 per centum; it had also the least pitch and was composed of the fraction $\frac{3}{10}$ths of the pitch; yet, this screw, if we omit the exceptional screw C, expended the greatest amount of power in overcoming the cohesive resistance of the water, namely, 8.53 per centum of the power applied to the screw shaft. We find also, that every increase of pitch and consequently of slip, was attended with a decrease in the economical efficiency, notwithstanding that with the increased pitches the power expended in overcoming the cohesion of the water, was reduced by reducing the fraction used of the pitch. The sum of the losses of useful effect by slip and by overcoming the cohesion of the water with screw B, was (13.85+8.53=) 22.38 per centum of the power applied to the shaft; and as this could not have been reduced by any further reduction of the fraction used of the pitch, it may be taken as the minimum obtainable with the given pitches, diameter and resistance. Hence, under the conditions of the experiments, $\frac{3}{10}$ths is the proper fraction of pitch to be employed in conjunction with a slip of 16.50 per centum.

In the strictly comparative experiments with screws B and C,—which were the same excepting that in C the hub and central portions of the blades were inclosed in a globe whose diameter was 35.2 per centum of the diameter of the screw—screw C gave a less economical efficiency of 2½ per centum, owing to the facts that the decrease of the blade surface, although made immediately around the axis, increased the slip; while the power expended by the globe in its rotatory movement to overcome the cohesion of the water, was greater than what would have been expended for the same purpose by the inelosed central portions of the blades moving in their helical paths. In addition to these increased losses, there is also the greater direct resistance of the large globe to the forward movement of the vessel, than what is opposed by the end of the ordinary hub and the sharp edges of the screw blades. Hence we find, that as this form of screw offers no practical advantages and entails considerable economical losses, it should never be employed except when feathering blades are used, in which case it is absolutely necessary for containing the mechanism that moves them.

In comparing screws D and E, which are the same in function of form, excepting that the former employs the fraction 0.25 of the pitch and the latter the fraction of 0.118 of the pitch, we observe that the relative economical efficiency of screw D was 2 per centum greater than that of screw E, the slip of the former being 22.41, and that of the latter 25,90 per centum ; whence appears, that in these cases the increase of slip was not compensated by the decrease in the power required to overcome the cohesion of the water, due to the lesser surface ; consequently, with slips of 22.41 per centum and over, there results a loss of economical efficiency by reducing the fraction employed of the pitch below 0.25.

In the strictly comparative experiments between screw E and the Boomerang propeller—which are quite fair, inasmuch as whatever pitch, fraction of pitch, diameter, or outline of blade may be employed for the one, can be employed for the other—screw E had very slightly the greatest economical efficiency, owing to its blades having less helicoidal though the same projected surface as the Boomerang, resulting from the fact, that the screw's blades were perpendicular to the axis, while the blades of the Boomerang were inclined fore and aft to the axis. The Boomerang, from this cause, has also the great practical inconvenience of requiring much more length (in the one experimented with double the length) fore and aft in the dead wood of the vessel, in order to accommodate the fore and aft inclination of the blades ; if its blades be not made with this inclination it is no longer a Boomerang but a true screw.

From the experiments with screws C and E, and the Boomerang, it appears how useless are any attempts to increase the efficiency of screws by modifying the outline of the blades; no taperings of the latter out or in, or inclinations of them from a perpendicular to the axis either in a longitudinal or lateral direction, and no removals radially of the surface by substitution of globes around the hub, or by other means, can add anything to the propulsive efficiency of the helicoidal surface, and they generally entail serious practical inconveniencies. The only improvement possible on the true screw of uniform length from hub to periphery, is that due to the use of an expanding pitch or curved directrix.

COMPARATIVE EXPERIMENTS

WITH THE

SCREW AND PADDLE-WHEEL.

AS APPLIED TO THE

U. S. STEAMERS "SPENCER" AND "McLANE."

Experiments to ascertain the Comparative Efficiency of the LOPER SCREW and of the PADDLE-WHEEL as applied to the United States Revenue Steam Cutters "SPENCER" *and* "McLANE;" *made by order of the United States Treasury Department, April* 15*th*, 16*th*, *and* 17*th*, 1846.

THESE experiments were conducted by Captain A. V. FRASER, of the U. S. Revenue Service; and were witnessed by Commodore M. C. PERRY and Engineer-in-Chief C. H. HASWELL, U. S. Navy. The latter two gentlemen made separate reports; from the conclusions in Mr. HASWELL'S report, I entirely dissent, and particularly from the calculated results (which contradict each other), where the power element, and other important data are evidently erroneously computed.

In the conduct of these experiments, undertaken for the sole purpose of determining the comparative efficiency of the two propelling instruments, which comparison rests wholly on the relations between the powers and speeds; it seems inexplicable that neither Indicator nor Dynamometer was fitted to the machinery; consequently, neither the resistance of the hull, nor the power developed by the engines, nor the pressure required to work the latter *per se* and overcome the friction of the gearing was ascertained; and the comparative economical efficiency of the two systems of propulsion, so far as it rests on the experimental data, was left as much undetermined as before these trials were commenced.

In the original reports, the consumption of fuel per hour in each case was given, and it might be supposed that this consumption could serve for an expression of the power; but as the trials lasted only a few hours, and as the consumption of fuel noted (except during the 1st Trial, April 17th) is simply what was put in the furnaces after starting, taking no account of the amount already in, and remaining at stopping, nor of the quantity of ashes and other refuse made, nor of the amount of water fed into or blown out of the boilers during the trials, it is manifestly impossible to use this element, especially as it continually contradicts itself; for instance: During the two trials made April 15th with the "SPENCER," the consumption of coal is stated for the 1st Trial at 1,634 pounds per hour, with steam of 42.3 pounds boiler pressure per square inch and 40.43 double strokes of engine piston per minute; for the 2d Trial, same throttle and measure of expansion for the steam, the consumption of fuel was but 1,155 pounds per hour, furnishing steam of 42.62 pounds boiler pressure per square inch, with 42.81 double strokes of piston per minute; that is to say, on the same day, with same machinery and fuel, firemen and engineers, the same boiler at an interval of a few hours furnished $6\frac{7}{10}$ per centum *more* steam with $41\frac{1}{2}$ per centum *less* fuel. Further, the fuel was supplied with air by a fan blast, and in both trials the blowers were driven at 280 revolutions per minute; as they furnished about the same quantity of air, there must have been consumed about the same quantity of fuel in equal times.

Again, during the 1st Trial, April 16th, with the "SPENCER," it is stated there was consumed 357 pounds of coal per hour, furnishing steam enough to make 35 double strokes of piston; during the 2d Trial the same day, under the same conditions of weather, water, throttle and measure of expansion of the steam, the "SPENCER," with 588 pounds of coal per hour, furnished steam enough for only 31.91 double strokes of piston per minute; and so on throughout all the experiments, except the 1st Trial, April 17th, in which, after steam was raised and the furnaces filled, 2,000 pounds of coal were weighed out for each boiler, and the steam being worked with equal expansion, though not with equal opening of the throttle, the vessels were run as long as the engines would continue in motion. In this case, the *total* amount of coal burned from starting fires being known, and that coal being entirely burnt out, it furnished a tolerably exact exponent of the relative efficiency of the two systems of propulsion in combination with the mode of using the steam, in function of fuel consumed, the only errors that could occur being due to the mode of firing, quality of coal, and amount of "feeding up" and "blowing off" done; all of which probably did not vary enough in the two cases to greatly vitiate the result. But the relative efficiency thus ascertained *in function of fuel consumed,* will not even be approximately a measure of the relative efficiency *in function of power exerted,* owing to the facts: that the screw and paddle-wheel, in order to give the vessel equal speeds, required a very different number of double strokes of engines' pistons to be made in equal times; and that the engines were of the same dimensions and non-condensing, consequently exhausting against the atmosphere, and having a back pressure on the pistons bearing a very high ratio to the mean effective or impelling pressure. Now, *ceteris paribus,* the weight of steam is an exact measure of the weight of combustible producing it, and as this back pressure and also the pressure required to work the engine *per se* were the same per stroke of piston with both the screw and the paddle-wheel engines, it follows: that the weight of steam to balance it, consumed in equal times, will be greater with the quicker working screw engine than with the slower working paddle-wheel engine, in the ratio of the number of strokes of piston made in equal times; and as this steam constituted a high per centage of the total quantity used, and was ineffective in the production of the power exerted, which is derived simply from the effective pressure or the pressure that remains after deducting from the absolute pressure that which is required to balance the back pressure and to work the engine *per se,* it follows, that with widely varying speeds of piston, the fuel consumed and the power generated by it, are not even approximately commensurable, but may vary to any extent.

Without adverting further to the conclusions of Messrs. PERRY and HASWELL, I shall take the elementary data as furnished by Captain FRASER, and draw my own conclusions from it.

The hulls of both vessels were of iron, and duplicates in all respects, being built in the same manner, from the same lines, and of the same dimensions. The model was peculiar, and originated from necessity, not choice, as these vessels were originally built for and fitted with "Hunter's submerged wheels," which could only be placed in a transverse section of peculiar form. These submerged wheels proving signal failures, were removed, and the common Paddle-wheel substituted in the "McLane," and two of Loper's screws, one under each counter, in the "Spencer." The principal portion of the submerged transverse section of the hull was nearly a parallelogram, the side being vertical, the bottom having but very little dead rise, and the bilge being almost a sharp angle instead of gently rounding with an easy curve. Just above the level of the top of the Hunter wheel and about 2 feet below the water line, the section swelled out rapidly in a reversed curve in order to give width of spar deck. The water lines were extremely sharp both fore and aft. Such a very defective model may be characterized as combining the minimum displacement with the maximum of rubbing surface.

The vessels were as deficient in sea going as in other good qualities; they were destitute of stability, and would not stand up under canvas in strong breezes. In fresh breezes on the wind and abeam, the lee wheel of the "McLane" would be immersed nearly to the shaft, and the weather wheel thrown proportionally out of water. The greatest immersed transverse section being placed very far abaft the centre of the load water line, the vessels were unmanageable in heavy weather, as they would neither "lay to," nor could be kept by the wind: for the same reason, they would not "stay," and they were difficult to "wear" in any reasonable space.

It will be observed, that from the use of two screws, one under each counter, and not overlapping each other, instead of one only, and that placed immediately behind the stern-post, the models of the vessels were about equally favorable for Screw and Paddle-wheel, as the water had easy access to both in a solid state. The paddle surface was large and of deep immersion in proportion to the size of vessel, and its considerable slip conclusively shows the hull to have had a very high coefficient of resistance. The surface of the two screws was very large and the pitch moderate in proportion to the size of the hull, so that their slip, as in the case of the paddle-wheel, proves the hull's coefficient of resistance to have been unusually great, especially for such sharp water lines. Such a model, it is evident, could not be of easy resistance.

The original boilers and engines were employed with the new systems of propulsion ; they were of precisely the same dimensions, but the speed of the engines relatively to the speed of the propelling instruments was modified in both vessels by cog-wheel gearing ; the loss of useful effect occasioned by the friction of the latter, was therefore the same in both ; the only difference in the gearing was, that the speed of the Paddle-wheel was geared *down* while the speed of the Screw was geared *up*.

In these experiments the distances run and the velocities of the tide were given by the Superintendent of the U. S. Coast Survey ; of the remaining data, there is much uncertainty as to the accuracy of the steam pressure, point of cutting off, and opening of the throttle. Besides which, the cylinder cut-off valves were quite different in the two vessels, being a "slide" in the "SPENCER," and a "puppet" in the "McLANE," which taken in connection with their very different speeds of piston, precludes all idea of determining the *relative* mean cylinder pressures from the boiler pressures, by making equal allowances for difference between them, and employing the same coefficient of expansion, and amount of back pressure. I have, however, in the "Table of Rectified Results," etc., hereinafter given, assumed as correct, the power required to propel the vessel at 7 geographical miles per hour which resulted from the mean of a number of accurate but detached experiments made at different times with the "McLANE" (paddle-wheel), and which I am convinced does not vary much from the truth.

§ *Hull and Machinery.*

The following are the dimensions, etc., of the hull and machinery of the two vessels, viz. :

Hull (iron).

Length between perpendiculars, ...	143 feet.
Beam at knuckle of bilge, ...	18 feet 6 inches.
Beam at load water line (9 feet 8 inches mean draught), ...	22 feet.
Beam on deck, ...	23 feet.
Depth of hold, ...	11 feet 10 inches.
Depth of keel, ...	1 foot.
Depth from rabbet of keel to load water line, ...	8 feet 8 inches.
Area of greatest immersed tranverse section (9 feet 8 inches mean draught)	166 square feet.
Displacement at 9 feet 8 inches mean draught, ...	460 tons.
Displacement at load water line per inch of draught, ...	5.11 tons.
Immersed surface of hull, ...	4,128 square feet.
Area of load water line, ...	2,142 " "
Area of load water line in proportion to circumscribing parallelogram, ...	0.681
Area of greatest immersed transverse section in proportion to circumscribing parallelogram, ...	0.871
Displacement in proportion to circumscribing parallelopipedon, ...	0.589
Displacement in proportion to cylinder having for base the area of the greatest immersed transverse section, ...	0.677
Angle of entrance of the load water line, ...	42°
Mean angle of entrance for the whole draught, ...	27°
Angle of clearance of the load water line, ...	57°
Mean angle of clearance for the whole draught, ...	27°

Angle of dead rise at the greatest immersed transverse section, ...	$7\frac{1}{4}°$

Engines.

Two non-condensing, horizontal engines for each vessel. The steam was cut off in the "SPENCER" by a slide valve, and in the "McLANE" by a puppet valve, at half stroke. The engines of both vessels were geared, and of the following dimensions, viz.:

Diameter of cylinders, ...	24 inches.
Stroke of pistons, ...	3 feet.
Space displacement of both pistons per stroke, ...	18.85 cubic feet.

Gearing.

("SPENCER," *Screw engine.*)

Extreme diameter of driving wheel, ...	3 feet $1\frac{1}{2}$ inch.
Extreme diameter of wheel on screw shaft,	2 feet 6 inches.
The driving wheel contains 75 teeth of wood.	
The wheel on the screw shaft contains 60 iron teeth.	
The screws make $1\frac{1}{4}$ revolution for each double stroke of engines' pistons.	

("McLANE," *Paddle-wheel engine.*)

Diameter of driving wheel on engine shaft, ...	4 feet 6 inches.
Face of ditto, ...	1 foot 4 inches.
Number of iron teeth in ditto, ...	47
Diameter of cog-wheel on paddle-wheel shaft, ...	7 feet.
Face of ditto, ...	1 foot 4 inches.
Number of wooden teeth in ditto, ...	72

These cog-wheels are formed of two sections, each 8 inches wide, placed together so that the teeth off-set or break joints to prevent back lash or jar, and to keep a greater number in contact. The Paddle-wheels make 0.6528 of a revolution for each double stroke of engines' pistons.

Boilers.

Each vessel had one boiler of iron with single return ascending flues. The natural draught, though strong, was entirely insufficient to burn enough coal to furnish the required amount of steam, and was aided by a powerful fan blast, the blowers of which were driven by a small independent steam cylinder. The fuel used was anthracite.

Length of the boiler, ...	22 feet 10 inches.
Breadth of boiler, ...	8 feet 10 inches.
Height of boiler (exclusive of steam chimney), ...	9 feet 5 inches.
Area of the total heating surface, ...	1,309 square feet.
Area of the total grate surface, ...	43 " "
Aggregate cross area of the two lower rows of flues, ...	7.309 " "
Aggregate cross area of the two upper rows of flues, ...	7.636 " "
Cross area of the smoke chimney, ...	7.876 " "
Height of the smoke chimney above the grates, ...	45 feet.
Capacity of steam room in the boiler, .	307 cubic feet.
Weight of sea water contained in the boiler, ...	37,300 pounds.

Proportions.

Proportion of heating to grate surface, .. 30.442 to 1.000

Proportion of grate surface to aggregate

cross area of the two lower rows of flues,	5.883 to 1.000
Proportion of grate surface to aggregate cross area of the two upper rows of flues,	5.631 " "
Proportion of grate surface to cross area of smoke chimney, ...	5.460 " "
Square feet of heating surface per cubic foot of space displacement of piston per stroke, ...	69.443
Square feet of grate surface per cubic foot of space displacement of piston per stroke, ...	2.281
Cubic feet of steam room per cubic foot of steam used per stroke of piston, ...	16.290

Paddle-wheel of the "McLane."

Diameter from outside to outside of paddles for the Trials April 15th and 16th, ...	16 feet 5 inches.
Diameter from outside to outside of paddles for the Trials April 17th, ..	15 feet 1 inch.
Number of paddles in each wheel, ...	14
Number of paddles in each wheel in water for the large diameter, ...	5
Length of each paddle, ...	5 feet 11 inches.
Breadth of each paddle, ...	10 inches.
Aggregate area of two paddles, ...	9.861 square feet.

Screws of the "Spencer."

Two Loper screws of wrought iron, one placed under each counter of the vessel and supported by hanging stirrups from the quarter. In this kind of screw, the pitch is uniform for the same element from fore to aft, but expanding radially from hub to periphery. The consequence is, that when the difference between the pitch at the hub and at the periphery is great, as in the case of the "Spencer's" screws, the central portion of the screw has a less longitudinal speed than the vessel and exercises no propulsive effort; while the loss of useful effect by the power required to overcome the cohesion of the water, is as great as though the normal propulsive effort was obtained. Another consequence is, that for every change of slip, the *acting* screw surface and the *acting* mean pitch changes ; the surface becoming less with the less slip and the pitch greater ; and with the greater slip, the *acting* surface becomes greater and the pitch less.

Diameter of the screw,.............	8 feet.
Diameter of the hub,...............	8 inches.
Number of blades,.................	4
Length of the screw in direction of axis at periphery, ...	2 feet 10 inches.
Tapering in to a length in direction of axis at $1\frac{7}{8}$ foot radius, of	2 feet 6 inches.
Length of the screw in direction of axis at $1\frac{7}{8}$ foot radius (2 inches offset on each side), ...	2 feet 2 inches.
Angle of blades at periphery from a line at right angles to axis, ...	36°
Angle of blades at hub from a line at right angles to axis, ...	60°
Pitch at periphery, ...	18.26 feet.
Pitch at hub, ...	3.65 feet.
The acting surfaces and the acting mean pitch will be found for each case of slip, in the Table of Experimental Data hereinafter given.	

The remaining data for the screw will be found in the following Table ; the calculations embrace *one* screw only ; for both screws the surfaces must be doubled, and also the power required for overcoming the cohesion of the water by the screw blades. This power has been calculated for the number (51.04) of revolutions required to be made by the screw per minute, with the normal slip of 17.63 per centum, to give the vessel a speed of 7 geographical miles per hour. The friction value of one square foot of helicoidal surface, moving in its helical path with a speed of ten feet per second, is taken at 0.45 pound, and to be in the ratio of the square of the speeds.

Pitches of the Elements, in feet,............	Radii of the Elements, in feet,..............	Circumferences normal to radii of Elements, in feet, ...	Length of the Elements, in feet,..............	Fractions used of the Pitches of the Elements,	Lengths used of the Elements, in feet,.........	Breadths of the Elements, in feet,.............	Helicoidal areas of the Elements, in square feet,	Projected areas of the Elements on a plane at right angles to axis, in square feet,...........	Speed of the Elements, in feet, per second,.......	Speed of the Elements, in feet, per minute,.......	Expression for the power required to overcome the Cohesion of the water by the screw blades.
A	**B**	**C**	**D**	**E**	**F**	**G**	**H**	**I**	**J**	**K**	
		2B × 3.1416	$\sqrt{A^2+C^2}$		D × E		F × G	C × E × G	$\frac{K}{60}$	D × 51.04	$\frac{J^2}{10^2} \times K \times 2H.$
4.5	0.417	2.618	5.206	1.926	10.027	0.667	1.671	0.840	4.429	265.714	174.16
6.1	0.625	3.927	7.256	1.421	10.311	0.25	2.578	1.395	6.172	370.346	727.49
8.0	0.875	5.498	9.707	1.083	10.513	"	2.628	1.488	8.257	495.445	1775.57
9.5	1.125	7.069	11.841	0.912	10.799	"	2.700	1.612	10.073	604.365	3311.20
10.8	1.375	8.639	13.830	0.802	11.092	"	2.773	1.731	11.765	705.883	5418.44
12.0	1.625	10.210	15.756	0.722	11.376	"	2.844	1.843	13.403	804.186	8222.00
13.0	1.875	11.781	17.544	0.718	12.597	"	3.149	2.115	14.924	895.446	12567.00
13.9	2.125	13 351	19.273	0.731	14.089	"	3.522	2.440	16.395	983.694	18625.30
14.7	2.375	14.922	20.943	0.690	14.453	"	3.613	2.574	17.819	1069.135	24530.00
15.4	2.625	16.493	22.565	0.682	15.389	"	3.847	2.812	19.195	1151.718	32650.30
16.0	2.875	18.064	24.128	0.667	16.086	"	4.021	3.010	20.525	1231.493	41721.70
16 6	3.125	19.365	25.506	0.654	16.681	"	4.170	3.166	21.697	1301.826	51111.50
17.2	3.375	21.205	27.337	0.641	17.523	"	4.381	3 398	23.255	1395.280	66113.00
17.6	3.625	22.776	28.785	0.636	18.307	"	4.575	3.622	24.487	1469.186	80603.00
18.1	3.875	24.347	30.338	0.626	18.992	"	4.748	3.810	25.808	1548.451	97937.06
											445487.72

and $\frac{445487.72 \times 0.45}{33000} = 6.075$ H.P. = Power required to overcome the cohesion of the water by *one* Screw, and 12.15 H.P. for *both* Screws.

Rig.

Both vessels were topsail schooner rigged. The "SPENCER" had three masts, the "McLANE" but two; yards were carried, however. on the foremasts only of both; and both vessels spread equal amounts of canvas.

§ *Experimental Trials.*

Two trials were made on each day, the vessels starting together, but running unequal distances through the water. The object was to test the comparative efficiency of the two systems of propulsion in smooth water and calms, with strong wind and rough sea ahead, and with strong wind and rough sea aft. The trials made on the 16th and 17th April, were in water perfectly smooth, and in calms and light airs. During the trials made on the 17th April, the paddles of the "McLANE" were *reefed* in towards the axis, reducing their diameter from 16 feet 5 inches to 15 feet 1 inch, and their immersion from 3 feet 9½ inches to 3 feet. In the 2d Trial, April 17th, the data with the "McLANE" was evidently widely erroneous—making the slip of the centre of pressure of the paddles 36 per centum—and totally disagreeing with the data of the other comparable trials; I have, therefore, omitted in this case the results from the "McLANE," and merely given those from the "SPENCER" as corroborative in their agreement of the accuracy of the results from the other trials made under similar circumstances of wind, water, etc.

The slips given by the screw in all the comparable trials made during the 16th and 17th April, were sensibly the same, showing that the resistances of the vessel were in the ratio of the square of its velocity, although that velocity varied from 5.473 to 7.705 geographical miles per hour.

The vessels' draught of water varied a few inches during the trials, but not enough to sensibly affect the results.

The power required to overcome the cohesion of the water by

the immersed surface of the hull, calculated for a speed of vessel of 7 geographical miles per hour, and in the same manner as with the screw, amounts to 55.97 Horses Power.

In the 1st Trial, April 16th, the throttle of the screw engines of the "SPENCER" was greatly closed to reduce their speed to 35 double strokes of piston per minute.

The 1st Trial, April 17th, was made to determine the relative performance of the two vessels, consuming an equal amount of fuel, but without regard to exact equality of time. For this purpose, 2,000 pounds of coal were weighed out in both vessels, and burnt at such rates as to maintain about the same boiler pressure in them; the throttle of the screw engine was partly closed, to maintain this equality of pressure, while that of the paddle-wheel engine was carried wide open. The coal was entirely consumed in both cases, and the engines operated as long as there was steam enough to move them. Hence, in this Trial, the relative economical efficiencies of the propelling instruments and motor combined, can be determined in function of fuel consumed from the experimental data, the steam being equally expanded in both cases, and exhausting against the constant atmospheric pressure. The distance run by the screw vessel "SPENCER" was 23.75 miles in 226 minutes, and by the paddle-wheel vessel "McLANE," 23.15 miles in 209 minutes. It is then necessary to ascertain what time would be required by the "McLANE" to run with the same fuel the distance 23.75 miles: this time will be the time 209 minutes increased in the ratio of the cubes of the distances 23.75 and 23.15 miles, which cubes compare as 1.08 and 1.00; consequently, $209 \times 1.08 = 226$ minutes, or precisely the same time as occupied by the screw vessel "SPENCER" in running the same distance. Hence in function of fuel consumed, the two systems—propelling instruments and steam machinery combined in each vessel—were of equal efficiency.

The *acting* mean fraction of pitch of the screw, when propelling normally in smooth water, uninfluenced by wind or current, was 0.65, and this increased as the slip increased from additional resistance of the vessel arising from any cause whatever.

The annexed Table contains all the Data of the Experimental Results of these Trials, and taken in connection with the preceding explanation and dimensions, gives all the information required. The loss of useful effect by the oblique action of the Paddles, has been *calculated* in the ratio of the squares of the sines of their angles of incidence on the water, modified in the direct ratio of their depths in feet below the surface of the water, plus a height of 33.84 feet above the surface of the water, the latter being the height of a column of water of equal weight with the atmosphere. The centre of pressure of the paddles was *calculated* for the same depths below the top of the watery column equal in pressure to the atmosphere. The acting mean pitch of the screws and their acting fraction of pitch, were calculated in function of the pitches and fractions of the elements and the square of their distances from the axis.

TABLE containing the Data of the Comparative Experiments made with the LOPER SCREW *of the "SPENCER" and the* PADDLE-WHEEL *of the "McLANE," by order of the United States Treasury Department, April 15th, 16th, and 17th, 1846.*

NAME OF VESSEL.	DATE OF TRIAL.	COURSE OF THE VESSEL.	DIRECTION AND KIND OF WIND.	STATE OF THE SEA.	Draught of the Vessel fore and aft, in feet and inches.	SPEED OF VESSEL.			ENGINES.				SCREW.							PADDLE-WHEEL.					
						Total distance run through the water, in geographical miles of 6,086 feet.	Total time, in hours and minutes, of running the total distance.	Speed of the vessel per hour, in geographical miles of 6,086 feet.	Steam pressure in boiler, in lbs. per square inch above atmosphere.	Proportion of Throttle.	Steam cut-off at from commencement of Stroke of Piston.	Number of Double Strokes of Piston made per minute.	Pitch, in feet, having a longitudinal speed equal to the speed of vessel.	Acting Helicoidal Area, in square ft. (both screws).	Acting Projected Area on a plane at right angles to axis, in sq. ft. (both screws).	Acting mean Pitch, in feet.	Number of revolutions made per minute.	Slip of the Screw in per centum of its speed.	Distance of the axis of the Screw below the surface of the water.	Diameter from outside to outside of Paddles, in feet and inches.	Immersion of the lower edge of Paddles, in feet and inches.	Number of revolutions made per minute.	Distance, in feet, travelled per revolution of wheel by centre of pressure of Paddles.	Loss of useful effect by oblique action of Paddles in per cent. of power applied.	Slip of the Centre of Pressure of Paddles in per cent. of their speed.
"SPENCER:" Screw, ...	1st Trial, April 17th, ...		Very light on bow, ...	Perfectly smooth, ...	9 .. 3 9 .. 6½	23.75	3 .. 46	6.306	35.4	Part closed first half of Trial.	1½	36.80	13.90	60.47	44.78	16.89	46.00	17.67	4.13	—	—	—	—	—	—
"McLANE:" Paddle-wheel, ...	Ditto.		Ditto.	Ditto.	9 .. 6 9 .. 7½	23.15	3 .. 29	6.646	39.0	Wide.	½	31.50	—	—	—	—	—	—	—	15 .. 1	3 .. 0	20.563	47.10	21.20	30.40
"SPENCER:" Screw, ...	2d Trial, April 17th, ...		Perfectly calm, ...	Perfectly smooth, ...	9 .. 3 9 .. 6½	21.19	2 .. 45	7.705	44.7	Wide.	½	45.00	13.90	60.47	44.78	16.89	56.25	17.74	4.13	—	—	—	—	—	—
"SPENCER:" Screw, ...	1st Trial, April 16th, ...	W.	Light airs from S., ...	Perfectly smooth, ...	9 .. 3 9 .. 6½	10.63	1 .. 46	6.017	39.0	$\frac{5}{16}$ths.	½	35.00	13.9	60.47	44.78	16.89	47.75	17.40	4.13	—	—	—	—	—	—
"McLANE:" Paddle-wheel, ...	Ditto.	W.	Ditto.	Ditto.	9 .. 3 9 .. 9	12.725	1 .. 49	7.005	47.0	Wide.	½	29.72	—	—	—	—	—	—	—	16 .. 5	3 .. 9½	19.40	49.33	25.16	25.76
"SPENCER:" Screw, ...	2d Trial, April 16th, ...	E.	Very light from S., ...	Perfectly smooth, ...	9 .. 3 9 .. 8	13.50	2 .. 28	5.473	22.5	Wide.	½	31.95	13.9	60.47	44.78	16.89	39.987	17.70	4.13	—	—	—	—	—	—
"McLANE:" Paddle-wheel, ...	Ditto.	E.	Ditto.	Ditto.	9 .. 3 9 .. 9	10.885	2 .. 11	4.993	22.1	Wide.	½	21.00	—	—	—	—	—	—	—	16 .. 5	3 .. 9½	13.709	49.33	25.16	25.11
"SPENCER:" Screw, ...	1st Trial, April 15th, ...	W. by S.	Strong gales from N.W.,	Turbulent sea on bow, ...	9 .. 5½ 9 .. 10½	24.742	4 .. 21	5.688	42.3	Wide.	½ on one engine, none on the other.	40.526	11.40	77.74	57.58	16.53	50.653	31.51	4.46	—	—	—	—	—	—
"McLANE:" Paddle-wheel, ...	Ditto.	W. by S.	Ditto.	Ditto.	9 .. 6 9 .. 11	25.820	6 .. 31	3.963	45.0	Wide.	½	24.333	—	—	—	—	—	—	—	16 .. 5	4 .. 0	15.885	49.50	25.16	48.83
"SPENCER:" Screw, ...	2d Trial, April 15th, ...	E.	Strong gales from N.W.,	Turbulent sea on quarter,	9 .. 5½ 9 .. 10½	24.00	3 .. 33	6.761	42.8	Wide.	½ on one engine, none on the other.	42.800	12.80	71.11	53.26	16.69	58.500	23.20	4.46	—	—	—	—	—	—
"McLANE:" Paddle-wheel, ...	Ditto.		Ditto.	Ditto.	9 .. 6 9 .. 11	23.60	3 .. 57	5.975	43.5	Wide.	½	27.813	—	—	—	—	—	—	—	16 .. 5	4 .. 0	18.156	49.50	25.16	32.57

To face page 112.

§ *Explanation of the annexed Table, exhibiting the Rectified Results and the Distribution of the Power, etc., for the Loper Screw of the* "SPENCER," *and Common Paddle-wheel of the* "MCLANE."

In this Table will be found grouped the comparative Results from the Loper screw of the "SPENCER" and the Paddle-wheel of the "MCLANE," for a uniform speed of vessel of 7 geographical miles per hour, and under the conditions of the Trials, whose data are given in the immediately preceding Table. The conditions, as regards weather and sea, are—1st, Smooth water uninfluenced by wind or current. 2d, Turbulent sea and strong gales on bow. 3d, Turbulent sea and strong gales on quarter.

Column 4 contains the slips of the propelling instruments in per centum of their speed. The slip of the Loper screw in smooth water, uninfluenced by wind or current, is the mean of all the trials made with it under these conditions. The other slips are what were experimentally determined in each case.

Column 5 contains the number of revolutions per minute required to be made by the propelling instruments, with the slips in Column 4, to give the vessel a uniform speed of 7 geographical miles per hour.

Column 1 contains the number of double strokes of engines' pistons per minute, in agreement with the number of revolutions of the propelling instruments in Column 5.

Column 6 contains the horses power required to work the engines *per se* and overcome the friction of the gearing, for the number of double strokes of piston in Column 1, calculated for a pressure of 2¼ pounds per square inch of pistons.

Column 9 contains the horses power required to overcome the cohesion of the water by the screw-blades; calculated for a value of 0.45 pound avoirdupois per square foot of helicoidal surface moving in its helical path with a velocity of 10 feet per second, and in the ratio of the square of the velocity, for the number of revolutions of the screw per minute in Column 5.

Column 12 contains the horses power required to propel the

simple vessel at the speed of 7 geographical miles per hour. It will be observed that this power (82 horses) is the same for the same conditions of smooth water, uninfluenced by wind or current; for the conditions of turbulent sea and strong gales on the bow and the quarter, this power is increased in the direct ratio of the increased slip of the screw in these cases; for the slip of the screw measures exactly the resistance upon it, a double slip indicating a double resistance, etc., and it is evident that with equal speeds of vessel, the power required will be in the direct ratio of the resistances. The normal power, 82 horses, required to propel the simple hull at 7 miles per hour in smooth water, uninfluenced by wind or current, is derived from the mean of a number of accurate experiments made with the paddle-wheel steamer "McLane" at various aftertimes, and is believed to be a very close approximation to the truth.

Column 11 contains the horses power expended in the slip of the propelling instruments, calculated from Column 12 in the ratio of the speed of the slip to the speed of the vessel.

Column 10 contains the horses power expended in the oblique action of the paddles, calculated as the square of the sines of their angles of incidence on the water, modified by the depth of their centre of pressure below a plane 33.84 feet high above the surface of the water; 33.84 feet being the height of a column of water equal to the pressure of the atmosphere.

Column 8 contains the horses power expended in overcoming the friction of the load. It is 7½ per centum of the aggregate of Columns 9, 10, 11 and 12, added to itself.

Column 7 contains the net horses power applied to the shafts of the propelling instruments. It is composed of the aggregate of Columns 8, 9, 10, 11 and 12.

Column 3 contains the gross horses power developed by the engines, and is composed of Column 7 increased by the number of horses power required to work the engines *per se*, as given in Column 6.

Column 2 contains the mean gross effective pressure on the pistons in pounds per square inch, in accordance with the gross

TABLE exhibiting the Rectified Results, and the Distribution of the Power in accordance with this Rectification, for the LOPER SCREW *of the "SPENCER" and the* PADDLE-WHEEL *of the "McLANE," under the Circumstances of the Comparative Experiments made by order of the U. S. Treasury Department during April 15th, 16th, and 17th, 1846, and for a Speed of 7 Geographical miles per hour. Also the Relative Economical Efficiencies of this Screw and Paddle-wheel in function of the Net and Gross Powers applied.*

NAME OF VESSEL.	CIRCUMSTANCES OF THE EXPERIMENTS.	TOTAL ENGINE POWERS.			Slip of the Propelling Instruments in per centum of their speed.	Number of Revolutions of the Propelling Instruments required to be made per minute to give the Vessel a speed of 7 Geographical miles per hour.	DISTRIBUTION OF THE TOTAL ENGINE POWERS.												RELATIVE ECONOMICAL EFFICIENCIES.		
							HORSES POWERS EXPENDED.							IN PER CENTUM OF THE NET POWER THAT REMAINS AFTER DEDUCTING THE POWER REQUIRED TO WORK THE ENGINES PER SE.							
		Number of Double Strokes of Engines' Pistons required to be made per minute.	Mean gross Effective Pressure on Pistons, in pounds, per square inch.	Gross Horses Power developed by the engines.			Working the engines *per se.*	Net power remaining after deducting from the Gross power what is required to work the engines *per se.*	Overcoming the Friction of the Load.	Overcoming the Cohesion of the Water by the Screw blades.	In the Oblique Action of the Paddles.	In Slip.	In Propelling the Vessel.	Overcoming the Friction of the Load.	Overcoming the Cohesion of the Water by the Screw blades.	In the Oblique Action of the Paddles.	In Slip.	In Propelling the Vessel.	Net powers, proportionally, remaining after deducting from the Gross power what is required to work the engines *per se.*	Gross powers, proportionally.	Weight of Steam consumed in equal times, proportionally.
		1	**2**	**3**	**4**	**5**	**6**	**7**	**8**	**9**	**10**	**11**	**12**	**13**	**14**	**15**	**16**	**17**	**18**	**19**	**20**
"SPENCER:" Loper Screw,.....	In smooth water, uninfluenced by wind or current,.............	40.83	20.23	185.87	17.63	51.04	15.11	120.76	9.06	12.15	—	17.55	82.00	7.50	10.06	—	14.53	67.91	1.0000	1.0000	1.0000
"McLANE:" Paddle-wheel,.....	In smooth water, uninfluenced by wind or current,.............. Diameter of wheel, 15 ft. 1 in. Immersion of Paddles, 3 feet.	32.41	32.57	173.63	30.40	21.16	11.99	161.64	12.12	—	31.70	35.82	82.00	7.50	—	19.61	22.16	50.73	1.3385	1.2780	1.0363
Do. Do.	In smooth water, uninfluenced by wind or current,*............. Diam. of wheel, 16 ft. 5 ins. Immer. of Paddles, 3 ft. 9½ ins.	30.25	34.17	170.03	25.43	19.75	11.19	158.84	11.91	—	36.97	27.96	82.00	7.50	—	23.28	17.60	51.62	1.3153	1.2515	0.9962
Do. Do.	Turbulent sea, and strong gales on bow,........................ Diameter of wheel, 16 ft. 5 ins. Immersion of Paddles, 4 feet.	43.98	59.47	430.41	48.88	28.71	16.27	414.14	31.06	—	96.38	140.14	146.56	7.50	—	23.27	33.84	35.39	3.4294	3.1678	2.0890
Do. Do.	Turbulent sea, and strong gales on quarter,...................... Diameter of wheel, 16 ft. 5 ins. Immersion of Paddles, 4 feet.	33.35	44.39	243.51	32.57	21.77	12.34	231.17	17.34	—	58.80	52.12	107.91	7.50	—	23.27	22.55	46.68	1.9143	1.7922	1.2957
"SPENCER:" Loper Screw, ...	Turbulent sea and strong gales on bow,......................	50.02	33.30	278.99	31.51	62.53	18.50	255.49	19.16	22.34	—	67.43	146.56	7.50	8.74	—	26.39	57.37	2.1157	2.0166	1.6182
Do. Do.	Turbulent sea and strong gales on quarter,......................	44.31	25.39	185.07	23.20	55.39	16.39	168.68	12.65	15.53	—	32.59	107.91	7.50	9.21	—	19.32	63.97	1.3968	1.3621	1.2218

To face page 115.

horses power in Column 3 and the double strokes of piston in Column 1.

Columns 13, 14, 15, 16 and 17, are Columns 8, 9, 10, 11 and 12 expressed in per centum of Column 7.

Columns 18, 19 and 20 exhibit the relative economical efficiencies of the propelling instruments under the different conditions of weather, etc. Column 18 is Column 7 proportionably, and exhibits the relative efficiencies in function of the net powers applied. Column 19 is Column 3 proportionally, and exhibits the relative efficiencies in function of the gross powers developed by the engines. Column 20 exhibits proportionally the weight of steam consumed in equal times in the different cases, and consequently the weight of fuel. It is calculated for cutting off at the same point, and for the same back pressure against the pistons of 16.2 pounds per square inch, from the mean gross pressure given in Column 2. Column 20, therefore, shows the relative economical efficiencies of the propelling instruments in function of fuel consumed. In thes columns the lowest numbers indicate the highest economical efficiencies.

Discussion of the Results of the Experiments with the Loper Screw of the "SPENCER," *and the Paddle-wheel of the* "MCLANE."

Referring to the foregoing "Table containing the Rectified Results," etc., of the experiments, we will first examine the effect of *reefing in* the paddles of the common paddle-wheel of the "MCLANE;" that is to say, of diminishing their diameter and the immersion of their lower edge beneath the water. During the trials on the second day, the diameter of the paddle-wheel was 16 feet 5 inches, and the immersion of the paddles 3 feet 9½ inches. During the first trial on the third day, the diameter was reduced to 15 feet 1 inch by reefing in the paddles 8 inches towards the shaft, which reduced their immersion from 3 feet 9½ inches to 3 feet; the discrepancy of 1½ inch being caused by difference in the mean draught of the vessel on the two days. The reduction in the diameter was 8.12 per centum, and the reduction in the immersion 20.93 per centum of the original. The result as regards slip, was an increase from 25.43 to 30.40 per centum, or very nearly one-fifth, the ratio of increase of the slip being sensibly the same as the ratio of decrease in the immersion of the paddle. With regard to the loss of useful effect by the oblique action of the paddles, it was with the deep immersion 25.16 per centum, and with the light immersion 21.20 per centum of the power applied to them, or a decrease of 15¾ per centum. We thus perceive, that in the case of the paddle-wheel applied to the "MCLANE," the reduction in the diameter and immersion of the paddles gave an increased loss by slip of one-fifth, and a decreased loss by the oblique action of nearly one-sixth. If these differences be measured by the net power applied to the paddle-wheel shaft, the losses with the original wheel were, by slip 17.60 per centum, and by oblique action 23.28 per centum, total 40.88 per centum; and with the reduced wheel these losses were, by slip 22.16 per centum, and by oblique action 19.61 per centum, total 41.77 per centum. The relative economical efficiency in the two cases of the paddle-wheel, measured by the net powers applied to the shaft, was, for the original wheel, 1.0000 against 1.0176 for the wheel of reduced diameter ; that is to say, the application of the power by the former was $1\frac{3}{4}$ per centum better than by the latter. If, however, the economical efficiencies be measured by the gross powers applied, the application of the power by the original wheel is $2\frac{1}{10}$ per centum better than by the reduced wheel, owing to the less power expended in working the engines *per se*, arising from the less number of double strokes of piston required for the same speed of vessel with the less slip. It must be borne in mind that these conclusions are only applicable to paddle-wheels having losses by slip and oblique action proportional to those of the "McLane ;" any variation in the slip, or in the oblique action, will vary the relative economical efficiency, and every problem requires a particular solution. If the comparison of economical efficiencies be made by weight of fuel consumed, the original paddle-wheel applies the power 4 per centum better than the wheel of reduced diameter.

We will now compare the results given by the original paddle-wheel with those from the Loper screw for the normal conditions of smooth water uninfluenced by wind or current ; and referring to Column 18 of the preceding Table, we perceive that the economical efficiency of the screw was $31\frac{1}{2}$ per centum greater than that of the paddle-wheel. Now, the net power applied to the shaft as given in Column 18, is the true measure of the relative economical efficiencies of the propelling instruments *per se*, and is what we must form our opinion from, abstractly from the modifications caused by difference in speeds of piston, and in ratio of back pressure to total absolute pressure, which are combined with the performances of the propelling instruments when either the gross powers developed by the engines, or the weight of fuel consumed, are taken for the measure of the cost. This difference of $31\frac{1}{2}$ per centum, though great, is no more than might be expected from the great difference in the slips of the screw and paddle-wheel ; the slip of the latter (Column 4) being 1.4424 times greater than that of the former. The losses of useful effect by the screw in per centum of the net power applied was, for overcoming the cohesion of the water by the screw blades

10.06, and expended in the slip 14.53, total 24.59 per centum against a total loss by the paddle-wheel of 40.88 per centum, The superiority of the screw could not be more decided, but it must not be overlooked that the cause lay in the very imperfect proportions of the paddle-wheel, whose losses of useful effect both by the slip and the oblique action of the paddles were excessive. The immersion of the paddles, which regulates the latter loss, was 46.19 per centum of their radius, a very unusual proportion, while the length of paddle was such as to give the excessive slip of 25.43 per centum. The screw, however, on its part, was by no means so perfect as it might have been, preserving the same dimensions in all respects except making the pitch uniform radially instead of expanding, and of the same length as the acting mean pitch, by which means the propulsively useless central portions of the screw would have been made of propelling efficacy. The central portion of the screw that was useless from having a less longitudinal speed than the speed of the vessel, was $4\frac{1}{2}$ feet, in diameter, or $56\frac{1}{4}$ per centum of the diameter of the screw; had this portion had the same pitch as the mean pitch of the acting peripheral portion, the slip of the screw would have been reduced from 17.63 to 14.49 per centum, with a nearly corresponding increase of efficiency; for this reduction would have been attended with but a slight increase of the power required to overcome the cohesion of the water. The central portion of the screw expended a considerable power for this purpose, and was only of use, mechanically, to attach the peripheral portion to the hub. If the gross power (Column 19) developed by the engines be taken for the measure of the cost, the efficiency of the screw is $25\frac{1}{7}$ per centum more than that of the paddle-wheel; while if the weight of fuel or steam expended (Column 20) be taken as this measure, the economical efficiencies are equal, owing to the causes already fully explained in the first part of this article.

We will now compare the performances of the paddle-wheel and screw during the 1st Trial, April 15th, in a turbulent sea with strong gale on the bow. In this trial, the absolute speed of the screw vessel "SPENCER" was 5.688 miles per hour, while the speed of the paddle-wheel vessel "McLANE" was only 3.963

miles per hour. The slip of the screw had increased from its normal amount of 17.63 to 31.51 per centum, or 1.7873 times; while that of the paddle-wheel had increased from 25.43 to 48.88 per centum, or 1.9221 times. It thus appears, that the increase of slip due to the opposing sea and wind, was greater with the paddle-wheel than with the screw. The reverse of this should have been the case, from the fact, that the paddle-wheel, as its slip is increased by additional resistance of the vessel, brings more paddle surface into propelling action, by giving the entering paddles a greater longitudinal speed than that of the vessel, while under normal conditions their longitudinal speed was less than that of the vessel: we must, therefore, look for the cause of this disagreement in the additional resistance offered to the wind by the paddle-box surface of the "McLane," and in the little stability of the hull, from which cause the rolling of the "McLane" was constantly decreasing the immersion of one wheel, and increasing the immersion of the other; but the increased resistance of the deeper immersed wheel by no means balanced the loss of resistance by the emersion of the other. From the same cause, the loss of useful effect by the oblique action of the paddles of the deeply immersed wheel, increased in a higher ratio than it decreased for the less immersed wheel. Now with the screw the rolling of the vessel neither diminished the resistance of the screw nor increased its loss by the power required to overcome the cohesion of the water; while with the paddle-wheel, this rolling increased its losses both by diminishing the resistance of the paddles and by augmenting their oblique action. The losses by the screw in per centum of the net power applied, was, in slip 26.39, and in overcoming the cohesion of the water, 8.74, total, 35.13 per centum, against a loss by the paddle-wheel in slip 33.84, and in the oblique action of the paddles 23.27, total, 57.11 per centum. The efficiency of the crew and paddle-wheel measured by the net power applied, was 62 per centum more with the former than with the latter; and if the gross horses power developed by the engines be taken for the measure of the cost, the efficiency of the screw was 57$\frac{4}{5}$ per centum more than the paddle-wheel. If the weight of fuel used be taken as the measure of the cost, the efficiency of the screw was $29\frac{1}{10}$ per centum more than that of the paddle-wheel.

Proceeding now to the case of the performances of the screw and paddle-wheel in a turbulent sea, with a strong gale on the quarter, 2d Trial, April 15th, we find that the absolute speed of the screw vessel "SPENCER" was 6.761, and that of the paddle-wheel vessel "MCLANE," 5.975 miles per hour. The slip of the screw had increased from its normal quantity, 17.63 per centum, to 23.20 per centum, or 1.316 times. The normal slip, 25.43 per centum of the paddle-wheel, had increased to 32.57 per centum, or 1.281 times. Hence, we observe that in the matter of slip, the increase with the screw was greater than with the paddle-wheel, doubtless owing principally to the effect of the wheel-houses of the "MCLANE," which offered a considerable surface to the wind, and acted propulsively as a sail. This result was exactly the opposite of that from the trial with the turbulent sea and strong gale on the bow. If, in the two cases of propelling in a turbulent sea against and with a strong gale, we compare the mean of the slips, we shall have for the screw $\frac{31.51+23.20}{2}=27.35$ per centum, and for the paddle-wheel $\frac{48.88+32.57}{2}=$ 40.72 per centum; making the normal slip of the screw to increase $(\frac{27.35}{17.63}=)$ 1.5513 times, and that of the paddle-wheel to increase $(\frac{40.72}{25.43}=)$ 1.6012 times, or about the same, if we consider the unavoidable errors of data. Hence we perceive, that in going before the wind, the paddle-boxes increased the speed of the vessel as much as they decreased it when going against the wind. In this trial, the efficiency of the screw, measured by the net power applied, was 37 per centum more than that of the paddle-wheel; and if measured by the gross horses applied, $31\frac{6}{10}$ per centum more; while if the weight of fuel used be taken as the measure of the cost, the efficiency of the screw was only 6 per centum more than that of the paddle-wheel. The general result of these trials, measuring the cost by the net power applied, shows that when propelling in smooth water, uninfluenced by wind or current, the screw had a very decided superiority of $31\frac{1}{2}$ per centum, which increased when propelling with a turbulent sea and strong gale on the quarter to 37 per

PERFORMANCE of the Paddle-wheel Steamer "McLANE" at Sea.

DATE.	Number of consecutive hours.	Speed of the Vessel per hour, in Geographical miles of 6,086 feet.	Mean Draught of the Vessel, in feet and inches.	ENGINES. Number of double strokes of Pistons made per minute.	ENGINES. Steam pressure in boiler, in pounds, per square inch above atmosphere.	ENGINES. Proportion of throttle open.	Pounds of Anthracite coal consumed per hour.	PADDLE-WHEEL. Immersion of lower edge of Paddles, in feet and ins.	PADDLE-WHEEL. Number of Revolutions made per minute.	PADDLE-WHEEL. Slip of the centre of Pressure of the paddles, in per centum of their speed.	State of the Sea.	Course of the Vessel.	WIND. Direction.	WIND. Kind.
UNDER STEAM ASSISTED BY SAIL.														
May 30, 1846,	20	6.90	9 .. 9	25.8	45.0	Wide.	908	3 .. 11	16.8	15.56	Smooth,	S.W.,	N.E. or aft,	Gentle breeze.
June 7, 1846,	16	6.25	7 .. 9	26.0	42.6	"	870	1 .. 11	16.9	23.96	Rough on quarter,	S.W.,	N.N.W. or abaft beam,	"
July 3 and 4, 1846,	18	6.17	9 .. 11	26.0	43.0	"	790	4 .. 1	16.9	24.93	Rough,	N.W.,	S. or on quarter,	Fresh breeze.
August 26, 1846,	12	6.00	9 .. 3	27.8	44.1	"	863	3 .. 5	18.1	31.07	Smooth,	S.S.E.,	N.W. or aft,	"
August 28, 1846,	14	5.40	9 .. 0	26.7	41.6	"	743	3 .. 2	17.4	36.19	Rough,	——	——	Gentle breeze.
June 6, 1847,	8	5.00	9 .. 1	21.1	32.1	"	750	3 .. 3	13.8	25.51	Do.,	N. by E.,	N.E. or sharp on bow,	Moderate breeze.
June 7 and 8, 1847,	24	5.50	8 .. 10	20.5	31.0	"	680	3 .. 0	13.4	15.60	Do.,	N.N.E.,	E.N.E. or on bow,	Fresh breeze.
June, 9, 1847,	12	5.67	8 .. 5	20.7	32.2	"	612	2 .. 7	13.5	13.65	Do.,	N.N.E.,	E. or nearly abeam,	Moderate breeze.
Means,		5.94	9 .. 0	24.33	39.1	Wide.	786	3 .. 2	15.88	23.09	Ordinary,		Abeam,	Moderate breeze.
UNDER STEAM ALONE.														
May 5 and 6, 1846,	20	7.50	9 .. 5	30.2	45.0	Wide.	1,050	3 .. 7	19.7	21.72	Smooth,	N.N.W.,	S. or on quarter,	Gentle breeze.
May 27 and 28, 1846,	38	5.65	10 .. 1	25.8	45.0	"	767	4 .. 3	16.7	30.44	Moderate,	S. by E.,	S.E. or on bow,	"
May 30 and 31, and June 1, 1846,	40	6.34	9 .. 4	26.1	43.4	"	880	3 .. 6	17.0	23.38	Smooth,	——	——	Calm.
June 2 and 3, 1846,	29	5.23	9 .. 0	25.1	43.5	"	905	3 .. 2	16.3	34.03	Rough ahead,	S.W. by W.,	S. W. or ahead,	Fresh breeze.
June 16 and 17, 1846,	36	4.92	9 .. 7	23.7	40.0	"	838	3 .. 9	15.5	34.93	Smooth,	——	Abeam,	Light breeze.
June 28 and 29, 1846,	20	5.00	10 .. 2	23.2	38.0	"	792	4 .. 4	15.1	31.92	Do.,	S.S.W.,	E.S.E. or abeam,	"
July 2, 1846,	24	5.33	10 .. 1	25.1	41.0	"	821	4 .. 3	16.4	33.17	Do.,	——	——	Calm.
August 19, 1846,	24	5 40	8 .. 11	25.4	45.0	"	820	3 .. 1	16.5	32.71	Do.,	S.W. by W.,	S. W. or ahead,	Gentle breeze.
August 27, 1846,	12	4.75	9 .. 2	25.6	40.2	"	867	3 .. 4	16.7	41.52	Do.,	S. by E.,	E. or abeam,	Fresh breeze.
Means,		5.60	9 .. 6	25.49	44.3	Wide.	854	3 .. 8	16.64	30.80	Smooth,		On bow,	Light breeze.
Means of the two Means,		5.72	9 .. 4	25.10	42.5	Wide.	831	3 .. 6	16.38	28.20	Light swell,		Forward beam,	Gentle breeze.

To face page 121.

centum, and which rose when propelling against a turbulent sea and strong gale on the bow, to 62 per centum. Making the comparison by weight of fuel consumed, the efficiency of the screw and paddle-wheel propelling in smooth water, uninfluenced by wind or current, was equal; when propelling with a turbulent sea and strong gale on the quarter, the efficiency of the screw was 6 per centum more than that of the paddle-wheel; while when propelling against the same turbulent sea and strong gale on the bow, this superiority rose to $29\frac{1}{10}$ per centum.

When propelling in strong winds, the paddle-boxes acted like a spread sail, diminishing the resistance of the vessel and the slip of the paddles when propelling with the wind, and increasing the resistance of the vessel and the slip of the paddles when propelling against the wind. Under the same conditions of wind, the slip of the paddles was decreased when going before it in about the same degree as the slip was increased when going against it.

It has already been stated that the power expended by the immersed surface of the hull in overcoming the cohesion of the water, was, for a speed of 7 geographical miles per hour, 55.97 horses, which was $68\frac{1}{4}$ per centum of the 82.00 horses power required to propel the simple vessel.

§ *Performance of the paddle-wheel vessel "McLane" at sea.*

The annexed table contains all that is extant of the steam log of the paddle-wheel vessel "McLane," showing the performance at sea under the conditions of ordinary service. During this steaming, the paddle-wheel was 16 feet 5 inches diameter, from outside to outside of paddles, which were of the same number and dimensions as before given. The steam was cut off at half stroke. The fan blast, for giving the boilers an artificial draught, required, in order to maintain the steam, to be constantly and violently driven.

The general results of the performance at sea are embraced in the following summary. The horses power required to propel the simple vessel is calculated from what is required to propel the same in smooth water, uninfluenced by wind or current, modified in the direct ratio of the slip of the centre of pressure of the paddles, and in the ratio of the cube of the vessel's speed. From this power, the entire gross horses power employed in propelling the vessel is derived in the same manner as hereinbefore described for the comparative experiments with the screw vessel "SPENCER."

	Under Steam assisted by Sail.	Under Steam alone.	Mean of the total performance under steam assisted by sail, and under steam alone.
OBSERVED.			
Number of hours,	124	343	367
Speed of the vessel per hour in geographical miles of 6,086 feet,	5.94	5.60	5.72
Steam pressure in boiler, in pounds per square inch above atmosphere,	39.1	44.3	42.5
Steam cut-off at in cylinders, from commencement of stroke in piston,	⅓	⅓	⅓
Proportion of Throttle valve open,	Wide.	Wide.	Wide.
Number of double strokes of engines' pistons made per minute,	24.33	25.49	25.10
Number of revolutions of the paddle-wheel made per minute,	15.88	16.64	16.38
Immersion of lower edge of the paddles, in feet and inches,	3 .. 2	3 .. 8	3 .. 6
Distance traversed, per revolution of the wheel by the centre of pressure of the paddles,	49.33	49.33	49.33
Mean draught of the vessel, in feet and ins.,	9.0	9.6	9.4
Greatest immersed transverse section of vessel, in square feet,	141	162	159
Displacement of the vessel, in tons,	419	450	440
Consumption of anthracite coal, in pounds per hour,	786	854	831
Consumption of anthracite coal, in tons per 24 hours,	8.42	9.15	8.90
Kind of breeze,	Moderate.	Light.	Gentle.
Direction of breeze,	Abeam.	On Bow.	F'rd of beam.
State of the sea,	Ordinary.	Smooth.	Light swell.
CALCULATED.			
Slip of the centre of pressure of the paddles in per centum of its speed,	23.09	30.80	28.20
Oblique action of the paddles in per centum of the power applied,	24.80	25.16	25.00
Mean gross effective pressure on pistons, in pounds per square inch,	23.50	27.48	26.14
Gross horses power developed by the engines,	94.05	115.26	108.09
Pounds of steam passed through the cylinders per hour,	3,051	3,557	3,386

§ *Further Experiments with the screw vessel "Spencer."*

On May 21st, 1845, the speed of the "SPENCER" was accurately ascertained by running the distance between Chester and Marcus Hook, 3.67 statute miles, of 5,280 feet, in the Delaware River, three times in each direction, making six runs in all. The throttle was carried wide open, and the steam cut off at half stroke. The following are the mean results, which, it will be perceived, do not differ sensibly from those obtained under similar conditions of smooth water, uninfluenced by wind or current, during the comparative trials with paddle-wheel steamer "McLANE;" the difference in the slip of the screw in the two cases is less than one per centum.

Steam pressure in boiler, in pounds, per square inch above atmosphere, ...	55.
Speed of the vessel per hour, in geographical miles, of 6,086 feet, ...	7.027
Number of double strokes of engines' pistons made per minute, ...	40.5
Number of revolutions made by the screw per minute, ...	50.625
Mean pitch of the acting surface of the screw, in feet, in function of the square of the velocity of that surface, circumferentially, ...	16.9
Slip of the screw in per centum of its speed, ...	16.69
Pitch of the screw in feet, having the same longitudinal speed as the vessel, ...	14.1
Acting helicoidal area of the two screws in square feet, ...	60.4
Acting projected area on a plane at right angles to axis of the two screws, in square feet, ...	44.7
Distance in feet and inches of the axis of the screw below the surface of the water........	4ft. 1½in.
Gross mean effective pressure on pistons in pounds per square inch, ...	20.43
Gross horses power developed by the engines, ..	136.12

After making the above runs, the experiment was continued by steaming down the Delaware Bay to the Breakwater, a distance from Newcastle of 69.17 statute miles; smooth water and calm. Throttle wide open, and steam cut off at half stroke. The following are the mean results, viz.:

Steam pressure in boilers in pounds per square inch above the atmosphere,................	49
Total distance ran through the water in statute miles, of 5,280 feet,......................	66.17
Total time of running the total distance through the water, in hours and minutes,............	7h. 27m.
Speed of the vessel per hour, in geographical miles, of 6,086 feet,......................	7.706
Number of double strokes of engines' pistons made per minute,............................	44.45
Number of revolutions made by the screw per minute,................................	55.57
Mean pitch of the acting surface of the screw, in feet, in function of the square of the velocity of that surface, circumferentially,...........	16.9
Slip of the screw in per centum of its speed,....	16.77
Pitch of the screw, in feet, having the same longitudinal speed as that of the vessel,.........	14.1
Acting helicoidal area of the two screws, in square feet,............................	60.4
Acting projected area on a plane at right angles to axis of the two screws in square feet,.....	44.7
Mean gross effective pressure on pistons, in pounds, per square inch,..................	24.
Gross horses power developed by the engines,...	175.49
Pounds of Anthracite coal consumed per hour with a strongly driven fan blast,............	1,210

The last experiment was a run at sea, from Cape Henlopen, Delaware Bay, to Sandy Hook, New York Bay, being in continuation of the two preceding trials. This run was made against a head sea and a fresh wind sharp on the bow, its direction being from N.E. No sail set. The following are the mean results, viz.:

Steam pressure in boiler in pounds per square inch above atmosphere,....................	45
Total distance run through the water in statute miles of 5,280 feet,.......................	142
Total time, in hours and minutes, of running the total distance through the water,...........	19h. 0m.
Speed of the vessel per hour in geographical miles of 6,086 feet, ...	6.484
Number of double strokes of engines' pistons made per minute,.........................	45.11
Number of revolutions of the screw made per minute, ...	56.39
Mean pitch of the acting surface of the screw, in feet, in function of the square of the velocity of that surface, circumferentially,...........	16.6
Slip of the screw in per centum of its speed,...	29.74
Pitch of the screw, in feet, having the same longitudinal speed as that of the vessel,.........	11.7
Acting helicoidal area of the two screws, in square feet,.............................	77.7
Acting projected area on a plane at right angles to axis of the two screws, in square feet,....	57.5
Mean gross effective pressure on pistons in pounds, per square inch, ...	27.43
Gross horses power developed by the engines,..	203.59
Pounds of Anthracite coal consumed per hour, with a strongly driven fan blast,...........	1,286.

I am of opinion that, during the preceding trials, the boiler pressure, cut-off, and throttle, cannot be depended on. The gross mean pressure on the pistons, and gross horses power developed by the engines, have therefore been calculated in the same manner, and on the same data as employed in the table containing the Rectified Results of the Comparative Trials with the paddle-wheel vessel "McLane."

§ *Extracts from a Report by Captain A. V. Fraser.*

The following extracts from Reports by Captain A. V. Fraser, U. S. Revenue Marine, who conducted the foregoing experiments, will have interest in this connection :

"From what I have seen of these vessels ['Spencer' and 'McLane'], I am confirmed in my former opinion, that they have not sufficient beam by 8 or 10 feet to enable them to perform under canvas, as was anticipated by the late Secretary of the Treasury, Mr. Spencer ; and that the principal reliance must be placed upon steam. The error was in allowing the projector of the plan of propulsion (Lieutenant Hunter, U. S Navy, for whose submerged wheel the 'Spencer' and 'McLane' were originally built), to control the model of the hull ; and for any defect in the sailing qualities he alone is accountable.

"The coal procured at Philadelphia [for the last experiment] contained a very large proportion of slate, which fouled the furnaces very rapidly, making it necessary very frequently to let the fires run down—the contracted space for the engine room rendering it impossible to remain below after the fires are raked out, or until the cinders are partially cooled.

"Some 50 feet in the body of the vessel is occupied by machinery ; and, notwithstanding that a current of air is forced into the engine room by a blower placed in the hatchway, the thermometer frequently ranges from 120° to 130° Fahrenheit.

"Under the present arrangement [of machinery] but six days' fuel can be carried, and the principal part of that quantity above the water line.

"The total cost of the 'Spencer'—including the alteration

from the Hunter submerged wheel to the Loper screw system of propulsion—from April, 1843, when commenced, up to December, 1846, was $105,013 10.

"The armament of the 'SPENCER' consisted of four iron 12-pounders, and one long, pivot, 18-pounder, one brass 9-pounder, and one brass 12-pounder."

Plate I.

SMITHERY BOILER. U.S. NAVY YARD, NEW-YORK.

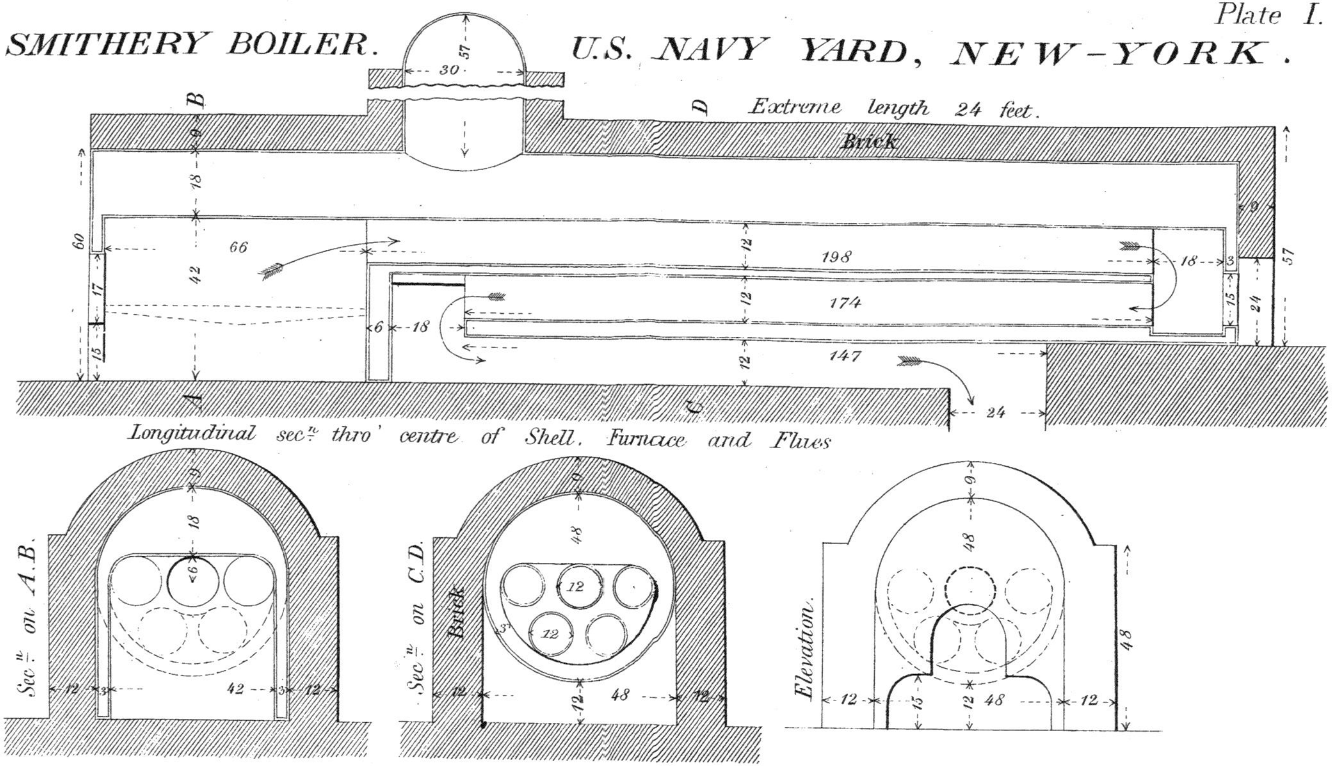
57
30
B
D
Extreme length 24 feet.
Brick
9
18
60
66
42
17
15
A
C
12
198
174
147
6
18
3
15
24
57
24
Sec.n on A.B.
Sec.n on C.D.
Brick
12
48
3
Elevation.

Longitudinal sec.n thro' centre of Shell, Furnace and Flues

Baillière Brothers, Publishers 440 Broadway N.Y.

ENGINEERING PRECEDENTS

FOR

STEAM MACHINERY;

EMBRACING THE

PERFORMANCES OF STEAMSHIPS,

EXPERIMENTS

WITH

PROPELLING INSTRUMENTS, CONDENSERS, BOILERS, ETC.,

ACCOMPANIED BY ANALYSES OF THE SAME;

THE WHOLE BEING ORIGINAL MATTER
AND ARRANGED IN THE MOST PRACTICAL AND USEFUL MANNER

FOR ENGINEERS.

BY B. F. ISHERWOOD,

CHIEF ENGINEER U. S. NAVY.

VOL. II.

NEW YORK:
BAILLIÈRE BROTHERS, 440 BROADWAY.
LONDON: H. BAILLIÈRE, 219 REGENT STREET.
PARIS: J. B. BAILLIÈRE ET FILS, RUE HAUTEFEUILLE.
MADRID: C. BAILLY-BAILLIÈRE, CALLE DEL PRINCIPE.

1859.

Thomas Holman, Printer,
Corner of Centre and White Streets, N. Y.

CONTENTS.

ERRATA.

Page 8, line 6 from the bottom, instead of 3,069 read 3.069.
" 25, " 3 " " top, " " 63.275 " 63,275.
" 26, " 10 " " " " " "desived" read desired.
" 55, " 30 " " " " " "loweriny" " lowering.
" 65, " 24 " " " strike out the words "of steam" after the word unit.
" 75, " 25 " " " change the word "description" into discussion.
" 86, bottom line, change $\frac{1}{2}$ to $\frac{5}{16}$.
" 100, line 30 from the top, insert "given" after the word as.
" 108, " 21 " " " change the word "would" into could.
" 109, " 29 " " " strike out the word "there."
" 115, " 16 " " " change the word "observed" into observe
" 117, " 8 " " " " " " "of" " with.
" 135, " 8 " " " strike out the comma.
" 200, " 17 " " " change the word "is" into was.
" " " 22 " " " " " " "was" " is.

PREFACE.

The flattering reception of the first volume of the "Precedents," has encouraged the Publisher to issue a second containing more matter and better illustrated. The contents consist of several papers relating chiefly to Boilers and Fuel, though incidental subjects are treated as they arise in natural connexion. Before proceeding to a separate enumeration of these papers, a few prefatory words in explanation may not be out of place.

With the exception of the last two—which are on the U. S. Steamships "NIAGARA," and "MASSACHUSETTS"—they are accounts of experiments ordered by the U. S. Navy Department, and made by Boards of Naval Engineers of which the writer was a member. The official reports were as brief as was consistent with such description of the methods employed as was necessary to inspire confidence in the results; but for permanent records and the satisfaction of persons unconnected with the Department, it is requisite that the accounts be full to the minutest detail, —the fuller the better, perhaps even to prolixity;—in fact the value of such records mainly depends on their circumstantial comprehensiveness, for although the reader must indeed credit the integrity of the experimenters, yet it is not necessary that their ability be also taken on trust or their conclusions accepted without scrutiny: they must therefore be accompanied by a complete exposition of the observations on which they were based, and of the inductive processes by which they were deduced, in order that the reader may clearly comprehend the one and judge of the soundness of the other. Furthermore, there occur incidentally in all experimental inquiries facts illustrating other results than those directly in view, but which, though interesting in themselves, are omitted in official reports because not pertinent to the questions at issue. Now as the information furnished by these experiments is believed by the writer to possess too much value for burial in the archives of the Navy Department, and as he had preserved full notes of them, he has re-written these reports in a more convenient form for reference, adding whatever had from any cause been omitted, and illustrating them by the necessary drawings. In this revision he has had the benefit in many cases of additional light thrown on the same subjects by after experiments; and in all of them the original notes have been carefully recollated and the calculations corrected of a few slight errors that had accidentally crept in.

It will be difficult to make the reader believe how very few *complete* records of reliable experiments of the nature of those descibed in this volume are to be found in print, but let him make the search, and although he will find statements of results and assertions of facts in abundance and in every degree of inconsistency and contradiction, he will not be oppressed with full descriptions of the apparatus employed, the manner of conducting the experiments, and the reasoning on which the conclusions depend. He must take all or reject all on the mere authority of the experimenters who have not thought proper to furnish the evidence that produced their own convictions. Such experiments are in effect always rejected and properly so, for we are naturally incredulous of the opinions of others and feel instinctively that the same facts according to surrounding circumstances admit of very different interpretations; we must then be furnished with a description of these circumstances that omits nothing, and it will be found that results are relied on just in proportion to the care and ability that have been exercised in arriving at them as exhibited in a full account of the processes employed. Some people substitute the imagination for the senses and jump at conclusions; others are not able to discover the various links of the chain connecting causes with effects, but laboriously draw from indisputable facts the most inconsequential conclusions. Now the true significance of a fact can only be obtained by coupling with it all the accessory facts and correctly estimating their influence; whether this has been done properly can only be judged by the reader from the account detailed, hence the necessity that it be above all things *complete*—nothing omitted, and in this respect the present volume will not be found with many companions on the shelves of the practical engineer, whatever be its value in others; and as the right interpretation of facts constitutes all real knowledge any addition to the means of making it must possess value.

The first paper describes the experiments made at the New York Navy Yard to determine the comparative evaporative efficiencies, etc., of the hard or true anthracite, the Trevorton semi-anthracite, and the Cumberland semi-bituminous coals; the three kinds in general use for steam vessel and land engines on the Atlantic coast of the United States. These are the only rigorously comparative and reliable experiments ever made for this purpose, and they were extended over a length of time and with the consumption of a weight of coal sufficient to neutralize errors and secure accuracy in the results. The experiments also determine the gain in evaporative effect to be obtained by simply perforating the ordinary furnace door with small holes to admit air above the solid fuel. The importance of these experiments can scarcely be exaggerated when the immense amount of these coals consumed in generating steam is considered; and they have the recommendation of having been made on a sufficiently large scale and under the ordinary conditions of use to give really practical results, so called in contradistinction to laboratory trials.

The second paper is a sequel to the first, but the experiments detailed in it were made solely with a view to determine the *practical* gain due to the use of steam very expansively over its use without expansion. In the discussion of the results, the causes of the enormous discrepancy between the gain as realized and as indicated by the theory of expansion are pointed out, and their numerical values given for the particular case of the experiment. At the present time when the mania for Patent Cut-offs is so prevalent, especially in the United States, and when certificates abound upon certificates of savings of fuel of from 25 to 50 per centum obtained by one patent Cut-off over a rival cutting-off at exactly the same point, and when the most exaggerated nonsense respecting the possible gain by slight variations of such contrivances is proclaimed by interested sellers and believed in by duped buyers, it is hoped for the sake of the latter and of truth, that the clear, indisputable, experimental facts may arrest attention and produce conviction, especially when accompanied by an exposition of the causes that restrict the gain by expansion to very narrow limits, even under favorable conditions, and that reduce to nothing the effects of very considerable variations in the measure employed. This is an important point; the simplification of steam engines—marine ones particularly—is of the first consequence to success and cheapness, and if it can be shown that complicated, variable expansion gear with a wide range and the ability to cut-off very short, does not economise fuel more than simple, fixed kinds, cutting-off longer and attached to smaller cylinders doing the same work with the power graduated by the throttle, then a great step will have been taken in the right direction. The wide difference between mechanical ingenuity and mechanical judgment has never received a more striking illustration than in the numerous variable expansion gear patented in the United States.

The third paper contains an account of the experiments made with the Prosser boiler, which though not a practicable one for general use, has nevertheless much merit of design for the accomplishment of the objects aimed at. The evaporating surfaces of this boiler are vertical and tubular, and although the products of combustion enter at once from the furnace into the tubes without passing through any mixing or combustion chamber, and although they are not broken up or mixed in the tubes but rise vertically and with unobstructed speed into the chimney, yet their excellent evaporation demonstrates not only the fact of the complete combustion of the fuel in the small time and space intervening between the grate and furnace crown, but also the advantage of the vertical arrangement of the evaporating surfaces as regards the rapid and easy extrication of the steam bubbles and the general vigor and regularity of the steam and water currents, both of which being in the same vertical direction offer no impediment to each other. In the experiments with this boiler the evaporation was—and for the first time to the knowledge of the writer—measured simultaneously by the Indicator and by the Tank, and the result is very instructive. It shows conclusively the great condensation that takes place in steam cylinders under the most favorable circumstances, as in the present case where the steam was superheated 30° Fahr. before entering the cylinder and where the proportion of steam room in the boiler to the capacity of the cylinder was so great as to preclude all possibility of priming. The results of these experiments with a type and proportions of boiler so unusual, are confidently recommended as well worthy the close attention of the Engineer. The boiler itself has been successfully employed for Steam Fire Engines for which it is admirably adapted from its lightness, strength, and little bulk especially on the ground plan. The small quantity too of water that it contains, is for this purpose the highest recommendation, because it permits steam to be raised in a few minutes from the lighting of the fire. It is proper to add that this boiler is claimed as their invention by Messrs. LEE and LARNED, the manufacturers of these engines.

The fourth paper contains an account of an experiment made to determine the economic evaporation of the boiler patented by the Messrs. ELLIS. This kind of boiler may in some cases be preferred to the usual arrangement with horizontal fire tubes when for a small boiler a cheap shell is required to withstand a high pressure. It is also useful to know what evaporation and strength of draught could be obtained with tubes of such unusually great length in proportion to their diameter.

The fifth paper contains the records of a set of comparative experiments made to determine the relative economic evaporation of the ordinary horizontal fire-tube boiler and of the vertical water-tube boiler as arranged and patented by Chief Engineer D. B. MARTIN, U. S. N. Now as it may be considered that for marine purposes these two kinds of boiler will eventually come into general use to the exclusion of others, the importance of a *rigorously comparative* experiment made to determine their relative value under the conditions of ordinary practice can hardly be overestimated; particularly when the result shows a great superiority of the vertical water-tubes not only in economic evaporation but in space occupied in the vessel by boiler and fuel for equal times of steaming at equal speeds; in the facility for the removal of scale—that *piece de resistance* in marine boilers,—in the less formation of the same, and in the less priming; in fact in all the characteristics of a first rate boiler. A more unexceptionable experiment could not possibly be made; the time was sufficient; the engines and all appurtenances were the same; the conditions were exactly those of ordinary practice on board marine steamers; and the boilers were of the first class in size; while the slowness of the combustion and the cleanness of the evaporating surfaces made the result a maximum for the horizontal fire-tubes to be continually reduced with use by the constantly accumulating thickness of scale impossible to prevent and almost impossible to remove. With the vertical water-tubes, the results obtained were an average that can be permanently sustained during the life of the boiler owing to the complete and easy manner in which they can be freed from scale: a proof of this assertion will be found in the next paper in the average evaporation per pound of combustible given by the boilers of the U. S. S. "NIAGARA" during her whole cruising. These boilers were of the same type and nearly of the same proportion as the vertical water-tube boiler of the U. S. S. "SAN JACINTO." It is believed that these experiments are the most important ever made on the subject of boilers; they exhibit on a large scale the best arrangement of the two best types practicable with marine steamers and indisputably determine their relative value.

The sixth paper contains the dimensions of the Hull and Machinery of the U. S. Steam Sloop-of-war "NIAGARA," and a digest of her performance as recorded in the Steam Log. The reader will appreciate the difference between such a performance and the delusive one of a trial trip of a measured mile duration. The results with this vessel are interesting on account of her great size, excessively sharp model, and altogether different *ensemble* to what is habitual with war steamers. A point of great value is the proof afforded by her *average* steaming of the high economic evaporation to be permanently obtained from vertical water-tube boilers. In this respect it will be seen that the mean evaporation by the "NIAGARA'S" boilers for all the steaming done is, per pound of *combustible*, almost precisely the same as given by the experiments with the same kind of boiler on board the U. S. Screw Frigate "SAN JACINTO."

The seventh and last paper contains a description of the Hull and Machinery of the U. S. Steamship "MASSACHUSETTS," and a digest of her performance as recorded in the Steam Log. She was a vessel of full model carried up high out of water, and propelled by a purely auxiliary power which like all other applications of small power to large vessels proved very unsatisfactory, though by no means useless, as for many purposes she was very efficient and economical. In addition to the engineering precedent furnished by the development of the power through such machinery on such a hull, the "MASSACHUSETTS" is worthy of a record on account of the peculiarity of the hoisting gear of her screw, a gear that may under many circumstances be judiciously imitated to the exclusion of the Well and hoisting through the deck system. The experiments too on the Drag of her Screw, are the only detailed and reliable ones with which the writer is acquainted, and they are on a point that ought to be well determined.

Before closing, a few words may be necessary in explanation of the "Distribution of the Power" made in analyzing the performance of the two screw steamers given in this volume. In some criticisms on this method of distributing the power in the case of the screw steamer performance contained in the preceding volume, although the correctness of the distribution itself was not impugned, yet an explanation was asked as to how the pressure required to work the engine *per se* was obtained; and how the value of the cohesive resistance of the water to separation by one square foot of cast metallic helicoidal surface moving in its helical path with a velocity of 10 feet per second, was known to be 0.45 pound.

As regards the first, it is impossible to have any other than the *general* result of Indicator diagrams taken from engines when disconnected from their load and running in their normal state. It has been found that when properly taken with a good Indicator,—and it should be an excellent one because the pressure per square inch required for this purpose is so small, that a slight imperfection in the instrument may easily double it—the pressure required to work medium sized engines, say of from 4 to 6 feet diameter of cylinder, is about 1½ pound per square inch of piston, decreasing as they become larger and increasing as they become smaller. It is quite useless, however, to affect exactness in this matter for the conditions do not admit it. The friction resistance of the same engine varies at different times with the tightness of its packings, the smoothness of its rubbing surfaces, the accuracy of its lining up, the closeness of its keying up, &c. &c.; even the quality of the oil used is perhaps the most influential condition of all, not to mention the more or less completeness of the lubrication itself. With different engines there is furthermore the difference of friction on the crank-pin due to the difference in the ratio of the leverage of the power to the load; and on the numerous guides, pillow-blocks, pins, and rock-shafts, due to the difference of the angles of the various links and connecting rods. Fortunately, however, for our purpose these differences at the widest, either for difference in the type of engine or in the conditions of the same engine, are comprised within very narrow limits; while the smallness of the pressure required to work the engine *per se* even at a maximum, in comparison with the gross mean effective pressure on the piston, makes a large error in it too insignificant to practically affect the result. It is indeed possible to so pack and key up an engine that a boiler pressure of 25 pounds per square inch would fail to move it, as the writer has witnessed; but it is understood that the average working conditions of packing and keying-up, and of lubrication, are above intended and not extreme cases,—the practical every day probabilities and not possibilities. The writer has, himself, made many experiments on the pressure required to work engines *per se*, and has found in general, that with marine, condensing engines the pressure required to work them disconnected from the load was, for cylinders of 2 feet diameter 3 pounds per square inch of piston decreasing as the diameter increased until it became 1½ pound for cylinders of 6 feet diameter. In many trials during a three years cruise in the U. S. Steam Frigate "SAN JACINTO," the pressure required to work her geared engines was found to vary at different and wide intervals of time from 1⅜ to 1¾ pound per square inch of pistons, the difference of ⅜ pound was quite insignificant compared with the gross mean effective pressure of which it formed a portion. It is believed, then, that any error arising from the assumed pressure required to work the engines in any given case, is too small to affect the practical result; and it must not be forgotten that this pressure though assumed for any particular case is the experimental mean of a wide generalization.

The friction of the engine itself, as above described, must be carefully separated from that other friction which the writer terms "of the load;" the two are very different, as will appear if we consider that as with the same engine the load may vary from nothing to the maximum, its friction will vary with it, being in fact a constant co-efficient of it; while, on the contrary, the engine friction will remain the same with all loads, and, sensibly, at all speeds of piston, because it is due purely to the resistances of the organs of the engine itself. The friction of the load then is that additional friction produced upon the moving parts of the engine by the pressure caused by the resistance of the load; it is taken at 7½ per centum of the load as a practical average from the experiments of MORIN. By "load" is, of course, understood the aggregate of all resistances to the movement of the piston, excepting the resistance of the engine *per se*.

The cohesive resistance opposed by the water to the passage of the helicoidal surface of the screw, moving in its helical path at the speed of 10 feet per second, is taken at 0.45 pound per square foot of that surface. This value is the mean of a collation of all the experiments I have been able to find from which the *surface* resistance of solids moving through water, or *vice versa*, could be deduced. The speed of 10 feet per second is selected for the standard simply on account of the facility it affords in calculation. It is impossible, for want of space, to here give the discussions of the experiments referred to, as they would occupy half the present volume, but they will be found *in extenso* in a work on the Screw Propeller that the writer proposes to publish as soon as his daily avocations permit. The laws of this cohesive resistance of the water to the passage of a physical superficies, have been clearly shown by reasoning, and confirmed by experiment, to be independent of pressure, to be in the direct ratio of the surface, and in the ratio of the square of the velocity.

In the case of the screw the helical velocity will vary at every point radially of the surface, increasing from the hub to the periphery, yet the calculation of the cohesive resistance of the water to the entire surface is by no means difficult, and can be done exactly by common arithmetic. To this resistance the term "friction of the screw surface on the water" has been frequently but improperly applied, as there is in fact no such friction.

In the "Distribution of the Power" we commence with the gross Indicated horses power developed by the engine, and from it we first deduct the power required to work the engine *per se,* as it is evident that the remainder only is the net power applied to the shaft and equilibrating the *load.* Next, there must be successively deducted from the net power the powers absorbed by the friction of the load and by the cohesive resistance of the water to the passage of the screw; for until these resistances as well as the friction resistance of the engine *per se*, are overcome, there can be no transmission of power to the watery fulcrum. Finally, the remainder of the power, that is the portion transmitted to the water, is distributed between the forward propulsion of the vessel, and that backward recession of the watery fulcrum to which the term "slip of the screw" is applied, and in direct proportion to the speeds of the two as an obvious consequence of the equality of pressure and resistance in opposite directions.

In conclusion, it may not be ill-timed to here remind the reader that all physical measurements are necessarily inexact; not even in the laboratory experiments of the chemist, or in the guarded observations of the astronomer, are the results *precise;* there is always a more or less probable error, to be diminished indeed by increasing the number of trials and taking their mean on the ground of the correction of errors, but never to be wholly eradicated. There is, however, a wide difference between a reasonably close approximation having for practical purposes all the value of a precise determination, and no knowledge at all in the premises; and unless we know the distribution of the gross power applied, how are we to improve the application? The final result of the speed of the vessel compared with the gross Indicated horses-power producing it, is influenced by the absolute size of the vessel, the form of its immersed solid, the portion of the gross power absorbed in working the organs of the engine, and lost in mal-application by the propelling instrument; and rarely in any two cases is the distribution alike, or the per centum of the gross power which is applied to the propulsion of the hull the same: hence, all attempts to solve the problem of steamship resistance by the gross Indicated horses power are absurd, for that power equilibrates many other and variable resistances besides those of the hull *per se*. To approach this question intelligibly we must know not the gross Indicated horses power developed by the engine, but the horses power applied to the hull alone, and until that quantity is determined and employed as a controlling element, all formulas and equations, and discussions of the squares and cubes of velocity, of displacements and amidship sections, can be passed over as mere futilities.

The writer can assert without arrogance, that as regards its bearing on future improvement, no problem of more importance in marine steam engineering has ever been brought forward than that of the "Distribution of the Power," as set forth in the present and preceding volume. When properly appreciated and correctly applied, it will point out not only the direction of advancement, but its limit too.

EXPERIMENTS

ON

BLACKHEATH ANTHRACITE,

TREVORTON SEMI-ANTHRACITE,

AND

CUMBERLAND SEMI-BITUMINOUS

COAL.

Experiments made with the Smithery Engine and Boiler at the United States Navy Yard, New York, to determine the Comparative Evaporative Efficiencies of the BLACKHEATH ANTHRACITE, *the* TREVORTON SEMI-ANTHRACITE, *and the* CUMBERLAND SEMI-BITUMINOUS *Coal.*

OF the following experiments to determine the comparative evaporative efficiencies of the BLACKHEATH ANTHRACITE, the TREVORTON SEMI-ANTHRACITE, and the CUMBERLAND SEMI-BITUMINOUS coal; those with the Trevorton and the first set with the Blackheath coal were made by the writer in conjunction with Chief Engineer J. W. KING, U. S. N., by order of the Navy Department; the last set of experiments with the Blackheath and those with the Cumberland coal were made by the writer alone.

The Trevorton coal was furnished by the Trevorton coal company (on whose application the experiments had been ordered by the Navy Department); the Blackheath and Cumberland coals were from the regular contract supplies to the New York Navy Yard. The Blackheath and Trevorton coals were from Pennsylvania; the Cumberland was from Maryland.

The only means at command for ascertaining the evaporation of the different coals, were one of the engines and boilers in daily use in the Navy Yard; and those of the Smithery were selected because the work performed by the engine was very regular (driving blowing fans), varying scarcely sensibly from day to day; and because the steam was used without expansion or condensation. Before detailing the manner of making the experiments and calculating their results, it is proper to give the dimensions of the boiler, engine, and fans, which were as follows, namely:—

Dimensions of the Boiler.—(Plate 1.)

The shell of the boiler, with the exception of the end occupied by the furnace, was cylindrical and 4 feet in diameter. The end occupied by the furnace was rectangular in plan and 6 feet 3 inches in length by 4 feet in width, its top was a semi-cylindrical extension of the cylindrical part of the shell. The extreme length of the boiler was 24 feet. It was, with the exception of the front at the furnace end and the top of the steam chest, entirely cased in brick masonry. The fire grate was 3½ feet wide and 5½ feet long: during the experiments made December 23d, 24th, 27th, 28th, and 29th, it was composed of nineteen cast iron bars, each of which was 1½ inch wide, leaving a total air space of 6.19 square feet or 32 per centum of the furnace area. These bars were then removed and during the remaining experiments were replaced by forty-two others having each a width of ½ inch, and leaving a total air space of 9⅝ square feet, or 50 per centum of the total furnace area; no appreciable effect resulted from the alteration.

The flues were five in number, cylindrical and 12 inches in diameter; they were arranged within the cylindrical part of the shell in two rows vertically. The first or upper row consisted of three flues extending 16½ feet from the furnace to the first smoke connection; thence the second row—lying beneath the first—extended 14½ feet directly back to the second smoke connection, which was placed immediately behind the furnace and below the first row of flues. The heated gases thus proceeded from the furnace through the first row of three flues to the first smoke connection, and thence returned in an exactly opposite direction through the second row of two flues to the second smoke connection, from which they descended into one large flue whose top was the bottom of the cylindrical part of the shell, and whose sides and bottom were composed of the brick masonry. In this flue the gases proceeded along the bottom of the boiler in their first direction 11¼ feet and then debouched into the chimney at a point 4 feet before the end of the boiler was reached. By this arrangement the heated gases descended from row to row of flues until they passed into the chimney; and, of course, their highest temperature was applied near the surface of the water, and their lowest temperature near the bottom where the feed water entered. The total length traversed by the heated gases from the furnace to the chimney, was 45¼ feet, in the course of which they passed through two smoke connections, where they had the opportunity of being mixed before proceeding farther. The water was carried 4 inches above the top of the furnace, which top was on the same level with the top of the first row of flues. The steam was taken from the top of the steam chest 5 feet 11 inches above the water level, and was conducted to the cylinder through a pipe 3¼ inches internal diameter and 50 feet in length, made of ⅛ inch thick wrought iron. This pipe rose vertically 6 feet and was then carried horizontally to a point 9 feet above the valve chest into which it descended vertically. In its length there were five right angled elbows, and both it and the cylinder were uncovered. The ash pit opening in front was 15 inches in height, giving an air area of 4.4 square feet.

The following are the remaining principal dimensions, namely:—

Area of fire grate..............			19.25	square feet.
Heating surface in furnace.......	41.10	square feet.		
Heating surface in first smoke connection......................	20.35	" "		
Heating surface in second smoke connection..................	8.50	" "		
Heating surface in boiler bottom..	62.80	" "		
Heating surface in the five flues...	246.70	" "		
Total heating surface in the boiler.			379.45	" "
Cross area of the first row of flues.			2.3562	" "

Cross area of the second row of flues		1.5708 square feet.
Cross area of the flue under the bottom of the boiler		5.7778 " "
Height of the chimney above the grates		60 feet.
Ratio of the heating to the grate surface		19.712 to 1,000.
Ratio of the grate surface to the cross area of the first row of flues.		8,170 " "
Ratio of the grate surface to the cross area of the second row of flues		12,255 " "
Steam room in the boiler	62 cubic feet.	
Steam room in the steam pipe and valve chest	4 " "	
Total steam room		66 cubic feet.
Weight of water under standard conditions in the boiler at 4 inches above top of furnace		7500 pounds.

The cross area of the flue under the bottom of the boiler was made large enough for a man to enter. As regards the proportions of the boiler it may be remarked, that the ratio of the heating to the grate surface was much smaller than is usual in this type; particularly when intended to burn as much as 14 pounds of coal per square foot of grate per hour. The ratio of the grate surface to the cross area of the flues was much larger than is usually given, or in other words, the calorimeter was much smaller than the usual practice. Both variations from the habitual standard were against obtaining a good economic evaporation from the fuel consumed.

Dimensions of the Engine.

One non-condensing engine with horizontal cylinder working upon a shaft carrying a large cast-iron wheel, which served both as a fly wheel and a drum from which to drive the fan blowers by belts. The steam valves were a short slide at each end of the cylinder, connected by a bar. The cut-off valves, one at each end of the cylinder, were two plates connected by a rod and sliding upon the same seat with the steam valves. The two steam valves moved between the two cut-off valves and worked them after the manner of a tappet, the distance between the inner edges of the cut-off plates being greater than the distance between the outer edges of the steam valves. The cut-off plates were attached to their connecting rod by right and left hand screws; the rod protruded through one end of the valve chest and could be turned by a handle so as to make the cut-off adjustable by bringing the plates nearer together or removing them farther apart. In the steam pipe there were two throttles; one, situated 9 inches above the top of the valve chest, was graduated by the governor; the other, situated 15 inches above the valve chest, was graduated by the hand at will. During the experiments the former was in action but the latter was kept wide open. The cut-off was not used and the steam (greatly throttled) from the boiler followed the piston during its whole stroke. The following are the principal dimensions of the cylinder, namely:—

Diameter of the cylinder....................	18 inches.
Stroke of the piston........................	4 feet.
Space displacement of the piston per stroke.	7.068 cubic ft.
Steam space at one end of cylinder between piston at end of stroke and steam valve....	0.259 "
Area of the steam port. (1¾ by 12 inches)..	21 sq. inches.
Area of the exhaust port. (2½ by 12 inches).	30 "
Clearance at each end of cylinder..........	⅜ths inch.

To the engine there is attached a heater by means of which the exhaust steam is made to raise the temperature of the feed water about 100° Fahr. before it enters the boiler.

Dimensions of the Fan Blowers.

The engine drives four fan blowers which furnish a superabundance of air for the forges of the large smithery. All the fans are geared to make 666⅔ revolutions per double stroke of engine piston, and they have the following dimensions, namely:—

	Three of these dimensions.	One of these dimensions.
Diameter over blades..........	34 inches.	32 inches.
Length of blade, radially.....	10 "	10 "
Width of blade at base........	10 "	14 "
Width of blade at periphery...	4½ "	6½ "
Number of blades.............	4.	4.
Diameter of inlet..............	13½ inches.	13½ inches.
Width of outlet..............	15 "	16 "
Height of outlet..............	11 "	13 "
Area of outlet	165 sq. in.	208 sq. in.
The blades are slightly curved.		

Manner of Making the Experiments.

During the experiments the boiler was operated in the usual manner to furnish the regular supply of steam. It was so large for the work that the fire required no forcing, and but few cinders were made. In the morning, the furnace having been well cleaned out, the temperature of the water in the boiler was noted, and a sufficient quantity of dry pine wood to kindle weighed out and lighted. The fire was allowed to nearly burn out just as the day's work was finished; the temperature of the water in the boiler was then ascertained from the steam pressure, and the waste from the coal in ashes and fine coal weighed. With the Cumberland semi-bituminous coal a small banked fire and steam in the boiler was generally kept during the night, in which case no wood was required for kindling. The coal was weighed out from time to time during the day, and very regularly fired by an experienced fireman. All the weighing was done with the same scales, and in the same box, which measured 25¼ by 17½ by 12 inches, giving a capacity of 3,069 cubic feet. The weight per cubic foot of the coals and their ashes hereinafter given, is the mean of many trials with this box levelled off. All the coals were screened, but not otherwise picked, and the lumps were about the size of a man's fist. The temperature of the air entering the ash pit was noted; and also the temperature of the feed water, which for this purpose was drawn from a cock in the pipe a few inches before entering the boiler. The steam pressure was shown by an Ashcroft guage; and the number of double strokes made by the engine piston was taken by a counter. The engine, though fitted with an adjustable cut-off valve, had never been worked with expansion; the cut-off plates being always run back to allow the steam to follow the piston full stroke; this was also the case during the experiments. A very excellent indicator was attached to the engine, and connected by a large pipe with each end of the cylinder. During the experiments diagrams were constantly taken from which the evaporation was calculated. A complete set of observations was noted every fifteen minutes.

In order to determine if any increased effect would follow the admission of air into the furnace through apertures in the door, the experiments were made both with and without them. The door was constructed in the usual manner of cast iron, with a ¼ inch thick wrought-iron lining to prevent the heat of the fuel from impinging upon it. This lining was a flat plate with a 1½ inch space between its periphery and the periphery of the door. The door was pierced over its whole surface and at regular spaces with sixty holes, each of ½ inch diameter, giving an aggregate area of 11.778 square inches. The lining was similarly pierced with one hundred and sixty-eight holes, each of ¼ inch diameter, giving an aggregate area of 8.232 square inches; in addition to which there was the area of the 1½ inch wide space by the length of the periphery of the lining which separated it from the door. The apertures when not in use were closed with fire-clay.

Attempts were made to obtain the temperature of the heated gases as they entered the chimney; this could not be effected exactly, as it was above 580° Fahr., the range of our mercurial themometer; but a loose roll of sheet lead which was placed at the mouth of the flue, supported on a fire-brick, was completely melted. Zinc, however, similarly placed, did not show the least trace of fusion, not even on the sharp fractured edges. The melting point of lead as given by Pouillet, Irvine, and Guyton Morveau, is respectively 608°, 590°, and 592° Fahr.; mean 597° Fahr. The melting point of zinc as given by Murray, Guyton Morveau, and Pouillet, is respectively 700°, 705°, and 680° Fahr; mean 695° Fahr. The temperature of the heated gases on entering the chimney was, therefore, between 597° and 695° Fahr.; we shall probably be near the truth if we take the mean of these two numbers, namely, 646° Fahr.

An approximation towards the temperature of the furnace was obtained by placing a loose coil of fine copper wire on a fire-brick, and putting the latter into the middle of the furnace, upon the top of the coal. A full charge of fresh fuel having been just previously thrown on, the brick was put in, and not withdrawn until the furnace required firing again. In this position the copper did not exhibit the slightest trace of fusing. The experiment was then repeated with the copper *overhanging* the brick and elevated about 2 inches above the level of the coal. In this position it remained some time intact, but finally the overhanging portion melted off, leaving the part on the brick as unfused as before. The maximum temperature of the gases as they rose from the incandescent coal must, therefore, have been about the melting point of copper, while the average temperature of the furnace above the fuel must have been much less. The melting point of copper is, according to Pouillet, 1922° Fahr.; and we will assume this as the temperature of the heated gases in their nascent state :—then as the temperature of the water in the boiler averaged 278° Fahr., there remained for producing evaporation (1922—278=) 1644° Fahr.; and as the temperature at which the heated gases passed into the chimney was 646° Fahr., the loss due to this cause was $\left(\frac{646 \times 100}{1922} =\right) 39\frac{3}{10}$ per centum of the heat applicable to evaporation.

Description of the Experimental Coals.

The BLACKHEATH COAL is a true anthracite of the hardest and dryest variety. When struck it gives a clear ringing sound; its cohesion is very great, and it breaks with a semi-conchoidal fracture exhibiting a brilliant jet of almost metallic lustre. The following is its composition exclusive of ash and the water mechanically present in its pores; namely:—

Carbon, 93.89. Hydrogen, 3.55. Oxygen, 2.56.

The hygroscopic water is 2½ per centum of the coal, and is very tenaciously retained. Specific gravity, 1.55.

This coal kindles slowly, and the very little flame it develops takes place only at the commencement of its combustion; this flame, which is at first bluish, merges soon into a faint yellow and quickly disappears. In the furnace the lumps neither soften, nor swell, nor split into fragments, but retain their form, and consume slowly away by their surfaces. From its behavior during combustion, it was evident that this coal did not contain a particle of bitumen; its oxygen and part of its hydrogen existed probably combined in the proportions to form water, the remaining hydrogen being in solid combination with the carbon.

The TREVORTON COAL is a semi-anthracite, but does not contain any bitumen. In mechanical structure it is completely opposed to the Blackheath anthracite; it has no tendency to the conchoidal fracture, but is lamellar and everywhere fissured by fine joints or clefts of easy cleavage, which present either a dull or a shining black appearance according to the directions of the cross partings. The faces, too, are frequently striated. It breaks or crumbles very easily, and compared with the Blackheath coal has greatly less cohesion; its weight per cubic foot in a merchantable state is also much less, the two in this respect being in the proportion of 1.000 to 1.124; the hand, too, is much more soiled by contact with it.

In the furnace the Trevorton coal kindles easily and the

lumps quickly divide and subdivide into small cuboidal fragments ; it burns without smoke but with considerable yellowish carbonaceous flame, which continues during nearly the whole combustion ; but the lumps retain their cuboidal form to the last and neither soften nor agglutinate nor intumesce.

The following are the proximate and organic analyses of this coal, as furnished by Professor JAMES R. CHILTON. They were made at different times on different samples :—

Proximate Analysis.

Fixed Carbon	85.66
Volatile combustible matter	6.67
Ashes	6.83
Water, expelled at 212° Fahr	0.84
	100.00

Organic Analysis.

Carbon	90.661
Hydrogen	1.726
Nitrogen	0.001
Oxygen	0.780
	93.168
Ashes	6.721
Loss	0.111
	100.009

Neglecting the ashes, nitrogen, and hygroscopic water, the composition is as follows, namely:—

Carbon, 97.310. Hydrogen, 1.853. Oxygen, 0.837.

A comparison of the above proximate and organic analyses shows, that the volatile matter with the exception of about 1 per centum is composed of combustible carbureted hydrogen, which exists as a free gas condensed in the pores of the coal, and not in the viscous state of bitumen.

The specific gravity of this coal is 1.38, and in the ordinary state of dryness its pores hold mechanically about $\frac{3}{4}$ of 1 per centum of water. The lightness of the coal is probably due to the fact of its pores being filled with carbureted hydrogen gas.

Omitting ashes and small constituents, the chief differences between Blackheath anthracite and the Trevorton semi-anthracite may be briefly summed as follows, namely:

In composition the Trevorton coal contains about $3\frac{2}{3}$ per centum more carbon, about one-half the quantity of hydrogen, about one-third the quantity of oxygen, and about one-fourth the quantity of hygroscopic water. In mechanical structure it is less dense, has less cohesion, and exhibits altogether different characteristics of fracture, &c.

The CUMBERLAND SEMI-BITUMINOUS is a free burning coal from Maryland. Its mechanical structure varies from slaty to columnar, and is chiefly the latter, which is semi-crystalline in texture while the slaty portions are amorphous; the columnar portions exhibit a deep shining jet black while the slaty portions show a dull black. Its cohesion is weak; it fractures easily, and the surfaces are frequently striated; it is very friable, crumbling under slight mechanical action into fine powder.

In the furnace it ignites readily and burns with a red flame of moderate length. While parting with its volatile constituents the lumps agglutinate slightly and intumesce considerably, the bulk of its coke much exceeding that of the coal from which it was derived. It is by no means a caking coal, only a small part of its volatile constituents being in the state of bitumen; part of its hydrogen probably unites with its oxygen in the proportion to form water, and the remainder is condensed into the pores of the coal in the state of free gas. It produces considerable smoke of a deep brown color.

Its weight in the merchantable state is less than that of he Blackheath anthracite, but more than that of the Trevorton semi-anthracite; and in its action in the furnace it differs from both in its production of smoke, in the rounding or melting off of the edges of the lumps, in their agglutination, and in the increase of bulk. The effect of the latter is, by increasing the porosity of the coal, to produce the rapid and complete combustion of its fixed carbon.

The following are the proximate and organic analyses of this coal, namely:

Proximate Analysis.

Fixed Carbon........................	80.75
Volatile combustible matter...........	13.00
Ashes................................	5.00
Water expelled at 212° Fahr...........	1 25
	100.00

Organic Analysis.

Fixed Carbon........................	86.50
Hydrogen............................	4.75
Oxygen..............................	2.50
Hygrometric moisture................	1.25
Ashes...............................	5.00
	100.00

Neglecting the ashes and hygrometic water, the composition is as follows, namely:

Carbon, 92.37. Hydrogen, 5.07. Oxygen, 2.66.
Specific gravity, 1.42.

The data of the experiments made with these coals in the manner described, will be found in the following three tables, namely:

Data of the Experiments made with the Smithery Boiler at the U. S. Navy Yard, New York, to determine the Evaporative Efficiency of the BLACKHEATH ANTHRACITE.

Date. 1858 and 1859.	Duration of each Experiment in Hours and Minutes.	State of the Weather.	Temperatures in Degrees Fahr.: Water in Boiler at starting Fire.	Water in Boiler at end of Experiment.	Feed Water supplied to Boiler.	Air entering Ash-pit.	Pressures in pounds per square inch.: In boiler above atmosphere per gauge.	In Cylinder at commencement of Stroke of Piston above atmosphere per Indicator.	In Cylinder at end of Stroke of Piston above atmosphere per Indicator.	Mean gross effective pressure on Piston per Indicator.	Number of Double Strokes made by the Engine Piston.: Total.	Per Minute.	Fuel.: Pounds of Coal consumed.	Pounds of Pine Wood consumed in kindling.	Pounds of Waste in Ashes, Fine Coal, &c.	Per Centum of waste of the Coal in Ashes, Fine Coal, etc.	Pounds of Coal consumed, estimating 2 pounds of Wood equal in evaporative value to 1 pound of Coal.
No Admission of Air through the Furnace Door.																	
Dec. 27.	7 .. 00	Fair.	96	259	131	60	33.9	16.9	9.7	11.60	10,795	25.702	1,950	298	2,333	20⅖	2,099
" 28.	7 .. 00	"	194	257	131	60	34.4	16.2	9.4	11.24	10,533	25.079	1,950	156			2,028
" 29.	7 .. 00	"	196	255	132	60	35.4	16.4	9.3	11.19	10,488	24.971	1,900	156			1,978
Jan. 3.	6 .. 56	"	108	255	134	65	29.8	16.8	9.5	11.50	10,600	25.481	1,920	226			2,033
" 4.	7 .. 10	Snowing	196	241	134	68	25.6	16.0	9.2	11.04	10,634	24.730	1,920	160			2,000
" 8.	7 .. 10	Fair.	204	241	136	70	25.5	15.1	8.8	10.47	10,225	23.779	1,800	158			1,879
Totals,	42 .. 16										63,275		11,440	1,154	2.333		12,017
Means.			166	251	133	63	30.7	16.2	9.3	11.17		24.951				20⅖	
Air admitted through Holes in the Furnace Door.																	
Jan. 11.	6 .. 55	Cloudy.	228	251	134	42	30.0	16.4	9.4	11.30	10,440	25.157	1,760	190	1,978	20¾	1,855
" 12.	7 .. 13	"	204	251	131	55	33.5	18.6	10.4	12.57	11,750	27.136	2,000	150			2,075
" 13.	7 .. 2	"	206	251	132	54	26.2	17.3	9.8	11.83	10,975	26.007	1,950	100			2,000
" 14.	7 .. 9	"	206	251	135	66	25.7	17.5	9.9	11.93	11,238	26.196	2,000	126			2,063
" 15.	7 .. 10	Raining. Foggy.	222	261	138	66	27.6	17.2	9.7	11.75	11,131	25.884	1,838	120			1,898
Totals.	35 .. 29										55,534		9,548	686	1,978		9,891
Means.			213	253	134	57	28.6	17.4	9.8	11.88		26.084				20¾	

Data of the Experiments made with the Smithery Boiler at the U. S. Navy Yard, New York, to determine the Evaporative Efficiency of the TREVORTON SEMI-ANTHRACITE.

Date. 1858 and 1859.	Duration of each Experiment in Hours and Minutes.	State of the Weather.	Temperatures in Degrees Fahr.				Pressures in pounds per square inch.				Number of Double Strokes made by the Engine Piston.		Fuel.				
			Water in Boiler at starting Fires.	Water in Boiler at end of Experiment.	Feed Water supplied to Boiler.	Air entering Ash-pit.	In Boiler above atmosphere per Gauge.	In Cylinder at commencement of stroke above atmosphere per Indicator.	In Cylinder at end of Stroke above atmosphere per Indicator.	Mean gross effective pressure on Piston per Indicator.	Total.	Per Minute.	Pounds of Coal consumed.	Pounds of Pine Wood consumed in kindling.	Pounds of waste in Ashes, Fine Coal, &c.	Per centum of waste of the Coal in Ashes, Fine Coal, &c.	Pounds of Coal consumed, estimating 2 pounds of Wood equal in evaporative value to 1 pound of Coal.
No Admission of Air through the Furnace Door.																	
Dec. 23.	6 .. 57	Fair.	84	241	131	65	34.1	16.4	9.4	11.27	10,476	25.122	1,704	298			1,853
" 24.	6 .. 58	Raining.	186	247	131	65	36.7	16.3	9.3	11.22	10,491	25.098	1,684	20			1,694
" 30.	6 .. 45	Snowing.	80	247	133	70	34.2	17.5	9.9	11.91	10,585	26.137	1,630	156			1,708
" 31.	6 .. 50	Raining.	154	261	131	75	34.1	17.7	10.0	12.07	10,816	26.380	1,620	90	1,252	12	1,665
Jan. 5.	7 .. 08	Fair.	186	241	131	75	30.3	18.1	10.1	12.30	11,455	26.764	1,684	180			1,774
" 6.	7 .. 05	"	162	241	133	75	32.5	17.9	10.0	12.17	11,280	26.541	1,680	90			1,725
Totals.	41 .. 43										65,103		10,002	834	1,252		10,419
Means.			143	246	132	71	33.6	17.3	9.8	11.83		26.010				12	
Air admitted through Holes in the Furnace Door.																	
Feb. 1.	7 .. 46	Fair.	95	241	139	60	29.2	18.2	10.2	12.33	12,481	26.783	1,916	180			2,006
" 2.	7 .. 48	"	160	241	142	67	31.0	19.1	10.6	12.89	12,924	27.616	1,800	60			1,830
" 3.	7 .. 52	Raining.	172	251	148	64	31.2	19.1	10.6	12.91	13,050	27.648	2,000	60	1,380	14¼	2,030
" 4.	7 .. 52	Fair.	160	245	154	63	31.5	19.4	10.7	13.07	13,159	27.879	2,000	60			2,030
" 5.	7 .. 56	"	172	241	152	61	33.5	18.7	10.4	12.66	12,984	27.277	1,970	60			2,000
Totals.	39 .. 14										64,598		9,686	420	1,380		9.896
Means.			152	244	147	63	31.3	18.9	10.5	12.77		27.442				14¼	

Data of the Experiments made with the Smithery Boiler at the U. S. Navy Yard, New York, to determine the Evaporative Efficiency of the CUMBERLAND SEMI-BITUMINOUS COAL.

Date. 1859.	Duration of the Experiments in Hours and Minutes.	State of the Weather.	Temperatures in Degrees Fahr.				Pressures in pounds per square inch.				Number of Double Strokes made by Engine Piston.		Fuel.				
			Water in the Boiler at starting Fire.	Water in Boiler at end of Experiment.	Feed Water supplied to Boiler.	Air entering Ash-pit.	In boiler, per gauge, above atmosphere.	In Cylinder at commencement of Stroke of Piston, per Indicator, above atmosphere.	In Cylinder at end of Stroke of Piston, per Indicator, above atmosphere.	Mean gross effective pressure on Piston per Indicator.	Total.	Per Minute.	Pounds of Coal consumed.	Pounds of Pine Wood consumed in kindling.	Pounds of Waste in Ashes, Fine Coal, &c.	Per Centum of waste of the Coal in Ashes, Fine Coal, etc.	Pounds of Coal consumed, estimating 2 pounds of Wood equal in evaporative efficiency to 1 pound of Coal.
No Admission of Air through Furnace Door.																	
Jan. 24.	7 .. 25	Fair.	83	245	137	61	29.8	18.1	10.1	12.30	11,890	26.719	1,850	160			1,930
" 25.	7 .. 28	"	180	251	137	59	29.6	17.5	9.9	11.96	11,742	26.210	1,840	None.			1,840
" 26.	7 .. 34	"	186	251	134	64	30.8	19.1	10.6	12.89	12,540	27.621	1,840	"	943	$10\frac{1}{6}$	1,840
" 27.	7 .. 33	"	175	251	136	63	30.6	18.4	10.3	12.47	12,225	26.987	1,850	"			1,850
" 28.	7 .. 36	Raining.	190	273	136	69	29.3	18.4	10.3	12.47	12,300	26.974	1,900	"			1,900
Totals.	37 .. 36										60,697		9,280	160	943		9,360
Means.			163	254	136	63	30.0	18.6	10.2	12.42		26.904				$10\frac{1}{6}$	
Air admitted through Holes in the Furnace Door.																	
Jan. 17.	7 .. 13	Fair.	136	261	135	66	32.6	18.8	10.5	12.73	11,840	27.344	1,800	160			1,880
" 18.	6 .. 26	"	184	251	132	59	30.9	17.8	10.0	12.12	10,212	26.456	1,440	None.			1,440
" 19.	7 .. 22	"	184	251	135	67	31.4	17.9	10.0	12.14	11,710	26.493	1,680	100	985	$11\frac{1}{2}$	1,730
" 20.	7 .. 25	"	184	251	134	68	30.9	18.1	10.1	12.28	11,876	26.688	1,800	None.			1,800
" 21.	7 .. 24	Raining.	192	261	135	72	32.7	18.9	10.5	12.76	12,179	27.430	1,800	"			1,800
Totals.	35 .. 50										57,817		8,520	260	985		8,650
Means.			176	255	134	67	31.7	18.1	10.2	12.41		26.892				$11\frac{1}{2}$	

Calculation of the Weight of Steam evaporated by the Coals.

The weight of steam or water evaporated is obtained by calculation, and is the sum of the following three quantities, namely:

1st. Of the weight of steam discharged from the cylinder at the end of the stroke of the piston: this is determined by the pressure at that point, as shown by the indicator.

2d. Of the weight of steam that would have been evaporated had the heat which was absorbed by the water in the boiler in raising its temperature the difference of its temperatures at the commencement and end of each experiment, been employed in evaporating it into steam of the same total heat as that in the boiler: this weight is determined from the temperatures of the water in the boiler at the commencement and end of the experiment, the weight of that water, and the total heat of the steam of mean boiler pressure during the experiment.

3d. Of the evaporation equivalent to the heat annihilated in the cylinder to produce the mechanical power developed by the engine. When this power is known, its thermal equivalent can be easily calculated; it is so much heat as will raise the temperature of one pound of water one degree on Fahrenheit's scale for every 772 foot-pounds accomplished by the engine.

These three quantities, though all that admit of calculation, do not constitute the whole weight of water actually evaporated by the fuel; they are exclusive of the losses of heat from the following causes, namely:

1st. *By conduction and radiation,* the losses due to which must have been considerable, as neither steam-pipe nor cylinder were covered. The former was 50 feet long, 3¼ inches inside diameter, and was made of ⅛ inch thick wrought-iron; the temperature of the steam within it was 278° Fahr.; of the air surrounding it 64° Fahr.

2d. *By leakage of steam past the valves and piston ;* a loss more or less serious with all engines, but which, though considerable in the present case, was probably not above the average.

3d. *By the use of the steam in what may be called the* VESICULAR *state;* that is, in minute globules contained within very thin envelopes or films of water, instead of being a homogeneous mass. This vesicular state is that in which steam is always found in boilers when in active evaporation supplying engines. It differs entirely from *priming* or *foaming*, which consists in the violent upheaval of comparatively solid masses of water consequent on the sudden reduction of the steam pressure in the boiler without a corresponding reduction of the temperature of the water beneath it. In other words priming is due to the abnormal relation of too high a temperature of the boiler water to the steam pressure upon it.

In the boiling of water, globules of steam, more or less minute, are first formed on the surface transmitting the heat; when their buoyancy becomes sufficient to overcome the cohesion of the superincumbent water, they rise through it and emerging at the upper surface occupy the steam room. On leaving the water a small envelope or film of it, due to its cohesion, remains around the ascending globule of steam and is carried by it to the cylinder. An aggregation of common soap bubbles will give a correct idea on an exaggerated scale of this vesicular condition of the steam, which is further maintained by the continuous condensation of the globules at their surface from the moment they leave the water. When steam issues from a boiler gauge-cock, it is nearly transparent and invisible at the opening, but at a short distance becomes visible and assumes a foggy appearance which is caused by the admixture of the minute globules of the vesicular steam and the atmospheric air ; for it appears to be a law of nature that the intimate mixture of two transparent media of different constitutions produces an opaque appearance, as in the case of beating up oils and water, or the powdering of glass, which is the intermixing of minute transparent fragments with the atmospheric air. The quantity of water thus carried from the boiler to the cylinder in the solid state as envelopes to the steam globule, is by no means inconsiderable.

4th. *By the quantity of water carried mechanically from the boiler to the cylinder by foaming or priming* which is caused by changes of *pressure* in the boiler without corresponding changes in the *temperature* of its water. This results from the fact that the withdrawal of steam from the boiler by the cylinder is intermitting, while the supply of heat to its water is uninterrupted; the sameness of the temperature of the water is also further maintained by its large mass. At each withdrawal, therefore, of a charge of steam from the boiler, its pressure is lowered, and as the temperature of the water remains the same, a sudden and violent evolution of steam follows, throwing up a mass of spray which it drives along with it to the cylinder. This state of things exists in all boilers to a greater or less extent, depending on their type and proportions. It is less, *ceteris paribus*, as the steam room is greater; because, then, the withdrawal of a charge of steam effects the pressure of the remainder in a correspondingly small degree. It is lessened, too, by taking the steam at a greater height above the water level, because there is more time given for the action of gravity to cause the lifted water to fall back. It is lessened, also, by the boiler having a greater area of water line, because the disengagement of steam from the larger surface will be greater in equal times, and the pressure will consequently be sooner replaced. It is lessened by greater facilities for the circulation of the water in the boiler. And, finally, it is lessened as the steam-pipe is supplied evenly from the whole area of the steam-room, instead of from one locality. When the latter is the case the pressure around the aperture of the pipe will be less than in other places, and the water there will have a local elevation due to this difference of pressure, exaggerated by the movement of the steam from remoter parts towards the pipe. The effect is to increase the priming by diminishing the distance between the water and steam-pipe. A boiler which primed excessively owing to the delivery of its steam at one extremity into a pipe but little above the water-line, was effectually cured by inserting a branch of the same pipe into the opposite extremity ; for by thus drawing the steam equally from both ends, the wave towards one aperture was completely prevented by the equal tendency in the opposite direction. It is difficult to estimate the quantity of water carried over by foaming, but for the average of boilers as proportioned in practice, it may be taken that 20 per centum of the water pumped in is carried in spray to the cylinder and swept from it by the exhaust of the steam. Great as this proportion appears it is known under unfavorable conditions to have been doubled. In the present case, the steam was taken 5 feet 11 inches above the water level, and the entire steam space from the water level to the valve seat contained nine charges of steam for the cylinder; but as the pressures of the steam in the boiler and in the cylinder at the end of the stroke were 45.2 and 24.0 pounds per square inch above zero, the nine charges become ($\frac{45.2}{24} = 1.883$, and $1.883 \times 9 =$) 16.947 charges, over fifty of which were withdrawn per minute and must have been attended with the carrying over of much water.

The loss of heat by the transvection of the boiler water to the cylinder, whether as envelopes to the steam globules or as spray in foaming, is caused by the fact that this water had already had imparted to it sufficient heat to raise its temperature from that of the feed water to that of the steam carrying it over; to balance the loss of this heat, there is only the insignificant value of the water's displacement of steam in the cylinder.

5th. *By the loss of heat due to the alternate cooling and heating of the metal of the cylinder during a stroke of the piston.* At the commencement of a stroke the piston is at one end of the cylinder, the interior of which is then exposed to the temperature of vapor of about atmospheric pressure in non-condensing engines, and of the condenser pressure in condensing ones. This temperature being always less than that of the entering steam, the interior surfaces of the cylinder will condense enough to furnish the requisite heat for raising them to its temperature. The loss from this source will be the greater, as the difference between the mean temperature of the entering steam during the stroke and of the vapor of the exhaust, is greater.

6th. *When the steam is used expansively, there is a very great loss of heat from the condensation due to that very expansion;* and the more expansively the steam is used, the greater will be this loss, though not in a direct ratio. It must be distinctly understood, that it is impossible to expand steam without reducing its temperature, and that the consequence of a reduction of temperature is a corresponding condensation. As soon, therefore, as the steam is cut off, the continuous retreat of the piston allows it to expand, and the temperature falling with the pressure, a condensation ensues, the result of which is a further expansion to fill the space that was occupied by the steam which has been condensed; there then follows from this further expansion, another fall of temperature, and consequent condensation of steam, and thus the process becomes continuous, propagating itself after having once commenced. It will be found that the condensation of steam in a close vessel having been once commenced, goes on with increasing rapidity, the tendency to condense becoming greater with each condensation, irrespective of the external refrigeration. From the moment, then, that the steam is cut off in the cylinder, and continuing to the end of the stroke of the piston, a large condensation is taking place, due wholly to the fact of the expansion, and becoming greater the shorter the steam is cut off.

From the foregoing it will be easily understood, that the evaporation by the same coal, *ceteris paribus*, *appears* very different when determined by the Indicator, and when the water is measured in a Tank previous to being pumped into the boiler; nor can the one be at all taken as a measure of the other; they vary greatly according to the already enumerated variable elements of type and proportions of boiler; tightness of the piston and of the valves of the engine; clothing of the boiler, steam-pipes and cylinder; temperature of the surrounding air, and of the steam ; point of cutting off ; etc. The evaporation as shown by the Indicator is generally from 25 to 50 per centum less than is shown by the Tank; and great even as this latter difference seems to be, it may easily, under a combination of unfavorable circumstances, be exceeded. Neither the Indicator nor the Tank, then, gives the *true* evaporation; the first makes it much too small, the last too great; but though they thus fail in determining an *absolute* quantity, yet either, under the *same conditions*, will give reliably correct *comparative results for those conditions, but for those only*, a change in them changing and sometimes even reversing the results.

Although, then, the experiments do not show the absolute evaporative power of the coals, which would furthermore be dependent on the quantity of water mechanically present at the time in their pores, on the temperature of the air entering the ash-pit, on the rapidity of the combustion, on the thickness of the fuel upon the grate, and on the hygrometric and barometric conditions of the atmosphere; yet as the experiments were made under almost rigorously the same conditions, with the same speed of piston and steam pressure, without expansion, and with nearly the same development of power by the engine; the coal too being burned by the same fireman; they can safely be accepted as exhibiting correctly the *comparative* evaporative power of the coals *under the conditions of the experiment.*

We will now illustrate the mode of ascertaining the weight of steam evaporated, by calculating it in the case of the Blackheath anthracite when burned with no admission of air through the furnace door.

And first for *the weight of steam discharged from the cylinder at the end of the stroke of the piston.* Let

a = the number of double strokes made by the piston.

b = the number of cubic feet filled by the steam per double stroke of piston.

c = the weight of a cubic foot of distilled water at standard temperature of 62° Fahr. Barom. 30 inches.

d = the number of volumes of steam of the pressure at the end of the stroke of the piston, generated from unit of volume of distilled water under standard conditions.

x = the number of pounds of water or steam discharged from the cylinder, and evaporated from the temperature of the feed-water entering the boiler.

Then $x = \frac{a \times b \times c}{d}$

And if the evaporation be desired, that would be given by the same weight of fuel from any other temperature of feed-water than the one at which the boiler was actually supplied: Let

e = total heat of steam of the boiler pressure in degrees Fahr.

f = the temperature in degrees Fahr. of the feed-water at which the boiler was actually supplied.

g = the temperature in degrees Fahr. of the feed-water from which the evaporation is desired.

$e-f$ = the number of degrees of temperature imparted to the feed-water to convert it into steam in the first case.

$e-g$ = the number of degrees of temperature imparted to the feed-water to convert it into steam in the second case.

x = the number of pounds of water or steam evaporated from the temperature f.

x = the number of pounds of water or steam evaporated from the temperature g.

Then $e-g : e-f :: \mathrm{x} : x$. and $x = \frac{e-f \times \mathrm{x}}{e-g}$

The total space filled by the steam per double stroke of piston was 14.654 cubic feet; the total number of double strokes made was 63.275; the steam pressure at the end of the stroke of the piston was 24 pounds above zero; the relative bulks of this steam, and the water under standard conditions from which it was generated, are 1084 and 1; and as the weight of a cubic foot of such water is 62.321 pounds, we have for the total weight of the steam discharged from the cylinder ($\frac{14.654 \times 63275 \times 62.321}{1084}=$) 53308.14 pounds, which was evaporated from the temperature 133° Fahr. of the feed-water entering the boiler. To ascertain now what this evaporation would be from a temperature of 100° Fahr. of feed-water The boiler pressure per square inch above zero was ($30.7 \times 14.7 =$) 45.4 pounds, the total heat of which steam is 1197.6 Fahr., and as the temperature of the feed-water was 133° Fahr., there remained to be imparted to convert it into steam (1197.6—133 =) 1064.6°, while with a temperature of feed-water of 100° Fahr. there will be required to be imparted (1197.6—100 =) 1097.6°, consequently for evaporation from a temperature of feed-water of 100° Fahr., the above 53308.14 pounds of steam would become ($\frac{53308.14 \times 1064.6}{1097.9}=$) 51705.40 pounds.

Next, *for the evaporation equivalent to the heat absorbed in raising the temperature of the boiler water from its temperature at the commencement to that at the close of the experiments* : Let

$h =$ the temperature in degrees Fahr. of the water in the boiler at the commencement of the experiment.

$i =$ the temperature in degrees Fahr. of the water in the boiler at the end of the experiment.

$e =$ the total heat of steam of the mean boiler pressure in degrees Fahr.

$j =$ the number of pounds of water in the boiler. (This weight was kept the same at the beginning and end of the experiments.)

$g =$ the temperature in degrees Fahr. of the feed-water from which the evaporation is desired.

Then $\frac{i-h}{e-g} \times j =$ the evaporation in pounds of steam or water from the temperature g of feed-water due to the heat expended in raising the boiler water from the temperature h to the temperature i.

The temperature of the water in the boiler at the commencement of the experiments was 166° Fahr., and at their close 251° Fahr., the difference being 85° Fahr. The total heat of the steam of the boiler pressure was, as before, 1197.6° Fahr., and the temperature of the feed-water from which the evaporation is desived is 100° Fahr., difference 1097.6° Fahr. The weight of the water in the boiler was 7,500 pounds. And $\frac{85}{1097.6} \times 7500 = 580.8127$ pounds. This, then, is the evaporation from a temperature of feed-water of 100° Fahr. due to the heat absorbed in raising the boiler water through 85° Fahr. of temperature. As the experiments were six in number, and as this quantity was the mean per experiment, the total evaporation will be $(580.8127 \times 6 =)$ 3484.88 pounds.

Lastly, for *the evaporation equivalent to the heat annihilated in the cylinder to produce the power developed by the engine.* The horse power being taken at 33,000 pounds raised one foot high per minute, and the thermal equivalent of 772 foot pounds being taken, according to JOULE, at one pound of water raised one degree of temperature on Fahrenheit's scale; then the thermal equivalent of an indicated horse power will be $\left(\frac{33000}{772} =\right)$ 42.7461 pounds of water raised one degree Fahr. Let

$k =$ the number of indicated horses power developed by the engine.

$e =$ the total heat of steam of the mean boiler pressure in degrees Fahr.

$g =$ the temperature in degrees Fahr. of the feed-water from which the evaporation is desired.

$t =$ the time in minutes during which the indicated horses power acted:—

Then $\frac{k \times 42.7461 \times t}{e-g}$ = the number of pounds of steam that would be evaporated in the time t, from a temperature g of feed-water, by the heat annihilated to produce the indicated horses power k developed by the engine; which heat was obtained by the condensation of steam in the cylinder.

The engine developed 17.193 horses power. The total heat of the steam of the boiler pressure was, as before, 1197.6° Fahr., and the temperature of feed-water from which the evaporation is desired is 100° Fahr., difference 1097.6° Fahr. The time during which the engine power acted was 42 hours and 16 minutes or 2536 minutes; hence we have $\left(\frac{17.193 \times 42.7461 \times 2536}{1097.6} =\right)$ 1698.06 pounds of steam evaporated from a temperature of feed-water of 100° Fahr. equivalent to the heat annihilated in the cylinder to produce the power developed by the engine.

Adding together the above three results, we shall have the following for the total weight of steam evaporated from a temperature of 100° Fahr. by the Blackheath anthracite when burned with no admission of air through holes in the furnace door, namely:

Pounds of steam discharged from the cylinder....	51705.40
Pounds of steam equivalent to the heat absorbed in raising the temperature of the boiler water from its temperature at the commencement to that at the close of the experiments	3484.88
Pounds of steam equivalent to the heat annihilated in the cylinder in producing the power of the engine..................................	1698.06
Total number of pounds..................	56888.34

Collecting the foregoing data and calculating their results in the manner described, we have, finally, the following exhibit of the comparative evaporative efficiency of the BLACKHEATH ANTHRACITE, the TREVORTON SEMI-ANTHRACITE, and the CUMBERLAND SEMI-BITUMINOUS coal with the boilers and under the conditions of the experiments.

Table exhibiting the Results of the Experiments made with the Smithery Engine and Boiler at the New York Navy Yard, to determine the comparative Evaporative Efficiency of the BLACKHEATH ANTHRACITE, *the* TREVORTON SEMI-ANTHRACITE, *and the* CUMBERLAND SEMI-BITUMINOUS *Coal.*

DATA.	BLACKHEATH ANTHRACITE.		TREVORTON SEMI-ANTHRACITE.		CUMBERLAND SEMI-BITUMIN'S.	
	No admission of air thro'h holes in Furnace door.	Air admitted through holes in Furnace door.	No admission of air thro'h holes in Furnace door.	Air admitted through holes in Furnace door.	No admission of air thro'h holes in Furnace door.	Air admitted through holes in Furnace door.
Duration of the experiments in hours and minutes,	42 : 16	35 : 29	41 : 43	39 : 14	37 : 36	35 : 50
Number of pounds of water contained in the boiler,	7,500	7,500	7,500	7,500	7,500	7,500
Temperature in degrees Fahr. of the water in the boiler at the commc't of the exper'ts,	166°	213°	143°	152°	163°	176°
Temperature in degs. Fahr. of the water in the boiler at the end of the experiments,	251°	253°	246°	244°	254°	255°
Temperature in degs. Fahr. of the feed water supplied to the boiler,	133°	134°	132°	147°	136°	134°
Temperature in degs. Fahr. of the air entering the ash-pit,	63°	57°	71°	63°	63°	67°
Time required to bring the boiler to steady action, in hours and minutes,	1 : 40	......	1 : 27	......	1 : 33	......
Pressure in pounds per square inch above the atmosphere of the steam in the boiler,	30.7	28.6	33.6	31.3	30.0	31.7
Pressure in pounds per sq. inch above the atmosphere of the steam in the cylinder at the commencement of the stroke,	16.2	17.4	17.3	18.9	18.6	18.1
Pressure in pounds per sq. inch above the atmosphere of the steam in the cylinder at the end of the stroke,	9.3	9.8	9.8	10.5	10.2	10.2
Total number of double strokes made by the piston (by counter)	63,275	55,534	65,103	64,598	60,697	57,817
Mean number of double strokes per minute made by the piston,	24.951	26.084	26.010	27.442	26.904	26.892
Mean gross effective pressure on piston in pounds per square inch (by Indicator)	11.17	11.88	11.83	12.77	12.42	12.41
Gross horses power developed by the engine,	17.193	19.116	18.982	21.618	20.613	20.587
Total number of pounds of coal consumed,	11,440	9,548	10,002	9,686	9,280	8,520
Total number of pounds of pine wood consumed (in kindling)	1,154	686	834	420	160	260
Total number of pounds of coal consumed, estimating two pounds of wood equal in evaporative value to one pound of coal,	12,017	9,891	10,419	9,896	9,360	8,650
Total number of lbs. of waste in ashes and in fine coal fall'g thro'h the grates unbur'd,	2,333	1,978	1,252	1,380	943	985
Per centum of waste of the coal in ashes and in fine coal,	$20\frac{2}{5}$	20	12	14¼	$10\frac{1}{6}$	11½
Total number of pounds of coal cousumed, exclusive of the waste in ashes, &c., estimating two pounds of wood equal in evaporative value to one pound of coal,	9,684	7,913	9,167	8,516	8,417	7,665
Pounds of coal consumed per hour per square foot of grate surface,	13.87	14.08	12.08	12.42	12.23	11.92
Pounds of coal consumed per hour per square foot of grate surface, exclusive of waste,	11.04	11.16	10.63	10.65	10.99	10.75
Weight of the coal in pounds per cubic foot,	54.50	54.50	48.50	48.50	51.47	51.47
Weight of the ashes, &c., in pounds per cubic foot,	47.91	47.91	44.17	44.17	38.00	38.00
EVAPORATION FROM A TEMPERATURE OF 100° FAHR.						
Pounds of steam discharged from the cylinder,	51,705.40	46,181.69	54,251.82	54,474.76	51,157.50	48,822.97
Pounds of steam equivalent to the heat absorbed in raising the temp'ure of the boiler water from its temperature at the commencem't to that at the close of the experi'ts,	3,484.88	1,373.75	3,515.20	3,142.65	3,109.91	2,698.09
Pounds of steam equivalent to the heat annihilated in the cylinder in producing the power of the engine,	1,698.06	1,593.26	1,848.33	1,981.51	1,811.55	1,723.16
Total number of pounds of steam evaporated	56,888.34	49,148.70	59,615.35	59,598.92	56,078.96	53,244.22
Pounds of water evaporated per pound of coal,	4.7340	4.9690	5.7218	6.0225	5.9913	6.1554
Pounds of water evaporated per pound of coal, exclusive of waste in ashes, &c.,	5.8744	6.2111	6.5033	6.9985	6.6626	6.9464

Discussion of the Results.

The coals, as regards their value for steam purposes, may be briefly compared as follows, namely:—

1st. Rapidity of Ignition.—The capability of rapid ignition, apart from its obvious convenience and utility in raising steam quickly, is valuable in coals, because it permits the steam pressure to be uniformly maintained in the boiler, which in ordinary cases is almost impossible with natural draught and coal of slow and difficult combustion. In those cases where, from any cause, the draught is feeble, the advantage of the coal of easiest ignition will be the more strongly marked. In this quality, the Trevorton coal stands first, the Cumberland next, and the Blackheath anthracite last.

2d. Preservation of Form.—The preservation of form under the constant attrition of handling and rolling about, is a cause of cleanliness, which on board ship has a commercial value in its saving of labor and material, independently of appearances and the comfort of the persons embarked. It has, also, a very great influence on the evaporative value; for when the coal has been reduced to powder, a large proportion of it falls unconsumed through the grate, and the part remaining on it impedes the draught and reduces the supply of steam. Coal in powder, then, is equivalent to a serious reduction of evaporative value per unit of weight; and it reduces also the boiler power of the vessel. As regards cohesive strength and consequent preservation of form, the Blackheath anthracite stands first; next, but at a considerable distance, comes the Trevorton semi-anthracite; closely to which follows the Cumberland semi-bituminous.

3d. Production of Smoke.—Both the Blackheath and Trevorton coals have a great advantage over the Cumberland in the non-production of smoke; which with the latter is considerable, and a constant source of soiling. It is furthermore highly objectionable in war steamers from its betrayal of their position at long distances.

4th. Waste from Ashes, Clinker, &c.—It is evident that it is only the portion of the coals which consumes that has an evaporative value. The waste, let it be ashes, clinker, or fine coal, is just so much abstracted from the weight of the coal: and in addition to this negative injury the presence of earthy matter is a positive one also; for the clinker, which is always produced with intense heat of furnace, covers the air spaces of the grate and obstructing the draught reduces the supply of steam. It also causes a loss of heat by the long opening of the furnace door to remove it, the cold air rushing in and cooling the flues.

The earthy matter uselessly occupying space in the furnace and intimately mixed with the fuel, prevents the contact of part of the combustible and the entering air, a larger portion of which will consequently pass off without giving up its oxygen than otherwise would. More air, therefore, passes through the grate in proportion to fuel consumed as the earthy matter constitutes a larger proportion of the coal, reducing the temperature of the furnace gases and correspondingly the evaporative efficiency of the unit of weight of coal, for it is only the difference of the temperatures of the gases within the flues and of the water surrounding them, that is available for evaporating. There is, also, the irretrieveable loss of heat in imparting to the air which is not deoxydized, the difference of its temperatures on entering and leaving the boiler.

The ashy residuum of the combustion of coal, is its earthy matter chemically and mechanically changed by the action of heat. To produce these changes an equivalent quantity of heat is absorbed, and this is just so much abstracted from the steam generating value of the remaining combustible: hence, the presence of earthy matter in coal not only diminishes its steam generating value by the weight of that matter, but to an additional amount measured by its specific heat and by the heat required for its chemical decomposition and mechanical change of form. It thus appears that the economic value of coal decreases more rapidly than in the proportion of its combustible, that is to say, of what remains after deducting the earthy matter, and this observation is fully confirmed by practice; in what ratio this extra decrease takes place is difficult to assign, but it is large enough to produce a very serious effect.

In the production of the chemical changes in the earthy matter, the requisite amount of oxygen is abstracted from the air entering the furnace, the supply of which to the combustible of the coal is thus diminished while the greater quantity of air that must be introduced for the combustion of the gross weight of coal is increased accompanied with the cooling effects due to its specific heat and to the difference of its temperature on entering the furnace and the chimney.

A chemical analysis,—which is made of only a few grains of a coal,—utterly fails to give the proportion of its ash that will be found in a large mass; because the earthy matter is not uniformly disseminated. Indeed, there can frequently be picked out of a pile large lumps composed of three parts earth to one part combustible, while on the other hand lumps of nearly pure combustible can be found. The quantity of *clinker* from a given weight of earth will depend on its composition partly, but chiefly on the intensity of the combustion, for at a sufficiently high temperature the whole of the earth would fuse, but the fusing point is not the same for all of its components. The *total* waste will depend not only on the quantity of ash, but on the fineness of the coal, the distance of the grate bars apart, the disintegration of the coal in the furnace, its agglutinating quality, and the more or less stirring of the fire.

With the hard anthracite, nearly the whole waste consists of earthy matter, and in all of this coal that I have burned the waste has been excessive:—the Blackheath anthracite of the experiments gave 20.54 per centum, which is certainly not above the average. The waste from the Trevorton coal was 13.37 per centum; and from the Cumberland 10.70 per centum. Of the former, I cannot speak from experience, but of the latter, the average waste is about 14 per centum. In the case of the experiments, the total waste with the two pulverulent coals must be considered a minimum as only lumps were thrown into the furnace.

Subtracting, now, the per centum of waste in ashes, etc., in the cases of the three coals, we have the following for the per centum of the remaining combustible, namely:—

Blackheath anthracite..................... 79.46 or 1.0000
Trevorton semi-anthracite.,............... 86.63 " 1.0902
Cumberland semi-bituminous.............. 89.30 " 1.1238

In rapport of cumbustible for equal weights of coal, therefore, their value stands in the above proportion.

As a cubic foot of the Blackheath, Trevorton, and Cumberland coals, weigh respectively 54.50, 48.50, and 51.47 pounds, their relative weights of cumbustible in equal bulks will be as follows, namely:—

Blackheath anthracite. (54.50×1.0000=) 54.5000 or 1.0307
Trevorton semi-anthracite. .... (48.50×1.0902=) 52.8747 " 1.0000
Cumberland semi-bituminous............ (51.47×1.1238=) 57.8420 " 1.0937

5th. Evaporative Efficiency.—The evaporative efficiency of the coals was determined with both admission and non-admission of air through holes in the furnace door. The results will be compared separately.

And first, *of the effect of the admission of air through holes in the furnace door on the evaporative efficiency of the same coal.* This is determined by comparing the evaporation given per unit of weight by each coal with air not admitted and admitted, and the results are as follows, namely:—

	Pounds of Steam evaporated per pound of Coal.		Gain by the admission of air, in percentum of the evaporation with no admission of air.
	No admission of air through holes in furnace door.	Air admitted through holes in furnace door.	
Blackheath Anthracite,.........	4.7340	4.9690	4.968
Trevorton Semi-anthracite,.......	5.7218	6.0225	5.255
Cumberland Semi-bituminous,....	5.9913	6.1554	2.739

If the same comparison be made, substituting the evaporation given per unit of weight of *combustible* for unit of weight of *coal*, we shall then have the following results, namely:—

	Pounds of Steam evaporated per pound of combustible.		Gain by the admission of air, in per centum of the evaporation with no admission of air.
	No admission of air through holes in furnace door.	Air admitted through holes in furnace door.	
Blackheath Anthracite,..........	5.8744	6.2111	5.732
Trevorton Semi-anthracite,.......	6.5033	6.9985	7.614
Cumberland Semi-bituminous,....	6.6626	6.9464	4.260

The latter table, which in this case is the proper one to be cited, shows that the evaporative effect of a given weight of combustible is, by admitting air through holes in the furnace door, increased with the two anthracitous coals, say, 6⅔ per centum; while with the semi-bituminous coal producing smoke, the gain is only 4¼ per centum. This, I am aware, is opposed to the generally received opinion; but the experiments were carefully made, and under their conditions the result can be confidently accepted.

Next;—*of the comparative evaporative efficiency of the unit of weight of the coals, and the unit of weight of their combustible, when burned without the admission of air through holes in the furnace door.* This is determined by comparing the number of pounds of steam evaporated under this condition from a temperature of water of 100° Fahr. by one pound of each coal, and by one pound of its combustible:—the results are as follows, namely:—

	PER POUND OF COAL.		PER POUND OF COMBUSTIBLE.	
	Pounds of Steam evaporated.	Compar'tive evaporative efficiencies.	Pounds of Steam evaporated.	Compar'tive evaporative efficiencies.
Blackheath Anthracite,..........	4.7340	1.0000	5.8744	1.0000
Trevorton Semi-anthracite,.......	5.7218	1.2087	6.5033	1.1071
Cumberland Semi-bituminous,....	5.9913	1.2656	6.6626	1.1342

Last;—*of the comparative evaporative efficiency of the unit of weight of the coals, and the unit of weight of their combustible, when burned with the admission of air through holes in the furnace door.* This is determined in the same manner as above, by comparing the number ef pounds of steam evaporated under this condition from a temperature of water of 100° Fahr. by one pound of each coal, and by one pound of its combustible:—the results are as follows, namely:—

	PER POUND OF COAL.		PER POUND OF COMBUSTIBLE.	
	Pounds of Steam evaporated.	Compar'tive evaporative efficiencies.	Pounds of Steam evaporated.	Compar'tive evaporative efficiencies
Blackheath Anthracite,.........	4.9690	1.0000	6.2111	1.0000
Trevorton Semi-anthracite,......	6.0225	1.2120	6.9985	1.1268
Cumberland Semi-bituminous,...	6.1554	1.2388	6.9464	1.1184

The general deduction from the two immediately preceding tables is, that exclusive of the waste in ashes, etc., the evaporative efficiency per pound of combustible of the Trevorton and Cumberland coals is about equal; and that it exceeds the evaporative efficiency of the Blackheath coal by one-eighth of the latter. Including waste in ashes, etc., the evaporative efficiency of the Cumberland coal is about 4 per centum greater than that of the Trevorton, and 25 per centum greater than that of the Blackheath coal.

Stowage.—The weights of equal bulks of the coals are, for the Blackheath anthracite 54.50, for the Trevorton semi-anthracite 48.50, and for the Cumberland semi-bituminous 51.47; the amounts of combustible remaining in them respectively after deducting the waste in ashes, etc., are 79.46, 86.63, and 89.30 per centum; consequently in rapport of combustible the weights for equal bulks will compare as (54.50×.7946=) 43.3057, (48.50×.8663=) 42.0156, and (51.47×.8930=) 45.9627. If these quantities be multiplied by the evaporative efficiencies of the coals after deducting the waste in ashes, etc., taking the case of non-admission of air through holes in the furnace door, which is the general one in practice; we shall have for the stowage value of equal bulks respectively (43.3057×5.8744=) 254.395, (42.0156×6.5033=) 273.240, and (45.9627×6.6626=) 306.231; or in other words, the weight of water that would be evaporoted by *equal bulks* of the coals, would be in the following ratio, namely:—

Blackheath Anthracite..................	254.395	or 1.0000
Trevorton Semi-anthracite..............	273.240	" 1.0741
Cumberland Semi-bituminous.............	306.231	" 1.2038

Additional Experiments with the Blackheath Anthracite.

After the foregoing was written, the evaporation by the Blackheath anthracite appeared so small in comparison with what was given by the two other coals, that I concluded to repeat the experiments with it in order either to confirm the previous results or to discover the error if any had been made. Accordingly, a new set of experiments, occupying five days, were made in precisely the same manner as before, with the coal burned without the admission of air through holes in the furnace door. The data of these experiments will be found in the following table, namely:

Table of the Additional Experiments made with the BLACKHEATH ANTHRACITE to determine the Evaporative Efficiency when burned in the Smithery Boiler of the New York Navy Yard, without the admission of air through Holes in the Furnace Door:

Date. 1859.	Duration of each Experiment in Hours and Minutes.	State of the Weather.	Temperatures in Degrees, Fahr.				Pressures in pounds per square inch.				Number of double strokes made by the Engine Piston.		Fuel.				
			Water in Boiler at starting Fires.	Water in Boiler at end of Experiment.	Feed Water supplied to Boiler.	Air entering Ash-pit.	In Boiler above atmosphere, per gauge.	In Cylinder at commencement of stroke above atmosphere per Indicator.	In Cylinder at end of stroke above atmosphere per Indicator.	Mean gross effective pressure on piston per Indicator.	Total.	Per Minute.	Pounds of Coal consumed.	Pounds of Pine Wood consumed in kindling.	Pounds of waste in Ashes, Fine Coal, &c.	Per centum of waste of the Coal in Ashes, Fine coal, &c.	Pounds of Coal consumed, estimating two pounds of Wood equal in evaporative value to one pound of Coal.
Feb. 7.	7 .. 58	Fair.	120	241	151	63	26.4	16.7	9.5	11.43	12,128	25.373	2,140	200	2,205	20	2,240
" 8.	7 .. 57	Cloudy.	202	249	149	65	24.8	16.7	9.5	11 44	12,116	25.400	2,230	154			2,307
" 9.	8 .. 07	"	200	251	150	66	23.5	16.4	9.4	11.25	12,219	25.090	2,150	160			2,230
" 10.	8 .. 12	Fair.	198	249	145	66	29.5	15.9	9.2	10.99	12,131	24.657	2,318	170			2,403
" 11.	8 .. 14	"	200	251	144	60	30.2	17.7	10.0	12.08	13,040	26.397	2,200	160			2,280
Totals,	40 .. 28										61,634		11,038	844	2,205	20	11,460
Means.			184	248	148	64	26.9	16.7	9.5	11.44		25.385					

Collecting the data in the above table and calculating their results in the same manner as heretofore, we have the following exhibit of the evaporation by the BLACKHEATH ANTHRACITE as given by the second set of experiments, burning it without admission of air through the holes in the furnace door.

DATA.

Duration of the experiments in hours and minutes	40..28
Number of pounds of water contained in the boiler	7,500
Temperature in degrees Fahr. of the water in the boiler at the commencement of the experiments	184°
Temperature in degrees Fahr. of the water in the boiler at the end of the experiments	248°
Temperature in degrees Fahr. of the feed water supplied to the boiler	148°
Temperature in degrees Fahr. of the air entering the ash pit	64°
Pressure in pounds per square inch above the atmosphere of the steam in the boiler	26.9
Pressure in pounds per square inch above the atmosphere of the steam in the cylinder at the commencement of the stroke	16.7
Pressure in pounds per square inch above the atmosphere of the steam in the cylinder at the end of the stroke	9.5
Total number of double strokes made by the piston (by Counter)	61,634.
Mean number of double strokes per minute by the piston	25.385
Mean gross effective pressure on piston in pounds per square inch (by Indicator)	11.44
Gross horses power developed by the engine	17.91
Total number of pounds of coal consumed	11,038
Total number of pounds of pine wood consumed (in kindling)	844
Total number of pounds of coal consumed, estimating 2 pounds of wood equal in evaporative value to 1 pound of coal	11,460
Total number of pounds of waste in ashes and in fine coal falling through the grates unburned	2,205
Per centum of waste of the coal in ashes and in fine coal	20
Total number of pounds of coal consumed, exclusive of the waste in ashes, etc., estimating two pounds of wood equal in evaporative value to one pound of coal	9,255
Pounds of coal consumed per hour per square foot of grate surface	14.07
Pounds of coal consumed per hour per square foot of grate surface exclusive of waste	11.26

EVAPORATION FROM A TEMPERATURE OF 100°.FAHR.

Pounds of steam discharged from the cylinder..............	50020.66
Pounds of steam equivalent to the heat absorbed in raising the temperature of the boiler water from its temperature at the commencement to that at the close of the experiments......	2189.78
Pounds of steam condensed in producing the power of the engine...	1696.02
Total number of pounds of steam evaporated...............	53906.46
Pounds of water evaporated per pound of coal..............	4.7039
Pounds of water evaporated per pound of coal exclusive of waste in ashes, etc....................................	5.8246

By comparing the above results with those obtained from the first set of experiments with the Blackheath anthracite burned under the same condition of no admission of air through holes in the furnace door, we shall find that they agree very closely in all respects. The evaporation from a temperature of water of 100° Fahr. per pound of coal was then 4.7340 pounds of steam; now it is 4.7039 pounds. The evaporation per pound of combustible was then 5.8744 pounds of steam; now it is 5.8246 pounds. We may, therefore, confide in the accuracy of the experiments.

ECONOMIC EFFECT

DUE TO THE

USE OF STEAM EXPANSIVELY.

Experiments made with the Smithery Engine and Boiler at the U. S. Navy Yard, New York, to determine the Relative Consumption of Coal for the production of equal Indicated Horses Power when using the Steam without Expansion, and when suppressing its admission into the Cylinder at $\frac{22}{100}$ of the stroke of the piston from the commencement, allowing it to expand through the remaining $\frac{78}{100}$ of the stroke.

After completing the foregoing experiments on "the Comparative Evaporative Efficiencies of the BLACKHEATH ANTHRACITE, the TREVORTON SEMI-ANTHRACITE, and the CUMBERLAND SEMI-BITUMINOUS coal;" in which the steam was used without expansion; the opportunity seemed favorable for an experimental determination of the gain in fuel to be obtained by using the steam expansively; and in order to make the result a marked one, I concluded to employ an early suppression, closing the expansion or cut-off valve at $\frac{22}{100}$ of the stroke of the piston from the commencement, and allowing it to expand through the remaining $\frac{78}{100}$ of the stroke.

The experiments were now repeated with this condition and in precisely the same manner as in determining the comparative evaporative efficiencies of the coals, using the same Blackheath anthracite, and burning it with both the admission and non-admission of air through the holes in the furnace door. The coal and ashes were carefully weighed by the same scales as in the previous experiments, and diagrams were continually taken with the same Indicator. The temperatures, pressures, etc., were noted every fifteen minutes in the same manner as previously. The data now obtained will be found in the two following Tables, namely:

Table exhibiting the Data obtained from the Boiler and Engine of the Smithery at the New York Navy Yard, burning Blackheath Anthracite without admission of Air through Holes in the Furnace Door, and "CUTTING-OFF" THE STEAM IN THE CYLINDER *at* 22 *per centum of the Stroke of the Piston from the commencement.*

Date. 1859.	Duration of each Experiment in Hours and Minutes.	State of the Weather.	Temperatures in degrees Fahr.				Pressures in pounds per square inch.					Number of Double Strokes made by the Engine Piston.		Fuel.				
			Water in Boiler at starting Fires.	Water in Boiler at end of Experiment.	Feed Water supplied to Boiler.	Air entering Ash-pit.	In Boiler above atmosphere per gauge.	In Cylinder at commencement of stroke above atmosphere per Indicator.	In Cylinder at point of cutting off the steam, above atmosphere, per Indicator.	In Cylinder at end of stroke above zero per Indicator.	Mean gross effective pressure on Piston per Indicator.	Total.	Per Minute.	Pounds of Coal consumed.	Pounds of Pine Wood consumed in kindling.	Pounds of waste in Ashes, Fine Coal, &c.	Per centum of waste of the Coal in Ashes, Fine Coal, &c.	Pounds of Coal consumed, estimating 2 pounds of Wood equal in evaporative value to 1 pound of Coal.
Feb. 16.	8 .. 27		200	251	142	69	34.1	27.2	20.5	14.7	11.26	12,723	25.095	2,025	174			2,112
" 17.	8 .. 24		197	255	144	72	30.5	25.1	18.9	13.6	10.56	12,059	23.927	1,908	160			1,988
" 18.	8 .. 25		199	252	139	74	32.6	25.7	19.3	13.9	10.75	12,255	24.267	1,800	160	1,500		1,880
" 19.	8 .. 15		200	240	140	73	33.0	26.9	20.2	14.5	11.14	12,324	24.897	1,800	160		19.91	1,880
" 21.	8 .. 35		78	251	144	71	31.7	30.6	22.8	16.2	12.36	13,816	26 827	2,300	240			2,420
" 22.	8 .. 38		196	243	145	68	32.7	29.9	22.3	15.9	12.13	13,712	26.471	2,200	160			2,280
" 23.	8 .. 35		200	241	143	75	30.4	29.8	22.3	15.9	12.11	13,622	26.450	2,200	160			2,280
" 24.	8 .. 39		200	245	136	74	33.3	28.7	21.4	15.3	11.73	13,425	25.867	2,000	160	2,212	20.67	2,080
" 25.	8 .. 44		198	257	139	74	35.8	29.6	21.6	15.5	11.82	13,624	26.000	2,000	160			2,080
Feb. 28.	8 .. 50	Fair.	80	249	137	74	34.3	27.0	20.2	14.5	11.16	13,224	24.951	2,000	160			2,080
Mar. 1.	9 .. 00	"	194	260	142	75	35.6	24.6	18.7	13.5	10.46	12,835	23.769	2,000	260			2,130
" 2.	8 .. 57	Cloudy.	200	257	141	70	31.9	25.3	19.0	13.7	10.60	12,895	24.013	2,000	160			2,080
" 3	8 .. 20	Fair.	202	251	143	70	32.8	28.6	21.4	15.3	11.71	12,918	25.836	2,000	160	1,940	19.40	2,080
" 4.	8 . 20	"	200	257	142	74	33.1	27.9	20.9	14.9	11.45	12,706	25.414	2,000	160			2,080
Totals.	120 .. 9											182.138		28,233	2,434	5,652		29,450
Means.			181	248	141	72	33.0	27.6	20.7	14.8	11.37		25.265				20	

Table exhibiting the Data obtained from the Boiler and Engine of the Smithery at the New York Navy Yard, burning Blackheath Anthracite, with the Admission of Air through Holes in the Furnace Door, and "CUTTING-OFF" THE STEAM IN THE CYLINDER *at 22 per centum of the Stroke of the Piston from the commencement.*

Date. 1858 and 1859.	Duration of each Experiment in Hours and Minutes.	State of the Weather.	Temperatures in Degrees Fahr.				Pressures in pounds per square inch.					Number of Double Strokes made by the Engine Piston.		Fuel.				
			Water in Boiler at starting Fires.	Water in Boiler at end of Experiment.	Feed Water supplied to Boiler.	Air entering Ash-pit.	In Boiler above atmosphere per Gauge.	In Cylinder at commencement of stroke above atmosphere per Indicator.	In Cylinder at point of cutting off the steam above atmosphere per Indicator.	In Cylinder at end of Stroke above zero per Indicator.	Mean gross effective pressure on Piston per Indicator.	Total.	Per Minute.	Pounds of Coal consumed.	Pounds of Pine Wood consumed in kindling.	Pounds of waste in Ashes, Fine Coal, &c.	Per centum of waste of the Coal in Ashes, Fine Coal, &c.	Pounds of Coal consumed, estimating 2 pounds of Wood equal in evaporative value to 1 pound of Coal.
Mar. 7.	9 .. 15	Fair.	110	257	142	72	35.1	28.2	21.1	15.1	11.57	14,236	25.650	1,950	260	2,321	20	2,080
" 8.	9 .. 15	Raining.	203	259	140	72	33.0	27.8	20.8	14.9	11.43	14,083	25.375	1,900	160			1,980
" 9.	9 .. 23	Fair.	201	257	142	71	33.2	27.3	20.5	14.7	11.29	14,156	25.144	1,920	160			2,000
" 10.	9 .. 20	"	202	251	144	71	35.0	26.9	20.2	14.5	11.16	13,970	24.946	1,920	160			2,000
" 11.	9 .. 25	Raining.	200	257	145	74	34.8	28.2	21.1	15.1	11.57	14,447	25.570	1,975	160			2,055
" 12.	9 .. 24	Cloudy.	203	245	144	74	35.3	28.1	21.0	15.0	11.54	14,412	25.553	1,975	160			2,055
" 14.	9 .. 28	Fair.	125	251	143	75	34.7	28.1	21.0	15.0	11.53	13,942	24.546	1,975	264	2,340	$19\frac{4}{5}$	2,107
" 15.	9 .. 35	Raining.	196	253	142	72	34.5	28.0	20.9	15.0	11.50	14,645	25.470	1,950	160			2,030
" 16.	9 .. 36	Fair.	200	249	144	73	36.0	26.4	19.9	14.3	11.01	14,219	24.686	1,975	160			2,055
" 17.	9 .. 40	"	204	245	143	70	34.3	27.3	20.5	14.7	11.27	14,574	25.128	1,975	160			2,055
" 18.	9 .. 40	Raining.	206	251	146	75	35.0	27.0	20.2	14.5	11.16	14,468	24.945	1,950	160			2,030
" 19.	9 .. 40	Cloudy.	204	245	144	75	37.0	25.9	19.4	14.0	10.80	14,126	24.351	1,950	160			2,030
Totals.	113 .. 41											171.278		23,415	2,124	4,661		24.477
Means.			188	252	143	73	34.8	27.4	20.6	14.7	11.32		25.110				$19\frac{9}{10}$	

Collecting the foregoing data, and making the calculations from them in the same manner as for the previous experiments on the Comparative Evaporative Efficiencies of the coals, we have the following exhibit of the results obtained when burning the BLACKHEATH ANTHRACITE, both with and without the admission of air through holes in the furnace door, and CUTTING OFF THE STEAM at $\frac{22}{100}$ of the stroke of the piston from the commencement:

DATA.	No admission of Air thro' Holes in Furnace Door.	Air Admitted through holes in Furnace Door.
Duration of the experiments in hours and minutes,......	120 : 9	113 : 41
Number of pounds of water contained in the boiler,.....	7,500	7,500
Temperature in degrees Fahr. of the water in the boiler at the commencement of the experiment,............	181	188
Temperature in degrees Fahr. of the water in the boiler at the end of the experiment.,......................	248	152
Temperature in degrees Fahr. of the feed water supplied to the boiler, ...	141	143
Temperature in degrees Fahr. of air entering the ash-pit,	72	73
Pressure in pounds per square inch above the atmosphere, of the steam in the boiler,.........................	33.0	34.8
Pressure in pounds per square inch above the atmosphere, of the steam in the cylinder at the comm't of the stroke,	27.6	27.4
Pressure in pounds per square inch above the atmosphere, of the steam in the cylinder at the point of cutting off,.	20.7	20.6
Pressure in pounds per square inch above the zero line, of the steam in the cylinder at the end of the stroke,..	14.8	14.7
Point of the stroke of piston at which the steam is cut off in the cylinder,..................................	$\frac{22}{100}$	$\frac{22}{100}$
Total number of double strokes made by the piston (by counter),..	182,138	171,278
Mean number of double strokes per minute made by pis'n,	25.265	25.110
Mean gross effective pressure on piston, in pounds per square inch (by indicator),...........................	11.37	11.32
Gross horses power developed by the engine,...........	17.721	17.494
Total number of pounds of coal consumed,..............	28,233	23,415
Total number of pounds of pine wood consu'd (in kindl'g,)	2,434	2,124
Total number of pounds of coal consumed, estimating two pounds of wood equal in evaporative value to one pound of coal,..	29,450	24,477
Total number of pounds of waste in ashes and in fine coal falling through the grate unburned,................	5,652	4,661
Per centum of waste of coal in ashes and in fine coal, ...	20	19$\frac{9}{10}$
Total number of pounds of coal consumed, exclusive of the waste in ashes, &c., estimating two pounds of wood equal in evaporative value to one pound of coal,.......	23,798	19,816
Pounds of coal consumed per hour per square foot of grate surface,....................................	11.97	10.59
Pounds of coal consumed per hour per square foot of grate surface, exclusive of waste,.........................	9.67	8.57
EVAPORATION FROM A TEMPERATURE OF 100° FAHR.		
Pounds of steam discharged from the cylinder, calculated from the pressure of the steam at the end of the stroke of piston,.....................................	94,754.57	88,412.66
Pounds of steam equivalent to the heat absorbed in raising the temperature of the boiler water from its temperature at the commence't to that at the close of the experi'ts,	6,398.36	5,239.70
Pounds of steam condensed in producing the power of the engine, ...	4,966.66	4,639.99
Total number of pounds of steam evaporated,...........	106,119.59	98,292.35
Pounds of water evaporated per pound of coal,..........	3.6034	4.0157
Pounds of water evaporated per pound of coal, exclusive of waste in ashes, &c.,............................	4.4592	4.9602

In order to make a proper comparison of the results obtained in the two cases of using the steam with and without expansion, the quantities necessary have been arranged in the following Table, and in separate columns for the results when the coal was burned without the admission of air through holes in the furnace door and when it was burned with the admission of air through them. The quantities in the first column are the mean of the original experiments with the BLACKHEATH ANTHRACITE, burned without the admission of air through the holes in the furnace door, and of the subsequent experiments made to verify those results :

Table exhibiting the Comparative Results obtained from the Smithery Engine and Boiler at the New York Navy Yard when Using the Steam Without Expansion and when Using it Expansively, suppressing its admission at $\frac{22}{100}$ of the Stroke of Piston from the commencement; the Fuel consumed being Blackheath Anthracite burned both with and without the Admission of Air through Holes in the Furnace Door:

	Using the steam without expansion		Using the steam with expansion; cutting it off at 22 per centum of the stroke of the piston from the commencement.	
	Burning Blackheath Anthracite without admission of air through holes in the furnace door.	Burning Blackheath Anthracite with air admitted through holes in the furnace door.	Burning Blackheath Anthracite without admission of air through holes in the furnace door.	Burning Blackheath Anthracite with air admitted through holes in the furnace door.
Pressure in pounds per square inch above the atmosphere of the steam in the boiler,.......... ..	28.8	28.6	33.0	34.8
Pressure in pounds per square inch above the atmosphere, of the steam in the cylinder at the commencement of the stroke,.................	16.4	17.4	27.6	27.4
Pressure in pounds per square inch above the atmosphere, of the steam in the cylinder at the point of cutting off,..........................	—	—	20.7	20.6
Pressure in pounds per square inch above the zero line, of the steam in the cylinder at the end of the stroke, ...	24.1	24.5	14.8	14.7
Temperature in degrees Fahr. of the air entering the ash pit (same as that of the boiler and engine room),......................	63½	57.	72.	73.
Mean gross effective pressure in pounds per square inch of piston,................................	11.36	11.88	11.37	11.32
Mean number of double strokes per minute made by the piston,................................	25.163	26.084	25.265	25.110
Gross horses-power developed by the engine (by Indicator),....................................	17.57	19.12	17.72	17.49
Pounds of coal consumed per hour,..............	275.4	271.1	230.5	203.9
Per centum of waste of the coal in ashes, fine coal, &c.,..	19¼	20.	20.	19 9-10
Pounds of combustible consumed per hour,........	222.2	216.9	186.2	165.1
Pounds of water evaporated per pound of combustible, calculated from the pressure at the end of the stroke of piston, from the power developed by the engine, and from the heat employed to raise the temperature of the boiler water the difference of its temperatures at the commencement and end of the experiments,...........	5.8495	6.2111	4.4592	4.9602
Pounds of coal consumed per hour per horse-power developed by the engine,....................	15.6744	14.1789	13.0080	11.6581
Pounds of combustible consumed per hour per horse power developed by the engine,................	12.6446	11.3442	10.5079	9.4403
Per centum of the total quantity of steam evaporated, according to the Indicator, condensed in the production of the power developed by the engine,	3.06	3.24	4.68	4.72

The first thing in the above Table that strikes us, is the great cost of an Indicated Horse Power in pounds of coal per hour ; but if the conditions under which the Smithery Engine worked be considered, this excessive cost can easily be accounted for. It is due to the high ratio which the back pressure bore to the total mean pressure, counting from zero ; and to the low evaporative efficiency of the boiler.

Let us examine this in detail. In the first place the pressure required to overcome the friction of the engine and shafting *per se*, was, as deduced from an extensive set of experiments, 2.5 pounds per square inch of piston. Now taking for illustration the third column in the Table, because the performance therein recorded is with expansion and without admission of air through holes in the furnace door, and therefore the nearest comparable with the usual conditions of practice ; we find the mean gross effective pressure to have been 11.37 pounds per square inch, to which if we add the atmospheric pressure of 14.7 pounds per square inch, and the mean pressure of 0.8 pound per square inch above the atmosphere in the cylinder during the exhaust, we shall have for the total mean pressure during the stroke counting from zero (11.37+14.7+0.8=) 26.87 pounds per square inch, of which the back pressure and the pressure required to work the engine and shafting *per se*, was (14.7+0.8+2.5=) 18 pounds per square inch, or ($\frac{18 \times 100}{26.87}$=) 67 per centum, leaving only (100—67=) 33 per centum to be utilized ; or out of a total mean pressure of 26.87 pounds, only 8.87 pounds were usefully applied. The evaporation given by the boiler was the low one of 3.6035 pounds of water from a temperature of feed-water of 100° Fahr. by one pound of coal. Great, therefore, as was the cost (13.008 pounds of coal per hour) of the horse-power, it was only what might have been anticipated from the conditions ; and it shows that not only were the proportions of the boiler very defective, but that the engine itself was greatly too large for the work to be performed.

The next thing that strikes us in the foregoing Table, is

the little difference of the cost in coal of a horse-power, when the steam is used without expansion, and when it is used with expansion being cut off in the cylinder at 22 per centum of the stroke of the piston from the commencement. The *theoretical* gain in fuel due to this measure of expansion over using the steam without expansion, is 1.515 times; that is to say, a given weight of steam when used with this measure of expansion *ought*, according to the law of MARIOTTE, to produce 1.515 times more indicated horses-power than when it is used without expansion. The first glance at the Table shows that this gain has not, with the *practical* conditions under which the steam was used, been even remotely approximated.

Taking, first, the quantities in the first and third columns when the coal was burned "without admission of air through holes in the furnace door," we find that with expansion the indicated horse-power cost 10.5079 pounds of combustible per hour, and without expansion it cost 12.6446 pounds; the gain being $(\frac{12.6446-10.5079 \times 100}{12.6446} =)$ 16.9 per centum. Taking the quantities in the second and fourth columns when the coal was burned "with air admitted through holes in the furnace door," we find that with expansion the indicated horse-power cost 9.4403 pounds of combustible per hour, and without expansion it cost 11.3442 pounds; the gain being $(\frac{11.3442-9.4403 \times 100}{11.3442} =)$ 16.8 per centum. The mean of both is $(\frac{16.9 \times 16.8}{2} =)$ 16.85 per centum; that is to say, that when using the steam expansively, cutting it off at 22 per centum of the stroke of the piston from the commencement, and allowing it to expand through the remaining 78 per centum of the stroke, a given weight of combustible produced 16.85 per centum, or about one-sixth more horses-power than when the steam was used without expansion.

The discrepancy between the theoretical prediction and the practical result, though enormous, may be accounted for by taking into consideration the facts which would naturally tend to modify the former in the direction of the latter, and determining their value.

In comparing the relative advantages of using steam with and without expansion, the weight of fuel consumed is taken as the measure of the cost, and the indicated horses power developed as the measure of the effect produced. Now to what part of this fuel does the fact of expansion apply? Evidently only to that part which has produced the steam actually used expansively in the cylinder. Upon all the remaining portion of the fuel, be it as large or as small as it may, the use of steam expansively has no influence.

In the first place, taking the average of boilers, the fuel produces upon the water only about two-thirds of its calorific effect, owing to the losses of heat in the products of combustion entering the chimney, and to the imperfection of the combustion itself. Of the fuel, too, a portion, probably 5 per centum, is lost in fine pieces falling unburned between the grate bars and in cleaning the fires. In marine engines there is also the further loss by "blowing off and feeding in" to prevent the formation of scale, and the loss from this source is on an average in practice, about one-sixth of the heat entering the boiler water: this, of course, includes the loss by "priming," as that forms in effect part of the boiler water to be extracted. Thus of the 100 per centum of the original fuel $(33+5=)$ 38 is lost without imparting heat to the water, and of the remaining 62, one-sixth, or say 10 per centum, is lost by the "blowing off," leaving only $(100-\overline{38+10}=)$ 52 per centum, or say one-half, applied to the generation of steam. It is plain enough now, that any saving of fuel by the use of steam expansively, can only be made upon that half of the total fuel consumed which is applied to the generation of steam. Upon the other half the fact of expansion has no influence, and this at once produces a practical reduction of one-half in the theoretical gain of fuel due to the measure of expansion employed for the steam. Of the steam, however, that is generated, but a portion produces a dynamic effect upon the piston, and it is to this portion only that the theoretical gain can be applied by using it expansively, and that gain will be practically greatly lessened by certain physical properties of the steam, and the conditions it is used under, all of which are ignored in the theoretical law of MARIOTTE.

The causes that prevent us from obtaining the full dynamical effect of the steam after it is generated, may be distributed under the four following heads, namely:

Annihilation of the steam by condensation.

The escape of steam by leakage.

The resistance of the back pressure in the cylinder to the movement of the piston.

Steam used in filling the cylinder clearance and ports.

The first head may be subdivided into, 1st. Condensation of steam due to the conduction and radiation of heat from the exterior surfaces of the boiler, steam-pipe, valve-chest, and cylinder. 2d. Condensation due to the difference between the temperatures of the interior surfaces of the cylinder, its valves and piston during a double stroke of the piston. 3d. Condensation due to the fact of the expansion of the steam *per se*.

The leakage consists of the steam which escaping past the valves and piston, passes to the condenser without producing any dynamical effect upon the piston.

The back pressure opposing the movement of the piston, is composed of the uncondensed vapor in the cylinder; to this pressure must be added in effect that which is required to work the engine and shafting *per se;* for it is evident that, like the back pressure, it must first be balanced before the piston can move.

That portion of the steam which is used in filling the space between the face of the valve and the piston when at the end of its stroke (comprised in the cylinder clearance and ports), produces no dynamical effect upon the piston when the steam is used without expansion. When it is used expansively, some dynamical effect is obtained from the portion filling the clearance and ports; but the loss from this cause is, nevertheless, greater than when the steam is used without expansion.

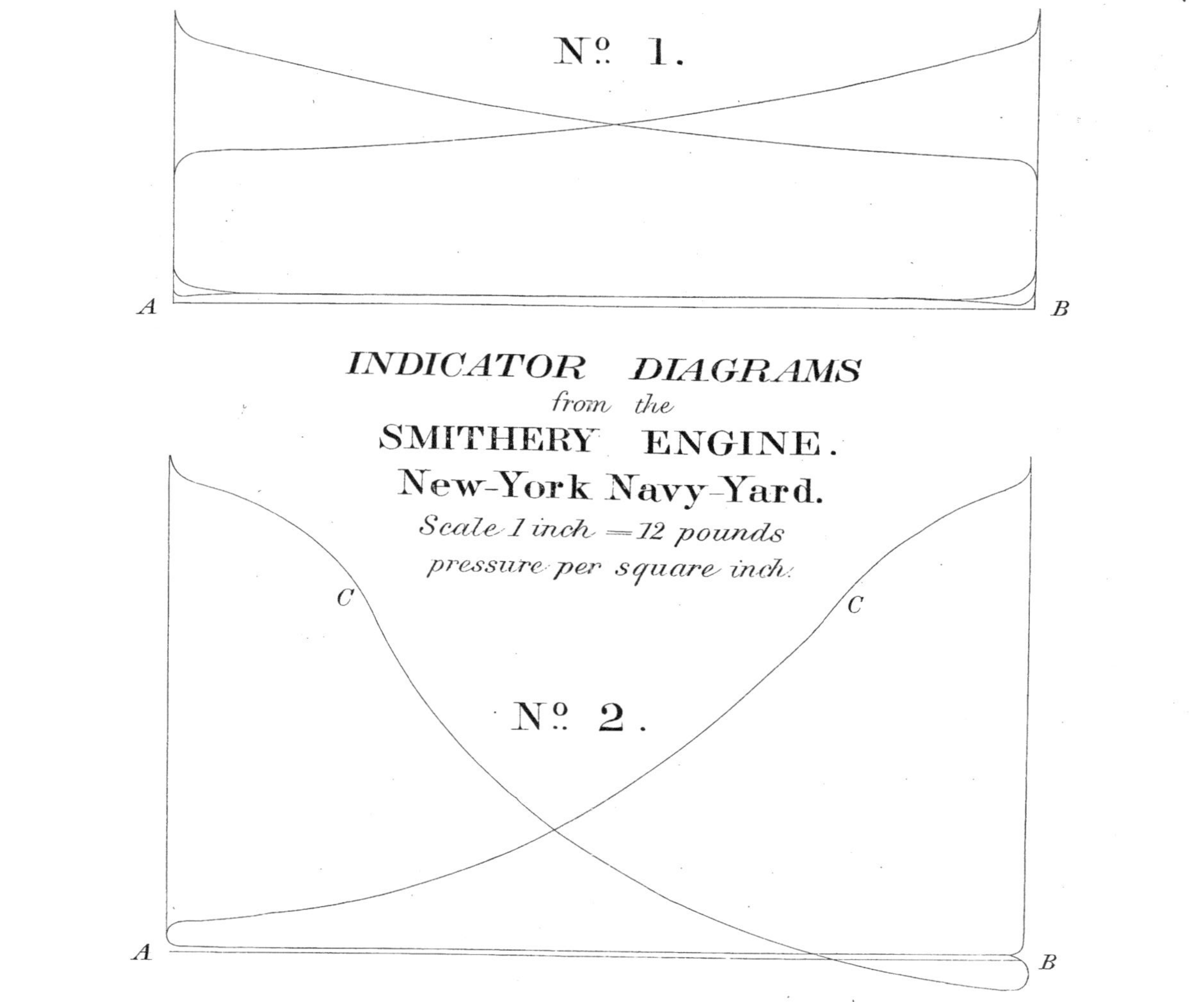
No. 1.
A
B
INDICATOR DIAGRAMS
from the
SMITHERY ENGINE.
New-York Navy-Yard.
Scale 1 inch = 12 pounds
pressure per square inch.
C
C
No. 2.
A
B

We will examine in detail the above enumerated causes of loss of dynamical effect by the steam, and distinguish their values in the cases of using it with and without expansion.

Of the condensation of steam due to the conduction and radiation of heat from the exterior surfaces of the boiler, steam-pipe, valve-chest, and cylinder. It is impossible to estimate the amount of loss from this cause, but that it is considerable will be granted by all whose experience has enabled them to observe the quantity of water formed by the condensed steam in the pipe during a short time with the engine at rest. This condensation will be influenced as to its absolute amount by the thickness and conductibility of the metal, and by the clothing given to the surfaces, but with equality in these respects, it will be in the ratio of the surfaces and the difference of temperature of the steam within and the air without.

In comparing steam used with and without expansion, it may be done under two conditions, making the engine under both to develop equal powers in equal times, for the object is to ascertain for a given power the most economical mode of using steam. We may condition, 1st. That the boiler pressure be the same in both cases, when the engine using the steam without expansion will employ a higher mean effective pressure per square inch of piston, will have much the smallest cylinder, and will lose the least by friction and back pressure, but the loss by radiation will be about the same. 2d. That the same cylinder and mean effective pressure per square inch of piston be employed; in which case the boiler pressure will be much the highest with the expanded steam, and the loss by conduction and radiation from the exterior surfaces of the boiler, steam-pipe, and valve-chest, will be proportionally great; but the radiation from the exterior surfaces of the cylinder and the condensation by the interior surfaces will be about the same. The friction and back pressure losses will also be about equal; but the higher the pressure, and consequently the temperature of the steam in the boiler, the greater with marine engines will be the loss by "blowing off and feeding in" to prevent the formation of scale ; for the temperature of the feed-water being constant, the higher the temperature of the blown out water the greater will be the loss of heat from this source ; besides which the concentration at which sea-water deposits scale lessens with increase of temperature, and a greater per centum of "blowing off" is then required with, of course, a *pro rata* loss. The 2d are the conditions under which the experiments with the Smithery engine and boiler were made; but as in them the steam pressure in the boiler was carried nearly the same—the difference being only between 43.4 and 48.6 pounds per square inch, counting from zero, the equality of the mean effective pressure on the piston being obtained by excessive "throttling"—the loss by radiation was very nearly equal; and as the boiler was supplied with fresh water, there was no loss in either case by "blowing off :" neither was there any sensible priming.

Of the condensation of the steam due to the difference between the temperatures of the interior surfaces of the cylinder, its valve and piston, during a double stroke of the piston. It is assumed that the interior surfaces of the cylinder and the surfaces of its valve and piston, will have the temperature of the steam or vapor with which they are in contact: this temperature will vary during a double stroke of piston between the temperatures of the entering steam and of the exhaust ; in fact, all the power of the engine—the latent heat apart—is due to their difference. Now, at the commencement of a stroke of the piston, these surfaces will have the temperature of the vapor of the exhaust or back pressure in the cylinder to which they are then exposed ; hence, when steam is admitted from the boiler, it will strike surfaces having a temperature less than its own, and will suffer the condensation due to the difference. The absolute amount of this condensation will be in the ratio of the area of those surfaces, of the conductibility and specific heat of the metal, and of the difference between the mean temperatures of the steam during a stroke of piston and of the vapor constituting the back pressure against it; and it will be further increased by the humidity which, like a dew, covers the surfaces at each condensation, and exercises more influence even than the metal itself whose capacity for heat is greatly less.

When the steam is used expansively, a small portion of the dew or condensed steam deposited during the first portions of the stroke of the piston, is doubtless reconverted into vapor under the lessened pressure of the expanded steam in the following portions, and exercises a useful pressure on the piston: this cannot be the effect in the case of steam used without expansion and of uniform pressure during the whole stroke, and so far as it goes makes the loss less by this condensation when using the steam expansively than when using it without expansion.

With the Smithery engine, the varying temperatures of the steam in the cylinder, and consequently of the metals of the cylinder, during a double stroke of the piston, can be ascercertained from the Indicator diagrams of which No. 1 and No. 2, Plate II., are fair representatives. No. 1 shows the average distribution of the steam in the cylinder when working without expansion: No. 2 show this distribution when working with expansion, cutting-off the steam at 22 per centum of the stroke from the commencement. In both cases the mean gross effective pressures are almost exactly the same, being 12.67 pounds per square inch with No. 1, and 12.79 pounds per square inch with No. 2, the piston making the same number of strokes in equal time. Dividing each of these diagrams into ten equal parts, and erecting an ordinate at the centre of each part at right angles to the atmospheric line A B, and taking from the diagrams the pressure above zero on each ordinate, the mean of the temperatures normal to these pressures will be the mean temperature on the steam side of the stroke, while the temperature normal to the back pressure will be the mean on the exhaust side of the stroke, and half the sum of the two will be the mean temperature of the cylinder. The temperatures of the steam on entering and leaving the cylinder will be those normal to the pressures at the commencement and end of the stroke of the piston as shown by each diagram. The results will be found in the following table ; namely :

Number of the Ordinate.	No. 1. Using the Steam without expansion.		No. 2. Using the steam with Expansion, cutting off at 22 per centum of the stroke from the commencement.			
	Right & Left-hand Diag's.		Left hand Diagram.		Right hand Diagram.	
	Pressure of the steam above zero in pounds per square inch	Temperature of the Steam in degrees Fahr.	Pressure of the steam above zero in pounds per square inch	Temper'ture of the Steam in degrees Fahr.	Temperature of the Steam in degrees Fahr.	Pressure of the Steam aover zero in pounds per square inch.
1	31.7	254.9	46.5	278.5	279.5	47.2
2	30.7	253.0	43.2	273.9	276.0	44.7
3	29.2	250.0	37.5	265.1	266.2	38.2
4	28.0	247.6	31.7	254.9	249.6	29.0
5	27.0	245.5	26.2	243.7	238.7	24.0
6	26.2	243.7	24.0	238.7	229.0	20.2
7	25.7	242.6	20.7	230.4	221.8	17.7
8	25.5	242.2	19.2	226.2	217.0	16.2
9	25.0	241.0	18.0	222.7	212.0	14.7
10	24.7	240.3	17.2	220.2	208.0	13.7
Means.	27.37	246.1	28.42	245.4	239.8	26.56

	No. 1.	No. 2.
Mean temperatures of both Diagrams on the steam side,	246°.1	242°.6
Mean temperature on the exhaust side,	214°.6	214°.6
Mean temperature of steam and exhaust sides,	230°.3	228°.6
Temperature of entering steam,	256°.3	280°.6
Temperature of steam on leaving,	240°.3	214°.1
Difference betw'n mean temperature of leaving and temperature of entering steam,	16°	66°.5

The condensation of steam in the cylinder due to the varying temperatures of its interior surfaces, is inherent to its use and cannot be prevented or modified by any external clothing or felting. The only means of prevention are to surround the cylinder with a jacket filled either with steam or with hot air, or to superheat the steam in the boiler, but they all produce the effect at the expense of fuel; an amount of heat equivalent to the refrigerating influence must be expended to counteract it, though it may be more economical to obtain that heat from the sources indicated than from normal steam in the cylinder. Whether it be or not, and to what degree, depends upon conditions too variable and exceptionable to be generalized here. The problem is whether the amount of heat thus expended in the last two cases could not be made to produce a greater economic effect upon the piston, if applied to the evaporation of more steam in the boiler. With boilers so proportioned that their heated gases are discharged into the chimney at too high a temperature for a good economic evaporation, there may undoubtedly be derived a gain by using a portion of the waste heat to superheat the steam, or to envelope the cylinder; this, however, is only a mode of recovering what ought never to have been lost, and will probably be found inexpedient, if carried far, on account of injury to the rubbing surfaces of the cylinder now so well lubricated by the water of the condensed steam. The gain by the steam jacket is not so clear, though strongly insisted on by many, as the condensation of steam in the cylinder can only be prevented by the condensation of an equal weight in the jacket, and the annihilation of equal weights of steam is the loss of equal powers, let it take place where it may.

Of the condensation of the steam in the cylinder that results from the lowering of the temperature due to the fact of the expansion per se.—The instant the introduction of steam into the cylinder from the boiler is suppressed—the movement of the piston continuing—the steam expands, and its temperature falling simultaneously with the expansion, a condensation inevitably follows and a part of the steam is precipitated in the form of water. A consequence of this condensation is a still further expansion of the steam (in addition to that which results from the continuous retreat of the piston) to fill the space due to the difference of the bulks of the steam before it was condensed and of the water resulting from that condensation; this second expansion is accompanied by a still further reduction of temperature, causing in its turn another condensation which again gives rise to another expansion, and so on until the end of the stroke. As it is impossible to expand steam without reducing its temperature, this process of condensation,—which is wholly irrespective of external refrigeration,—is an inherent function of the steam and becomes continuous after being once commenced; and will be the greater the greater the measure of expansion employed for the steam. It results from the fact, that although the total heat of steam of higher pressure is greater than the total heat of steam of lower pressure, yet as the latent heat of the latter increases in a much higher ratio than its total heat diminishes, and as this increase in the latent heat is at the expense of the sensible heat, it becomes a cooling process and produces the condensation stated.

As it is then impossible to expand steam without lowering its temperature, and as this lowering is inseparably accompanied by a condensation, and as these effects of the reducing of temperature and the precipitating of water after having once commenced, propagate themselves in a rapidly increasing or geometrical ratio, it follows that if any vessel filled with steam be a little enlarged so as to allow the within steam to expand, though ever so slightly, condensation produced by that expansion *per se* will instantaneously take place and proceed with continuously increasing rapidity until all the steam be converted into water, and this without any aid from external cooling.

The experiments with the Smithery engine enable us to ascertain for that particular case the amount of condensation in the cylinder due to the fact of expansion *per se.* This amount will be determined by the difference between the weights of steam discharged from the cylinder at the end of the stroke of piston per pound of combustible when using the steam with and without expansion. The evaporation due to the condensation produced by the development of the power, and to the heat employed in raising the temperature of the boiler water from that at the commencement to that at the end of the experiments, is not included, because from the method of their calculation they are unaffected by the fact of expansion *per se.* Now as the *real* evaporation in the boiler per pound of combustible must have been the same whether the steam was used with or without expansion,—and as precisely the same coal was burned, giving the same per centum of refuse, in the same boiler, by the same fireman, with the same engine doing the same work, at the same speed, the boiler pressure being nearly the same, and the cylinder pressures being ascertained by the same Indicator which was a most excellent and reliable one,—therefore, whatever difference results in the two cases, must be *apparent* only and due entirely to greater condensation of steam in the cylinder: consequently, excluding the evaporation due to the difference of the temperature of the boiler water at the commencement and end of the experiments, and to the power developed by the engine, which, from the manner in which they were calculated, will be in both cases in the same ratio to the combustible, there remains to compare the weight of steam discharged in a given time from the cylinder at the end of the stroke of its piston, with the weight of combustible consumed in the same time, and the difference in the two cases will correctly give the per centum that the condensation in the one exceeds the condensation in the other.

Previous to this determination, however, we will examine if there be any difference in the two cases in the loss of heat by external radiation, for if there be, it will affect the result. Referring now to the table containing the comparative experimental results obtained by using the steam with and without expansion, and taking the mean when burning the coal with and without the admission of air through holes in the furnace door, we find that in the first case the steam in the boiler was 33.9 pounds pressure per square inch above the atmosphere, and had consequently a temperature of 281.°3 Fahr.; the temperature of the engine and boiler room was 72.°5 Fahr., difference 208.°8 Fahr. In the second case, using the steam without expansion, the pressure in the boiler was 28.7 pounds per square inch above the atmosphere, with a temperature of 274.°2 Fahr.; the temperature of the engine and boiler room was 60° Fahr., difference 214.°2 Fahr., or nearly the same as before. Consequently, the difference between the evaporative results, calculated as set forth in the immediately preceding paragraph, will be caused entirely by the condensation due to the expansion itself.

Taking the mean of all the Smithery experiments when burning Blackheath anthracite with and without the admission of air through holes in the furnace door, and *using the steam without expansion*, we have for the weight of steam discharged from the cylinder at the end of the stroke of its piston 1265.5341 pounds per hour. The weight of combustible consumed per hour being 225.9611 pounds, we have 5.6007 pounds of steam per pound of combustible.

In the same manner, taking the mean of the experiments when burning Blackheath anthracite with and without the admission of air through holes in the furnace door, and *using the steam expansively*, we have for the weight of steam discharged from the cylinder at the end of the stroke of its piston 783.3239 pounds per hour. The weight of combustible consumed per hour being 186.5175 pounds, we have 4.1997 pounds of steam per pound of combustible.

The *apparent* difference in the evaporation in the two cases, is, therefore, $(\frac{5.6007-4.1997 \times 100}{4.1997}=)$ 33.36 per centum of the amount when using the steam without expansion, and must have been produced entirely by condensation in the cylinder due to the expansion *per se*, because all the other conditions were almost rigorously the same.

In estimating the gain to be derived from using steam expansively, a great error is made by supposing that the weight of steam passed into the cylinder is correctly measured by the Indicator, and is per stroke of piston a cylinder full of steam of the pressure at the end of the stroke as shown by the instrument. Such, however, is not the case; the Indicator does indeed measure correctly the weight of steam *discharged* from the cylinder at the end of the stroke, or the weight *present* in it at any point of the stroke, but not the weight of steam that has at the end or at any point of the stroke of the piston been *received* into the cylinder; for the Indicator being simply a measurer of existing pressure, cannot, it is manifest, show the weight of steam that has been condensed in the cylinder by any cause whatever.

In the experiments, the final pressure in the cylinder by Indicator when using the steam without expansion, was 24.3 pounds per square inch above zero; and when using the steam expansively 14.75 pounds; the number of double strokes of piston made per minute in the two cases was 25.623 and 25.187, and if the Indicator were a correct measurer of the quantity of steam received into the cylinder, then the weight of combustible consumed in the two cases would have been nearly in the ratio respectively of (24.3×25.623=) 622.6389 and (14.75×25.187=) 371.5156 or of 1.0000 and 1.6759, instead of which we find it to have been by actual weighing in the ratio of only 1.0000 and 1.1685.

Of the modification of the theoretical result of expansion made by the leakage of the valves. When we say that the steam is cut off at such or such a point of the stroke of the piston, we mean that the introduction of the steam into the cylinder from the boiler is intended to be suppressed at that point by the mechanism, and would really be so did the valve move steam tight on its seat. This freedom from leakage, however, is from physical causes, and the forms habitually given to the valves almost an impossibility ; and of the large number of indicator diagrams that I have examined, from many engines of various types and proportions, I have never seen one which did not evidence a very considerable leakage. That this should be so is easily understood when we reflect, that the valves employed, with the exception of the poppet and piston-valves, are in general form, large flat pieces of metal depending for tightness on the accuracy with which two metallic surfaces, one moving freely on the other, can be made to fit; that the metal of the valves has a different texture and a different coefficient of expansion from the metal which forms the valve-seat; that the valves are faced to their seats *cold*, but when in use have one side exposed to the temperature of the boiler steam, while the opposite side is exposed to only the temperature of the exhaust; this difference of temperature on opposite sides of a large flat thin piece of metal, acts uncontrollably to warp it and to cause it to leak; the same cause also warps the valve-seat, and increases the leakage, to which must be added what is due to the flutings or channels soon produced by use and corrosion.

In the case of the double poppet-valve, almost universally employed for the American river and marine engines whose rotary velocity will permit it, there is to be overcome the great difficulty of making their two connected discs steam tight; it is easy to grind one tight, but a very delicate manipulation is required to grind the other tight at the same operation. There is furthermore the leakage due to the difference between the expansion of the connecting stem of the discs, and of the metal of the valve-chest; this could indeed be in a great measure obviated by grinding in the valves hot, but owing to the inconvenience of so doing it is rarely or never done, the valves are habitually ground in cold and of course leak when hot. The single poppet-valve, which is one flat, thin disc, can be ground tight; but it is now scarcely ever employed.

The piston-valve, which depends for its tightness on an *elastic packing of the full circular form*, is the only kind of slide-valve that can be made and kept tight under the ordinary conditions of practice; the elasticity of the packing permitting it to accommodate itself to changes of form without losing its tightness; but I have known this valve to be used only in a very few cases.

It may be supposed that if the valve and its chest were

made of the same metal poured at the same time, both would have the same texture and the same coefficient of expansion; such, however, will not be the practical result; for the two masses being comparatively very small and large, the difference in their rate of cooling will produce a complete change in the quality of the metal. Neither do I overlook the fact that the considerable difference of pressure on the two sides of the valve tends mechanically to keep it flat and in contact with its seat; but this force will be found a feeble antagonist to that resulting from the unequal expansion of the metal by difference of temperature. Let us pause here for a moment and determine what this difference is.

Referring to the Table of Comparative Results, and taking the mean of the two columns when using the steam without expansion, we find its pressure when entering the cylinder to have been 16.9 pounds per square inch above the atmosphere, the temperature of the steam in the valve-chest must then have been at least 254.6 degrees Fahr., and as the temperature of the exhaust was 214.6 degrees Fahr., there was a difference of 40 degrees to warp the valve. Again, taking the mean of the two columns when using the steam with expansion, we find its pressure when entering the cylinder to have been 27.5 pounds per square inch above the atmosphere; its temperature in the valve-chest must then have been at least 272.6 degrees Fahr., and the temperature of the exhaust being as before, 214.6 degrees Fahr., there was a difference of 58 degrees to produce warping.

That a large portion of the leakage was due to the cut-off valve, is very evident from an inspection of the indicator diagrams, Fig. 2, Plate II. These diagrams were taken at one double stroke of the piston. The cut-off valve closed at the point C, which is precisely at the same distance from the commencement for both strokes. At the point C, too, the steam pressure in the cylinder was precisely the same; and had the cut-off valves (consisting of two flat plates, one at each end of the cylinder) been equally tight, the steam pressure at the end of the stroke would have been the same also;

that it was not the same is evident at a glance; the right hand diagram shows it to have been 1⅔ pound per square inch *above* the atmosphere, while the left hand diagram shows it to have been 1⅔ pound per square inch *below* the atmosphere; this difference of 3⅓ pounds per square inch can only be owing to the different tightness of the two cut-off valves. To estimate its value we must consider, that in the one case the total steam pressure at the end of the stroke, counting from zero, was 16.03 pounds per square inch; while in the other it was only 13.37 pounds; the differential of leakage was, therefore, nearly $(\frac{16.03-13.37 \times 100}{13.37}=)$ 20 per centum.

The leakage due to the steam-valve cannot be determined from the diagrams, as the valve had no lap; it can only be inferred from the low *apparent* evaporation by the boiler, for such a leakage would pass a large body of steam directly from the valve-chest into the atmosphere without producing any effect upon the piston, indeed without even entering the cylinder; now, as the *real* evaporation of the boiler, known from experiments on others of the same type and similar proportions, was much greater than the calculations give, there must have been a considerable leak past the steam-valve as well as past the cut-off valve.

The steam and cut-off valves of the Smithery engine have been described in the account of the experiments made to determine the comparative evaporative efficiencies of the Anthracite, Trevorton, and Cumberland coals. They were slide valves and leaked, as we have seen, considerably; the amount of this leakage, and the modification of the theoretical gain by expansion produced by it, we will now determine in the following manner, namely:—

The fact of expansion, of course, does not apply to the steam leaked past the valves and piston directly to the exhaust, and the quantity thus leaked, therefore, went to decrease in direct ratio the proportion of the total fuel uninfluenced by the expansion, and consequently to decrease in the same ratio the theoretical gain due to the measure of expansion employed.

As regards the steam leaked past the cut-off valve into the cylinder after the steam port was closed, it will evidently produce a dynamical effect upon the piston, but will decrease by its amount the measure of expansion *intended* to be employed, and consequently lessen the theoretical gain due to the cutting off at the point where the valve closed, but it will not lessen this gain for the *true* measure of expansion obtained, let that be what it may. In the case of the Smithery engine, the steam space between the piston and cut-off valve at one end of the cylinder, is 0.259 cubic foot, equal to an extension of the space displacement of a stroke of the piston of 0.146 foot; the length of the stroke is 4 feet, and as the expansion-valve closed at 22 per centum of the stroke, or at 0.88 foot, the relative bulks of the steam before and after expansion were 0.88 and 4.146; and the steam pressures in the cylinder, according to the law of MARIOTTE, at the point of cutting off, and at the end of the stroke should be inversely as these numbers. Referring now to the table of Comparative Results, and taking the mean of the third and fourth columns, it will be observed that the pressure of the steam in the cylinder at the point of cutting off was 20.65 pounds per square inch above the atmosphere, or (20.65+14.7 =) 35.35 pounds above zero; consequently it should have been, according to the law of MARIOTTE, (4.146 : 35.35 : : 0.88 :) 7.5 pounds per square inch above zero at the end of the stroke of the piston; whereas, we perceive by the table, that it was 14.75 pounds, or nearly double. Hence it is evident, that after the closing of the cut-off valve, as much steam leaked past it from the boiler into the cylinder as had entered the cylinder previous to the closing of the valve, supposing no reëvaporation had taken place towards the end of the stroke of the piston of the steam condensed in the cylinder in the first part of the stroke. In fact, however, much more than this quantity had entered, because had the valves been perfectly tight, the pressure at the end of the stroke would have been considerably less than according to the law of MARIOTTE. We thus perceive that although the cut-off valve closed at 22 per centum of the stroke, yet the measure of the expansion was far from $\left(\frac{4.146}{0.88}=\right)$ 4.71 times; what the true measure was can be reasonably approximated by comparing the pressure at the end of the stroke of piston with the pressure at the point of cutting off. The pressure at the latter point was 35.35 pounds per square inch above zero, and at the former 14.75 pounds; the measure of expansion was consequently $\left(\frac{35.53}{14.75}=\right)$ 2.397 times instead of 4.71 times. The theoretical gain in fuel due to the measure 2.397 of expansion over using the steam without expansion is 0.874 times; that is to say, a given weight of steam when used with this measure of expansion ought, according to the law of MARIOTTE, to produce 0.874 times more indicated horses-power than when it is used without expansion. Now, when steam is used with the measure 4.71 of expansion, this theoretical gain ought to be 1.515 times the effect produced without expansion; consequently, we perceive that while we have been expecting the gain due to the greater measure of expansion, because the cut-off valve closed at the proper point to produce it, we ought, owing to the leakage of the valves, to have expected only the gain due to the lesser measure of expansion.

Of the modification of the theoretical effect due to the expansion of steam by the back pressure against the piston. That the existence of back pressure influences the economy of expanded steam very materially, will be at once comprehended when we consider that the back pressure is constant, while the steam pressure, counting from zero, is a continuously decreasing one from the point of cutting off; consequently, from that point the back pressure continuously becomes a greater and greater per centum of the steam pressure as the end of the stroke is approached. Hence results, that with the same initial pressure, and the same back pressure, the greater the expansion of the steam the greater will be its loss of useful effect caused by the back pressure; and the greater the back pressure the greater will be the lessening of the theoretical gain due to expansion.

If we suppose the expansion to be carried to such a degree that the steam pressure at any point of the stroke previous to its termination becomes less than the back pressure, then it is plain that the engine is now not only exerting no power, but that some of the power developed by it during the previous portion of the stroke will be abstracted to uselessly overcome the differential of the steam and back pressures. We thus perceive that owing to the existence of back pressure it is possible to carry the expansion of steam so far as to cause its economical effect to be greatly less than if it were used without expansion, a result which would be impossible were there no back pressure. For example, suppose the case of steam of any total pressure, say 30 pounds per square inch, used with an expansion of four times, that is to say, cut off at one-quarter of the stroke of piston from the commencement; suppose also there were no back pressure and that the steam expanded according to the law of MARIOTTE, then the mean effective pressure throughout the stroke would be, say, 18 pounds per square inch. Without expansion this pressure would, of course, be 30 pounds per square inch, but there would have been consumed in producing it four times as much boiler steam as when employing expansion; dividing, then, the 30 by 4 we obtain $7\frac{1}{2}$, which expresses the pressure obtained per unit of steam of fuel using the steam without expansion, while the pressure 18 was obtained from the same fuel using the steam with expansion; hence the gain would be $\left(\frac{18}{7\frac{1}{2}}-1=\right)$ 1.4; that is, the same fuel with the expanded steam would produce 1.4 times additional effect to the effect produced by it without expansion. Now, let us suppose a back pressure in each case of 8 pounds per square inch, then the relative mean effective pressures will be $(18-8=)$ 10 with expansion, and $(30-8=)$ 22 without, and as in the latter case four times as much fuel was used, the relative pressures per unit of fuel will be $(\frac{10}{1}=)$ 10 and $(\frac{22}{4}=)$ $5\frac{1}{2}$, and the gain by expansion will be only $\left(\frac{10}{5\frac{1}{2}}-1=\right)$ 0.8 instead of the 1.4 when there was no back pressure. If the back pressure be increased to 16 pounds per square inch and the same process repeated, we shall find that the mean effective pressure with the expanded steam will be (18—16 =) 2 pounds, and with the unexpanded steam (30–16=) 14 pounds. The weight of fuel consumed in the two cases being as 1 and 4, we obtain per unit of fuel the pressures ($\frac{2}{1}$=) 2 and ($\frac{14}{4}$=) 3½; that is to say, the economical effect of the steam used without expansion exceeds that which is obtained from the steam used with expansion in the ratio of 3½ to 2.

The same results would evidently be obtained if, with the same initial steam pressure and the same back pressure, we were to increase the measure used of expansion, that is to say, cut off shorter and shorter ; in which case the mean effective pressure with the expanded steam would become less and less per unit of fuel ; while with the unexpanded steam it would remain constant ; a point would then soon be reached where the gain due to the expansion would be balanced by the back pressure, and if the expansion were carried beyond this it would occasion a loss.

Practically, in some engines, as for instance that of the Smithery with which the experiments were made, the loss from back pressure is equal whether the steam be used with or without expansion, the engine doing the same work in the same time with the same speed of piston. This, however, is owing entirely to a mal-proportion between the size of the engine and the work to be done, which latter required when working with unexpanded steam a very low pressure, while it permitted with the expanded steam a comparatively high initial pressure, the mean effective pressures in the two cases being identical. The Smithery engine, if it had been worked without expansion and with steam whose cylinder pressure equalled the pressure at the point of cutting off when the steam was used with expansion, could have been greatly reduced in size and still have developed the same power with greater economy of fuel, because the loss by back pressure would then have been much less than when using the steam with expansion. For example : in the Table of Comparative

Results, we find the pressure at the point of cutting-off when using the steam expansively to have been 20.65 pounds per square inch above the atmosphere or a total pressure of (20.65+14.7=) 35.35 pounds ; the back pressure was $15\frac{1}{2}$ pounds per square inch, and the mean effective pressure per indicator was 11.35 pounds. With the same back pressure and using steam of the same total pressure, namely, 35.35 pounds, but without expansion, the mean effective pressure would have been (35.35—15.5=) 19.85 pounds ; and the capacity of the cylinder would have been reduced in the ratio of $(\frac{19.85}{11.35}=)$ 1.75 to 1.00, and could still have developed the same power with the same speed of piston, while the loss from the back pressure, which with the expanded steam was $(\frac{15\frac{1}{2}\times 100}{11.35+15.5}=)$ $57\frac{4}{5}$ per centum, would have been only $(\frac{15\frac{1}{2}\times 100}{19.85+15.5}=)$ $43\frac{4}{5}$ per centum. The equality of loss, then, with equal back pressures, in the cases of using steam with and without expansion, can only be obtained on the supposition of employing too large a cylinder when working without expansion and one of the proper size when working with expansion, the equality not being inherent but accidental, depending entirely on a mal-proportion of size of engine to quantity of work done and in favor of expanded steam. Hence it is manifest that as whatever initial cylinder pressure can be carried in one case can be carried in the other, and starting with equality in this respect, there must always be a great decrease of the theoretical gain due to the existence of back pressure. In fact, could the volume of the cylinder of the Smithery engine have been decreased, when using steam without expansion and of the same pressure as at the point of cutting-off when using steam with expansion, until it performed the same work with the same speed of piston as when working expansively the result from expansion would have been reversed, and instead of showing a gain of nearly 17 per centum, would have shown a loss exceeding that ratio ; beside which there would be obtained all the practical advantages of a smaller engine—too obvious to be dwelt on.

In estimating the practical effects of expansion, the enormous influence of such large back pressures as we have to deal with even in the case of good condensing engines, have been quite overlooked, as have also been the advantages to be derived from the less capacity of cylinder required for equal developments of power when steam is used without expansion and of the same initial pressure as with expansion.

Still as it may be replied, and with truth, that in many cases, particularly of marine condensing engines, a considerable gain has been realized by using the steam with a greater measure of expansion than before ; it becomes incumbent to show that this fact when rightly interpreted, is not in contradiction to the foregoing remarks. In these cases it must be remembered that there were employed the same cylinder with the same area of steam-ports, and the same boiler furnishing the same quantity of steam. The gain realized by cutting-off shorter was obtained almost entirely from changes accidentally produced in the action and virtual proportions of the mechanism, and not from the fact of any increased measure of expansion *per se*. The sizes of the cylinder and boiler had been in bad proportion to each other, the former being much too large for the latter, as is almost universally the case ; and not only was the boiler too small to furnish as much steam of the proper pressure as the cylinder could work off, but it was too small in steam room also. Let us now trace the consequences of this mal-proportion. The first is, that the steam when using the less measure of expansion had necessarily a lower initial pressure in the cylinder and therefore lost the gain it would have realized from the less proportion of the back pressure had the cylinder been small enough to maintain, with equal development of power, the same initial pressure as when using the steam with a greater measure of expansion. Again, as with the less measure of expansion a greater bulk of steam had to be discharged in equal time through the same steam-port, the *absolute* back pressure against the piston was increased ; consequently, when using the steam with the less measure of expansion, instead of the back pressure being absolutely the same and relatively less, it was both relatively and absolutely greater than when using the steam with the greater measure of expansion. An inspection of indicator diagrams from any condensing engine using steam with different measures of expansion, will show at once how much greater is the back pressure when following far with the steam than when cutting it off shorter. The vacuum in the condenser may be the same, and also the *maximum* vacuum in the cylinder, but the *average* in the latter will be less, and there will be observed a greater and greater rounding of the diagram at the exhaust end as the masses of steam discharged in equal times through the same port become greater and greater, owing to the maximum condensation becoming later and later. Now, as marine condensing engines rarely work with an average pressure exceeding 16 pounds per square inch of piston above the back pressure, and generally with pressures greatly below it, the effect of increasing the back pressure 1 pound per square inch is equivalent to neutralizing more than one-sixteenth of the power, for allowing the friction resistance of the engine to be 1½ pound per square inch, the net pressure is (16—1½ =) 14½ pounds, of which 1 pound is nearly 7 per centum. In engines of ordinary sized ports, I have known the back pressure to increase between 2 and 3 pounds per square inch when the point of cutting-off was changed from one-fifth to one-half the stroke, the vacuum in the condenser remaining the same. This increase of back pressure was of course an accidental effect and would have disappeared on a proper enlargement of the port, but the great economical difference due to it was erroneously attributed to the fact of expansion *per se*.

It may be said with truth that nearly all boilers, and particularly marine ones of the tubular type, have too little steam room; and as a deficiency in this respect seriously impairs the economical effect produced by the fuel, any increase of steam room becomes a source of gain, and every decrease a cause of loss. Now the steam room of a boiler is not an absolute but a relative quantity, and is to be compared with the bulk of steam drawn from the boiler in a given interval of time ; hence, if the steam room contain ten charges of steam for the cylinder when the cut-off valve closes at one-fourth the stroke of piston, it will contain only five charges when the valve closes at half stroke; the throttle-valve opening remaining the same in both cases. In this illustration, by simply changing the point of cutting-off there has been withdrawn in the same time twice the bulk of steam from the steam room which is thus virtually reduced one-half. The effect of such reduction is to increase the quantity of water worked over from the boiler to the cylinder, where it increases the back pressure by obstructing the exhaust port and where it impedes the movement of the piston near the end of the stroke by its want of elasticity and facility of escape. It also lessens the condenser vacuum and increases the load upon the air-pump owing to the large quantity of injection water required to reduce its temperature from that of the boiler to that of the condenser. This additional amount of primed over water with its attendant additional amount of injection water, fills the channel way from the condenser to the air-pump to the exclusion of the air and uncondensed vapor to be extracted: the result is, as has been stated, a lessened vacuum in the condenser and an increased load upon the pump. The water primed over from the boiler carries with it the difference of the feed water and boiler water temperatures, which has thus been uselessly imparted to it at the expense of the fuel if a surface condenser be employed: with a jet condenser there is no loss of fuel in this respect, as a certain amount (about 57 per centum) of the water pumped into the boiler must be withdrawn to prevent the formation of scale, and it is immaterial whether this withdrawal be effected by priming through the cylinder or by blowing-off through the valve provided for that purpose.

The advantageous results of increasing the measure employed of expansion for the steam due to the above causes, would disappear by simply increasing the steam room and enlarging the cylinder steam-ports, and the gain, which is now usually ascribed to the fact of expansion *per se*, would then be credited to its proper source. Or, retaining the same absolute amount of steam room and reducing the size of the cylinder so that when working with the less measure of expansion and with the same initial pressure as with the greater measure of expansion, the engine developed the same power, we would obtain about the same advantageous results in this rapport. I know that in many cases where experiments have been faithfully made with a wide range in the measure of expansion employed, no sensible gain has followed; I am aware, also, that there have been many particular cases where a marked gain has followed an increase of the measure of expansion; the discrepancy proves the existence of other and modifying causes acting with unequal influence. All errors of opinion in physics have been supported by an appeal to facts, but these are an infallible umpire only when they are rightly interpreted, and the tendency is always to generalize too broadly and to ascribe whatever results follow a change wholly to that change *per se* without inquiring whether these results be not due to other causes brought into action by the change and which when removed, and the change left to act alone no longer follow or with very diminished intensity.

Of the loss of dynamic effect due to the steam used in filling the cylinder clearance and ports. As it is impossible to place the valve in such contact with the piston at the commencement of its stroke, that there shall be no space between them, and as the intervening space is filled with steam from the boiler, and as this steam is exhausted at each stroke of the piston, it becomes necessary to ascertain what dynamical effect, if any, is obtained from it. The problem divides into two cases: 1st. When the steam is used without expansion. 2d. When it is used expansively.

In the first case it is plain, that as the pressure of the cylinder steam is unchanged during the stroke of the piston, the portion of it comprised in the cylinder clearance and ports, which are filled from the boiler at the commencement and exhausted at the end of the stroke of the piston, acts only as so much filling, produces no dynamical effect, and serves no other purpose than to transmit the boiler pressure to the piston. In this case, then, it is a complete loss measured in quantity by the contents of the space and the weight of the steam. For instance: let the space displacement of a piston per stroke be 100 cubic feet, and the space comprised in the clearance and steam ports 7 cubic feet, then the loss from this source, if there be no leakage past the valves and piston to the exhaust, will be $(\frac{7 \times 100}{100+7}=)$ $6\frac{1}{2}$ per centum of the quantity entering the cylinder. If there be leakage it will, of course, diminish this per centum, for then more steam in equal time will enter the cylinder while the contents of the clearance and ports will remain the same; for instance: If, in the above example, there had leaked per stroke of piston 10 cubic feet of steam, then the loss of steam in the clearance and ports instead of being $6\frac{1}{2}$ per centum would have been $(\frac{7 \times 100}{100+7+10}=)$ 6 per centum of the total quantity entering the cylinder.

In the case of using the steam expansively, a portion of that part of it which fills the space in the clearance and ports produces a dynamic effect because as the expansion of the steam in this space extends to the end of the stroke it increases the pressure upon the piston over what it would have been had no such space existed, but the remainder of the steam filling this space after deducting the portion of it producing an increase of pressure on the piston, is entirely lost; and as this remainder is a higher proportion of the whole quantity of steam used than in the case of no expansion, and the higher the greater the measure employed of expansion—because the space in the clearance and ports is a constant quantity while the total quantity of steam used decreases in the ratio of the portion of the stroke at which the steam is cut off plus the length of the stroke to which the space in the clearance and ports is equal—it follows that the loss of economical effect from the steam filling this space is greater when the steam is used expansively than when it is used without expansion, and the more expansively the steam is used the greater will be this loss.

In order to appreciate the amount of this loss and the degree in which it is affected by using the steam expansively, we will take the case of a cylinder of, say, 8 feet stroke of piston and having a space comprised in its clearance and steam-port at one end equal to the area of the cylinder by a length of, say, 0.6 foot, which is about the average in practice, and let the steam be used first without expansion, and then with expansion cutting it off successively at such points of the piston as to produce including the space in the clearance and port, expansions of twice, four times, and eight times.

And first, using the steam without expansion, taking its pressure at unity, supposing the cylinder to have no clearance or port, and representing the weight of steam used by 8, we shall have a mean pressure on the piston during its stroke of 1. and an economical effect from the steam per unit of weight of $(\frac{1.}{8.}=)$ .12500. With the clearance this effect is $(\frac{1.}{8.6}=)$ .11628; consequently the loss caused by the clearance and port is $(\frac{12500-11628 \times 100}{12500}=)$ 6.98 per centum.

Next, still taking the initial pressure of the steam at unity but expanding it twice, it would produce were there no clearance and port to fill, a mean pressure on the piston during its stroke of .84657 obtained by an expenditure of a weight of steam represented by 4. Now suppose the clearance of 0.6 of a foot to be added, then the same measure of expansion (twice) being used as before the steam will be cut off at 3.7 feet of the stroke from the commencement instead of at 4 feet as before, and the average pressure on the piston during the stroke will be .83506 obtained by an expenditure of a weight of steam represented by (3.7+0.6=) 4.3. Without clearance, then, we have an economical effect from the steam per unit of weight of $(\frac{.84657}{4})$ .21164; while with clearance this effect is $(\frac{.83506}{4.3}=)$ .19420, consequently the loss is $(\frac{21164-19420\times100}{21164}=)$ 8.24 per centum due to the clearance and port.

Proceeding in the same manner and expanding the steam four times, it would produce were there no clearance and port to fill, a mean pressure on the piston during its stroke of .59657 obtained by an expenditure of a weight of steam represented by 2. Now, suppose the clearance of 0.6 of a foot to be added then still using the same measure of expansion the steam will be cut off at 1.55 foot of the stroke from the commencement instead of at 2 feet as before, and the average pressure on the piston will be .56631 obtained by an expenditure of a weight of steam represented by (1.55+0.6=) 2.15. Without clearance, then, we have an economical effect from the steam per unit of weight of $(\frac{.59657}{2}=)$ .29829; while with clearance this effect is $(\frac{.56631}{2.15}=)$ .26340, consequently the loss is $(\frac{29829-26340\times100}{29829}=)$ 11.70 per centum due to the clearance and port.

With an expansion of eight times, the steam, were there no clearance and port to fill, would produce a mean pressure on the piston during its stroke of .38493 obtained by an expenditure of a weight of steam represented by 1. Adding now the clearance and port space of 0.6 of a foot and still using the same measure of expansion, the steam will be cut off at 0.475 foot of the stroke from the commencement instead of at 1 foot as before, and the average pressure on the piston will be .33880 obtained by an expenditure of a weight of steam represented by (0.475+0.6=) 1.075. Without clearence the economical effect of the steam per unit of weight was $(\frac{.38493}{1}=)$ .38493, while with clearance it was $(\frac{.33880}{1.075}=)$ .31516, consequently the loss is $(\frac{38493-31516\times100}{38493}=)$ 18.13 per centum due to the clearance and port.

Collecting the above, we have in the different cases the following for the loss of economical effect from the steam due to the space comprised in the clearance and port of the cylinder, and expressed in per centum of the effect that the steam would have produced had there been no such space to have been filled with it:

Using the steam without expansion.......... 6.98 per cent.
Using the steam with an expansion of twice.. 8.24 "
Using the steam with an expansion of four times..............................11.70 "
Using the steam with an expansion of eight times................................18.13 "

By observing this rapid increase of loss when employing increased measures of expansion, and its large per centum with high measures, we shall perceive how greatly it affects the economy of using steam very expansively, and what a serious practical modification it causes in the theoretical results. This loss, which when expanding the steam twice was 8.24 per centum, rises to 18.13 per centum when the steam is expanded eight times. If we suppose, then, that one-half of the heat of the fuel enters the cylinder with the steam, 8.24 per centum of it, or ($50 \times .0824 =$) 4.12 per centum of the fuel thrown into the furnaces, is thus lost when expanding the steam twice; and 18.13 per centum, or ($50 \times .1813 =$) 9.06 per centum of the fuel thrown into the furnaces, when the expansion is carried to eight times.

From the preceding description it appears, that the theoretical gain due to expansion can only be obtained when the steam is generated and used under purely theoretical conditions; that is to say, when the combustion of the fuel is perfect and the entire heat developed from it is applied to the evaporation of the water, and when the steam so generated suffers no loss either by leakage or condensation, and when its effect is not impaired by friction resistance, by back pressure, or by the space intervening between the expansion valve and piston at the commencement of the stroke. Just, however, in the proportion that these physical conditions are found to exist, will be the modification practically effected in the theoretical gain due to the use of steam expansively. It will be observed that the obtaining of a higher result in any of the operations intermediate between the combustion of the fuel and the production of the power is a cause of obtaining a higher result from the expansive use of the steam; and that on the degree of evaporative efficiency given by the boiler, on the amount of back pressure against the piston, on the space comprised in the cylinder clearance and port, on the tightness of the valves, on the more or less thorough felting of all the radiating surfaces, and on the general propriety of the proportions of the organs of the machinery and of its dimensions to the power developed, will depend the measure of expansion to be employed for obtaining the highest duty from the steam, and not on any theoretical derivations from the law of MARIOTTE, which though rigorously true for the imaginary conditions upon which they are based, are yet subject to such wide modifications by the practical conditions actually encountered with steam machinery, that the predicted advantages may be lessened to any extent, and may even disappear under very unfavorable circumstances, while under the most favorable ones possible there will always remain an enormous discrepancy. We can now understand why in some cases increasing the measure of expansion with which the steam was used notably increased the economical efficiency of the fuel, while in others no sensible gain, and sometimes a loss, followed.

When the cylinder valves are not arranged for cutting-off the steam, it does not necessarily follow that the steam is used without expansion, on the contrary, it will be found practically that owing to insufficient area of the cylinder ports, or to a contraction of the steam-pipe by the throttle-valve, the steam within the cylinder is used with a certain measure of expansion though the communication with the boiler be not closed. To this effect produced on the steam the name of "throttling" or "wire-drawing" is given; and as it influences the results obtained when using the steam without expansion,—that is to say, of uniform pressure during the stroke derived from uniform supply from the boiler,—and as the steam was throttled in the case of the Smithery experiments when using it without expansion nominally, the expansion valve not being employed and the steam-valve being without lap, it will be proper before concluding to make the following discussion :

Of the effect of "throttling" the steam, or of "wire drawing" it at the throttle-valve so as to cause it not only to enter the cylinder considerably below the boiler pressure, but to suffer a continual decrease of pressure during the stroke of the piston. The first effect of throttling obviously is to establish a marked difference between the pressure in the boiler and in the cylinder, and thus virtually to increase the steam room in the former; because the latter at each stroke of the piston withdraws a less quantity or weight of steam than it otherwise would do. So far, therefore, as value of steam room in the boiler is concerned, there is a decided advantage to be derived from "throttling," especially in the case of deficient steam room. On the other hand, however, it is attended with a loss arising from the fact that, as the total heat of steam increases with the pressure, there is required more heat or fuel to evaporate a given weight of water into steam of a high than into steam of a low pressure: and there is, furthermore, too, an increase in the specific heat of water as its temperature increases. Now if we generate steam under a high pressure and use it under a low one, which is precisely the case in throttling, (and also in using steam expansively) we evidently lose the difference in the cost of evaporation at the two temperatures. But if we use the steam in the cylinder at the pressure it is generated under in the boiler then, *ceteris paribus*, the higher the pressure the greater is the gain in fuel, because as the pressure is increased the temperature or sensible heat is also increased, and the tension becomes greater from this cause than what is due to the *weight* of water contained in a given bulk of steam. This additional tension due to the increase of temperature is equal to that which would result from heating the steam out of contact with water the difference of the degrees of temperature in the two cases; and is, according to Regnault $\frac{1}{491}$ of its value for each degree on Fahrenheit's scale. The gain that is obtained with steam of higher pressure by means of this additional tension, is greater than the loss by its increased total heat; but if we include in the account, as we ought to do, the important practical fact, that as the evaporation depends on the difference between the temperatures of the furnace and of the water in the boiler, and as this difference becomes less and less as the pressure of steam is increased, the fuel with the higher pressure steam will produce a less evaporative result;—and add to this, too, the greater loss due to the greater radiation of heat from steam of higher pressure;—we shall have the practical result actually obtained of the sensible economical equality of the fuel whether low or high pressure steam be used.

When steam is changed from a higher to a lower pressure by throttling, there is the same loss by condensation that always follows such a change of pressure, be it from any cause whatever. This loss is due to the fact, that as the pressure is lowered the latent heat increases faster than the total heat decreases, the difference being found in the heat of the weight of steam precipitated into water. An opposite result is the erroneous opinion of many persons who, only considering that the total heat is greater with higher pressures, imagine that the effect of throttling is to "superheat" instead of to condense the steam; that is to say, that the steam of lower pressure resulting from the throttling of steam of higher pressure, will have a greater temperature by the difference of the total heats in the two cases than is normally due to its pressure; and on the ground that as the greater total heat existed previously to throttling, the same quantity must be present afterwards; quite overlooking the important fact of the change in the amount of latent heat in the two cases, which has so increased with the steam of lower pressure as to overbalance the decrease of the total heat and produce a condensation instead of a superheating of the wire-drawn steam. By *superheated steam* is meant steam of a temperature higher than is due to its pressure were that pressure obtained wholly by evaporation from water.

There is still another effect of throttling to be considered. It is, when working without a cut-off valve, the continuous decrease of pressure suffered by the steam during the stroke of the piston; the result of which is that the steam is used to a certain extent expansively, the measure of expansion employed being obviously determined by the relation of the final to the initial pressure; and the more the steam is throttled the more expansively it will be used. That such is the effect produced becomes evident if we attend to the causes in action. With a fixed opening of throttle-valve (too small to admit the steam at a pressure at all approaching that in the boiler) the steam enters the cylinder at a certain pressure at the commencement of the stroke of the piston where the velocity of the latter is the minimum, this velocity continuously increases to the centre of the stroke and consequently the piston in equal intervals of time has continuously increasing space displacements which the throttle-valve opening, owing to its smallness, is only able to fill with steam of continuously decreasing pressure from the commencement of the stroke ; the result is that as the piston advances the spaces it vacates not being filled from the boiler with steam of equal pressure to that in the earlier parts of the stroke, the steam already in the cylinder admitted during those parts expands to the equilibrium and in so doing develops expansively an additional power which is a gain as it is obtained without direct cost of fuel. From the centre of the stroke of the piston to its end, the velocity continuously decreases, but as the spaces to be filled are still greater and greater while the throttle-valve opening through which they are to be filled remains the same, enough steam cannot be admitted from the boiler, notwithstanding the lessening velocity of piston, to fill them with steam of equal pressure to that admitted during the preceding parts of the stroke, the pressure will therefore continue to fall, but not nearly so rapidly as during the first half of the stroke, and the steam already admitted into the cylinder during the previous parts of the stroke will continue to expand and develop power expansively as before though not to so great a degree. The general result is, that the effect of throttling steam is to use it expansively the measure of that expansion continually varying from one end of the stroke to the other, becoming continuously greater from the commencement to the centre of the stroke, and continuously smaller from the centre to the end of the stroke.

To obtain the full benefit of throttling, the throttle-valve must be placed as near the cylinder-port as possible, for the effect of whatever expansion results is spread over the space from the throttle-valve to the piston when at the end of its stroke, and the dynamic effect developed by the expansion in the space between the throttle-valve and the piston when at the commencement of its stroke is entirely lost. In fact in this respect the same consideration applies to the throttle as to the expansion-valve, namely; that it is essential to its proper action that as little space as possible intervene between it and the piston at the commencement of the stroke. In the case of the Smithery engine, the throttle-valve was so distant from the steam-valve that much of the benefit otherwise derivable from it was lost.

The advantages and disadvantages of throttling, *per se*, may be briefly summed as follows: The advantages are the virtual increase of the steam room in the boiler, and the use of the steam more expansively. The disadvantages are the losses by evaporating steam under higher pressure; by the condensation due to the greater expansion; and by the greater radiation from the boiler and steam-pipes due to the higher pressure of the steam. Whether the advantages are greater than the disadvantages, or *vice versa,* depends upon conditions which cannot be generalized. In the majority of cases, under the conditions and with the proportions actually existing in the average of practice, there will be found a gain by throttling; the value of the increase of steam room in the boiler and the consequent greater dryness of the steam, as Engineers phrase it, or feedom from water in the vesicular state, being more than enough to overbalance all the disadvantages.

In the case of the Smithery engine, referring to the table of Comparative Results, and taking the mean of the first and second columns, we find that when the engine was worked without the cut-off valve the pressure of the steam at the commencement of the stroke was (16.9+14.7 =) 31.6 pounds per square inch above zero, while at the end of the stroke it was only 24.3 pounds per square inch above zero; difference 7.3 pounds per square inch. In comparing the results, however, of the experiments when using the steam with and without expansion, it must be remembered that it was throttled in both cases; the difference in the cylinder between the initial pressure and the pressure at the point of cutting-off with the expanded steam being 7 pounds per square inch. The degree of throttling was therefore the same in both cases and neutralized its effect in a comparison.

On a review of the preceding discussion, there is no difficulty in comprehending how the results from the fuel when cutting-off the steam at 22 per centum of the stroke of the piston from the commencement, was only 16.85 per centum more than when using it without expansion. The measure of expansion really employed, it must be remembered, instead of that due to the point of cutting-off, namely, 4.71 times, was, owing to leakage only 2.397 times, the theoretical gain due to which is .874.

In the first place, of the total heat due to the combustion of the fuel, only about 60 per centum was used in the generation of the steam, reducing the theoretical gain at once to (.874×.60 =) .5244. Supposing the loss of heat by radiation from the boiler and steam-pipe to have been 10 per centum, this amount will be reduced to (.5244—$\overline{5244\times.10}$ =) .4720; and as of the quantity of heat entering the cylinder with the steam, there was lost by the condensation due to the fact of expansive *per se* 33.36 per centum or (.3336×.4720 =) 15.75 per centum of the fuel, this amount will be further reduced to (.4720—.1575 =) .3145 of which there was actually realized .1685, leaving (.3145—.1685 =) .1460 for the losses due to leakage of steam past the cylinder valves and piston without producing dynamic effect upon the piston, and to the space comprised in the cylinder clearances and ports. The effects of throttling, back pressure, and radiation, were sensibly the same in both cases. The space in the clearance and port of the Smithery engine at one end of the cylinder was very small, being only 3⅜ per centum of the space displacement of the piston per stroke, and as the actual measure of expansion was only 2.397 times, the loss from this source when using the steam expansively was about 4.60 per centum, leaving for the loss by leakage past the valves and piston (14.60—4.60 ≐) 10 per centum.

It is, of course, not supposed that the *proportions* in the above distribution are *rigorously* correct, for from the nature of things they can only be approximated, but the distribution is right in kind, the final result is right, and the proportions are sufficiently near the truth to clearly show why the experimental result should be as it was, and to practically enable us to discern the direction and limit of improvement.

THE

PROSSER BOILER.

Experiments made in April and May, 1859, *on the Multitubular Boiler of* THOMAS PROSSER, *at No.* 28 *Platt Street, New York City, by Chief Engineers* B. F. ISHERWOOD, WM. E. EVERETT, *and* J. W. KING, *U. S. N., by order of the Navy Department.*

Mr. THOMAS PROSSER having invented a new method of constructing close surface condensers and multitubular boilers for the purpose of using at sea steam of very high pressure with condensation but without an air pump, and of supplying and recuperating the boiler with distilled feed-water, invited the attention of the United States Navy Department to a specimen of the machinery constructed on his system and regularly performing the work of his shop at number 28 Platt Street, New York City. Accordingly, Chief Engineers B. F. ISHERWOOD, WM. E. EVERETT, and JAMES W. KING were ordered by the Secretary of the Navy to form a Board; and they were directed to examine the system of Mr. PROSSER, to experiment with his machinery, and to report the results. This Board, after making a very careful set of experiments, reported *in extenso* upon the proposed system, upon the plan of constructing the condenser, and upon the boiler, as the subject naturally separated into these divisions. In the present paper will be found the facts ascertained and the inferences drawn as regards the boiler alone. The Report is followed as closely as possible, something more fully explanatory of the matter is occasionally added, and sometimes paragraphs are transposed for convenience; the calculations also have been revised and some slight corrections made, but nothing has been changed to alter in the least the substantive facts and opinions arrived at by the Board.

Conditions to be satisfied by the Boiler.

Before proceeding to a description of the boiler, it is proper to premise with the conditions that it was designed to fulfill; they may be briefly summed as follows, namely:

1st. Great economical evaporative efficiency; to accomplish which the proportion of the heating to the grate surface was made enormously large beyond all precedent for boilers employing only a natural draught, while the iron composing the heating surface was of the minimum thinness. By great economical efficiency is meant the evaporation of a great weight of water per unit of weight of fuel.

2d. The superheating of the steam to such a degree that after the reduction of its temperature by external radiation, by expansion in the cylinder, and by refrigeration due to the varying temperatures of the interior surfaces of the cylinder, it would retain sufficient heat from the moment of its generation to that of its exhaustion from the cylinder, to prevent any condensation, and consequently to entirely save the large loss from that source. To accomplish this in an easy and economical manner, the heating surface was placed in a vertical position and the products of combustion were made to traverse it vertically, passing first through the water and afterwards through the steam-room of the boiler.

3d. As the system proposed by Mr. Prosser was based on the employment of steam of an excessively high pressure, the boiler was designed for much greater strength than is possessed by the usual forms of high pressure boilers. To obtain this unusual degree of strength, it was composed almost entirely of cylinders, all of which, with one exception, were tubes not exceeding 2 inches in diameter: the flat surfaces were very limited and closely braced by the tubes themselves.

4th. Minimum weight both of the boiler and of the water within it. To accomplish this the width of much of the water space was made ½ inch, and but very little of it exceeded 1¾ inch. The material of the boiler was chiefly thin tubes, and there was a total absence of bracing.

5th. Minimum space occupied by the boiler. To accomplish this the heating surface was not only composed of tubes of very small diameter but many of them were arranged to form couples, one tube being placed within the other, and there was no space lost between the furnace and the tubes.

6th. The boiler was intended for evaporating only *pure distilled water.* Not even the purest spring or river water can be used with it. Its employment, therefore, is only possible in connection with a surface condenser and a system of recuperative supply that will replace the loss by leakage with distilled water also.

Of the Type of Prosser's Boiler.

The mechanical means of satisfying all the preceding conditions happily meet in the type of boiler to which Mr. PROSSER'S belongs ; and although this type has never achieved a permanent success, yet as it has been long known and used in practice on a respectable scale, that fact deprives Mr. PROSSER of the merit of its invention and restricts his claim solely to his novel method of arranging the tubes in connection with their plates. The general features of this type of boiler (an account of a specimen of which may be found on pages 68 and 69 of the Treatise on the Steam Engine by the Artisan Club, published in 1846) are as follows, namely :

The tubes are placed vertically immediately over the firegrate, and the lower tube-plate forms the crown of the furnace. The products of combustion ascend through the tubes and emerge into a dome-shaped smoke connection whence they are discharged into the chimney. The upper tube-plate forms the bottom of the smoke connection. A continuous cylindrical shell envelopes furnace and tubes, and between them are the water and steam, the latter surrounding the upper part of the tubes, and the former surrounding the lower part of the tubes and the furnace. That the upper part of the tubes shall be surrounded by the steam while their lower part is immersed in the water, is a necessity of this arrangement, and forms coincidently a very convenient method of superheating the steam, by which is meant heating it above the temperature normal to its density as 'saturated steam or steam raised directly from water. For not only is the steam superheated by this arrangement without requiring any separate vessel or additional parts for the purpose, but it is superheated without danger in the case of *stationary* boilers, because the temperature of the products of combustion are reduced far below a red heat before they impinge upon that portion of the tubes which is unprotected by water. The low specific heat and conducting power of steam render it so poor a transmitter of heat that a very considerable extent of tube surface at the temperature of from 450° to 550° Fahr. is required to produce the moderate superheating of from 35° to 40° Fahr., and this extent of surface can be easily obtained in this type of boiler by a mere elongation of the tubes. To produce the amount of superheating just mentioned, and of the degree and under the conditions stated, will require a heating surface above the water-line of about twenty-four times the area of the fire grate. To obtain this in a separate vessel, or by additional parts, involves a bulk, cost, inconvenience, and danger, that has thus far prevented recourse to superheating with other types of boiler. Even with this type the certainty of safety is restricted to *stationary* boilers, for it is well known that metals when at a black heat or about 700° Fahr. evaporate water with excessive rapidity, and in the case of sea-going steamers whose violent and irregular movements would occasionally swash the water high upon the upper and highly-heated part of the tubes, a sudden evolution of steam might take place in such quantities as to produce rupture; particularly upon starting the engine after it had been some time at rest with full fires burning and the damper nearly closed. It may be answered that the mass of matter in the part of the tubes out of water in conjunction with the specific heat of the metal, is not equal to this effect, especially when the short time is considered during which the metal and water would be in contact by the swashing ; but an area of iron or brass tubes of twenty-four times the grate surface and having the temperature stated, will evaporate and with great suddenness a large quantity of water thrown upon it at a temperature varying from 250° to 300° Fahr. ; and a permanent careening of the vessel might on starting the engine after it had been some time at rest with full fires burning, bring a large mass of water in permanent contact with the upper part of the tubes when in their most highly heated state.

In comparing the space occupied by this type of boiler and by the usual multitubular boiler having horizontal fire tubes returned above the furnace, it must be premised that the only practicable method of putting in the vertical tubes or of taking them out, is through the smoke connection on top. This connection, therefore, must be made of the height of the tubes, for although they could be divided lengthwise into one or more parts and screwed together, and thus be got in with proportionately less height of smoke connection, yet the difficulty, cost, and uncertainty of such an operation, would prevent its being had recourse to in large boilers, and even then there must be left sufficient height in this smoke-box for men to work in fitting the tubes to their plates, and also for sweeping the tubes as they cannot be swept from below. In small land boilers the top of the smoke-box may be entirely removed for these purposes, but with large boilers, particularly in the hold of a vessel and closely decked over, such an operation is out of the question, and under the most favorable circumstances the labor and time required would be serious objections. If, then, we make this smoke connection of the same height as the tubes, it will be found that for equal grate and heating surfaces and capacity of steam room, the two types of boiler will displace about the same space; the greater bulk of this smoke connection above the tubes in the one type compensating the space which with the other type intervenes between the bridge-wall or further end of the grate and the nearest tube plate of the horizontal tubes. This space, it will be observed, is, with the type of boiler we are discussing, entirely saved, because the crown of the furnace is the bottom plate of the tubes; and there is also saved, additionally, the water space of about 6 inches in width, which surrounds it.

The shell of the usual horizontal tubular boiler is rectangular, while that of the other type is cylindrical, consequently, the latter will require more space in the vessel due to this difference of form, because, were several boilers employed, the greater part of the spandrels would not be available for other uses. The cylindrical form of shell is with this type a necessity, because, as its entire interior is occupied by tubes, it cannot be braced across. If much pressure is to be carried the diameter of the shell will be obviously very restricted, and a large number of boilers will be required to furnish a moderate amount of power.

The usual horizontal tubular boiler possesses a great advantage in the less height under which it can be conveniently arranged, for this dimension is of the first importance with marine boilers though not for land ones. Now the type of boiler with which we are comparing it properly requires a height of about 14 feet, which is inadmissible on board any but first class vessels and would exclude it from smaller ones even were there no other objections.

In comparing the weights of the two types of boiler, it will be seen that the usual horizontal tubular one has a mass of bracing and the water-casing to the smoke space intervening between the bridge-wall and first tube plate, which are wanting in the other; but this type, on the other hand, has a greater weight of shell, even if only a very moderate power is to be furnished, owing to the restricted diameter of the shell imposed by conditions of strength and by arrangement of furnaces. A compensation is thus established between the two, that would probably leave but little difference of weight in favor of either. As regards weight of water in the boilers, the horizontal tubular one contains the most.

The vertical position of the tubes immediately over the grate—whose area and form are precisely those of the tube plate—gives the type of boiler we are considering an important advantage over the horizontal tubular boiler in the distribution of the heat to the tubes; for it is evident that as each tube, with such an arrangement, must receive the products of combustion from that portion of the grate which lies immediately beneath it, every tube will receive the same quantity of heat, and as all have the same position relatively in solid water and foam, they must all have equal evaporative efficiency and discharge their gases at the same temperature; whereas in the horizontal tubular boiler such equal distribution of the heat is, from the arrangement of the tubes one above the other, impossible, and the heated gases are discharged at temperatures which vary widely for the upper and lower rows owing to the difference of their heat-absorbing efficiencies due to the fact that the upper rows are immersed in mere foam, while the lower ones are surrounded by comparatively solid water. The temperature of the gases as they emerge from the upper rows of horizontal tubes, is frequently high enough to melt zinc (773° Fahr.), while the temperature of those emerging from the lower rows will scarcely melt tin (440° Fahr.).

The type of boiler we are describing is utterly unfit for use with any other than distilled water, on account of the inaccessibility of the tubes. They can neither be examined, nor scaled, nor washed free of mud; while the tube plate forming the crown of the furnace is, from its horizontal position, the recipient of all solid matter in the water, and is exposed to the direct and most intense heat of the fire.

As regards the circulation of water within the boiler, it must be precisely the same as within a dinner-pot, and for the same reason, namely; that the entire horizontal projection of the boiler is placed over a uniform fire of the same form and area, and receives an equal amount of heat on every unit of its surface.

Having thus pointed out the general features of this type of boiler, we will now describe the particular variation invented by Mr. PROSSER.

Description of the Prosser Boiler. (Plate III.)

The point of difference between the multitubular boiler of Mr. PROSSER and others of the same type, consists in the *ensemble* of the tubes and the tube plates. The peculiarity is purely a mechanical one and does not involve any new application of physical principles, nor it is attended with any difference of result as regards the generation of the steam or the combustion of the fuel. The heat is developed and applied to precisely the same kind of surfaces and in the same relative position; and the steam is generated and treated throughout in precisely the same manner as in all boilers of this type.

A conception may be obtained of the PROSSER boiler from the following description of the one experimented on at No. 28 Platt street, New York; reference being had to Plate III., where it will be found represented in complete detail.

First, as regards the tubes and their plates: Suppose a rectangular box or hollow parallelopipedon, 17 inches square and 1¾ inch in height, to be placed immediately over the fire-grate and 19½ inches above it: this box is called by the inventor a hollow slab. Immediately above it and at a distance of 28 inches there is placed a hollow cylinder of 30 inches diameter and 26 inches height: the axis of the cylinder is vertically over the centre of the slab. Into the *upper* side of this slab and *lower* end or base of the cylinder there are fastened twenty-five iron tubes of 2 inches external diameter and 28 inches length in the clear; and through each of these 2 inches tubes—with the exception of the centre one—there is passed an iron tube of 1¼ inch external diameter and 55¾ inches total length, one end of which is fastened into the *lower* side of the slab and the other end into the *upper* end or top of the cylinder. These tubes are thus disposed in

MULTITUBULAR BOILER

Plate III.

at 28 Platt Street, New York City
by
THOMAS PROSSER.

Scale one inch=1foot.

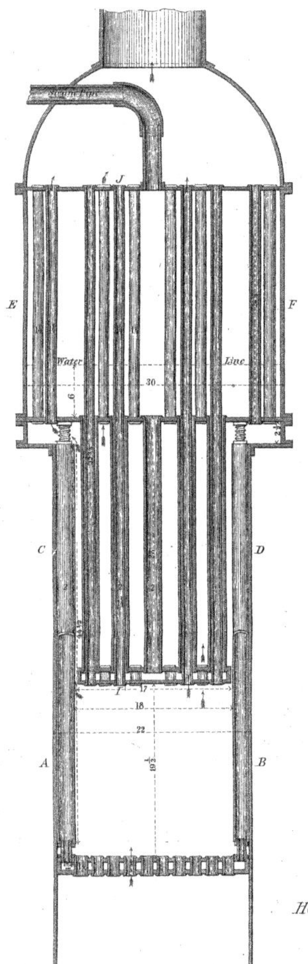

Vertical Section on GH through Axis of Boiler.

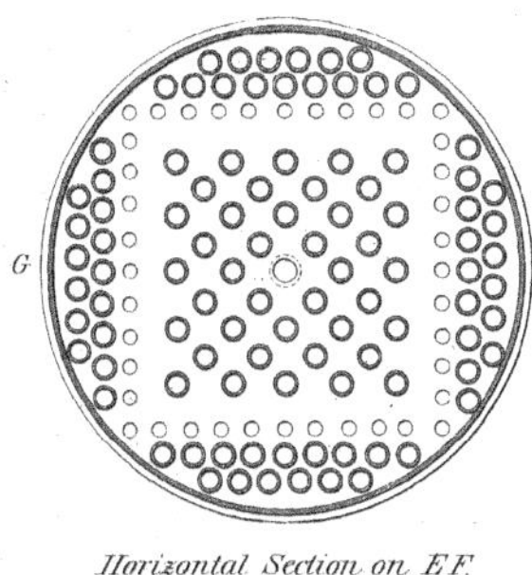

Horizontal Section on E.F.

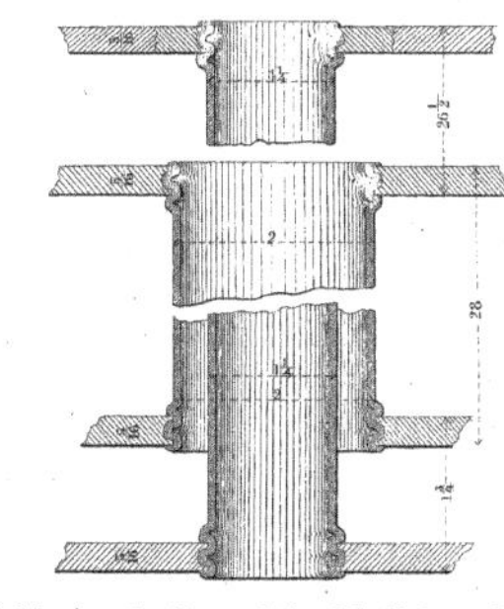

Half size Section of double Tube at I & J
showing movable Screw Plug to allow the fastening of the outer Tube into its plate.

Horizontal Section on C.D.

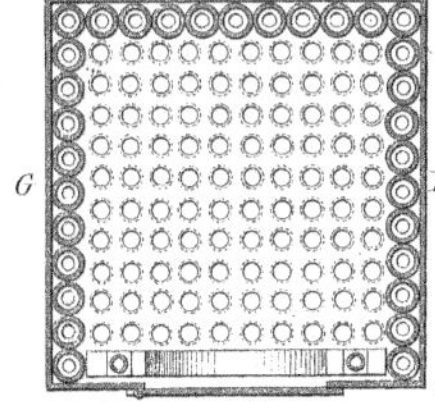

Horizontal Section on A.B showing top view of Water grate.

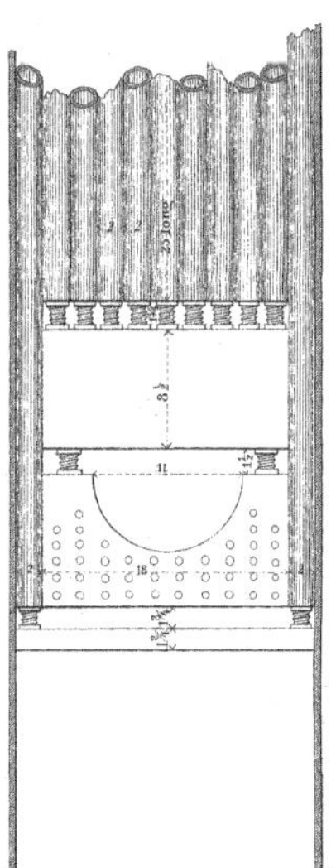

Elevation of Furnace, with door & casing omitted.

Baillière Brothers Publishers 440 Broadway N.Y.

pairs, the tubes of each pair having their axes coincident and forming an annular space between them. The water occupies the interior of the slab, the annular spaces between the 2 and 1¼ inch tubes, and the lower part of the cylinder to the depth of 6 inches: the cylinder may be made of any height required to give the necessary steam space above the water. The 1¼ inch tubes pass, of course, through and through both slab and cylinder.

In order to fasten the ends of the 2 inches tubes to the base of the cylinder and to the upper side of the slab, there must be made in the upper end or the top of the cylinder and immediately opposite to the tubes, holes of about 2¼ inches diameter which, after the 2 inches tubes have been secured to their two plates, are closed by screw plugs into which the upper ends of the 1¼ inch tubes passing through the 2 inches ones, are in their turn fastened. The hollow slab is composed of $\frac{5}{16}$ inch thick iron plate; the top and bottom are got out in separate pieces with an edge turned up on the four sides, these edges are then doweled together by wrought-iron pins and the whole being heated the halves are welded together.

The slab is a little less in horizontal dimensions than the fire-grate immediately over which it is placed; this is requisite in order to allow part of the products of combustion to pass up around the sides and obtain access to the outside of some of the 2 inches tubes. To allow the remainder of these products to reach the outside of the rest of the 2 inches tubes the top and bottom of the slab are perforated and connected across by short vertical tubes or thimbles 1¾ inch long and 1¼ inch external diameter, one of which occupies the centre of each square formed by four 2 inches tubes. In order to carry the products of combustion into the chimney from the space surrounding the 2 inches tubes, the upper and lower ends of the cylinder are similarly connected by iron tubes of 1¼ inch external diameter and 26½ inches length—the height of the cylinder: these tubes are placed vertically immediately over the corresponding ones in the slab beneath, and it is by passing a brush through them that the outside of the 2 inches tubes are swept of soot.

The fire-grate is a hollow parallelopipedon or slab $1\frac{3}{4}$ inch in height and 18 inches square; its top and bottom are perforated and connected directly across by one hundred short vertical tubes or thimbles $1\frac{3}{4}$ inch in length and 1 inch in external diameter. This slab is filled with water and forms a water-grate upon which the combustion of the coal takes place, the air obtaining access to it from the ash-pit beneath through the one hundred thimbles.

A row of iron tubes 2 inches in external diameter and $44\frac{1}{2}$ inches long in the clear, touching along their entire length and having no interval between, is placed around three of the four sides of the water-grate and connected with it so that the interior of the tubes and of the grate communicate. These tubes rise vertically and passing the slab that forms the crown of the furnace, are fastened into the base or lower end of the hollow cylinder; thus joining the water spaces of the grate and cylinder, and forming the sides of the furnace, and enclosing the space around the pairs of tubes between the lower end of the cylinder and the slab that forms the crown of the furnace. Immediately over the fourth side of the grate and separated from it by a space $1\frac{3}{4}$ inch high, is a hollow slab $1\frac{3}{4}$ inch thick, 15 inches wide, and 10 inches high, forming the lower portion of the front of the furnace. This slab contains water, and the two sides of 15 by 10 inches are perforated and connected directly across by forty-two short horizontal tubes or thimbles of $\frac{5}{16}$ inch external diameter and $1\frac{3}{4}$ inch length; through these thimbles air is admitted into the furnace above the solid fuel according to the plan recommended by WILLIAMS. The opening or door for firing the furnace is through this slab, and is a semi-circle of 11 inches diameter, the diameter coinciding with the top of the slab and the curve being below. The space above mentioned of $1\frac{3}{4}$ high which intervenes between the grate and this slab, is for the purpose of slicing up the fires and raking out the ashes and refuse; it also admits air to the solid part of the fuel. Immediately above the hollow slab just described and separated from it by a space of $1\frac{3}{4}$ inch, there is another hollow slab of $1\frac{3}{4}$ inch thick, 15 inches wide, and $8\frac{1}{2}$ inches high, forming the upper portion of the front of the furnace; this slab contains water also and communicates with the one beneath it through two short vertical tubes—one at each end—of 1 inch external diameter and $1\frac{3}{4}$ inch length in the clear. Into the top of this slab and communicating with it, there is fastened a row of vertical iron tubes similar to the row already described around three of the sides of the grate. These tubes are 2 inches in external diameter and 25 inches in length in the clear; they touch each other along their entire length and have their upper ends fastened into the base or lower end of the cylinder, thus joining the water spaces of the two hollow slabs that form the furnace front with the water space of the cylinder, and making the fourth side of the space around the pairs of tubes between the lower end of the cylinder and the slab that forms the crown of the furnace. The rows of 2 inches tubes just described and which form the four sides of the boiler below the cylinder, are fastened at their extremities in the following manner, namely: The ends—top and bottom—are closed up solid; they are then tapped and into them are screwed short pipes $1\frac{3}{4}$ inch long in the clear for the bottom and $2\frac{1}{2}$ inches long in the clear for the top end; the thread is cut upon the whole length of these pipes and before they are screwed into the ends of the tubes two nuts are placed on each pipe; the remaining end of each pipe is then screwed either into the top of the hollow slab or into the base of the cylinder as the case may be, after which the nuts are set up to form a joint. The periphery of the cylinder overhangs the square water-grate slab equally on its four sides, and each projecting segment contains fifteen iron tubes of $1\frac{1}{4}$ inch external diameter and $26\frac{1}{2}$ inches length, through these tubes part of the products of combustion pass on their way to the chimney. These products obtain access to the $1\frac{1}{4}$ inch tubes through the spaces, $\frac{3}{4}$ inch wide by $2\frac{1}{2}$ inches high, between the short pipes which connect the upper ends of the 2 inches tubes with the base or lower end of the cylinder.

The cylinder is surmounted by a hemisphere of the same diameter, and the products of combustion from all the tubes are received into it and discharged through a chimney 12 inches in diameter placed at the summit.

The steam-pipe has an interior diameter of 1½ inch; it rises from the centre of the upper end of the cylinder, describes a quadrantal arc through a portion of the dome, and passes out horizontally to the engine.

The feed-water enters through a pipe of 1 inch diameter which passes entirely through the hollow slab that forms the upper part of the furnace front and discharges into the hollow slab that forms the crown of the furnace. The inventor deems it essential that the feed-water should be received into this particular slab.

The exterior of the vertical rows of 2 inches tubes which form the four sides of the boiler between the cylinder and water-grate, was cased up with boiler plate which descending 16 inches below the grate formed the ash-pit.

The following are the general dimensions and proportions of the boiler. The heat-absorbing surface is calculated for the area acted on by the products of combustion—not the area from which water is evaporated:

Extreme height of the boiler from bottom of ash-pit to top of dome		8.75 feet.
Diameter of the cylindrical part of the boiler (its greatest horizontal dimension)		2.50 "
Contents of a parallelopipedon circumscribing the boiler		54.69 cub. ft.
Area of fire-grate (18 inches square)		2.25 sq. ft.
Water-heating surface on top of water-grate	1.3167 sq. ft.	
" " in hollow slab forming top of furnace	3.7320 " "	
" " " the 1¾ inch long tubes or thimbles in ditto	0.6542 " "	
" " " base or lower end of the cylindrical part of the boiler	4.1180 " "	

Water-heating surface in	2 inches tubes connecting the cylindrical part with the hollow slab forming the top of the furnace	28.6320 sq. ft.
" "	" 1¼ inch tubes inside the above 2 inches tubes	23.5618 " "
" "	" 1¼ inch tubes inside the cylindrical part of the boiler	12.4354 " "
" "	" 2 inches tubes joining water-grate and cylindrical part	35.7853 " "
" "	" hollow slab forming the lower part of the furnace front	1.2639 " "
" "	" hollow slab forming the upper part of the furnace front	1.3889 " "

Total surface in boiler immersed in water and acted on by the products of combustion	112.86 sq. ft.
Total surface in boiler immersed in the steam and acted on by the products of combustion to superheat it (contained in the 1¼ inch tubes in the cylindrical part)	54.40 " "
Minimum calorimeter or aggregate area for the passage of the products of combustion	0.615 " "
Cross-section of the chimney	0.7854 " "
Height of the chimney above the level of the grate	48.5 feet.
Weight of water contained in the boiler at 212° Fahr., at 6 inches above upper end of cylinder	340. pounds.
Capacity of steam-room	6.14 cub. ft.
Area for admission of air through the water-grate	0.69 sq. ft.
Ratio of water-heating surface to grate surface	50.160 to 1.000
" steam superheating surface to grate surface	24.178 " "
" air-openings in grate to total grate surface	0.307 " "
" minimum calorimeter to grate surface	0.273 " "

From the foregoing description of the boiler, it is obvious that its use is only practicable with distilled or absolutely pure water, as its evaporating surfaces are wholly inaccessible. Even river or spring water could not be used, for the slight deposit from it would soon choke up the $\frac{5}{16}$th inch annular space between the double tubes. It is indeed proposed to use it with distilled water only, but as it is manifestly impossible to rely with certainty on the perfect action of any surface-condensing and recuperating mechanism, it would be absurd to adopt a boiler which in the event of a failure of the full supply needed of distilled water would render the machinery useless.

The exteriors of the 2 inches double tubes are very difficult to sweep of soot; and in the event of leaks in most of the tubes, either in their length or joints, it would be impossible to discover the tube or place, and if discovered, the removal of the tube, and its replacement would require a great deal of time and labor, and possibly a degree of skill not always to be commanded.

For marine purposes the height required by this boiler is inadmissible except for vessels of the largest size; the least height in which it could be placed with due regard to cleaning and repairing being 14 feet. It is true that the extreme height of the experimental boiler was 8¾ feet, but in order to sweep its tubes or replace them the dome and chimney had to be removed. This is practicable enough with a boiler whose greatest horizontal dimension is 2½ feet—about that of a large stove—but with boilers of the dimensions required for steamers of the most moderate size, the idea of such an operation is not to be entertained.

The novelty as regards this boiler consists, as has been observed, in the arrangement of the tubes in conjunction with the hollow slabs, by which means the steam pressure for all parts except the hollow cylinder is exerted within 2 inches diameter tubes, upon 1¼ inch and 1 inch diameter tubes, and within hollow rectangular slabs of the very shallow dimension of 1¾ inch in one direction while in the other their flat surfaces are braced about every inch by the tubes themselves. The hollow cylinder itself is, it is plain, precisely the same except in proportions as the hollow slabs; in fact it is a deep, instead of a shallow slab, and round in plan instead of rectangular. If the depth of the hollow cylinder could have been made the same as that of the slabs, namely, $1\frac{3}{4}$ inch, then the whole boiler would have presented a distribution of material which for the weight employed will give the maximum resistance to internal pressure. In fact it may be confidently said, that the arrangement of small tubes in conjunction with shallow hollow slabs as designed by PROSSER, is unapproachable by any other possible distribution of the material for the resistance of internal pressure in cases where a number of tubes is required; and in this respect it is worthy of praise and admiration, and may prove of great utility in the experimental solution of many problems in natural philosophy. The weakest part of the boiler, then, is the deep hollow cylinder containing the steam-room; its weakness lies in its sides and is caused by its depth, for although its two ends are flat surfaces, yet as they are closely braced across by tubes, they present a resistance to bursting pressure equal to that of the tubes themselves. What is the measure of the strength of this hollow cylinder? Is it *ceteris paribus*, in the direct ratio of the diameter? It would be so were it of indefinite length, but as its length is only 26 inches, and as it has solid ends braced rigidly apart at close intervals by stiff tubes so as to be incapable of receding from, or approaching each other without first tearing asunder or crushing them, this ratio will be modified and possibly to a very considerable extent in favor of strength.

Let us examine this matter a little in detail. The problem is one of a hollow cylinder with solid ends braced directly apart, subjected to internal steam pressure. What is the measure of the strength that prevents the cylinder from dividing on two opposite lines parallel with its axis? And what is the measure of the total pressure tending to produce that division? This pressure is evidently measured by the product of the length and diameter of the cylinder and the pressure per unit of surface. The strength is as evidently measured by the area of metal required to be torn directly asunder. What is that area? It would be the sum of the sections through two opposite sides of the cylinder provided the solid ends were absent, but as they are present the cylinder cannot divide on these sections without at the same time dividing the two solid ends on the line of the diameter connecting the sections through the two opposite sides of the cylinder ; hence the strength to resist bursting will be measured by the area of the metal on the two sections of division on the cylindrical surface, and on the two sections of division on the diameter of the ends. Supposing the thickness of the metal of the cylinder to be uniform, then the strength will be in the ratio of twice the length of the cylinder plus twice the diameter of the cylinder, or more simply in the ratio of the sum of the length and diameter of the cylinder, while the bursting pressure will be in the ratio of the product of that length and diameter. We thus perceive that with the cylinder the same in all respects except length, the total bursting pressure will increase in the direct ratio of the length while the strength to resist this pressure will decrease in the ratio of the sum of the diameter and length; hence, as the length of the cylinder is increased, the diameter being constant, there will be a continual decrease of strength, the longest cylinder being the weakest.

In the case of the hollow cylinder of the Prosser boiler, there is a modification of the general law due to the fact that one-half the section of the lower end is cut out by the tubes though they only cut through one-third the section of the upper end ; consequently the strength of this cylinder, which is 26 inches long and 30 inches in diameter, will be measured by $(26+\frac{30}{2}=)$ 41, while by the calculation based on the resistance of the sides alone, it will be, comparatively, 26. The relative strength as by the two methods of calculation, will then be as 26 to 41 or as 100 to 158 nearly, showing a gain of strength of 58 per centum due to the solid ends.

In rapport of strength, the distribution of the materials in the Prosser boiler produces the maximum effect, and is unequaled by any other form; and this, too, without the employment of a single brace. The same arrangement also, incidentally, reduces the weight of contained water to a minimum;

but these advantages are purchased at the expense of accessibility—a fatal price—and would be too dearly paid for by the host of resulting disadvantages. Inaccessibility alone is conclusive against the permanent success of any kind of steam machinery. The pressure of steam to be carried in practice is not regulated by the maximum strength of boiler possible to be obtained, but by many other conditions wholly unconnected with this strength; and in no case yet has the pressure been approximated to the strength of boiler attainable with the usual forms by well known modes of bracing and hooping; consequently the practical value of the superior strength of the Prosser boiler, however desirable in itself, is not great enough to enter as a very important factor in the determination of its adoption.

A description and engraving of a boiler of this type, but having its heating surface arranged in the simplest form, will be found on pages 68 and 69 of the edition of 1852 of the "Treatise on the Steam Engine," originally published by the Artisan Club in 1846. It was employed on board a tug steamer plying on the river Thames. All the tubes extended vertically from the tube-plate which formed the crown of the furnace to the tube-plate which formed the bottom of the smoke connection, and the water, using PROSSER'S proportions, would cover two-thirds of their length leaving one-third for superheating the steam in precisely the same manner as in the Prosser boiler. The steam pressure is wholly on the outside of the tubes which are enveloped by a cylindrical shell of the same diameter as the hollow cylinder of Prosser's boiler, still using his proportions. Now the strength of a boiler is measured by that of its weakest part, and the weakest part of both Prosser's boiler and the one we are describing is this cylinder; but it is the strongest owing to its less length in Prosser's. How much stronger? Employing the proportions of the Prosser boiler, which are as good and as convenient for one variety of the same type of boiler as for the other, the diameter of the cylinder would be the same in both, namely, 30 inches; but its length, which is only 26 inches with PROSSER'S, would with the other boiler be 77 inches, which is the length from the top of the cylinder to the bottom of the fire-grate with PROSSER'S, and cutting out equal portions of the solid ends for the tubes, we shall have, with equal pressure and thickness of metal, the strength represented by ($77+\frac{30}{2}=$) 92; while by the calculation based on the resistance of the sides alone, it will be comparatively 77. The relative strength by the two modes of calculation will then be as 77 to 92 or as 100 to 120, showing a gain of only 20 per centum, while with the Prosser boiler this gain was, as we have seen, 58 per centum. Again, taking the strength of the cylinder in the Prosser boiler to be represented by 41 as before determined, the pressure may be represented by the product of its diameter and length, namely ($30\times26=$) 780, and the division of the former by the latter will give ($\frac{41}{780}=$) .0526. In the same manner the strength of the cylinder of the other boiler being represented by 92 and the pressure as before by the product of its diameter and length, namely, ($30\times77=$) 2310, we obtain by dividing the former by the latter ($\frac{92}{2310}=$) .0399. Hence the relative strengths of the cylinder in the two boilers will be as .0526 to .0399, which is an excess of strength in favor of PROSSER'S of ($\frac{.0526-.0399\times100}{.0399}=$) 33 per centum.

This boiler requires the same height as PROSSER'S, and it contains more water ; but a considerably larger amount of grate and heating surface can be placed within the same circumscribing parallelopipedon, using tubes of the same diameter. The tubes can be easily swept of soot, and removed, and replaced ; and if a leakage occur it can at once be discovered. The whole boiler, in fact, from the greater simplicity of its construction contains in a given circumscribing parallelopipedon more power, is cheaper to make and repair, and is practically attended with the least trouble and inconvenience. If such a type of boiler were to be employed, this arrangement is preferable to PROSSER'S, but neither is admissable for marine purposes.

The boiler of the tug steamer just described exploded, as was reasonably to be anticipated as it used the water of the river Thames and could neither be examined nor scaled. Previously much difficulty was caused by the cracking of the lower tube-plate between the tubes.

The Prosser boiler has now been in use about 20 months for 10 hours of each day excepting Sundays, and it shows no appearance of deterioration, but it has always been supplied wholly with distilled water.

The conditions controlling the advantages to be derived from the use of superheated steam have yet to be discovered by experience. No attempts to use it have thus far been permanently successful, and it is doubtful whether under any circumstances it can judiciously be carried very far on account of the practical inconveniences resulting from the high temperature. When the heating surface of the boiler is insufficient to properly absorb the heat of the products of combustion, and they pass off at a very high temperature causing a great waste of fuel, then the addition of more surface even in the steam room is beneficial, as whatever additional heat is extracted by the steam is so much clear gain. The addition of the tubes of the superheating apparatus increases by their capacity the steam room of the boiler and goes to mitigate the evil of priming; this is in itself a great advantage with boilers of limited steam room; besides which the water primed over lodges in these tubes and is there evaporated into steam, and the waste heat from the boiler tubes proper is thus profitably applied to the production of more steam as well as to the superheating of that which has already been generated. But in properly proportioned boilers of good type where the heating surface is large enough to absorb all the heat from the products of combustion excepting what is necessary to produce the draught, and where the steam room is high enough and capacious enough to prevent priming, there will brobably be found but little advantage in reducing the temperature of the products of combustion to the same degree by less heating surface in water and superheating the steam. It is only badly proportioned boilers that can be made to give greatly increased results by superheating their steam.

Description of the Steam Engine by means of which the following Experiments were made with the Prosser Boiler.

The steam engine with which the experiments on the Prosser boiler were made, consisted of one vertical cylinder fitted with an unpacked short slide steam valve, and a slide expansion valve working on a separate seat immediately in front of the steam valve; both moved vertically and were actuated by eccentrics. In front of the expansion valve and close to it, was a butterfly throttle valve controlled by a governor; and in the steam pipe, but at a considerable distance from this throttle, there was another controlled by hand; both were in use during the experiments. The cylinder had no relief valves for discharging the water resulting from condensation of steam in it. The steam pipe was about ten feet in length and composed of 1¾ inch diameter gas pipe; it was well protected by felt, as was also the feed pipe to the boiler; but the cylinder itself was uncovered. The hollow cylinder of the boiler containing the steam was well felted. The Indicator was attached to the cylinder top and bottom by pipes of a few inches in length.

The engine had a Surface Condenser but no air-pump, and in addition to this condenser for condensing the exhaust steam there was a Still Condenser of the same construction for replacing with distilled water the feed water lost by leakage. There was yet another vessel (the duplicate of the Still Condenser) attached to the condensing apparatus and called the Heater Condenser into which the steam was first exhausted from the cylinder and through which it passed on its way to the Main Condenser. The water of condensation from the Main Condenser and the recuperative supply from the Still Condenser, were drawn off by the feed pump, and forced through the Heater Condenser in order to obtain from the exhaust steam an increase of temperature before entering the boiler. There was no circulating pump for supplying the injection water, which was obtained from the Croton Acqueduct and ran off by its gravity after reaching the overflow pipe in the condenser. The back pressure in the condenser against which the steam from the cylinder exhausted, was always greater than that of the atmosphere, but by giving a sufficient supply of injection water it could be reduced below that of the atmosphere; for it was impossible that any air could become mixed with the steam unless it were condensed below the atmospheric pressure, and there happened at the same time to be a leakage in the exhaust pipe. The engine, therefore, used steam of high pressure with expansion and condensation, but without an air-pump and exhausting against a greater than the atmospheric pressure; and it fed its boiler with distilled water of a temperature closely approximating the corresponding boiling point.

The experiments, as has been already stated, embraced the condensing apparatus as well as the Boiler, but as this paper is devoted to the latter alone, the former is only so far described as is incidental and necessary to the understanding of the experiments with the former.

The following are the dimensions of the cylinder and appendages, namely:—

Diameter of the cylinder..............	8.	inches.
Diameter of the piston rod............	1.5	"
Stroke of the piston...................	18.	"
Point at which the expansion valve closes from the commencement of the stroke of piston....................	5.08	"
Space displacement of the piston per double stroke, exclusive of piston rod.	1777.8	cubic inches.
Space comprised at both ends of cylinder in clearance........................	25.0	" "
Space comprised at both ends of cylinder in passages from clearance to steam valve.........................	49.5	" "

Space comprised in the valve chest between the steam and expansion valves.	65.5 cubic inches.
Bulk of steam of the pressure at the end of the stroke, used per double stroke of engine piston..................	1.07193 cubic ft.

Mode of Conducting the Experiments and Calculating the Results.

The entire machinery was situated in the cellar of house No. 28 Platt street, New York city, and was not exposed to currents of air.

Thermometers were placed in deep narrow cups filled with mercury, and the cups were inserted in the steam and water spaces of the boiler,—in the top of the Main Condenser,—and in the feed-pipe between the Heater Condenser and the boiler. They indicated respectively the temperature of the superheated steam, the temperature of the water from which that steam was generated, the temperature of the vapor rising from the injection or condensing water at the locus of its discharge from the Main Condenser, and the temperature of the feed-water entering the boiler. These thermometers were large and excellent instruments made expressly for the purpose and graduated to the Centigrade scale, but for the sake of convenience, their indications have been reduced to Fahrenheit's scale. The temperature of the injection water before entering the condenser, and of the engine and boiler room, were also noted by thermometers. In the experiments of April 28th and 29th, and May 2d, the feed-water was drawn from the Main Condenser and emptied into a Tank whence it was taken by the feed-pump and driven through the Heater Condenser into the boiler. During these experiments the temperature of the water in the Tank was noted by a thermometer in addition to the other temperatures.

The steam pressure in the boiler, and the back pressure of vapor in the Main Condenser against which the steam from the cylinder exhausted, were given by large manometer gauges. The Indicator used was an excellent instrument and diagrams were taken from both ends of the cylinder: average specimens of these diagrams will be found in Plate IV. The number of double strokes made by the piston was registered by a Counter worked by the engine itself.

The fuel used was the first quality of Trevorton coal, a dry free-burning Semi-Anthracite from middle Pennsylvania, destitute of bitumen, burning without smoke, and containing but little earthy matter: in steam generating value it stands in the first class of coals. The quantity consumed was carefully weighed by a steelyard, as was also the waste in ashes and fine coal in a dry state.

As the regular work of the establishment required only about one-third of the power that the machinery could produce, there was added during the experiments the resistance of a friction brake, which possessed the further advantage of rendering the load more uniform.

The injection, or condensing water, was obtained from the Croton Aqueduct supplying the city, which furnishing any quantity required by its own head alone rendered the employment of a circulating-pump unnecessary.

The duration of the experiments was necessarily limited by the working hours per diem of the establishment. In making them no account was taken of the coal required to raise steam to the working pressure; but at the commencement of each experiment the condition of the fire was estimated by the eye, and the height of the water in the boiler and the pressure of the steam carefully noted: at the end of each experiment the water and steam were left the same as at the commencement, as was also the condition of the fire as nearly as could be judged. During the continuance of each experiment a complete set of observations and an Indicator diagram were taken every fifteen minutes, the mean of all which together with the results of the calculations made from them, will be found in the subjoined table. It would have been more satisfactory could the experiments have been continued through a greater number of *consecutive* hours, so as to have diminished the effects of error in the estimation of the condition of the fire at the commencement and end; but if the size of the grate be considered—only 18 inches square—it will be admitted that on so small a space the eye could closely estimate ; beside which the precaution was taken to fire at regular intervals very nearly the same weight of coal up to the last; it is, therefore, believed that full confidence can be placed in the amount of coal consumed as well as in the other elements of the experiments.

The experiments were made on the 18th, 19th, 28th, and 29th days of April, and on the 2d day of May, on each of which the conditions were varied. With the experiments made April 18th, 19th, and May 2d,—embraced in the first three columns of the subjoined table,—the steam was used expansively: with the remaining experiments made April 28th and 29th, the steam was used without expansion: in all it was very much throttled.

The experiment of April 28th was made with the maximum weight of coal the furnace would consume; and the experiment of May 2d, was made with the highest mean pressure on the piston that the friction brake would be loaded to: could the brake have borne a greater strain the power developed by the engine might have been increased about 25 per centum, or up to 11½ horses per Indicator.

The weight of water evaporated has been calculated from the pressure per Indicator in the cylinder at the end of the stroke of piston for all the experiments: and for the experiments of April 28th and 29th, and May 2d, the evaporation was also obtained by measurement of the water in a Tank, previous to its being pumped into the boiler. To the weight of water evaporated by calculation from the steam pressure at the end of the stroke of the piston, there has been added the weight of steam condensed in the cylinder to produce the power developed by the engine. It has been calculated according to Joule's equivalent of one pound of water raised one degree on Fahrenheit's scale for every 772 foot-pounds developed by the engine. In making these calculations the tables of REGNAULT have been used, and the weight of a cubic foot of water at 62° Fahr. has been taken at 62.321 pounds.

In obtaining the evaporation by Tank measurement, the feed pipe was put in communication with a Tank or reservoir, into which was carefully measured by a standard gallon measure of 231 cubic inches, all the water of condensation furnished by the Main Condenser. This water was drawn from the condenser by hand by means of a pipe and cock, and the usual feed-pump delivered it into the boiler after passing it through the Heater Condenser in order to give it an increase of temperature as it rapidly cooled in the open Tank. When the Tank was employed, the Still Condenser was not used, and the deficit of feed water was made good by measuring into the tank the requisite quantity of Croton water as needed.

Whence came this deficit? During the experiments, the pressure on the exhaust steam side of the condensing tubes in the Main Condenser varied from 0 to 6 pounds per square inch above the atmosphere, mean 1½ pound; the pressure of the injection water on the opposite side of these tubes was a little above that of the atmosphere at the top of the condenser and about 1¼ pound per square inch above it at the bottom; the probability of leakage from the exhaust steam to the injection water side of the condenser was thus very small even had the tubes not been tight, and there was no reason to believe they were not. Now had the boiler and feed pipe also been tight, it is plain that no recuperative supply of feed water would have been required, for were there there no loss by leakage the condensation of the exhaust steam would afford exactly the required amount of feed, and the same water would pass in a continuous round from condenser to boiler in the liquid form, and from boiler to condenser in the form of vapor. The boiler was set upon four legs upon a brick platform with a clear passage way all around it, so that any external leakage could not have escaped detection, but none appeared; nevertheless, it was found that not only was there a deficit in the feed water but that it increased with the boiler pressure. In fact there was no doubt that sensibly the whole of this deficit was due to leakage from the boiler and internally, and probably from the fastenings of the 2 inches diameter tubes joining the hollow cylinder and the slab forming the crown of the furnace; and also from the joints in the base of the hollow cylinder of some of the 1¼ inch diameter tubes employed for superheating the steam. Neither the joints of these 2 inches and 1¼ inch diameter tubes, nor the surrounding spaces, could be seen, and from the construction of the boiler they were the most likely to be defective. The quantity of water leaked was so small that it could easily be evaporated by the heated gases as rapidly as it exuded, consequently, as it did not run down into the furnace, there was no means of discovering it by the eye. Of course, as the evaporation of this weight of water was effected by the fuel, it must be credited to the boiler the same as though it had been evaporated normally from the heating surfaces; and the steam generated from it must have materially increased the draught of the chimney. During the experiment of April 28th, the deficit of feed water was 4.85 per centum of the whole quantity pumped into the boiler, and the boiler pressure was 101.2 pounds per square inch above the atmosphere. During the experiments of April 29th, when the boiler pressure was 112 pounds, this deficit became 6.38 per centum. And during the experiments of May 2d, when the boiler pressure was increased to 137.9 pounds, this deficit rose to 7.89 per centum. In the calculation by the evaporation by Tank measurement, as given in the subjoined table, these deficits are included; and the proper corrections for differences of temperature have been made throughout.

The results in rapport of fuel have been given both for the pound of coal consumed and for the pound of combustible, the latter being the former less the waste in ashes and fine coal. The pound of combustible is, of course, the proper unit by which to measure the cost, because the waste is a quantity variable from many causes. In all the experiments

TABLE exhibiting the DATA and RESULTS of the EXPERIMENTS with the MULTITUBULAR BOILER, of THOMAS PROSSER.

		Using the steam expansively, cutting-off at 0.28 of the Stroke of Piston from the commencement.			Using the Steam without Expansion.	
		April 18.	April 19.	May 2.	April 28.	April 29.
	Duration of the Experiments in Hours and Minutes	7 .. 0	10 .. 0	7 .. 0	6 .. 18	8 .. 0
	Total number of Double Strokes made by the Piston	24,783	34,565	16,933	20,311	21,420
	Mean " " " per Minute	59.00	57.61	40.31	53.71	44.63
PRESSURES. per Gauge.	Mean pressure in pounds per square inch above the atmosphere of the Steam in the Boiler	106.0	101.3	137.9	101.2	112.00
	" " " " " " " Vapor in the Condenser	3.1	2.0	1.2	0.4	0.4
per Indicator.	" " " " " " " Steam in the Cylinder at the commencement of the stroke	59.2	65.0	94.0	38.3	39.0
	" " " " " " " " " " point of cutting-off	43.9	46.7	77.3	——	——
	" " " " " " " " " " end of the Stroke	9.8	12.0	24.5	26.6	28.6
	" " " " " " " Back pressure in the Cylinder against the Piston	6.1	4.9	3.5	1.6	1.9
	Gross Mean effective pressure on the Piston during its stroke in pounds per square inch	21.8	25.8	51.4	27.5	29.4
	Gross Horses Power developed by the Engine	5.774	6.672	9.302	6.634	5.890
COAL.	Total number of Pounds of Trevorton Semi-Anthracite Coal consumed	177	275	216	237	257
	" " Refuse in Ashes and Fine Coal unburned	19	35	25	42	40
	Per Centum of the Refuse in Ashes and Fine Coal unburned	10.74	12.73	11.58	17.72	15.56
	Number of Pounds of Coal consumed per Hour per square Foot of Grate surface	11.25	12.22	13.71	16.72	14.28
	" " Combustible " " " " "	10.03	10.66	12.12	13.75	12.05
	" " Coal " " Horse-Power developed by the Engine	4.382	4.122	3.317	5.671	5.454
	" " Combustible " " " " " "	3.905	3.597	2.933	4.666	4.605
TEMPERATURES.	Mean Temperature in Degrees Fahrenheit of the Engine and Boiler Room	76	77	74	70	77
	" " " " " Condensing Water when entering the Condenser	50	51	55	52	53
	" " " " " " " " leaving " "	212	203	214	212	212
	" " " " " Water in the Boiler	346	343	365	343	350
	" " " " " Steam " " (superheated)	380	374	392	382	376
	" " " " " Feed-Water when entering the Boiler	207	200	187	178	184
	" " " " " " " in the Tank	——	——	132	123	130
EVAPORATION.	Number of Pounds of Steam evaporated from the temperature of the feed-water, discharged from the Cylinder into the Condenser; calculated from the pressure of the Steam at the end of the stroke of Piston	1,556.01	2,348.53	1,634.67	2,057.38	2,267.37
	Number of Pounds of Steam evaporated from the temperature of the feed-water, equivalent to the heat annihilated in the Cylinder to produce the Power of the Engine; calculated from JOULE'S equivalent	102.54	168.28	161.12	103.16	116.76
	Total number of Pounds of Steam evaporated from a temperature of Feed Water of 212° Fahr.; by INDICATOR measurement	1,666.79	2,546.86	1,840.17	2,233.63	2,450.42
	" " " " " " " " " " 100° " " " "	1,499.81	2,291.47	1,656.74	2,009.68	2,205.16
	" " " " " " " " " " 212° " " TANK "	——	——	2,492.11	2,555.62	2,836.74
	" " " " " " " " " " 100° " " " "	——	——	2,243.68	2,299.39	2,552.81
ECONOMIC RESULTS.	Pounds of Steam evaporated from a temperature of Feed-Water of 212° Fahr., by One Pound of COAL, by INDICATOR measurement	9.417	9.261	8.519	9.424	9.535
	" " " " " " " " " " " " " " TANK "	——	——	11.538	1^.783	11.038
	" " " " " " " 100° " " " " " INDICATOR "	8.474	8.333	7.670	8.480	8.580
	" " " " " " " " " " " " " TANK "	——	——	10.388	9.702	9.933
	" " " " " " " 212° " " " " COMBUSTIBLE, " INDICATOR "	10.550	10.612	9.634	11.454	11.292
	" " " " " " " " " " " " " TANK "	——	——	13.048	13.106	13.072
	" " " " " " " 100° " " " " " INDICATOR "	9.492	9.548	8.674	10.306	10.162
	" " " " " " " " " " " " " TANK "	——	——	11.747	11.792	11.764

See Page 111.

Plate IV.

INDICATOR DIAGRAMS.

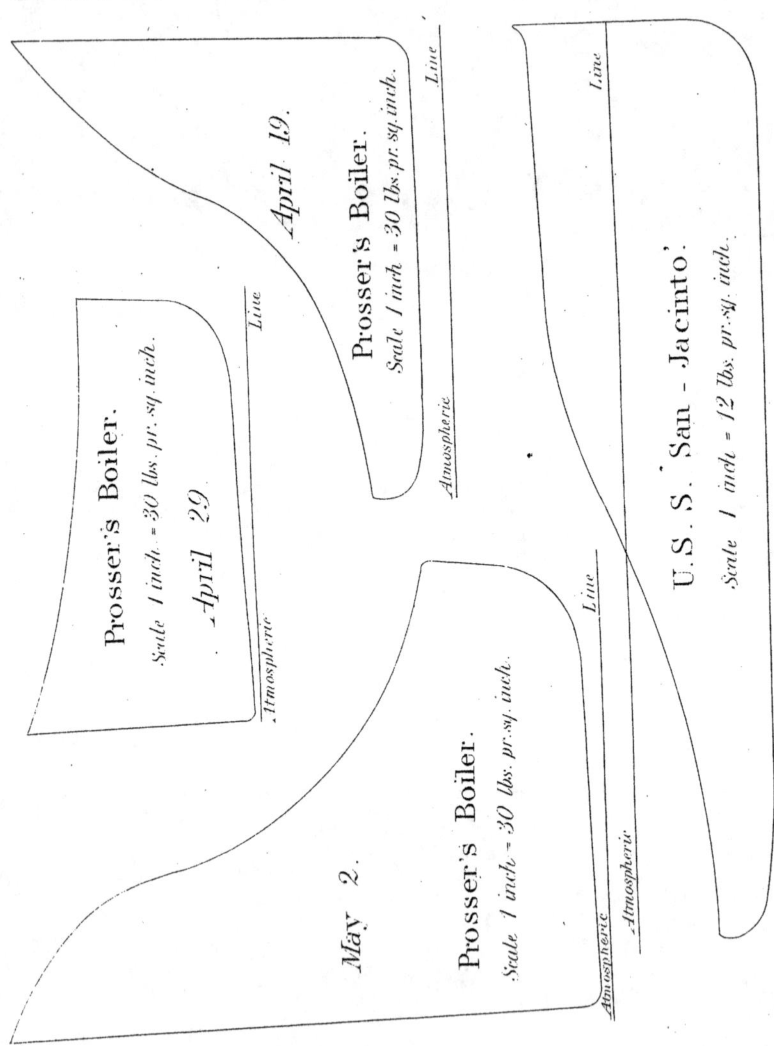

the coal was precisely the same, there was not a particle of clinker formed, and the earthy matter probably did not vary sensibly. The difference in the per centum of waste found, was due to the greater quantity of fine coal falling through the one inch diameter holes of the grate, when more rapid combustion was maintained by more slicing of the fire. It will be observed that the per centum of waste increased with the rate of consumption of coal per square foot of grate per hour. As, in experiments of this kind, the evaporation is sometimes measured from a temperature of feed water of 100° Fahr. and sometimes from a temperature of 212° Fahr. it has been calculated for both for convenience of comparison.

The data by the experiments and the evaporation by the boiler, obtained and calculated in the manner described, will be found in the subjoined table:—

Results of the Experiments.

An observation of the particulars of the preceding Table shows, that on different days—the conditions being different—the indicated horse-power was obtained by very different weights of combustible consumed per hour. It will be useful to investigate the causes producing this result in the cases of the three experiments during which the steam was used expansively; for in the cases of the two experiments in which it was used without expansion, the difference in the conditions being very slight, there was but a correspondingly slight difference in this result.

What are the different conditions of those experiments that influence the final result, and in what degree did they affect it? They are:—1st. The ratio borne by the gross mean pressure on the piston above zero to the back pressure against it; for it is only their differential that constitutes the pressure element of the indicated horse-power; but the fuel consumed is the same, *pro rata*, for the back pressure as for the portion of the mean gross pressure utilized, consequently the higher this ratio the greater will be the economic effect of the fuel. 2nd. The gain due to the employment of steam of higher pressure, which consists in the fact that the pressure of steam increases in a higher ratio than its density while the evaporation of equal weights under different pressures requires, within the limits of our experiments, sensibly equal weights of combustible; consequently the higher the pressure used the greater will be the economic result from the fuel. In considering this condition, however, we must keep in mind that the gain just described applies not to the steam as generated in the boiler but as used in the cylinder; hence, in any determination of its value for different cases, we must compare the mean pressures on the piston above zero during the whole stroke, and not the boiler pressures. 3d. The temperature of the feed-water; for of the total quantity of heat required to be imparted to the feed-water to convert it into steam, there is furnished by the fuel only the differential of the heat of the feed-water and the total heat of the boiler steam generated from it; the higher the temperature, therefore, of the feed-water the greater will be the economic effect of the fuel. 4th. The relative evaporative efficiency of the pound of combustible in the different experiments as measured by the Indicator—not by the Tank—because the indicated horse-power is produced by only that portion of the steam which remains such throughout the stroke of the piston and propels it from one end of the cylinder to the other, and that portion is what is measured by the Indicator but cannot be by the Tank. The higher this evaporative efficiency, the greater will obviously be the economic effect of the fuel. Let us now ascertain the value for each of these conditions and observe if the ratio of the economic results from the fuel in the different cases as determined by them, is the same as given by a direct comparison of the weight of combustible consumed per hour per indicated horse-power.

Beginning then with the experiment of April 18th, we have (referring to the Table) for the mean pressure on the piston above zero (21.8+14.7+6.1 =) 42.6 pounds per square inch; and for the back pressure (14.7+6.1 =) 20.8 pounds; the portion of the mean pressure utilized will then be $\left(\frac{42.6-20.8 \times 100}{42.6}=\right)$ 51.17 per centum.

With the experiment of April 19th, the mean pressure on the piston above zero was (25.8+14.7+4.9 =) 45.4 pounds per square inch; and the back pressure was (14.7+4.9=) 19.6 pounds; the portion of the mean pressure utilized will then be $\left(\frac{45.4-19.6 \times 100}{45.4}=\right)$ 56.83 per centum.

With the experiment of May 2d, the mean pressure on the piston above zero was (51.4+14.7+3.5 =) 69.6 pounds per square inch; and the back pressure was (14.7+3.5 =) 18.2 pounds; the portion of the mean pressure utilized will then be $\left(\frac{69.6-18.2 \times 100}{69.6}=\right)$ 73.85 per centum.

These per centum of utilization have now to be modified for the ratio of the density of the steam to its pressure in the respective cases. The density is expressed relatively by the volume of steam of the given pressure to the volume of water from which it was generated. This pressure is the mean pressure on the piston throughout the stroke above zero. The products resulting from the multiplication of the volumes by the respective pressures will give, relatively, the gain in fuel due to the use of higher pressure steam *per se.* During the experiment of April 18th, the mean pressure on the piston above zero was 42.6 pounds per square inch, as above shown, the volume due to which is 640.6 and 640.6×42.6=27289.56. During the experiment of April 19th, this pressure was 45.4 pounds, and the corresponding volume 605.2, and 605.2×45.4 =27476.08. During the experiment of May 2d, this pressure was 69.6 pounds, the volume corresponding to which was 416.0, and 416.0×69.6 = 28953.60. Multiplying the per centum of pressure utilized in the respective cases by these quotients, we have (51.17×27289.56=) 1396406.7852, (56.83×27476.08=) 1561465.6264, and (73.85×28953.60=) 2138223.3600.

These products in their turn require modification according to the different temperatures of feed water in their respective cases. In the first case that temperature was 207° Fahr., and as the total heat of the steam of the boiler pressure was 1218° Fahr., there were required (1218—207=) 1011° Fahr. to be imparted to the feed water to convert it into steam. Making the calculation in the same manner in the second and third cases, we have respectively 1017° and 1036° Fahr. required to convert the feed water into steam of the respective boiler pressures. These degrees are in the inverse ratio of 1.0000, 0.9941, and 0.9759; and multiplying the final products of the immediately preceding paragraph by these numbers respectively, we have (1396406.7852×1.0000=) 1396406.7852, (1561465.6264×0.9941=) 1552252.9792, and (2138223.3600×0.9759=) 2086692.1770.

Finally, these numbers have to be modified in the ratio of the evaporative efficiency of the pound of combustible per Indicator measurement in their respective cases, namely:

10.580, 10.646, and 9.682, multiplying by which we obtain (1396406.7852×10.580 =) 14773983.7874, (1552252.9792×10.646 =) 16525285.2166, and (2086692.1770×9.682 =) 20203353.6577, which are in the ratio of 1.000, 1.118, and 1.367.

In these cases the cost of the Indicated horse-power in pounds of combustible per hour, was 3.905, 3.597, and 2.933, which inversely are in the ratio of 1.000, 1.086, and 1.332, which is nearly the ratio of 1.000, 1.118, and 1.367, as just obtained. If, however, we compare the last two numbers of both ratios, we shall have $\frac{1.367}{1.118}=1.2227$ and $\frac{1.332}{1.086}=1.2265$, or sensibly the same. These results, therefore, closely verify each other.

In comparing the results of the experiments of April 19th and May 2d, in both of which the steam was used expansively but with widely differing pressures, we observed a very strongly marked fact, namely; that the evaporative efficiency of the pound of combustible per Indicator measurement decreases in some ratio as the steam pressure in the cylinder increases; and that too, notwithstanding the superheating of the steam in the boiler about 30° Fahr. in both cases: this effect is unquestionably due to the following circumstances, namely: The temperature of the interior surfaces of the cylinder during the exhaust stroke remains nearly the same, but as the temperature of the steam increases with its pressure, there must necessarily be when steam of a higher pressure is employed, a greater condensation of it *pro rata* due to the greater difference of the temperatures of these interior surfaces during the steam and exhaust strokes. Also, the leakage of steam past the piston and the cylinder valves is greater with the higher pressure. And, finally, the loss of heat by radiation from the external surfaces of boiler, steam pipe, and cylinder, will be greater, too, with the higher temperature steam. Of none of these losses does the Indicator measurement take any account; that instrument shows only the weight of steam in the cylinder at any point of the stroke of the piston *at that particular instant of time;* it does not show any of the losses sustained by the steam since its generation in the boiler. The *apparent* evaporation by Indicator measurement may therefore vary greatly, according as these losses have been greater or less, while the *true* evaporation continues precisely the same.

If, now, in the experiments of April 19th and May 2d, we compare the boiler pressures, we shall find them to be 100.3 and 137.9 pounds per square inch above the atmosphere, the the temperatures corresponding to which are 342½° Fahr. and 366½° Fahr., difference 24° Fahr., consequently, there must have been a greater loss on the 2d in radiation from the external surfaces of the boiler and steam pipe due to this difference of temperature; and there must also have been a greater loss by leakage from the boiler due to the difference of (137.9—100.3 =) 37.6 pounds pressure per square inch above the atmosphere. If we compare the mean pressures in the cylinder during the stroke of the piston we shall find that on the 19th, that pressure was (25.8+14.7+4.9 =) 45.4 pounds per square inch above zero, the temperature corresponding to which is 277° Fahr.; the back pressure was (14.7+4.9 =) 19.6 pounds per square inch above zero, the temperature corresponding to which is 227° Fahr.; the difference then of the temperatures of the interior surfaces of the cylinder during the steam and exhaust strokes was (277—227 =) 50° Fahr. On the 2d, the mean pressure in the cylinder was (51.4+14.7+3.5 =) 69.6 pounds per square inch above zero, with a corresponding temperature of 305½° Fahr.; the back pressure was (14.7+3.5 =) 18.2 pounds per square inch above zero with a temperature of 223½° Fahr.; the difference then of the temperature of the steam and exhaust strokes in this case was (305½—223½ =) 82° Fahr., or nearly one and two-thirds the difference on the 19th. Of course, there must have been a much greater cylinder condensation in the latter than in the former experiments, for a difference of (82—50 =) 32° Fahr. of temperature possesses, *ceteris paribus*, a very serious condensing power. In addition to this difference of temperature there was the difference of leakage past the cylinder valves and piston due to the difference between the mean effective pressures of 51.4 and 25.8 pounds per square inch, or in one case double the other. Under these conditions the evaporation per Indicator measurement of the pound of combustible in the two cases was, from a temparature of feed water of 212° Fahr., 10.612 and 9.634 pounds of water; the loss of the high pressure due to the cause above stated being $\left(\frac{10.612-9.634 \times 100}{10.612}=\right)$ $9\frac{1}{5}$ per centum of the evaporation with the low pressure. How much of this is caused by the greater condensation effected by the greater difference of the temperatures of the interior surfaces of the cylinder during the steam and exhaust strokes it is impossible to determine, but be it what portion it may, it would, of course, have been greater had the steam not been superheated, for one effect of that superheating is to impart during the steam stroke the heat to the interior surfaces of the cylinder which is abstracted during the exhaust stroke, without reducing the normal heat of the steam for its pressure as received from the boiler. Were the superheating sufficient to produce this effect there could be no loss from condensation; though there would be in the pressure of the steam considered as a fixed gas, due to the reduction of the superheated temperature and amounting to $\frac{1}{490.463\text{th}}$ for each degree Fahr.

In observing the evaporation per pound of combustible by Tank measurement, we find it to have been sensibly the same in all cases, whether the steam be used with higher or lower pressure, or with expansion or without it; and this is as it should be, for the Tank measurement gives the true evaporation except in so far as it affected by external water leakage from the boiler, and from the priming over of the water from the boiler to the cylinder. When, therefore, in different cases these causes operate to the same extent or not at all, the results will agree. Now as regards priming or the passage of *solid* water from the boiler to the cylinder, there could have been none; because, independently of the superheating of the steam, the disparity of the bulks of the steam within the boiler and of the steam withdrawn per stroke of piston was too great to allow it. When the steam was used expansively the boiler contained about thirty-five charges for the cylinder, and as the pressure in the cylinder at the point of cutting-off was only about two-thirds of the boiler pressure these thirty-five charges became over fifty charges. When the steam was used without expansion, the boiler contained about twelve charges for the cylinder which, as the cylinder pressure at the end of the stroke was only about four-tenths of the boiler pressure, became thirty charges. The mean of the experiments by Tank measurement gives an evaporation per pound of combustible of $13\frac{1}{12}$ pounds of water from a temperature of 212° Fahr.

If, however, we observe the evaporations per pound of combustible by Indicator measurement, we shall find under the different conditions of the different experiments, very great discrepancies, and not only between the results as compared with the Tank measurement but as compared with themselves. There has been already shown in comparing the results of the experiments of April 19th and May 2d, the causes producing a difference of 9 per centum in the evaporation per Indicator measurement, but there still remains other facts of interest to be observed in this matter.

And first, as regards the difference in the Indicator evaporation when, *ceteris paribus*, the steam is used with and without expansion. To determine this we may compare the mean of the results of the experiments of April 18th and 19th when using the steam expansively, with the mean of the results of the experiments of April 28th and 29th when using the steam without expansion; the difference of the boiler and cylinder pressures not being great enough to cause any marked difference of result. The mean boiler pressure during the experiments of the 18th and 19th was 103.15 pounds per square inch above the atmosphere, and the mean effective pressure on the piston was 23.8 pounds per square inch. During the experiments of the 28th and 29th, the mean boiler pressure was 106.6 pounds per square inch above the atmosphere, and the mean effective pressure on the piston was 28.45 pounds per square inch. The difference between the respective quantities in the two cases is too little to much affect the result by difference of leakage, of radiation, and of condensation by the interior surfaces of the cylinder. There remains then only the effect of the expansion of the steam *per se* to ascribe it to. Now the mean evaporation per pound of combustible by Indicator measurement was for the experiments of April 18th and 19th, when the steam was used expansively $(\frac{10.550+10.612}{2}=)$ 10.581 pounds of water from a temperature of 212° Fahr.; while during the experiments of April 28th and 29th when the steam was used without expansion this evaporation was $(\frac{11.454+11.292}{2}=)$ 11.373 pounds of water; the difference being (11.373—10.581=) 0.792 pound, or $(\frac{11.373-10.581\times 100}{10.581}=)$ 7½ per centum of the evaporation using the steam expansively. This difference would, of course, have been much greater had the steam not been superheated; for it is unquestionably produced by the condensation due to the fact of expansion *per se*. In explanation of this it may be remarked, that all bodies in expanding absorb heat, and that particularly in the case of steam this absorption is attended by a great condensation which propagates and exaggerates itself. The first effect of the expansion is an increase of the latent and a decrease of the sensible heat of the steam, whence follows a precipitation of a corresponding portion of the steam into water. This conversion of part of the steam into water occupying a greatly less bulk, leaves space for a further expansion of the steam followed by the inevitably accompanying condensation, which in its turn causes another expansion followed by another condensation, and so on till all be condensed. The only means of preventing this result is to superheat the steam, and as this was done in the case of our experiments to the extent of about 30° Fahr., it must have prevented the condensation to a considerable degree, though not completely so, as we have seen from the experimental results. A portion of the steam condensed during the first moments of expansion is undoubtedly recovered by reëvaporation under the lessened pressure towards the close of the stroke of the piston, as is shown by the greater pressures at the end of the stroke than is due to the measure of expansion employed ; a large part of this latter effect is, however, unquestionably due to the leakage of the valves, but the final result is, as has been stated, a very serious loss inherent to the fact of expansion and taking place notwithstanding the superheating given to the steam before it entered the cylinder. The greater the measure used of expansion the greater will be the condensation due to it, which having once commenced will propagate itself in some geometrical ratio of the time ; that is to say, the condensation due to an expansion of four times will be more than twice as much as what is due to an expansion of twice.

In comparing the evaporation by Tank and by Indicator measurement, taking the case of using the steam without expansion, and the mean of all the experiments, we find that by Tank measurement one pound of combustible evaporated 13.083 pounds of water from the temperature of 212° Fahr., while by Indicator measurement this evaporation was only 11.373 pounds of water, the difference being (13.083—11.373 =) 1.710 pound or $\left(\frac{13.083-11.373 \times 100}{11.373}=\right)$ 15 per centum of the Indicator evaporation. If, now, this comparison be made for the case of using the steam expansively, taking the mean of the experiments of April 18th and 19th, we find that the evaporation per Indicator measurement was $\left(\frac{10.550+10.612}{2}=\right)$ 10.581 pounds of water from the temperature of 212° Fahr. per pound of combustible. The difference then between this and the Tank measurement is (13.083—10.581 =) 2.502 pounds or $\left(\frac{13.083-10.581 \times 100}{10.581}=\right)$ 23.65 per centum of the Indicator evaporation. If, in the experiment of May 2d, when the steam was likewise used expansively, we compare the evaporation by Tank and Indicator measurements, we find that by the latter it was 9.682 pounds of water from a temperature of 212° Fahr. per pound of combustible ; the difference between that and the Tank measurement being (13.083 —9.634 =) 3.449 pounds or $(\frac{13.083-9.634 \times 100}{9.634}=)$ 35.80 per centum of the Indicator evaporation.

If, in these experiments where there was no priming and but little leakage, and where furthermore the steam was superheated about 30° Fahr., there exists such great discrepancies between the two methods of measurement, how much greater must that discrepancy be in cases where there is no superheating of the steam and where there is both considerable priming and leakage? in fact in the cases of ordinary practice.

Again: we find that in these experiments the evaporation by indicator measurement is variously 11.373, 10.581, and 9.634 pounds of water from a temperature of 212° Fahr. per pound of combustible, according as the conditions varied of using the steam without expansion, expansively, and with higher or lower pressures; during all of which the Tank evaporation remained sensibly the same. These variable and great discrepancies we have seen are caused by the difference of the losses by leakage, by radiation, and by condensation in the cylinder due to the difference of the temperatures of its interior surfaces during the steam and exhaust strokes, and to the fact of expansion *per se*. And they teach us how great should be our caution in estimating the efficiency of different types or proportions of boilers by their evaporation as given by the Indicator, unless we are assured that the conditions in their cases are precisely the same as in those with which they are compared.

The experiments enable us to determine the gain in fuel by using the steam expansively over working it for the whole stroke without further expansion than was given by the throttling. When the steam was used expansively it was cut off at 0.28 of the stroke of piston from the commencement, but if there be included the space comprised between the piston at the end of its stroke and the cut-off valve, the steam was expanded almost exactly three times. In this case, too, the steam was throttled from the point of admission to the point of cutting off; the throttling in both cases then may be considered to have produced equal effects. When the steam was used without expansion the cut-off valve was disconnected and its ports left wide open. In making this comparison the pounds of combustible required per hour to produce an indicated horse-power is taken as the measure of the cost of the power in fuel, and we must select comparable cases for it; that is, those in which the boiler pressure, mean effective pressure on the piston, back pressure, and temperature of the feed-water do not vary much. We shall then take the mean of the experiments of April 18th and 19th for the data when using the steam expansively, and the mean of the experiments of April 28th and 29th for the data when using the steam without expansion.

In the experiments of April 18th and 19th, the mean boiler pressure was 103.15 pounds per square inch above the atmosphere, the temperature corresponding to which is 344° Fahr., while the temperature of the boiler-room was 76½° Fahr.; and in those of April 28th and 29th this pressure was 106.60 pounds with a temperature of 346½° Fahr., while the temperature of the boiler-room was 73½ Fahr. The losses by boiler radiation and leakage were therefore somewhat the greatest with the unexpanded steam. The mean effective pressure on the piston during the experiments of April 18th and 19th was 23.8 pounds per square inch, and as the mean pressure above zero was 44 pounds per square inch, there was utilized $\left(\frac{23.8 \times 100}{44} =\right)$ 54.09 per centum of the mean pressure above zero. The mean effective pressure on the piston during the experiments of April 28th and 29th was 28.45 pounds per square inch, and as the mean pressure above zero was 44.9 pounds, there was utilized $\left(\frac{28.45 \times 100}{44.9} =\right)$ 63.36 per centum of the mean pressure above zero, making a difference in favor of the unexpanded steam of 9.27 per centum. The temperature of the feed-water with the expanded steam was 203½° Fahr., and as the total heat of the boiler steam was 1217½° Fahr., the heat already in the feed-water was $(\frac{203\frac{1}{2} \times 100}{1217\frac{1}{2}} =)$ 16.71 per centum of the total heat of conversion into steam. With the unexpanded steam, the temperature of the feed-water was 181° Fahr., and as the total heat of the boiler steam was 1218° Fahr., the heat already in the feed-water was $(\frac{181 \times 100}{1218} =)$ 14.86 per centum of the total heat of conversion, making a difference of (16.71—14.86=) 1.85 per centum in favor of the expanded steam. Deducting this from the previous 9.27 per centum, we have still a balance of (9.27—1.85=) 7.42 per centum in favor of the unexpanded steam. The temperature of the interior surfaces of the cylinder during the exhaust stroke was, with the expanded steam, 229° Fahr.; and during the steam stroke 275° Fahr.—difference 46° Fahr. With the unexpanded steam the mean temperature of the exhaust stroke was 218° Fahr., and of the steam stroke 276° Fahr.—difference 58° Fahr. With the unexpanded steam, therefore, there was the disadvantage of the greater condensation due to the difference of (58—46=) 12° Fahr. of temperature by the interior surfaces of the cylinder; and there was also the disadvantage of a difference of effective pressure of (28.45—23.80=) 4.65 pounds per square inch of piston to produce leakage. We have already seen that a difference of 32° Fahr. of temperature, and (51.4—25.8=) 25.6 pounds per square inch of pressure produced a difference of economic result of 9⅓ per centum; it is therefore fair to estimate the difference due to 12° Fahr., and 4.65 pounds pressure to be, say, 3.42 per centum, which would leave a balance in favor of the unexpanded steam of (7.42—3.42=) 4 per centum. That is to say, that independently of the effect of expansion *per se*, the conditions with the unexpanded steam would have produced 4 per centum more economic result from the fuel than the conditions with the expanded steam would have allowed; consequently, 4 per centum must be added to the experimental gain by expansion. This method gives the maximum result possible from using the steam with the experimental measure of expansion; for it supposes the mean effective pressure on the piston and the back pressure against it to be the same as with the unexpanded steam, and of course allows the steam at the commencement of the stroke of the piston to be carried sufficiently high to produce these results which render in both cases the losses by back pressure the same, and by condensation by the interior surfaces of the cylinder nearly the same.

What was the experimental gain given by expansion? The mean of the experiments of April 18th and 19th when the steam was used expansively, gave 3.751 pounds of combustible per hour for the cost of the Indicated horse-power; while the mean of the experiments of April 28th and 29th gave 4.636 pounds of combustible per hour for the cost of the same power. The gain in fuel then due to the expansion was $(\frac{4.636-3.751 \times 100}{4.636}=)$ 19.09 per centum of the cost of the power with unexpanded steam, to which, if we add the 4 per centum above obtained and due to the difference of conditions, we shall have a gain of, say, 23 per centum as the practical maximum obtainable from the expansion supposing in the two cases equal back pressures, mean effective pressures, temperatures of feed water, and a superheating of the steam of 30° Fahr., which latter should materially increase the gain by expansion over what it would have been, had saturated or normal steam been used. The gain *theoretically* due to cutting off the steam at 0.28 of the stroke of piston from the commencement and expanding it through the remaining 0.72 of the stroke and including the effect in the space between the piston at the end of its stroke and the cut-off valve, is 1.0986; that is to say, this measure of expansion (three times) should, according to the law of MARIOTTE, have increased the work done by the unit of weight of combustible 1.0986 time, whereas the actual increase was only 0.24 time, leaving the enormous discrepancy of 0.8586.

The foregoing deductions regarding the apparent evaporation by Indicator measurement, and as regards the discrepancy between the practical and theoretical gain by expansion, have been made without reference to any effect that may have been produced by the superheating of the steam. The data itself, rests independently upon an accurate experimental basis.

The amount of superheating given to the steam averaged about 30° Fahr. The steam in this respect was very sensitive to reduction in the temperatures of the products of combustion. The admission of a stream of cooler air by opening either the furnace door, or the damper wider in the chimney, or by a variation in the thickness or in the openness of the fuel on the grate, would be immediately shown by a fall of the thermometer in the steam room relatively to the thermometer in the water spaces of the boiler, which latter would scarcely show a sensible diminution. It must be remembered that the raising of the temperature of saturated steam 30° Fahr. by superheating it, is a very different matter to imparting the same number of degrees of temperature by increased tension due to the evaporation of more saturated steam; the amount of heat in the latter case exceeds vastly that in the former, and the sensibility to refrigerating influence will be correspondingly less. Before a reduction of 30° Fahr. can be made in the temperature of saturated steam, some 966° Fahr. of heat in a large portion of it must be rendered latent; a reduction of its saturated temperature will therefore be slow, while its superheated temperature which, on account of the rarity of steam, is acquired with difficulty and lost with facility, will fluctuate rapidly with slight variations of refrigerating condition.

In considering the evaporation given by the Prosser boiler, there must be kept in view the very favorable circumstances under which it was obtained. In the first place, the very small area of the fire grate allowed it to be fired with all the care of a laboratory experiment; secondly, the coal was of the very best kind for generating steam and of first rate quality of the kind. The fireman was thoroughly experienced with the boiler, and the shortness of the experiments—the longest being only 10 hours—prevented any waste in the cleaning of the fires. There were no clinkers formed, and the refuse consisted entirely of ashes and fine coal. It will be noted that the per centum of refuse increased with the intensity of combustion, that is to say, with the number of pounds of coal burned per hour per square foot of grate. The rate of combustion was as great as is usual in practice, and the coal was a dry semi-anthracite from the Trevorton mines of Pennsylvania.

The proportion of heating to grate surface was enormous, being in the water alone over 50 to 1; while there was additionally 24 to 1 for superheating the steam; making altogether the excessive ratio of 74 of heat absorbing surface to 1 of grate,—over double of what is habitually given with tubular boilers.

The temperature of the gases as they entered the chimney, was as near as could be ascertained by tin, about the melting point of that metal, namely, 440° Fahr., or only 60 degrees above the temperature of the superheated steam. The supply of air to the furnace both through and above the incandescent fuel was ample.

ELLIS' BOILER.

Plate V.

ELLIS' BOILER AT WILLARD'S HOTEL. WASHINGTON D. C.

Longitudinal section on C. D. — Cross section on A. B.

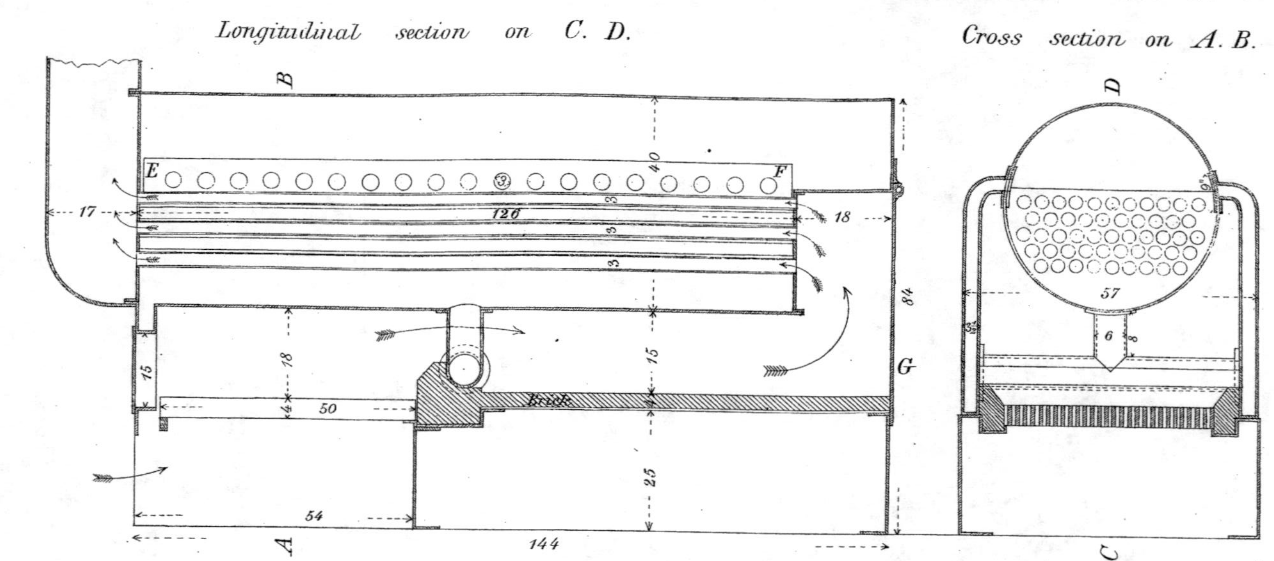

Experiments made in January, 1859, *on* ELLIS' *Boiler, at Willard's Hotel, Washington City, D. C., by Chief Engineers* W. W. W. WOOD, B. F. ISHERWOOD, *and* J. W. KING, *U. S. N., by order of the Navy Department.*

In the month of January, 1859, a Board of Chief Engineers of the Navy composed of W. W. W. WOOD, B. F. ISHERWOOD, and J. W. KING, were ordered by the Navy Department to examine a boiler then in operation at Willard's Hotel, Washington City, D. C., which had been patented April 13th, 1858, by WM. M. and JONAS B. ELLIS; to make the requisite experiments for determining its evaporative efficiency; and to report upon its merits for naval steamers. The Board accordingly ascertained by a careful experiment the number of pounds of water evaporated in this boiler per pound of coal consumed, and then made a Report to the Secretary of the Navy embracing the facts hereinbelow given. The inferences and description of detail in the present paper are by the writer, but the general conclusions are in substance the same as those arrived at by the Board.

Description of the Boiler.

The boiler (Plate V.) consists of a cylindrical shell 10½ feet in length, with an extension of the top at the back end 18 inches long in the form of a segment of a cylinder 17 inches high the flat part of which forms the top of the uptake. The cylindrical portion, which has the uniform diameter of 40 inches from end to end, contains in its lower half fifty iron tubes, each 10½ feet long and 3 inches external diameter, firmly expanded around the heads which act as tube-plates. On both sides of this cylinder and precisely at its horizontal diameter, there is riveted along its length (10½ feet) a strip of iron plate E F 9 inches broad by ½ inch thick. Through each strip and the shell behind it there are pierced nineteen holes of 3 inches diameter connecting the interior of the cylinder with flat water-legs riveted upon each side and along the whole length (12 feet) of the boiler. The object of the plate is to make the portion of the shell it covers equally strong with the rest of the cylinder, notwithstanding the perforations. These legs are 3½ inches wide and extend 39 inches below the axis of the cylinder, at the front end of which and beneath it and between the water-legs the furnace is placed. Behind the furnace there is a brick bridge-wall, and beyond that a brick floor which, together with the ash-door G and the remainder of the water-legs and cylinder-bottom, form the conduit leading the heated gases from the furnace to the tubes. Immediately behind the brick bridge and partly bedded in it, there is a horizontal wrought-iron pipe 6 inches in diameter; this pipe extends across between the water legs and connects them at right angles :—from its centre a vertical branch of the same diameter joins it to the bottom of the cylindrical shell. The purpose of this pipe and branch is to allow a free circulation of water between the bottoms of the legs and shell. A smoke connection with suitable ash-door is attached to the front of the cylinder, and the chimney is carried up from it. The whole boiler, as described, is elevated 25 inches to allow an ash-pit beneath the furnace-grate.

The following are its principal dimensions and proportions, namely:

Extreme length....................	13 feet.
" breadth..................	4 feet 9 inches.
" height	7 feet.
Contents of circumscribing parallelopipedon..........................	432.25 cubic feet.
Numer of tubes (iron)	50.
External diameter of tubes	3 inches.
Length of tubes....................	10 feet 6 inches.

Width of grate	3 feet 6 inches.
Length of grate	4 feet.
Total grate surface................	14 square feet.
Heating surface in tubes..........	412. "
Heating surface other than in tubes..	151. "
Total heating surface..............	563. "
Calorimeter or area of tubes for draught	2.062 "
Height of smoke chimney above the grates	70 feet.
Contents of steam-room.............	31.46 cubic feet.
Weight of water up to 4 inches above tubes	4310. pounds.
Ratio of heating to grate surface ...	40.214 to 1.000.
" grate surface to cross area of tubes for draught.......	6.790 " "

Discussion of the Design of the Boiler.

From the foregoing description it is apparont, that as regards the arrangement of its evaporating surfaces this boiler belongs to the horizontal fire-tube type with the tubes returned above the furnace ; the only peculiarity is in the shape of the shell or envelope containing them. Now as the evaporative efficiency depends on the arrangement and proportions of the evaporating surfaces alone, irrespective of the shape of the shell, provided the usual provisions for circulation be secured; it is evident, that the evaporation given by this boiler will, according to its proportions of calorimeter, grate and heating surfaces, be the same as that given by others of the same type having equal facilities of circulation. There remains, then, to compare these facilities and to contrast the advantages and disadvantages resulting from the peculiar form of the shell with those resulting from the form habitually given.

The original idea of Ellis' boiler has been a plain cylinder placed over a furnace and having its lower half filled with evaporating tubes ; it has been produced by the attempt to form a shell of sufficient strength to resist high pressure steam without the expense and obstructions of stays or bracing. Such a shell must of necessity be cylindrical, and as the conditions of strength required its diameter to be as small as possible, it was made just large enough to contain the tubes without the furnace which, as it could not be placed within the cylinder without greatly enlarging its diameter, had of necessity to be placed beneath it. If, now, we suppose the simple cylinder to be supported upon walls of masonry so arranged as to form the sides of the furnace and smoke conduit below, we shall have the primitive conception ; but in this case there would result two considerable disadvantages : first, the want of provision for the proper circulation of the water in the cylinder ; second, the loss of the sides of the furnace and smoke conduit as evaporating surfaces. The former, however, is of the most consequence though the latter, too, is important. The first can be secured and the second avoided by replacing the walls of masonry with flat water-legs and attaching them to the cylinder in such a manner as to maintain its integrity of form and yet allow a free communication between them. This has been done by perforating that part of the cylindrical shell against which the water-legs are rivetted, with small holes having considerable spaces of solid metal between them. Notwithstanding the metal thus left, however, it is obvious that the strength of the section on the line of the perforations has been lessened, and in a higher ratio than the proportion of metal cut out ; hence it is necessary to strengthen that section, which has been done by rivetting over it an additional strip of iron of such width and thickness that when similarly perforated the aggregate strength of the remaining metal on the line of the centre of the perforations shall be equal to the strength of any other section of the cylindrical shell, either in the direction of or at right angles to its axis. To perfect the arrangement for circulation it was further necessary to connect the bottoms of the cylinder and water legs; this has been done by the horizontal pipe and its vertical branch situated behind the bridge wall, and about midway the length of the cylinder. Were it not for this pipe, and if the length of the cylinder were just the length of the fire-grates beneath it, the mass of water in the cylinder being equally heated by the furnace below could have no descending currents, and as a consequence no ascending ones except those made by the gradual boiling-off and pumping in of the feed-water; instead, therefore, of solid water being constantly presented to the heating surface by the currents sweeping away the steam bubbles as fast as generated, these bubbles would remain for some time in contact with the metal and only be detached at intervals when they had attained a large size. In this manner a film of steam, as it were, would for a considerable portion of the time be interposed between the heat and the water, and as steam is a very poor conductor of heat the effect would be not only a great diminution of the evaporative efficiency of the heating surfaces, but also their rapid destruction. When, however, the length of the cylinder considerably exceeds the length of the fire-grates these effects are proportionally diminished, because the heat not being as great at the back end of the cylinder as at the end over the furnace, currents would be generated sweeping the cylinder longitudinally from the back to the furnace end, rising at the latter and descending at the former. The circulation thus established would, in the case of a short boiler like Ellis', be too feeble, but the addition of the pipe connecting the bottom of the shell and water-legs furnishes an avenue for motion, and the heated currents rising vertically among the mass of tubes, pour over laterally through the perforations into the water-legs down which they descend vertically to the cross-pipe whence they rise again and enter the cylinder at its lowest point to be again submitted to the heat, and to perform their circuit anew.

Invention, or Novelty Embodied in the Boiler.

Having thus described the boiler and pointed out the conditions that determined its design, it is proper to next ascertain what are the novel features, or new combination of known features, which distinguish it from other boilers and give validity to the patent of the designers. In their letters patent, issued April 13th, 1858, the "claim" is narrowed to the following precise limits, namely :—"*Connecting the water-legs extending from the front to the rear end of the boiler continuously to the shell* [cylinder] *of the boiler at the point of the greatest horizontal diameter of the boiler,*" [cylinder.] It is, as will be perceived, a very restricted one and consists merely in the substitution of a rectangular for a cylindrical water conduit; for essentially the same device and for the same purpose has been frequently practised in another form, namely: by uniting the upper water spaces in a boiler with the lower ones by means of a number of separate pipes placed at regular intervals, instead of a flat water-leg or continuous pipe pierced with holes at regular intervals. The two methods are precisely the same in principle and in practical effect also; they differ simply in the shape of the section of the water conduit, which in one case is a single parellelogram and in the other a number of equivalent circles whose diameter is the same as the width of the parallelogram. As a mechanical device the water-leg is superior in one respect to the pipes and inferior in others, but the thing is so obviously the same that a patent could only be obtained by coupling its use with the condition of its application to the cylinder at precisely the horizontal diameter of the latter. If attached at any other point there would be no infringement of the patent, and it is difficult to understand how one was ever granted on so meaningless a fact; for the proper point of attachment will depend not at all upon the horizontal diameter of the cylinder but upon the level of the water within it ; because it is evident that if this level be below that diameter, as it easily may be, then the water-leg if attached there would be inoperative for circulation, for it would not communicate with the upper water spaces of the cylinder. And again, if the water level were carried considerably above the horizontal diameter, that line would not be the proper point of attachment as it would leave a mass of water above it cut off from circulation. The water-leg should communicate with the cylinder at such a point as would secure the perforations, being always just submerged when the water was at or near its working level. The aim should be to connect the extreme top and bottom of the water, and this condition and not the horizontal diameter of the cylinder determines where the water-leg should enter it.

I have said that the flat water-leg was, as a mechanical device, superior to the pipes in one respect and inferior in others. It is superior inasmuch as it adds a considerable amount of evaporating surface; but, on the other hand, if the pipes are not evaporating surfaces they are from that very fact better as a means for circulation, because their temperature will be lower and the specific gravity of the water in them consequently greater. It is inferior in requiring stays, as it is a flat surface; while the surfaces of the pipes being circular require none.

Advantages and Disadvantages of the Boiler.

It is well first to inquire the merit of this boiler as advocated by its inventors. They assert in a note dated January 21st, 1859, addressed to the Board of Engineers, that it "consists in connecting the water-legs to a cylinder *at or near the working water line* the whole length of the boiler, and we claim to have gained by this device, 1st. The production of dry steam by perfect and rapid circulation. 2d. Economy of space. 3d. Strength equal to any other form of boiler, with less bracing. 4th. Convenient access to the boiler for cleaning or repairs. 5th. Economy in the consumption of fuel."

It will not be difficult to show that of these five assumptions not one is true. We will investigate the whole five in detail, comparing them respectively with the same qualities in the common horizontal fire-tube boiler of the same type as ELLIS'. Before doing so, however, we will remark *en passant*, that in this very note the inventors have abandoned their invention which was for connecting the water-legs to the cylinder *at its horizontal diameter*, and have attributed the merit to the fact of the attachment being made *at or near the working water level*, a point having no connection whatever with the horizontal diameter, as appears in the boiler experimented with in which the legs were attached above the horizontal diameter of the cylinder, as shown in Plate V.

1st. *Of the production of dry steam by perfect and rapid circulation.* The great effect of vigorous circulation is to increase the evaporative efficiency of the boiler by sweeping the steam bubbles from the evaporating surface as fast as they are generated, and continuously replacing them with solid water. Coincidently, the more complete the circulation the greater will be the facility with which the steam bubbles are extricated from the water, and the shorter will be the time occupied between their leaving the evaporating surface and emerging into the steam room. Both of these effects tend to the production of dry steam, but so far is ELLIS' boiler from being preëminent in causing them that a careful inspection of the design of the boiler as exhibited in Plate V, will show how languid and imperfect the circulation of the water must have been, and how difficult it was to disengage the steam bubbles from the evaporating surface, and to replace them with solid water. The boiler was a short one, the length of the cylinder being only 2½ times the length of the fire-grates, and although the hottest part of the combustion was under the first half of the cylinder yet the coolest part was in the portion of the tubes immediately over this half, while the last half of the cylinder and the portion of the tubes over it were subjected to the mean temperature of the fuel. The mean temperature, then, of the water in the cylinder throughout its length was nearly the same, and there could scarcely have been any longitudinal currents for the want of sufficient differences of temperature to produce them. The entire circulation, therefore, was what was due to the cross pipe and vertical branch connecting the bottoms of the water-legs and cylinder; this pipe was of small diameter, there was but one for the entire boiler, and its effect was chiefly local. In addition, the tubes were arranged not vertically over each other as is usually done and which allows the freest ascent to the vertical currents, but they were so positioned that the tubes of each row were placed over the open spaces between those in the adjacent rows, thus impeding by obstruction what feeble currents did form, and hindering the disengagement of the steam bubbles. The tubes were furthermore situated very close together, their distance apart in the clear being only ½ inch, a space quite inadequate for the passage of the ascending steam and water currents. So far, then, was this boiler from having "a perfect and rapid circulation," that it might be characterized as possessing the very reverse property.

The ordinary horizontal fire tube boiler of the same type as Ellis' has a much superior circulation. It has flat water-legs extending in effect from the water surface to the top of the furnace, and formally from the furnace top to the flat water bottom which reaches clear across the boiler and entirely connects the top and bottom water spaces at all points. The tubes, being arranged vertically over each other, offer for this type of boiler the least possible obstruction to the ascending currents which, by sweeping off the steam bubbles and replacing them by solid water more rapidly, enables a less surface to evaporate an equal amount of water in equal time. The foaming too, and wetness of the steam, will be in measure prevented by the greater steam room obtained with the ordinary horizontal fire-tube boiler in the same circumscribing parallelopipedon owing to the rectangular form of the shell. In these respects, therefore, Ellis' boiler is inferior to others of the same type as habitually arranged.

2d. *Economy of Space.* This is a relative term, and means quantity of grate and heating surface and steam room comprised within a given parallelopipedon. Now, as it is at once evident that the cubical contents of a given parallelopipedon cannot be equaled by any inscribed solid, it is plain that a circular shell can never contain the space of a rectangular one with sides equal to the diameter of the circle; hence, ELLIS' boiler cannot possibly be made to hold the same grate and heating surface and steam room as the ordinary horizontal fire-tube boiler with rectangular section. A simple inspection will show that the large spandrels above the grates, which are wholly useless as furnace, cannot be filled with tubes as in the usual arrangement and are therefore lost; while the upper spandrels of the cylinder are similarly lost for steam room. As regards "Economy of Space," then, this boiler is much inferior to others of the same type having the habitual form of shell.

3d. *Strength equal to any other form of boiler with less bracing.* The proper manner of stating this quality would be "Equal Strength with less Material than in any other form of boiler." And first, of the flat surfaces. It is obvious that they will require the same staying as the flat surfaces of any other boiler; there remains then only the cylinder containing the tubes, and as its diameter is determined by the width of the furnace beneath it, there would, for a large boiler, be required as many cylinders as furnaces, and having flat water-legs of double width between them. The quantity of metal in this succession of cylinders would far exceed that required for the corresponding portion of the shell and its staying in the case of an ordinary horizontal fire-tube boiler of rectangular section and embracing from four to seven furnaces, the greater the number of furnaces, the greater would be the gain for the ordinary boiler. Neither must it be overlooked that the perforated strips of plate E F replace to a great extent, both as regards weight and workmanship, the stays rendered unnecessary by the circular form of the cylinder. So far then from ELLIS' boiler having equal strength with less material, that it requires more material when several furnaces are employed than the ordinary horizontal fire-tube boiler.

4th. *Convenient access to the boiler for cleaning or repairs.* In this respect it is scarcely equal to the ordinary tubular boiler with circular topped furnaces, which permits a man to easily enter between the furnace crown and lower row of tubes and perform any repairs or cleaning within reach.

5th. *Economy in the consumption of fuel.* This is a point only to be ascertained by an actual experiment. It was made by the Board of Engineers which found the evaporation of water by ELLIS' boiler to be, under very favorable circumstances, and measured in a Tank before being pumped into the boiler, 9.070 pounds from a temperature of 100° Fahr. by one pound of first quality steam coal. This, under the conditions of the case, and considered in connection with the proportion of grate and heating surface employed, must be consideed a mediocre result, and less than would have been given by an ordinary horizontal fire-tube boiler of the same type and proportions. The experiment was made as hereinbelow described.

Manner of Conducting the Experiment, and the Experimental Data and Results.

A portion of the steam from the boiler was used to supply a very small engine doing the hotel work; but the principal part was consumed for warming, washing, and cooking purposes. The drain of steam from the boiler was, therefore, nearly continuous, and not intermittent as in the case of its being worked off by a steam engine; consequently, at no time did the boiler show the slightest indication of priming; on the contrary, when one cock showed solid water, the next, two inches above it, showed clear dry steam.

As it was impossible to use an Indicator in the case, the evaporation was determined by measuring the water in an open Tank previously to its being pumped into the boiler. The dimensions of this Tank were 6 feet by 2 feet by 2 feet; it contained exactly 24 cubic feet, and was made of wood and lined with sheet lead. As often as evacuated it was re-filled through a pipe from a large cistern situated above it. From the Tank, the water was forced into the boiler by a small steam pump. Exactly eleven tankfuls were evaporated.

The coal consumed was excellent Cumberland, a first quality steam coal, dry, free-burning, and semi-bituminous, giving the very small residuum of 12¾ per centum. The coal and ashes were carefully weighed with a sensitive balance; the ashes were in a perfectly dry state no water having been allowed to wet them.

During the experiment, the pressure of the steam per gauge, and the temperature of the water in the Tank and of the air in the boiler room were taken every half hour. The extreme temperatures of the water were 48° and 53° Fahr., mean 49°. The boiler room was a portion of the hotel and its temperature did not sensibly vary.

The temperature of the products of combustion when they entered the chimney, were approximately determined by placing separately upon a brick, and immediately in front of the tubes, a piece of tin and a piece of sheet lead, and allowing them to remain for several hours. The tin was completely melted, but the lead did not show even on its sharp edges the least trace of fusion. The melting points of tin and lead are respectively 458° and 600° Fahr. The temperature of the products of combustion as they left the boiler, was between these points, and probably at about 500° Fahr.

The experiment was commenced at precisely 9 A. M., January 22d, and continued until 9 P. M. of the same day. At the commencement, a large, clean fire was upon the grate; the steam pressure in the boiler was 30 pounds per square inch above the atmosphere by an Ashcroft guage; and the height of the water in the boiler was carefully noted on a glass gauge situated several feet from the boiler and connecting with it by tubes. At the close of the experiment the water was left at precisely the same height in the glass guage; the steam at the same pressure in the boiler; and the fires in the same state, as nearly as could be estimated, as at the commencement. This method was the only one at command as the Hotel could not dispense with the use of the boiler for an hour. The objection to it is the possible error in the estimation of the coal on the grate; but with experienced Engineers and so small a grate, it is highly improbable that any error could be made large enough to be of practical importance.

In calculating the results the weight of water evaporated was found for its mean temperature of 49° from its known weight of 62.321 pounds per cubic foot at the temperature of 62° Fahr.; the relative specific gravities being taken at 1.00000 and 0.99908 respectively. As there were eleven tankfuls of 24 cubic feet each, we shall have for the weight of water evaporated from the temperature of 49° Fahr. $\left(\frac{24 \times 11 \times 62.321 \times 1.00000}{0.99908} =\right)$ 16467.9 pounds.

The mean boiler pressure was 35 pounds per square inch above the atmosphere, and taking the total heat of steam of that pressure at 1199°3. Fahr., we shall have for the weight of water evaporated from 100° Fahr. $\left(\frac{16467.9 \times \overline{1199.3-49}}{1199.3-100} =\right)$ 17231.9 pounds: and from 212° Fahr. $\left(\frac{16467.9 \times \overline{1199.3-49}}{1199.3-212} =\right)$ 19186.7 pounds.

The following are the experimental data and results, namely:—

Duration of the experiment, in hours	12.
Mean temperature of the feed-water in the tank, in degrees Fahr	49.
Mean pressure of the steam in the boiler, in pounds per square in. above the atmosphere	35.
Total weight of water evaporated from temperature of 49° Fahr	16467.9
Total weight of water evaporated from temperature of 100° Fahr	17231.9

Total weight of water evaporated from temperature of 212° Fahr., in pounds	19186.7
Total weight of Cumberland coal consumed, in pounds	1900.
Total weight of ashes, clinker, and fine coal withdrawn from ash-pit, in pounds	242.
Per centum of ashes, clinker, and fine coal	12¾.
Pounds of coal consumed per hour per square foot of grate surface	13.57
Pounds of combustible consumed per hour per square foot of grate surface	11.84
Pounds of water evaporated from a temperature of 100° Fahr. by one pound of coal	9.070
Pounds of water evaporated from a temperature of 212° Fahr. by one pound of coal	10.098
Pounds of water evaporated from a temperature of 100° Fahr. by one pound of combustible	10.393
Pounds of water evaporated from a temperature of 212° Fahr. by one pound of combustible	11.572
Mean temperature of the boiler-room, in degrees Fahr.	65.

The experiment showed that the temperature of the products of combustion was about 500° Fahr., after having been subjected to a heat absorbing surface of over forty to one of the grate surface. The ratio of the diameter to the length of the tubes was one to forty-two. The calorimeter was 1 to each 6.79 of grate area, a proportion that practice has determined to be about the best. The combustion was by no means forced, being only 13.57 pounds of semi-bituminous coal per square foot of grate per hour, which is not above the average in practice. Yet notwithstanding all these favorable proportions, more favorable far than are habitually given, the evaporation measured by the Tank was only 9.070 pounds of water from a temperature of 100° Fahr. per pound of first quality coal. This must be considered a mediocre result.

HORIZONTAL FIRE-TUBE

AND

VERTICAL WATER-TUBE BOILERS.

*Experiments made by order of the U. S. Navy Department on board the Screw Frigate "*San Jacinto,*" at the New York Navy Yard, June,* 1859, *to determine the Relative Evaporative Efficiencies of the* horizontal fire-tube, *and the* vertical water-tube boiler.

Upon the return to the New York Navy Yard of the U. S. Screw Frigate "San Jacinto," in 1858, from a three years' cruise in the East Indies, it was found necessary to remove her original three copper flue boilers; and the opportunity was embraced in replacing them with two iron Tubular boilers, to make one of them of the horizontal fire-tube type, and the other of the vertical water-tube type, for the purpose of ascertaining their relative evaporative efficiencies by an unexceptionable experiment.

In order that the comparison might be purely between the two *types* of boiler, it was determined that it should not be influenced by difference of furnace, of calorimeter, of smoke connections, or of chimney, or of anything—excepting the tubes—that could differently affect the evaporation in the two cases. It was determined, also, with the view of obtaining a *rigorously comparative* result under the conditions of actual practice on board marine steamers, that the experiment should be made by operating the engines and screw with the vessel secured to the dock, and measuring the weight of steam discharged from the cylinders at the end of the strokes of their pistons by means of the Indicator. Accordingly, after the new tubular boilers were placed in the vessel and the entire machinery had been put in complete repair for another cruise, a Board of Chief Engineers composed of B. F. Isherwood, Wm. E. Everett, Jas. W. King, and John Faron, were convened by an order of the Secretary of the Navy to make the proper experiments, and to report the results. This duty was performed by the Board with the utmost care and fidelity; and in the present paper will be found all the facts and inferences contained in their report, together with several others, and more explanatory matter. The writer has carefully revised the calculations in that report, and has made a complete analysis of all the indicator diagrams, for the purpose of verifying or correcting the statements of the Board. The result has been to slightly modify the figures of some quantities, but the important facts remain substantially unchanged. In order to render the account of the experiment as complete and as intelligible as possible, it will be prefaced by a description of the rival boilers, the engines, and the screw employed.

Description of the Boilers.

The boilers, shown in Plates VI. and VII., were placed fronting each other and separated by a fire-room 8½ feet wide extending in the fore and aft direction of the vessel. There was one telescopic chimney in common and it was situated at the centre of the boilers immediately over the fire-room. The shells were precisely the same, both as regards form and dimensions, which was also the case with the furnaces, ash-pits, smoke connections, grate-bars, doors, and water-ways. The only difference was in the tubes, which in one boiler were according to the type known as the common marine tubular, having the tubes arranged horizontally above the furnaces, surrounded with water, and containing the products of combustion; while in the other boiler they were according to the vertical water-tube type, and arranged vertically above the furnaces as patented by Chief Engineer D. B. MARTIN, U. S. Navy, being surrounded by the products of combustion, and containing the water within. The two kinds of tubes, then, though performing the same function of transmitting the heat of the products of combustion to the water, were diametrically opposed in the mode of doing it; in the one case they were horizontal fire-tubes; in the other they were vertical water-

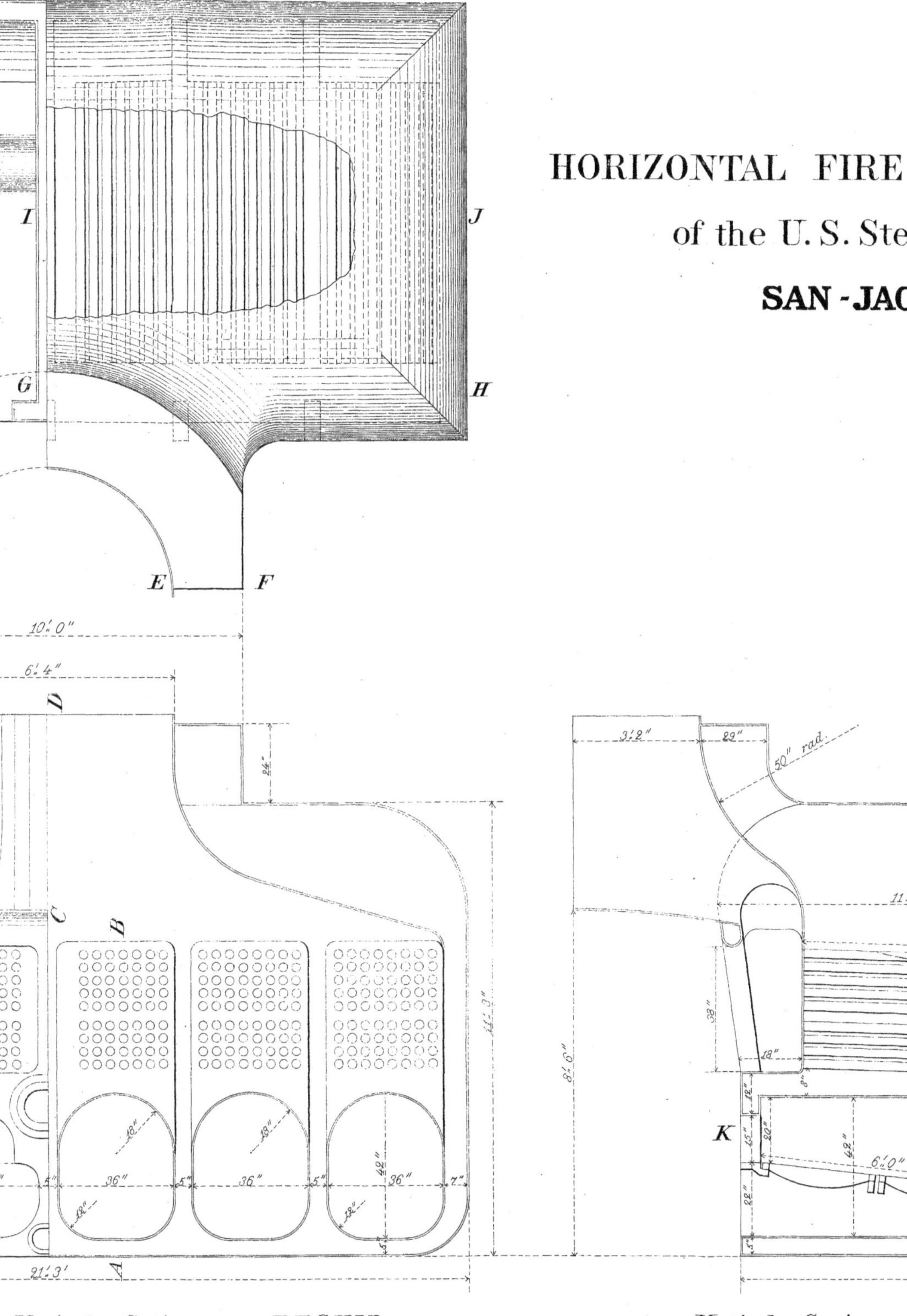
K L: Top View.
HORIZONTAL FIRE
of the U. S. Ste
SAN-JAC
I
J
G
H
E
F
10' 0"
6' 4"
D
C
B
A
24"
11' 3"
36"
5"
7"
18"
42"
21' 3'
3' 2"
22"
50" rad.
11'
38"
18"
8' 6"
8"
12"
K
15"
20"
42"
6' 0"
22"
5"
Vertical Section on EFGHIJ.
Vertical Section on

Plate VII.

VERTICAL WATER - TUBE BOILER
of the U. S. Steam Frigate
SAN - JACINTO.

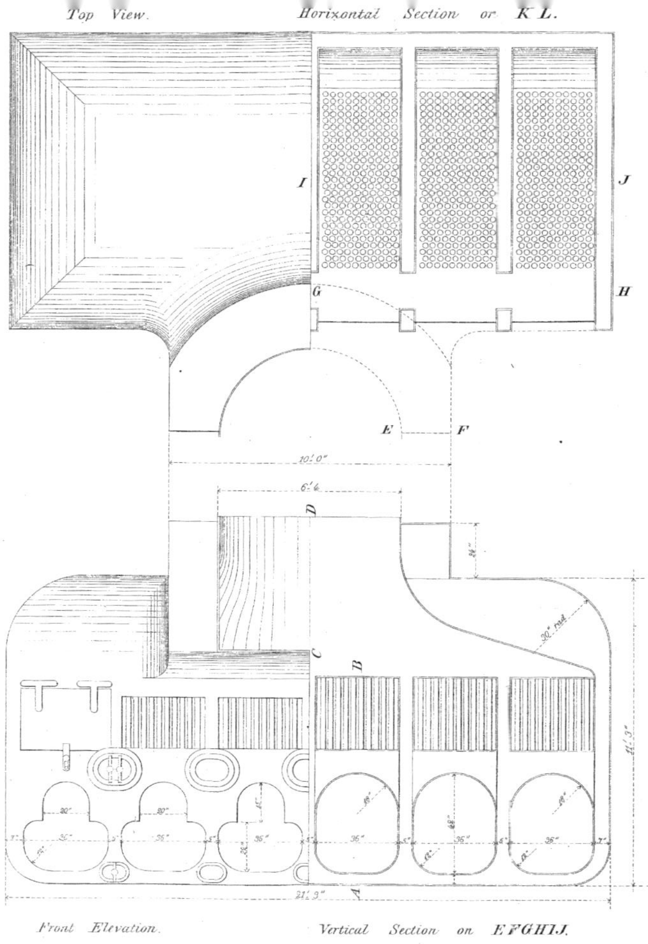

Top View.

Horizontal Section on K L.

Front Elevation.

Vertical Section on E F G H I J.

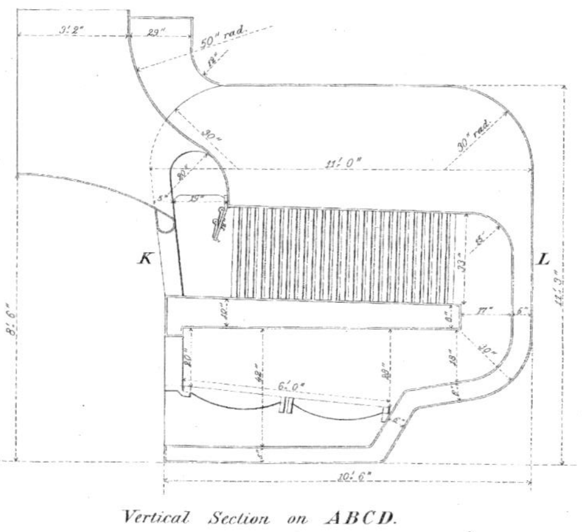

Vertical Section on A B C D.

Baillière Brothers, Publishers 440 Broadway N.Y.

tubes ; both occupied the same space and had the same relative position to the furnace and chimney; and the object of the experiment was to determine the difference of evaporation due to this difference of type *per se*, irrespective of all extrinsic influence. In both boilers the tubes appertaining to each furnace occupy nearly the same space, namely, a length of 7 feet, a breadth of 3 feet, and a height with the horizontal fire-tubes of 37 inches, and of 33 inches with the vertical water-tubes. The distance between the crown of the furnace and the lower tube-plate with the vertical water-tubes, is 10 inches at the front and 8 inches at the back of the boiler; with the horizontal fire-tubes these distances are respectively 8 and 6 inches, and they could be reduced to 4 inches, while with the vertical water-tubes the 10 and 8 inches are indispensable for putting them in. The two kinds of tubes could have been so placed that the tops of each would have been at the same height above the crown of the furnaces, the additional 4 inches of height with the horizontal fire-tubes being provided for in the 4 inches less space required between them and the furnace crown; but in the actual arrangement the tops of the horizontal fire-tubes rose 2 inches above the level of the tops of the vertical water-tubes, and diminished the steam room by that space. The distances, however, of 8 and 6 inches between the furnace crown and lower row of horizontal fire-tubes, are no more than what are properly required for the accommodation of the steam and water currents.

In the vertical water-tube boiler there was placed at the top of the tubes at the point where the products of combustion are delivered from them into the chimney, a hanging bridge composed of two pieces of iron plate, each 6 inches wide and hinged for turning up or throwing back when required. The object of this bridge was to retain the products of combustion around the upper part of the tubes until the heat was sufficiently abstracted, as experiment has amply shown that without this bridge the portion of the products of combustion which passes along the upper tube-plate is delivered into the chimney at a much higher temperature than those from the lower portions of the tubes. The bridge was arranged to leave a clear space of 2 inches at its top between it and the upper tube-plate, so as to greatly lessen without completely stopping the draft at that point.

The centres of the tubes of each longitudinal row of vertical water-tubes instead of being placed in straight lines from the back to the front smoke connections, were slightly zig-zagged that the tubes might be the more directly exposed to the currents of the heated gases. The lines of the centres of every other tube of the same row diverged from the back tube so as to be $\frac{1}{8}$ of an inch apart at the front tube. This, of course, made the direct calorimeter or area for draft, measured at the front tubes, considerably less than the same measured at the back tubes. Transversely to the furnaces, the rows of tubes had their centres in the same straight line.

The centres of the tubes of each perpendicular row of horizontal fire-tubes are in the same straight line. In both boilers man-holes give easy access between the bottoms of the tubes and the crown of the furnaces; the braces being arranged to allow the passage of a man from front to back of boiler without disturbing them. As far as practicable both boilers were braced alike, the same quantity of the same T iron being used in each, and in the same places; when finished they were subjected to a cold hydrostatic pressure of 50 pounds to the square inch. The shells were of $\frac{3}{8}$ inch thick iron plate, with the exception of the bottom and ash-pits which were $\frac{7}{16}$ inch thick; the furnaces and smoke connections were of $\frac{1}{2}$ inch thick plate. The tube-plates for the vertical tubes were $\frac{1}{2}$ inch thick iron—for the horizontal tubes $\frac{9}{16}$ inch thick. Every seam except where in contact with fire, was double riveted and caulked on both sides. The furnace doors had each nine perforations, giving in the aggregate 9 square inches of area for the admission of air above the incandescent fuel; this air was distributed by an interior lining of the size of the door, perforated over its whole surface with $\frac{3}{16}$ inch diameter holes. All the tubes were of drawn brass (not brazed); the vertical ones were No. 13 wire gauge in thickness; the horizontal ones were No. 10 wire gauge in thickness; both tubes were expanded on the inner side of their sheets and riveted over on the outer side. The smoke connexion doors were the same except in height, which with the horizontal fire-tubes was 37 inches, while with the vertical water-tubes it was only 24 inches, no more being required with the latter for sweeping them of soot; and this less height is a great practical convenience. With the horizontal fire-tubes one vertical row of the two centre furnaces was omitted, in order to make room for the turn-buckles setting up the cross braces.

The following are the dimensions, proportions, and weights of the two boilers:

	Horizontal Fire tube Boiler.	Vertical Water-tube Boiler.
Breadth of boiler; (fore and aft direction of the vessel) in feet and inches	21 .. 3	21 .. 3
Length of boiler (athwartship) at furnaces; in feet and inches	10 .. 6	10 .. 6
Length of boiler (athwartship) extreme in feet and inches	11 .. 0	11 .. 0
Height of boiler, exclusive of steam chimney or drum, in feet and inches	11 .. 3	11 .. 3
Height of boiler, inclusive of steam chimney or drum, in feet and inches	13 .. 3	13 .. 3
Number of furnaces	6 ..	6 ..
Width of furnaces, in feet	3 ..	3 ..
Length of fire-grate, in feet	6 ..	6 ..
Aggregate area of fire-grate surface, in square feet	108 ..	108 ..
Number of brass tubes	414.	1,620.
External diameter of the tubes, in inches	3.	2.
Internal diameter of the tubes, in inches	2.732	1.810
Length of the tubes, in inches, extreme	84¼.	33.
Length of the tubes, in inches, between plates	83⅛.	32.
Distance between centres of tubes vertically, in in's.	4.	—.
Distance between centres of tubes crosswise the furnaces, in inches	4¼.	$3\frac{6}{10}$.
Distance between centres of tubes lengthwise the furnaces, in inches	—	3.
Number of rows of tubes vertically	9.	—.
Number of rows of tubes crosswise the furnaces	8.	10.
Number of rows of tubes lengthwise the furnaces	--	27.
Length of the space occupied by the tubes of each furnace, in inches	84¼.	84.
Width of the space occupied by the tubes of each furnace, in inches	36.	36.
Height of the space occupied by the tubes of each furnace, in inches	37.	33.
Space between crown of furnace and bottom of tubes, in inches	7.	9.
Thickness of metal of the tube, in inches	0.134	0.094
Weight of the tubes in pounds	10,115.	9,856.
Calorimeter or area for draft through the tubes, in square feet — at back	16.854	21.555
Calorimeter or area for draft through the tubes, in square feet — at front	16.854	16.889
Heating surface in the six furnaces, in square feet	289.20	289.20
Heating surface in the back smoke connexions, in square feet	159.36	119.36
Heating surface in the front smoke connexions, in square feet	136.40	106.40
Heating surface in the tubes measured on their exterior circumference, in square feet	2,282.67	2,332.64
Heating surface in the tubes measured on their interior circumference, in square feet	2,078.92	2,111.00
Heating surface in the sides, tops, and bottoms of tube-boxes, in square feet	———	447.65
Total heating surface, the tube surface being measured on the exterior circumference, in square ft.	2,867.63	3,295.25
Total heating surface, the tube surface being measured on the interior circumference, in square feet.	2,663.88	3,073.61
Diameter of smoke pipe, in feet and inches	6 .. 4	6 .. 4
Height of smoke pipe above fire-grate, in ft. and in.	51 .. 6	51 .. 6
Steam-room in boiler and steam chimney or drum, in cubic feet	636.	675.
Weight of water in boiler at 243° Fahr., measured to 9 inches above tubes, in pounds	46,600.	39,200.
Weight of boiler, exclusive of water, grate bars, and valves, but inclusive of tubes, and man-hole and hand-hole plates, and doors, in pounds	86,412.	86,860.
Ratio of heating to grate surface, the tube surface being measured on the exterior circumference	26.552 to 1.000	30.511 to 1.000
Ratio of heating to grate surface, the tube surface being measured on the interior circumference	24.666 to 1.000	28.460 to 1.000
Ratio of grate surface to minimum calorimeter through the tubes	6.470 to 1.000	6.395 to 1.000
Ratio of grate surface to cross area of smoke-pipe (the whole pipe to the grate of each boiler)	3.429 to 1.000	3.429 to 1.000

The proportions adopted for the vertical water-tube boiler were the best as determined by an extensive experience ; and it is not probable they could have been changed with any advantage as regards evaporative effect per pound of combustible. The proportions of the horizontal fire-tube boiler were made as nearly as possible the same, in order to determine the difference in value of the tube surface *per se.* The proportions given to this kind of boiler vary greatly in practice, but it is believed that those of the experimental boiler are about the average. A tube having a length of 7 feet for an external diameter of 3 inches, a draught area of about one-sixth the grate surface, and a heating surface of about 26½ to 1 of grate, does not differ materially from the practice of the most successful builders. That these proportions, however, are not the best for high evaporative effect, was very clearly shown during the experiments. The tube was too short for its diameter, the ratio of calorimeter employed too great, and the ratio of heating to grate surface too small. Could these proportions have been advantageously changed with the tubes occupying the same space ? They could, by simply decreasing the external diameter of the tubes to 2¼ inches, and increasing their number to about 580. The dimensions of the space in which the horizontal fire-tubes were placed, were not favorable for properly proportioning them for maximum economic evaporation. It was too high and too short. It would have been better in occupying the same number of cubic feet of space with a given width, to have had it longer and lower, but that would have increased the length of the boiler. Under no conditions, however, is it possible to have as good proportions in as small a space with the horizontal fire-tube as with the vertical water-tube ; in this respect—and it is a most important one—the latter is unapproachable by its rival, and equality can only be obtained at the expense of a considerably increased space. For good proportions in minimum space, the superiority of the vertical water-tubes is so great that it is probable in the case of the experimental boiler, the length occupied by the tubes could, with the weight of coal consumed per square foot of grates per hour, have been much shortened without sensibly impairing the economic result.

If the calculations of the heating surface in the preceding Table be observed, it will be perceived that they are made for both the external and the internal area of the tubes ; and as the difference is very considerable, it is of importance to determine which is the correct measurement. In the case of the horizontal fire-tubes, their exterior is in contact with the water and their interior with the products of combustion ; while in the case of the vertical water-tubes this distribution is exactly reversed, the products of combustion being on the outside of the tubes while the water is within them. Hence in calculating the heating surfaces of the two kinds of tubes, if the area in contact with the water be the proper one, the comparison will be between the exterior surfaces of the horizontal fire-tubes and the interior surfaces of the vertical water-tubes ; but if the area in contact with the products of combustion be the correct one—as it unquestionably is—then these quantities will be exactly reversed, and the comparison will be between the interior surfaces of the horizontal fire-tubes and the exterior surfaces of the vertical water-tubes. Let us now ascertain the difference in the total heating surface of the two boilers due to the two modes of measurement.

With the horizontal fire-tube boiler, the total area of heating surface measured on the outside of the tubes, is 2867.63 square feet ; with the vertical water-tube boiler the total area of heating surface measured on the inside of the tubes, is 3073.61 square feet ; the difference being 205.98 square feet or $\left(\frac{3073.61-2867.63 \times 100}{3073.61}=\right)$ 6.7 per centum of the surface of the horizontal fire-tube boiler in favor of the vertical water-tube boiler, making the comparison by area in contact with the water.

But if the comparison be made correctly—that is, for the areas in contact with the products of combustion—then the heating surface of the horizontal fire-tube boiler measured on the inside of the tubes, is 2663.88 square feet ; while with the vertical water-tube boiler measured on the outside of the tubes, it is 3295.25 square feet; the difference being 631.37 square feet or $(\frac{3295.25-2663.88 \times 100}{2663.88}=)$ 23.7 per centum of the surface of the horizontal fire-tube boiler in favor of the vertical water-tube boiler.

It thus appears that with the proportions of the experimental boilers, the vertical water-tube had the great superiority of containing 23.7 per centum more heating surface in the same bulk; nor is it possible by any change of the proportions of the horizontal fire-tubes to much modify this fact, for it is an advantage inherent to the vertical water-tube type in connection with the heating surface contained in the tube boxes.

That the measurement of the surfaces in contact with the products of combustion is the correct one, will be apparent if we consider that the power of the water to absorb heat greatly exceeds that of any metal to transmit it. Now the area for the reception of the heat is evidently that in contact with it, and as the tube can transmit no more than what enters by this area, it is plain that this area is the correct measure of the heating surface of the boiler.

The weight of water contained in the boilers up to 9 inches above the top of the tubes, is calculated for fresh water and at the steaming temperature of 243° Fahr. The weight of a cubic foot at that temperature is taken to be 59.073 pounds, on the supposition that the specific gravity of the water lessens as much from 212° to 243° as from 181° to 212° Fahr., and that the weight of a cubic foot at 62° Fahr. is 62.321 pounds. The specific gravity of water at 62° being 1.001010 and at 212° Fahr. 1.042986, the weight of a cubic foot at the latter temperature will be 59.813 pounds. The specific gravity of water at 181° Fahr. is 1.030237, consequently the weight of a cubic foot at that temperature will be 60.553 pounds; and 60.553—59.813 = 0.740, and 59.813—0.740 = 59.073, the weight in pounds of a cubic foot of fresh water at 243° Fahr.

In comparing the weights of water contained in the experimental boilers, it will be perceived that the vertical water-tube has an advantage in lightness of (46600—39200 =) 7400 pounds, and that it contains ($\frac{46600-39200 \times 100}{46600}$ =) 15.9 per centum less water than its rival.

In weight of tubes—which being of brass are expensive—the vertical water-tube boiler has the advantage of (10115—9856 =) 259 pounds less than the horizontal fire-tube boiler, or the vertical water-tubes weigh ($\frac{10115-9856 \times 100}{10115}$ =) 2.56 per centum less than the horizontal fire-tubes, although the former contain the most heating surface ; this is, of course, due to the greater thinness of their metal.

The gross weight of the two boilers, including tubes, etc., but exclusive of water, differs only by (86860—86412 =) 448 pounds or ($\frac{86860-86412 \times 100}{86860}$ =) 0.52 per centum of the weight of the vertical water-tube boiler in favor of the horizontal fire-tube. This is caused, notwithstanding the 259 pounds less weight of the tubes, by the additional weight of the sides of the tube-boxes and of the top and bottom tube-plates with the vertical water-tube boiler.

If, however, the gross weight of both boilers, inclusive of water, be compared, we have for the horizontal fire-tube (86412+46600 =) 133012 pounds against (86860+39200 =) 126060 pounds with the vertical water-tube, difference 6952 pounds or ($\frac{133012-126060 \times 100}{133012}$ =) $5\frac{1}{4}$ per centum of the weight of the horizontal fire-tube boiler in favor of the vertical water-tube.

Description of the Engines.

There were two horizontal, condensing, geared engines, placed on the same side of the vessel, and connected upon the main shaft at right angles to each other. The cylinder valves were of the usual double poppet kind, and the steam was cut off by the steam valve with the adjustable arrangement patented by ALLEN & WELLS. The two engines have one surface condenser in common, constructed according to the Patent of J. P. PIRSSON. It is not a close surface condenser, but the spaces within and without the refrigerating tubes are in communication with each other by means of large apertures, so that whatever steam escapes condensation by the tubes passes through the apertures and is condensed by the shower of refrigerating water falling freely in vacuo among the tubes. There is consequently the same vacuum on the outside of the tubes as within them, and were there no air-leaks this vacuum could always be made equal to a column of mercury 27 inches high let the tube surface be efficient or not, for whatever steam passed it would be condensed by the shower as in the usual jet condenser ; any deficiency of vacuum, therefore, with this condenser, is due purely to air-leaks. Of course, whatever steam passes the tubes and becomes condensed by the shower or jet, is so much loss of distilled water to the boiler. The condenser is exhausted by two large air pumps (one to each engine) in communication with the space outside the tubes ; that is, between them and the shell ; and the distilled water resulting from the condensation of the steam by the tubes, is drawn off by one small air-pump (in common for both engines) in communication with the space inside the tubes.

Just previous to the experiments the cylinders had been newly bored, the engines relined, and most of the principal journals provided with new brasses. The entire cylinders, valve-chests, and steam pipes up to the boilers, were covered with a thick coat of felt cased over with wood.

The following are the dimensions required to be known in connection with the experiments, namely :—

Diameter of the forward cylinder................	70⅛ inches.
" " after "	70⅜ "
" " piston rod (one to each engine)...	7 "
Stroke of piston of both engines	4 feet.
Aggregate area of both pistons, exclusive of area of piston rods................................	7713.516 sq. inches.
Space displacement of both pistons per double stroke, exclusive of bulk of piston rods..............	428.528 cub. ft.

Space comprised between pistons and steam valves (which are also the cut-off valves) at both ends of both cylinders per double stroke of piston ..	19.220 cubic feet.
Total space filled with steam of the final cylinder pressure, per double stroke of both pistons....	447.748 "
Total number of refrigerating tubes (copper) in condenser..................................	1210
Length of tubes................................	5 feet.
External diameter of tubes......................	1 inch.
Area of condensing surface in tubes..............	1584 square feet.

Description of the Screw.

As it may be useful to some reader to know the dimensions of the screw in connection with the facts of these experiments, they are given as follows, namely :—

Diameter of the screw.................................	15 feet.
Diameter of the hub	26 inches.
Pitch (uniform)......................................	22 feet 6 inches.
Length of the screw in the fore and direction of the vessel,	32 inches.
Number of blades	3
Multiple of Gearing..................................	$2\frac{2}{7}$

Mode of Conducting the Experiments.

As the experiments were made for the sole purpose of determining the relative evaporative efficiencies of the two kinds of boilers, it was unnecessary to take the ship to sea ; and for the sake of convenience the engines and screw were operated with the vessel securely lashed to the dock of the New York Navy Yard. The object being to ascertain the evaporation under the ordinary conditions of actual practice, the experiments with each boiler were continued uninterruptedly for ninety-six hours in order to include the effects of average care in firing, of dirty fires, and of losses in cleaning the fires. During the experiments regular sea-watches were kept by the Firemen and Assistant Engineers of the vessel, superintended by the Board. A log was kept by the senior Engineer of the watch, who entered in it at the close of each hour the average boiler steam pressure for that hour as shown by an open syphon mercurial gauge with glass top ; the average vacuum in the condenser as shown by a close barometer gauge ; the temperature of the engine room, of the fire-room, of the salt and fresh water hot-wells, and of the injection water ; the weight of coal thrown into the furnaces, and of dry refuse in ashes, clinkers, and fine coal withdrawn ; the saturation of the water in the boiler, and the number of inches in depth blown out and fed in from the salt water hot-well to maintain it at one and a half time the natural concentration. The number of double strokes made by the engines' pistons, was taken by a self-registering counter and entered every hour. An Indicator double diagram was taken at the end of each hour from both cylinders, and from the mean of the final pressures as given by these diagrams the evaporation was calculated. The thermometers were placed in the centre of the engine and fire-rooms, and those showing the temperatures of the hot-wells had their bulbs constantly immersed in the water.

In making the experiments every precaution was taken to insure exact similarity of circumstance with both boilers. The same Indicators (one permanently fixed to each engine), thermometers, gauges, and scales, were employed ; and the same Firemen fired both and were directed by the same Assistant Engineers. The cut-offs, set to suppress the admission of the steam into the cylinders at $\frac{48}{100}$ of the stroke of piston from the commencement, were secured to prevent accidental alteration ; and the throttle (a butterfly valve) was kept unchanged at two holes open on the arc, eight holes being wide open.

The experiments with both boilers were begun and concluded at mid-day. They were first made on the horizontal fire-tube boiler, commencing at noon on the 10th of June and ending at noon on the 14th ; at which time precisely—the steam in the vertical water-tube boiler having previously been raised for some time and blowing off, and the fires brought to steady action,—the screw stop valve of the horizontal fire-tube boiler was closed and that of the vertical water-tube boiler opened without stopping the engines, and the experiments continued without interruption until they ended at noon on the 18th of June. They thus embraced exactly ninety-six consecutive hours with each boiler.

The experiments were conducted in precisely the same manner with both boilers. At the commencement they were filled with sea water, and no account was taken of its temperature, or of the weight of fuel required to raise the steam to a pressure of 22 pounds per square inch above the atmosphere ; but as soon as it reached that point, the height of the water in the boiler was noted upon the glass water guage, the condition of the fires was carefully observed, and the engines were started. At the end of each experiment the height of water and the steam pressure in the boiler were left the same as at the commencement, as was also the condition of the fires as nearly as could be estimated by the eye.

The indicators were large, excellent instruments, and had been properly tested and put in complete order for these experiments ; they worked very satisfactorily and gave smooth-lined diagrams in whose correctness it is believed every confidence may be placed. A fair specimen of these diagrams will be found in Plate IV. A careful analysis was made of all the diagrams taken, and the respective quantities will be found in the following Table.

The coal used was hard Pennsylvania anthracite of very inferior quality, giving for a mean with slow combustion the excessive amount of over 25 per centum of dry refuse. Every pound of the coal and of the refuse was weighed in the same scales.

The boilers with the exception of the bottoms, were thoroughly covered by a thick coat of new felt ; the tops and the steam chimney were additionally protected by sheets of lead soldered together over the felt, and for the steam chimney there was still over the lead a casing of wood.

The great advantage of continuing the experiments with each boiler for so long a period as four consecutive days, was the certainty of obtaining correct practical results whose probable error would not equal one per centum. Experiments of this kind on such large boilers are reliable, *ceteris paribus*, in proportion to their duration ; the longer the time the less becomes any error from a single observation because it is distributed among quantities so large that it forms but an inappreciable fraction of them. In extended experiments where there are a great many numerical observations, there also results great accuracy in their means from the correction of errors, and the greater the more numerous the observations. A short experiment with such large boilers containing so many furnaces, would be comparatively unsatisfactory from the impossibility of knowing how near the condition of the fires was the same at the commencement and end ; from the inequality in firing ; from the different proportion of refuse found even in different shovelfuls of the same heap of coal ; from the fluctuations in the draught ; from the losses by cleaning the furnaces ; from the different quantities of air in proportion to fuel admitted at different times ; and from the more or less perfect combustion of the coal which depends so much on the size of the lumps, the thickness of the bed of coal on the grates, the cleanness of the fires, and the absence of holes in them, &c.; the average of which conditions, though sensibly the same for long times and large quantities, may vary greatly for short times and small quantities.

Data and Results of the Experiments.

The following Table contains the observed data and the calculated results of the experiments with the two boilers : the quantities given are the means of all the observations taken. The weight of water evaporated is obtained by calculation from the pressure of the steam at the end of the stroke of the pistons as given by the Indicator ; and to this is added the evaporation due to the heat required for producing the power of the engine, which heat was obtained by the condensation of steam in the cylinders. This evaporation is calculated for JOULE's equivalent of one pound of water raised one degree on Fahrenheit's scale for every 772 foot-pounds developed by the engines. There is also added the evaporation due to the difference of the heat in the water blown out of the boiler and pumped-in from the salt water hot-well to maintain the boiler water at one and a half time the concentration of sea-water, as there was a small deficit in the distilled water furnished by the condenser for feeding the boiler. The total evaporation is the sum of these three quantities. It is, of course, too small by the weight of steam condensed in the boilers, steam pipes, and cylinders from any causes whatever ; and by the heat lost in water leaking from the boilers or priming over into the cylinders.

The boilers had been tested cold and made tight under a hydrostatic pressure of 50 pounds per square inch above the atmosphere, and there was during the experiments no perceptible leaks, but there might have been a slight leakage in the connexions not discerned. I have known this to be the case when the most careful examination failed to detect it.

The boilers did prime though not inconveniently, and this was what might have been expected, notwithstanding the throttling of the steam and the slow speed of piston, from the small capacity of the steam-room compared with the capacity of the cylinders; for it must be remembered that only half the steam-room was in use owing to the boilers being separately experimented with. The steam-room was the greatest with the vertical water-tube boiler but the difference was not important. It may be taken during the experiments, including 132 cubic feet in the long steam pipes, at 787 cubic feet; the capacity of both cylinders per stroke of piston was, say, 224 cubic feet, making the ratio as $3\frac{1}{2}$ to 1. But if we consider that the steam was cut off at $\frac{48}{100}$ of the stroke of piston from the commencement, and that its pressure at the point of cutting off was, say, 16.8 pounds per square inch above zero, while the boiler pressure was, say, 25.6 pounds above that point, it will be found that the weight of steam used per stroke of pistons compared with the weight in the boiler and steam-pipes is nearly as 1 to $10\frac{3}{4}$. At the same time the piston had the low velocity of 88 feet per minute, making only eleven double strokes in that time.

The deficit of distilled water for feeding the boilers given by the surface condenser was, as nearly as could be ascertained by careful observation, one twelfth; that is to say, there was returned to the boiler as distilled water eleven twelfths of the steam leaving it. Now, as the concentration of the boiler water was maintained at one and a half time the density of sea water, there was lost by the necessary "blowing off and feeding in" to produce it, the heat due to the difference of the temperatures of the blown out and fed in water for one twelfth of the total feed-water. The time required to raise the water in the horizontal fire-tube boiler from the density of sea-water to a density one and a half time greater was 19 hours, and for the vertical water-tube boiler 16 hours, owing to the difference in the weight of water contained in them. Hence, with the horizontal fire-tube boiler the loss by blowing off continued for (96—19=) 77 hours of the total 96 of the experiment; and with the vertical water-tube boiler for (96—16=) 80 hours. On this data the loss by blowing off has been calculated.

In determining comparatively the evaporation of two boilers when steam of the same pressure is worked off in the same manner by the same engine, and when the same instruments are employed, the Indicator measurement is more reliable than the direct measurement of the water in a Tank previously to being pumped into the boiler; particularly in the case of boilers like these having very small steam-room and priming. The priming depends on many accidental conditions during an experiment, and also on the type of boiler employed; now, by the Tank measurement the whole of it is credited to the evaporation of the boiler, making the boiler that primes the most the greatest apparent gainer in the result, and in the direct ratio of the difference of the priming; while by the Indicator measurement a considerable difference of priming would produce but a slight error in the results, because the latent heat of steam so greatly exceeds the sensible heat. In the case, too, of a difference of leakage from the two boilers, the one that leaked the most would obtain the greatest apparent evaporation, because the leakage is included in the Tank measurement, and increases it in direct ratio; while with the Indicator measurement, unless the difference in leakage be excessive, there would result but a trifling error for the same reason as in the case of difference of priming. The Tank measurement gives too great an evaporation by the priming and leakage of the boiler; the Indicator gives too small a one by the weight of steam condensed in the boiler, steam pipes, and cylinders, and by the heat due to the difference of the temperature of the boiler-water and of the feed-water required to replace the losses by priming and leakage; but, as before remarked, it will give in the case of the experimental boilers very correct *comparative* results, which the Tank measurement would not have done, unless by the improbable accident of equality of leakage and priming with both. The Indicator measurement is also the most convenient, and it is the most useful practically because habitually employed.

In calculating the evaporation, the tables of REGNAULT are employed, and the results are given in pounds of steam evaporated per pound of coal and also per pound of combustible from a temperature of feed-water of 100° and of 212° Fahr. for convenience of reference as both are used. The combustible is the coal less the refuse in ashes, clinkers, and fine coal and is, of course, the proper unit of comparison, the per centage of refuse being a mere accident of the coal itself, and to be eliminated when the purely evaporative results are to be compared.

Table Containing the Data and Results of the Experiments.

		Horizontal Fire-tube Boiler.	Vertical Water-tube Boiler.
	Duration of the experiments in consecutive hours.......	96.	96.
PRESSURES.	Steam pressure in boiler in pounds per square inch above atmosphere, per guage...........	10.43	11.41
PRESSURES. PER INDICATOR.	Steam pressure in cylinder in pounds per square inch above zero, at commencement of the stroke..........	19.44	20.30
	Steam pressure in cylinder in pounds per square inch above zero, at point of cutting off....................	16.40	17.13
	Steam pressure in cylinder in pounds per square inch above zero, at end of stroke.........................	9.11	9.45
	Mean back pressure against pistons in pounds per square inch above zero	5.50	5.85
	Mean gross effective pressure on pistons in pounds per square inch..	9.18	9.58
ENGINES.	Vacuum in condenser in inches of mercury, per guage...	21.48	20.80
	Total number of double strokes of pistons made by the engines, per counter...............................	62,518.	64,196.
	Mean number of double strokes of pistons per minute made by the engines...............................	10.854	11.145
	Portion of stroke of piston at which the steam is cut off, from the commencement...........................	0.48	0.48
	Gross horses power developed by the engine, per indicator	186.32	199.65
COAL.	Total number of pounds of anthracite consumed.........	100,436.	92,512.
	Total number of pounds of refuse in ashes, clinkers, and fine coal..	24,908.	24,178.
	Total number of pounds of combustible consumed.......	75,528.	68,334.
	Per centum of the anthracite in refuse.................	24.80	26.14
	Number of pounds of anthracite consumed per hour.....	1,046.21	963.67
	Number of pounds of combustible consumed per hour....	786.75	711.81
	Number of pounds of anthracite consumed per square foot of grate per hour..............................	9.687	8.923
	Number of pounds of combustible consumed per square foot of grate per hour..............................	7.285	6.591
	Number of pounds of anthracite consumed per hour per indicated horse-power..............................	5.615	4.827
	Number of pounds of combustible consumed per hour per indicated horse-power..............................	4.223	3.565
	Total number of pounds of water blown out of boiler to maintain its density at one and a half time that of sea water...	111,492.	123,144.
TEMPERATURES.	Temperature in degrees Fahr. on deck.................	61.	74.
	Temperature in degrees Fahr. of engine room..........	96.	106.
	Temperature in degrees Fahr. of fire room.............	99.	112.
	Temperature in degrees Fahr. of salt water hot-well.....	100.	102.
	Temperature in degrees Fahr. of fresh water hot-well....	100.	100.
	Temperature in degrees Fahr. of injection-water.........	62.	65.
EVAPORATION.	Pounds of steam evaporated from a temperature of feed-water of 100° Fahr., and discharged from the cylinders at the end of the strokes of their pistons, calculated from the pressure by indicator at the end of the stroke.	657,570.70	699,056.30
	Pounds of steam evaporated from a temperature of feed-water of 100° Fahr., equivalent to the heat lost in "blowing off" to maintain the boiler water at 1½ time the density of sea water..............................	14,492.93	16,250.88
	Pounds of steam evaporated from a temperature of feed-water of 100° Fahr., equivalent to the heat annihilated in the cylinders in producing the power of the engines..	42,203.55	45,193.86
	Total number of pounds of steam evaporated from a temperature of feed-water of 100° Fahr.................	714,267.18	760,501.04
	Total number of pounds of steam evaporated from a temperature of feed-water of 212° Fahr.................	796,316.33	847,798.48
ECONOMIC RESULTS.	Pounds of steam evaporated from a temperature of feed-water of 100° Fahr. by one pound of anthracite......	6.827	7.892
	Pounds of steam evaporated from a temperature of feed-water of 100° Fahr. by one pound of combustible......	9.079	10.684
	Pounds of steam evaporated from a temperature of feed-water of 212° Fahr. by one pound of anthracite......	7.611	8.798
	Pounds of steam evaporated from a temperature of feed-water of 212° Fahr. by one pound of combustible......	10.122	11.910

Comparative Merits of the Horizontal Fire-tube and the Vertical Water-tube Boilers for Marine Steam Machinery.

The qualities of boilers for marine purposes are as follows, namely :—

The relation which the bulk, weight, and potential and economic evaporation of the boiler, bear to the aggregate bulk and weight occupied in the vessel by boiler and coal. This relation depends upon the absolute weight of steam which a boiler of given dimensions of shell can furnish in a given time ; and on the weight of steam furnished per unit of weight of combustible.

The accessibility of the *heating surfaces* for *scaling.*

The accessibility of the whole for sweeping out soot and ashes, and for repairs.

Durability.

Cost.

We will compare the experimental boilers on these points, separately.

1st. Of the absolute weight of steam which the experimental boilers can furnish in a given time.—This depends upon the maximum rate of combustion of the two boilers, and their economic evaporation. In the preceding Table it will be perceived that the rate of combustion during the experiments was nearly the same both with the horizontal fire-tube and the vertical water-tube boilers ; the vertical water-tube consuming only $(\frac{7.285-6.591 \times 100}{7.285}=)$ $9\frac{1}{2}$ per centum less of combustible per square foot of grate per hour than the horizontal fire-tube. It must not, however, be concluded from this that their maximum rates of combustion were in that proportion ; for this close approach to equality was designedly caused in order to test the economic evaporation of the two types of tube *per se,* which required for this purpose that equal quantities of heat should be thrown upon them in equal times. Now, as the maximum rate of combustion of anthracite with the vertical water-tube boiler was known previously from others of sensibly the same arrangement and proportions, the quantity to be burned per square foot of grate per hour with both boilers was fixed at this maximum which is from 9 to 10 pounds. The horizontal fire-tube boiler, however, as ascertained from trials before and after these experiments, could burn under the same conditions of atmosphere, etc., 14 pounds of anthracite per square foot of grate per hour, but this increased rate of combustion was accompanied by a very great falling-off in the economic evaporation of the unit of weight of combustible; how great, the trials were not sufficiently long to determine with exactness, but the difference was certainly as much as one-sixth; that is to say, if the evaporation from a temperature of feed-water of 100° Fahr. was 9.079 pounds of water per pound of combustible when burning at the rate of 9.687 pounds of anthracite per square foot of grates per hour, it would be 7.566 pounds of water when this rate is raised to 14 pounds. That it should be so is obvious enough when we consider that the increased rate of combustion depends on an increased draught, to obtain which, *ceteris paribus*, the products of combustion must be delivered into the chimney at a correspondingly higher temperature. In other words, if an increased rate of combustion be desired, a portion of the heat that was previously applied to evaporation must be taken to produce the increased draught necessary to give it; consequently it is obtained entirely at the expense of the economic evaporation. As nearly as could be ascertained, an increase of $\frac{2}{5}$ths in the rate of combustion was accompanied by a decrease of $\frac{1}{6}$th in the evaporation per unit of weight of combustible. And in this connection must be remarked a striking difference in the two boilers: in the horizontal fire-tube the rate of combustion could be easily increased by simply supplying the furnace with more coal; while in the vertical water-tube the additional supply remained unconsumed. The reason of this will be hereafter given. If now we deduct the $\frac{1}{6}$th decrease of economic evaporation from the $\frac{2}{6}$th increased weight of coal consumed in equal times, we shall have remaining ($\frac{1.4}{6} = 0.23$, and 1.40—0.23 = 1.17) 17 per centum more absolute weight of steam produced. The maximum evaporation of the horizontal fire-tube boiler can then be taken at 17 per centum more than given by the experiments. With the vertical water-tube the rate of combustion given in the Table was the maximum that could be obtained.

During the experiments, the weight of steam produced by the two boilers from the feed-water temperature of 100° Fahr., was 714267.18 pounds for the horizontal fire-tube, and 760501.04 pounds for the vertical water-tube; difference in favor of the latter 6½ per centum of the former; deducting which from the above 17 per centum, there remains finally 10½ per centum in favor of the horizontal fire-tube. *If, therefore, the maximum absolute weight of steam that can be produced in equal times be alone considered, the horizontal fire-tube boiler for equal dimensions has an advantage of* 10½ *per centum over the vertical water-tube.*

2d. Of the weight of steam per unit of weight of combustible furnished by the two boilers.—In determining the relative economic evaporation in the two cases, it is obviously proper to compare the weights of steam obtained per unit of weight of combustible and not per unit of weight of coal; for it is only the part consumed of the gross weight that is applied evaporatively, the remaining refuse is a proportion of the gross weight of the coal variable from many accidental circumstances and is in no way influenced by the type of boiler.

With the horizontal fire-tube boiler there was evaporated from the temperature of 100° Fahr. of feed-water, 9.079 pounds of steam per pound of combustible; and with the vertical water-tube boiler, 10.684 pounds; difference in favor of the latter, ($\frac{10.684—9.079 \times 100}{9.079}$ =) 17⅔ per centum of the former. Hence, we perceive, that *the vertical water-tube boiler had the great superiority of evaporating with the same fuel* 17⅔ *per centum more water than the horizontal fire-tube boiler.* And at the same time it produced $6\frac{1}{2}$ per centum more weight of steam in equal times.

If the economic evaporation with both boilers be compared when at their maximum rates of combustion, then the vertical water-tube will evaporate ($\frac{1}{6}$th$+0.17\frac{2}{3}=$) $34\frac{1}{3}$ per centum more water with the same fuel than the horizontal fire-tube; but the latter will produce in equal times $10\frac{1}{2}$ per centum more weight of steam.

3d. OF THE TOTAL OR ABSOLUTE WEIGHTS OF STEAM THAT WOULD BE FURNISHED BY BOILERS OF THE EXPERIMENTAL TYPES, SUPPOSING THE SAME SPACE IN THE VESSEL TO BE ALLOTTED FOR BOILER AND FUEL WITH BOTH; AND SUPPOSING BOTH TO FURNISH EQUAL WEIGHTS OF STEAM IN EQUAL TIMES.—From the foregoing we perceive, that to furnish the same absolute weight of steam at the maximum rate of combustion, there would be required $10\frac{1}{2}$ per centum more vertical water-tube boiler than horizontal fire-tube boiler, but that with the former the steam would be obtained with $34\frac{1}{3}$ per centum less coal. On board the "SAN JACINTO" the bunkers stowed 360 tons of anthracite occupying 15000 cubic feet of space; the circumscribing parallelopipedon of the two boilers and fire-room between them was 7291 cubic feet; if, now, we add $10\frac{1}{2}$ per centum more boiler we shall add to this space ($7291\times.10\frac{1}{2}=$) 766 cubic feet which will be subtracted from the coal bunker space of 15000 cubic feet leaving for coal ($15000-766=$) 14234 cubic feet. We shall then have for the space occupied by the vertical water-tube boiler ($7291+766=$) 8257 cubic feet, and by the coal 14234 cubic feet; while for the space occupied by the horizontal fire-tube boiler we have 7291 cubic feet, and by the coal 15000 cubic feet; both boilers furnishing at their maximum rates of combustion equal quantities of steam in equal times. But this steam will, with the horizontal fire-tube boiler, cost $34\frac{1}{3}$ per centum more coal to obtain it. Taking in the two cases the cubic feet of space occupied by the coal to represent the weight of the coal itself, the coal stowed with the vertical water-tube boiler will produce a total weight of steam represented by $(\frac{14234}{1.00}=)$ 14234; while with the horizontal fire-tube boiler it will produce a weight of only $(\frac{15000}{1.34\frac{1}{3}}=)$ 11166; consequently, taking the space allotted for boiler and coal on board the "SAN JACINTO" for the basis of comparison, there could be placed in it a vertical water-tube boiler producing in equal times equal weights of steam with a horizontal fire-tube boiler at its maximum rate of combustion, and having the ability to steam nearly $(\frac{14234-11166 \times 100}{11166}=)$ $27\frac{1}{2}$ per centum *longer time.* The first cost of this boiler would be $10\frac{1}{2}$ per centum more, but it would cause a constant saving of $34\frac{1}{3}$ per centum of all the fuel consumed. If ability to steam equal times were required in the two cases, there could be saved with the vertical water-tube boiler $(14234 \times 0.27\frac{1}{2}=)$ 3914 cubic feet of space which is $(\frac{3914 \times 100}{7291+15000}=)$ $17\frac{1}{2}$ per centum of the total space allotted to the horizontal fire-tube boiler and its fuel. The weight of two vertical water-tube boilers, like the experimental one, and their water would be 252120 pounds or, say $(\frac{252120}{7291}=)$ $34\frac{3}{4}$ pounds per cubic foot of circumscribing parallelopipedon, including fire-room; the weight of a cubic foot of anthracite is, say 54 pounds; hence the substitution for coal of an equal bulk of boiler would lessen the weight in the vessel.

Finally, we perceive, then, that *the weight of steam furnished in equal times by both boilers being equal, and equal space being occupied in the vessel for boiler and coal, the vertical water-tube boiler at its maximum rate of combustion has the great superiority of furnishing $27\frac{1}{2}$ per centum more total weight of steam than the horizontal fire-tube boiler at its maximum rate of combustion, while at the same time the aggregate weight of boiler and coal will be the least.* On board the "SAN JACINTO" the vertical water-tube boiler and coal would weigh $(766 \times \overline{54-34\frac{3}{4}}=)$ 14,745 pounds less than the horizontal fire-tube boiler and coal.

4th. OF THE ACCESSIBILITY OF THE HEATING SURFACES FOR SCAL-

ING.—It is of the highest importance that all the heating surfaces of marine boilers should be accessible for being freed mechanically from scale; for it is impossible to keep them from becoming covered with it, or when once formed to remove it by chemical means without destroying the metal. Universal experience has shown that all marine boilers, how well soever they may be managed, and carrying steam of the lowest temperature under the most favorable conditions, form scale which cannot be taken off except by hammers, scrapers, and picks. To use these implements the surfaces must be accessible, and in this respect *the vertical water-tubes have a decisive superiority from the complete and easy manner in which they can be reached by a scaling tool and cleaned mechanically.* The bracing and man-holes are so arranged that access can be had to both ends of the tubes—on top and below—and the room between the shell and top of the tubes required for putting them in is sufficient to allow of easy working and the convenient handling of the cutters and scrapers. A very little labor therefore at the end of each voyage will completely remove all the scale formed; the operation will require but little time when so frequently repeated, and then the boiler is in the condition of a new one so far as evaporation from its surfaces is concerned. The writer has seen these tubes thoroughly cleaned of indurated scale $\frac{3}{8}$ of an inch thick which had been suffered to accumulate by neglect. The operation was performed with a tool having four narrow cutters, that on being forced down the tube made as many slots from end to end of the interior cylinder of scale which then broke out and fell to the bottom. With the vertical water-tube boilers of the large Frigates of the United States Navy, now in use from three to four years, and which are scaled at the end of every voyage, the scaling is done with great quickness and in a very thorough manner by a simple steel spring scraper split and fitting the tube.

With the horizontal fire-tube boiler the operation of scaling is excessively tedious and difficult, and only partial at the best. In fact it is impossible to scale the whole of the horizontal tubes without the removal of a consideraple portion of them in order to render the remainder accessible. In many boilers one vertical row of tubes to each furnace is omitted in the construction to make space for a man to descend and use a scaling tool on the level of each horizontal row. This method, while it is not effective, is at the expense of about one-ninth of the heating surface,—already much too small. All attempts to remove hard scale by suddenly expanding the tubes with a quick blaze from shavings will be found futile; and they can only be made at the imminent hazard of the joints. It being then practically impossible to keep the surfaces of the horizontal fire-tubes free from scale, they will become more and more coated as their age increases, and their evaporative efficiency will be continually impaired to the extent of the heat thus intercepted.

In the case of the experimental boilers, it will be observed that both being new the surfaces of their tubes were equally clean. The vertical water-tubes can be maintained in this state; the horizontal fire-tubes cannot. Were the experiments to be repeated after the lapse of a year, the gain of $17\frac{2}{3}$ per centum by the vertical water-tube boiler would probably be found increased to 20 or 25 per centum due to the difference in cleanliness alone.

5th. OF THE ACCESSIBILITY OF THE BOILER FOR SWEEPING OF SOOT AND ASHES, AND FOR REPAIRS.—The horizontal fire-tubes can be swept of soot and ashes much more easily, rapidly, and completely than the vertical water-tubes, and in this respect have the advantage; but the difference is not considerable enough to be of consequence practically. Both can be swept from the fire-room when steaming, the tubes of each furnace in succession, by allowing the fire to burn down.

If the tubes or their joints rupture when steaming, the horizontal fire-tubes are much the most accessible for plugging; further, as they are only about one-fourth the number of the vertical water-tubes, the liability to leakage is correspondingly lessened. The leaking horizontal fire-tube can be seen at once, but it is often a difficult matter to discover the leaking vertical water-tube, as the water from it spreads out over the lower tube-plate and embraces several, while the tubes themselves can only be partially seen by inserting a candle in the narrow space separating the rows. Under these circumstances it is easy to understand how difficult it may be to find the leaking tube in the centre of a nest. The much greater time required to find a leaking tube and then to plug it, and the greater labor involved—for the boiler must be blown entirely out and cooled, and the man-holes opened before it can be entered—are strong objections to the vertical water-tube, particularly for war steamers if iron tubes be used, indeed these are the only objections of any moment; but with the drawn brass tubes now generally adopted for both kinds of boiler, the liability to leakage is so trifling that most of their importance is lost. The horizontal fire-tubes can be plugged from the smoke connexions as soon as the steam is blown off and the water blown down below the level of the leak; we have neither to open the boiler nor to wait for it to cool, for as soon as the fire is drawn the strong rush of cold air through the furnaces and tubes to the chimney makes it practicable to enter the back smoke connexions after a few minutes delay.

6th. Durability.—The experience of several years with the boilers of a large number of United States Steamships has not shown the failure of a single vertical water-tube, and they are now apparently in as good a condition as ever. It is true that in some merchant steamers many of the tubes have pitted deeply and wasted away; but then as others adjacent remained intact, the cause of injury must be looked for in the mal-composition of the metal of the tube, and not in the fact of its being a vertical water-tube. Had the latter been the case the destruction would be general and in all boilers of this type, whereas instead of being the rule it has been the exception only.

We have not had sufficient experience with brass horizontal fire-tubes to institute a comparison as to durability, but there is no reason to believe that in general the one kind of tube has any superiority in this respect over the other.

7th. COST.—As regards materials the vertical water-tube boiler is the cheapest from the fact of the less weight of its brass tubes, although the weight of iron in it slightly exceeds that in the horizontal fire-tube boiler. But as regards workmanship it is a little the dearest, owing to the greater amount of labor in preparing the tube-plates, fastening the tubes, and making the tube-boxes. The aggregate cost of materials and workmanship is a trifle the greatest with the vertical water-tube boiler, but the difference is too little to enter into a practical estimate.

8th. FINALLY.—It is clear from the foregoing comparison, that the superiority is so great of the vertical water-tube boiler both in potential and economic evaporation, and in the facility and completeness with which its heating surfaces can be scaled—the qualities of paramount importance with Marine Boilers—that unquestionably it should be preferred to the horizontal fire-tube boiler.

TEMPERATURE OF THE PRODUCTS OF COMBUSTION WHEN DISCHARGED FROM THE TUBES.—During the experiments with the boilers the temperature of the heated gases when emerging from the tubes into the uptake was frequently obtained between certain limits by placing just within the tubes small pieces of tin and lead supported on a tripod of slender iron wire with the horizontal fire-tubes, and suspended by the same kind of wire with the vertical water-tubes. With the latter it was found impossible to fuse the tin even on the sharp cut edges and in the hottest part of the current. A thermometer placed in a cylindrical vessel of copper 6 inches deep and 2 inches diameter, filled with oil and suspended beneath the hanging bridge midway between it and the bottom of the uptake, averaged 290° Fahr., which was only about 47 degrees above the temperature of the steam.

With the horizontal fire-tubes there was selected over one of the middle furnaces and in the middle vertical row, the centre tube, and the second tube from the top and from the bottom, and in the mouths of these three tubes were placed on separate tripods of slender iron wire about 1¼ inch high, small pieces of lead and tin ; the purpose being to ascertain not only the absolute temperature of the emerging gases but whether the heat was equally diffused among the tubes vertically. The result was strongly marked ; in the lowest tube the tin was not melted, in the centre tube—situated half way between the top and bottom—the tin was melted but not the lead, while in the upper tube the lead was melted ; consequently, in the lower tubes the temperature of the emerging gases was less than 440° Fahr., in the middle tubes it was more than 440° but less than 600° Fahr., while in the upper tubes it was more than 600° Fahr.; the mean temperature was probably about 500° Fahr.

The difference in the temperature of the products of combustion when leaving the tubes in the two boilers was then about (500—290 =) 210° Fahr., and it was curiously verified by the marked difference in the temperature of the corresponding sides of the chimney during some after experiments, when both boilers were used together. Now as the chimney is in common to the two boilers and the gases are free to mingle in it, it might be supposed that its temperature would be uniform on both sides ; this, however, was far from being the fact, for on the side of the horizontal fire-tube boiler the radiant heat was sufficient to affect paint on wood at a distance of 3½ feet, while on the side of the vertical water-tube boiler there was no danger from this cause. By applying the hand, also, the great difference of temperature on the two sides became very sensible.

We have seen that with the horizontal fire-tube boiler the temperature of the heated gases emerging from different horizontal rows of tubes varies enormously, probably 300° Fahr. for the extreme top and bottom rows. Now to what are we to ascribe this great difference? Is it to the fact that the gases find the easiest exit through the top rows and that the calorimeter of these rows is sufficient to pass them with such facility as to rob the lower rows of their proper share leaving them thus comparatively inoperative as heating surfaces? Or is it because the upper rows in consequence of being enveloped in the total mass of steam produced by the furnaces and by the lower rows lying beneath, are not in contact with enough solid water to reduce the temperature of the gases passing through them as low as the temperature of the gases emerging from the lower tubes, which lying in the steam produced by the furnaces only, are in contact with much more solid water and produce a higher economic evaporation from the more complete absorption of the heat of the gases? The latter is undoubtedly the true cause. The upper rows of tubes must necessarily be surrounded with a mass of mere foam composed of water finely divided by and mixed with the steam generated from the lower rows of tubes and the furnaces; in fact nearly all the steam produced by the boiler has necessarily to pass between the tubes of the upper rows, displacing the solid water and replacing it with a soap-bubble like mass possessing a far less heat-absorbing power. The result is, that from the lower row to the upper one, the tubes have a continuously decreasing evaporative efficiency owing to their absorbing a less and less amount of heat as we ascend and as a consequence delivering their heated gases into the chimney at a continuously increasing temperature.

That this is the true solution, is proven by the fact that, *ceteris paribus*, a higher economic evaporation is obtained from the horizontal fire-tubes in measure as the vertical rows are numerous and the horizontal rows few. Also, that their evaporative efficiency increases with each increase of the space between the vertical rows to a distance much greater than is given in practice. In many cases a gain has followed from taking out one or two vertical rows over each furnace, due to the additional space thus left for the passage of the steam rising from the furnaces and lower rows of tubes. On the other hand, by lessening the number of vertical rows and increasing the number of horizontal ones, there will be found a great falling-off in the evaporative efficiency of the tubes; and if the aggregate height of the horizontal rows exceed 3½ feet, scarcely any evaporation will be obtained from the upper rows which will pass their heated gases into the chimney at about 1000° Fahr., owing to deficiency of solid water for absorbing their heat. In effect, these rows will become mere superheating tubes for the steam instead of evaporating tubes for the water.

The economic evaporation of the tubes is then very greatly affected by their distribution; the maximum, *ceteris paribus*, being obtained from the fewest number of horizontal rows and with the widest spaces between the tubes. But this desirable arrangement can only be remotely approximated in practice owing to the fact that the number of vertical rows is limited by the breadth of the furnace, and that in order to place in this space the greatest number of these rows the distance between them must be reduced to a minimum; at the same time the necessity of providing a proper proportion of heating surface and of calorimeter, compels recourse to the maximum number of horizontal rows; and thus we finally obtain a boiler that satisfies the numerical proportions by ignoring the physical laws and paying the penalty in a reduced evaporation.

Now can this state of things be improved? It can, in a measure, by making the tubes of each vertical row to decrease in diameter as we ascend from the lower to the upper tube. The effect of this modification is to retain the same number of tubes and the same number of rows both vertically and horizontally, but the calorimeter of the tubes of each horizontal row will be decreased in the ratio of the square of their diameter, and the velocity and mass of the gases through them being thereby greatly lessened more time will be given for the extraction of the heat. Also, owing to the decreasing diameter of the tubes as we ascend from the lower to the upper ones, the distance between the vertical rows will continuously increase from the bottom to the top and thus furnish increasing spaces for the increasing quantities of steam to be passed through them. By this system of proportioning the tubes, making the diameter of the top ones two-thirds the diameter of the bottom ones, with a distance between the latter of not less than $\frac{45}{100}$ of their diameter ; and by restricting their aggregate height within 2½ feet; and by making the aggregate calorimeter about one seventh of the grate surface, with a proportion of the latter to the total heating surface of the boiler measured on the *interior* circumference of the tubes, of not less than 1 to 28 ; we shall obtain the highest economic evaporation from the horizontal fire-tube boiler consistent with practical conditions. These proportions could not be obtained with a grate exceeding 5 or 5½ feet in length. For diameters of the tubes 3 inches for the bottom row and two inches for the top one will be found convenient, and the intermediate rows can be distributed among diameters increasing by ⅛ inch. Such an arrangement gives also greater facility for scaling, for apart from the obvious advantage of the reduced aggregate height of the tubes, those of each horizontal row project a little beyond those of the row immediately above and expose the scale to be broken by a downward blow from a tool. Although the lessened length of grate with these proportions may appear a disadvantage as requiring more frontage of boiler for equal areas, yet with equal frontage or width of grate it will be found that the same weight of steam will be furnished in equal times as with the additional length and proportions habitually employed, and at a much less cost of coal ; both results being produced by the higher evaporation per unit of weight of combustible.

A great defect of the Horizontal Fire-tube as a transmitter of heat to water, consists in the fact that the temperature of the cylindrical mass of heated gases passing through it, is not equally reduced from axis to periphery; but that while the temperature of the external film in contact with the metallic envelope may be sufficiently lowered, that of the axial thread may remain nearly the same upon leaving as upon entering the tube. After the gases enter the tube there is nothing to continually break them up and mix them so as to successively present fresh particles to the metal in order that the temperature of the whole may be equally reduced. To enable the tube surface to have a maximum evaporating effect, the moment the temperature of a particle of the gas in contact with it is sufficiently lowered, that particle should be removed and replaced by another having a higher temperature, which in its turn should give way to still another, and so on until the temperature of the mass when leaving the tube should be uniform and low enough for a good enonomic result. With the Horizontal Fire-tube this effect is impossible owing to the smoothness of the tube, the want of obstruction in it, the straightness of its direction, and the small instant of time elapsing between the entrance and the exit of the gas. The want of time together with the momentum of the particles due to the velocity of the draught, prevent those in contact with the upper half of the tube surface from obeying the law of gravity and exchanging places with the hotter and therefore lighter particles beneath; while those in contact with the lower semi-circumference of the tube cannot possibly exchange places with the hotter and lighter particles above because they already occupy the lowest position. We thus perceive that not only is the temperature of the products of combustion very unequal upon leaving the whole system of tubes considered as an aggregation, being higher at the top than at the bottom; but that in the case of each particular tube there is the same want of uniformity, the axial thread or core being the hottest and the peripheral film in contact with the metallic envelope being the coolest.

As far back as 1853 during some experiments with the boilers of the U. S. Steamer "PRINCETON," the idea was suggested by Chief Engineer D. B. MARTIN of placing within the tubes a thin strip of iron twisted helically, the width of the iron being equal to the diameter of the tubes. The object was to continually break up and mix the gases by the helical or convolved movement that would be caused by the twisted strip, and to thus present successively fresh particles to the tube surface. The idea was not carried into effect from the belief that if a sufficient number of convolutions were given to the strip to cause a proper mixing up of the gases, the draught would be completely shut off. This method of mixing the gases in a horizontal fire-tube has lately been proposed in England, but it will be found impracticable for the above reason.

The mixing of the gases and the resulting successive presentation of fresh particles to the heat absorbing surface, which is found to be impossible with the horizontal fire-tubes, is easily and completely accomplished with the vertical water-tubes; for it is a natural consequence of the position of their surfaces which, lying at right angles to the stream of the gases, constantly break them up mechanically by obstruction into a mass of eddies and whirlpools, so that the course of any particle from its entrance among the tubes to its exit, instead of being a straight line as in the horizontal fire-tubes, is one of sinuosities and angular deflections that bring it many times into and out of contact with the heat absorbing surfaces. Every particle of the entire mass is, by thus being brought at some time during its course into contact with the tube-surfaces, made to give up its heat before escaping from among the tubes.

With the vertical water-tubes there is found, as with the horizontal fire-tubes, a considerable difference in the temperature of the gases emerging from around the upper part of the tubes and from around the lower part. This difference, though due to the same cause as in the case of the horizontal fire-tubes, is not near so great; for although the upper part of the vertical water-tubes, like the upper rows of the horizontal fire-tubes, is surrounded by mere foam while the lower part is immersed in comparatively solid water, yet as the two parts, unlike the top and bottom rows of the horizontal fire-tubes, are the same piece of metal, the heat of the top strata of the gases not absorbed by the foam surrounding the upper part of the tubes, instead of passing off to the chimney is, in large measure, carried downward by the conductivity of the metal to the solid water beneath which absorbs it and thus obtains from it its proper evaporative effect.

The application of a hanging bridge across the upper part of the tubes at the smoke connexion or uptake leading directly into the chimney, produces a still further equalization of the temperature of the heated gases emerging from among the tubes, and to so great a degree that the difference between the top and bottom strata is not of importance practically; in this respect the bridge is a valuable adjunct and should never be omitted. It can be roughly made of iron plate and supported on inclined brackets; it should be divided vertically into two or three parts hinged—the upper on the brackets and the lower on the upper—in order that a part or the whole may be employed or thrown back at will. It should also be divided lengthwise into as many parts as there are furnaces, so that it can be used for all or for any number desired. A space, about 2 inches wide, should be left between the top of the bridge and the top of the tubes in order that the direct movement of the gases along the upper tube sheet may not be entirely prevented. When the bridge is thrown back the draught is improved, the difference between the temperatures of the top and bottom strata of the gases emerging from the tubes becomes considerably increased, and the economic result from the fuel is diminished.

A much less depth of water may with safety be carried over the vertical water-tubes than over the horizontal fire-tubes; for if the former be left uncovered the conductivity of the metal will rapidly carry off the heat to the water below and preserve the tube from injury, while if the upper rows of the latter be left uncovered for even a very short interval, they will be burned out and ruined. The loss of the tubes is the least evil, but the danger to life and the vessel, and the loss of time required for putting in new ones even when there are enough on hand, are so serious, that in order to be on the safe side the water is carried high at the expense of the steam-room whose proportions at the best with tubular boilers are greatly too restricted.

Of the circulation of the water and the extrication of the Steam.—The circulation of the water and the disengagement of the steam bubbles from the evaporating surfaces, are much the most rapid with the vertical water-tubes. With the horizontal fire-tube boiler the water replenishing that which is evaporated by the tubes, comes partly from between the furnace crown and the lower row, and partly from the water spaces between the aggregations of tubes belonging to each furnace. The cross currents from the latter strike the ascending currents from the former at right angles and the velocity of both is lessened as a consequence, in addition to which these currents are greatly impeded by the mechanical obstruction of the tubes themselves, lying at right angles to the direction of both.

With the vertical water-tubes, all the water evaporated by them is supplied from the space between the crown of the furnace and the lower tube-plate, and the ascent of the current not being impeded by either the crossing of other currents or by any mechanical obstructions, and being guided in vertical lines by the tubes themselves, the path of each ascending particle of water will be the shortest possible and its speed the maximum due to the conditions of temperature and height of column. Hence in a given time a much greater number of particles of water would be brought into contact with the vertical water-tube surface than with the horizontal fire-tube surface, and a greater evaporation would necessarily result from a given unit of surface in equal times. A consequence of this greater evaporation would be that the temperature of the metal of the vertical water-tubes would be kept lower than that of the metal of the horizontal fire-tubes, and there would follow the important practical result of a much less formation of scale under equal conditions of density and temperature of the water.

That the temperature of the metal of the evaporating surfaces in boilers is really above that of the water in contact with them, is proven by the different character of the scale deposited upon the furnaces, the tubes, and the shell of the boiler. On the first it is highly crystalline in structure and excessively indurated; on the second the crystalline character and the hardness are much less and gradually decline as we approach the chimney; on the last the scale has become sedimentary in structure and comparatively soft. The *quantity* of scale deposited follows the same law of change with the *quality*, becoming less and less as we recede from the furnace towards the chimney. These differences result entirely from the differences in the local heat causing the deposition of scale on the different parts; and as the temperature of the water on every part was the same, the different temperatures causing the difference in the quality and quantity of the scale precipitated, must have been local and in the metal of the evaporating surfaces themselves. Had the temperature of those surfaces been uniform the scale would have been uniform too in all respects both of quality and quantity instead of exhibiting the marked differences of both found in all boilers.

When a bubble of steam first forms on an evaporating surface it is extremely minute, and if it be not swept off mechanically it will not at once disengage itself and ascend because it will not have sufficient buoyancy to overcome the cohesion of the superincumbent water and force a passage; it will therefore continue in contact with the surface until by the addition of more evaporated particles its buoyancy exceeds the cohesion of the water when it will detatch itself and rise. If, however, the evaporating surfaces be swept by a current, the bubbles of steam will be brushed off mechanically and carried onward with the general stream. Just, then, in proportion to the strength of this current, to its parallelism with the surface swept, and to its coincidence of direction with the natural ascensional direction of the steam, will be the rapidity with which the nascent bubbles are swept off and replaced by solid water. The Vertical Water-tube boiler contains all the conditions for maximum evaporative effect in these particulars, and as regards them is far superior to the Horizontal Fire-tube boiler.

With both kinds of boiler all the steam generated by the furnaces must pass upwards through or between the tubes; and the steam generated by the lower part of the tubes must, in addition, pass through the upper part; but with the vertical water-tube the steam and water currents move vertically in precisely the same direction without obstruction or interference, and being parallel to the surface of the tube sweep it constantly in their ascent brushing off the steam bubbles and replacing them with solid water unintermittingly; thus keeping the temperature of the metal as nearly as possible to the temperature of the water and preventing whatever formation of scale would be due to a greater difference. With the horizontal fire-tube the evaporating surface lies across both the steam and water currents, and the mechanical efficiency of the latter in sweeping off the steam bubbles is consequently greatly decreased and in addition to the decrease due to the less velocity of the water current itself; the horizontal water currents and the vertical steam currents interfere and oppose each other, and the extrication of the bubbles is rendered still more difficult by the obstruction of the tubes themselves; the steam bubbles consequently remain longer in contact with the evaporating surfaces before becoming disengaged and prevent during that time the contact of solid water; the temperature of the metal, therefore, of the horizontal fire-tube, with equal temperature of water, must be greater than with the vertical water-tube, and the formation of scale, *ceteris paribus*, will be greater accordingly.

Owing, also, to the more rapid circulation of the water and easier extrication of the steam, there will be less priming with the Vertical Water-tube than with the Horizontal Fire-tube boiler; and it will be free, too, from the violent intermitting and percussive priming so frequently experienced with the other when its tubes are too crowded and its water-ways too narrow.

On the whole, then, we find, 1st. That the evaporating surface with the vertical water-tubes is not only greater in equal spaces, but that per unit of surface it has a greater evaporative efficiency than the horizontal fire-tubes and will generate more steam in equal times. 2d. That it is so disposed that per unit of surface it extracts in equal times a much greater amount of the heat in the products of combustion. 3d. That it delivers these products into the chimney at a more uniform temperature for the whole mass. 4th. That the temperature of the metal of the tubes is lower and the formation of scale less. And 5th. That the priming is less, owing to the easier and more rapid extrication of the steam from the water.

The superiority of evaporating surfaces arranged in vertical water-tubes immersed in and lying at right angles to the currents of the products of combustion is so great in every respect, that when it becomes properly appreciated the arrangement in horizontal fire-tubes will doubtless be definitively abandoned.

UNITED STATES STEAM SLOOP

"NIAGARA."

UNITED STATES STEAM SLOOP

"NIAGARA."

The "NIAGARA" is an enormous steam sloop-of-war completed in 1856 by the U. S. Navy Department simultaneously with the steam frigates "WABASH," "COLORADO," "ROANOKE," "MERRIMAC," and "MINNESOTA," from all which she differs widely in dimensions, model, sparring, and battery; in fact in everything. She was designed by the late GEORGE STEERS, builder of the yacht "AMERICA," who was temporarily employed for this duty by the Navy Department.

The "NIAGARA," though but a sloop, is larger than the above named frigates; her water lines are excessively sharp and her coefficient of displacement very small, all calculated to produce an immersed solid of little resistance for the length, breadth, and depth. In fact the employment of large lineal dimensions with small capacity—the secret of all brilliant performance as regards *speed*—has been carried in this vessel to extremes.

BATTERY.—The battery consists of twelve shell pivot guns of 11 inches bore; five are placed on each side and one on each end of the vessel. Each gun weighs 15,000 pounds net, and with its carriage and appendages 25,000 pounds; it throws a shell of 136 pounds, and requires a charge of 15 pounds of powder. None of the guns throw solid shot, and the vessel carries ammunition for one hundred and twenty-five rounds.

Up to the present time the "NIAGARA" has never carried her battery, as the only services on which she has been employed were the laying of the Atlantic Telegraph Cable, and the transportation from the United States to Liberia of a number of kidnapped Africans.

PERSONNEL.—The full war complement is 750 men exclusive of officers; but on the service for which the vessel was detailed, she carried only 514 men, of whom 30 were firemen and 28 were coal heavers belonging to the Engineer Department.

Hull.

The hull, which is excessively sharp fore and aft, has the appearance and indeed the qualities of a first class clipper ship; the sharpness forward being continued up to the rail. The following are the principal dimensions, namely:

Extreme length from taffrail to figure-head	345 feet
Length on deck from fore part of stem to after part of stern post above the spar deck	337 "
Length on load line	328 ft. 10½ in.
Breadth of beam at amidship section, molded	53 ft. 8 in.
Breadth of beam at amidship section, extreme	55 feet.
Depth of hold	23 "
Depth of hold to spar deck	31 ft. 3 in.
Constructor's deep load draught	23 feet.
Depth from load line to rabbet of keel	21 ft. 3 in.
Area of greatest immersed transverse section at 23 feet draught	911 square ft.
Distance of greatest immersed transverse section abaft centre of length on load line	7 ft. 3 in.
Molded displacement at 23 feet draught	5110 tons.
Total displacement at 23 feet draught	5440 tons.
Centre of buoyancy abaft centre of length on load line	8 ft. 7¾ in.
Centre of gravity of displacement below load line	8 feet.
Meta centre above load line	5 ft. 6 in.
Area of load water line	12755 square ft.
Displacement per inch of draught at load draught of 23 ft.	30.428 tons.
Immersed surface of hull at load draught of 23 feet	19760 square ft.
Ratio of length to breadth on load line	5.979 to 1.000
Ratio of greatest immersed transverse section to circumscribing parallelogram	0.779
Ratio of load water line to circumscribing parallelogram	0.705
Ratio of displacement to circumscribing parallelopipedon	0.494
Angle of load water line at bow	30°
Angle of load water line at stern	52°

Angle of water line midway between rabbet of keel and load water line at bow.. 25°

Angle of water line midway between rabbet of keel and load water line at stern.. 37°

Angle of dead rise.. 12°

Spars.

The vessel is three masted, ship rigged, and has spars of the following dimensions, namely:

Spars.	Extreme Length. ft. inc.	Diameter. inches.	Spars.	Extreme Length. ft. in.	Diameter. inc.
Main Mast, above deck 84 feet 6 inches..................	111 .. 0	37½	Fore Topgallant Yard.........	48 .. 9	11
Fore Mast, above deck 74 feet 3 inches..................	101 .. 0	35	Mizzen Topgallant Yard.......	37 .. 3	8
Mizzen Mast, above deck 72 feet......................	89 .. 0	30	Main Royal Yard.............	34 .. 9	8
Main Top-mast..............	70 .. 0	21	Fore Royal Yard.............	32 .. 3	7½
Fore Top-mast...............	62 .. 0	20¼	Mizzen Royal Yard......	25 .. 0	6
Mizzen Top mast.............	52 .. 6	15	Spanker Boom...............	67 .. 0	15
Main-Top-gallant-mast........	38 .. 0	12½	Spanker Gaff................	43 .. 0	10¼
Fore Top-gallant-mast........	34 .. 0	11¾	Main Gaff....................	42 .. 8	9½
Mizzen Top-gallant-mast......	29 .. 6	8⅞	Fore Gaff....................	41 .. 3	9
Main Royal-mast.............	24 .. 6	10	Main Trysail Mast............	68 .. 0	11
Fore Royal-mast.............	22 .. 6	9⅜	Fore Trysail Mast............	59 .. 0	11
Mizzen Royal-mast...........	19 .. 0	6⅞	Mizzen Trysail Mast..........	49 .. 0	10
Bowsprit, outboard 20 feet....	53 .. 0	{22¾ 23¾	Swinging Boom...............	62 .. 0	11½
Jib-boom....................	38 .. 0	13	Lower Steering-sail Yard.....	35 .. 6	8
Flying Jib-boom.............	13 .. 0	8½	Fore Top-mast Steering-sail-Boom....	49 .. 0	10½
Main Yard...................	106 .. 0	25	Fore Top-mast Steering-sail Yard......................	28 .. 0	6¾
Fore Yard...................	94 .. 0	22½	Fore Top-gallant Steering-sail Boom......................	37 .. 6	7½
Cross-jack Yard.............	76 .. 0	16¼	Fore Top-gallant Steering-sail Yard.........	21 .. 0	5
Main Topsail Yard...........	81 .. 3	19¾	Main Top-gallant Steering-sail Boom......................	41 .. 0	8¾
Fore Topsail Yard...........	73 .. 4	17½	Dolphin Striker..............	15 .. 6	9
Mizzen Topsail Yard....	58 .. 0	12½	Whisker Boom................	11 .. 6	7
Main Top-gallant Yard........	53 .. 9	11			

Area of Sails.

Main sail..................	7,308	square	feet.	Fore skysail...............	704	square	feet.
" topsail................	5,808	"	"	" spencer...............	3,624	"	"
" top-gallant sail.......	2,990	"	"	Mizzen topsail....	3,284	"	"
" royal.......	1,551	"	"	" top-gallant sail	1,862	"	"
" skysail...............	816	"	"	" royal................	1,008	"	"
" spencer...............	3,904	"	"	" skysail..............	567	"	"
Fore sail..................	6,016	"	"	Spanker..............	3,568	"	"
" topsail................	4,958	"	"	Flying Jib.................	1,938	"	"
" top-gallant sail........	2,623	"	"	Jib........................	2,988	"	"
" royal..................	1,408	"	"	Fore topmast staysail.......	1,831	"	"

Total..................................58,756 square feet.

Surface of Fore and Aft sail, namely : Jib, Flying Jib, Fore-topmast stay-sail, Fore and Main Spencers and Spanker..........................17,853 square feet.

Surface of the Plain sail, namely : Courses, Topsails, Top-gallant sails, Jib and Spanker..41,405 " "

Surface of the plain sail in proportion to area of load water line..............3.246 to 1.000

" " " " " greatest immersed transverse section..45.550 " "

Square feet of plain sail per ton of displacement..................................7.611

Total weight of Spars, rigging and sails..225 tons.

The "NIAGARA" has frames of live oak. Floors *molded* 20½ inches, and 8 inches at heads; *sided* 15 inches. Frames 40 inches apart at centres. They are filled in solid with yellow pine to a line 6 feet above the base line; and crossed diagonally on the outside with two sets of iron straps 5 inches by ⅞ inch, crossing each other in opposite drections. The hull is also further strengthened by similar iron straps laid diagonally across the beams of the upper deck. The planks of the bottom and deck are of yellow pine. Having a very fine run, the vessel is of course weak at her quarters, in consequence of which her constructor fitted on each side a large 2 inch stay or brace, which lies along the upper deck beams, passes through the decks below, and steps upon the stern post.

The following are the materials used in the construction of the hull:

Live Oak timber................	40,000	cubic feet.
White Oak timber	11,000	"
Yellow Pine timber	42,000	"
White Pine timber	3,000	"
White plank	11,000	superficial feet.
Yellow Pine plank	60,000	" "
White Pine plank..............	42,000	" "
Iron bolts.....................	400,000	pounds.
Galvanized iron and Spikes	25,000	"
Copper bolts	140,000	"
Composition bolts..............	16,000	"
Diagonal iron braces	169,000	"
The total weight of the hull ready for launching, is	2750	tons.

Or 50½ per centum of the displacement at load line of 23 feet draught.

Machinery.

The whole of the machinery and fuel is placed below the berth deck and occupies a space 100 feet in length by the entire breadth of the vessel. The bunkers, which surround the engines and boilers, contain 825 tons of coal, and the total weight of the machinery including the iron of the bunkers, spare pieces for engines, and water in boilers, is 625 tons ; making with the coal 1450 tons or 26⅔ per centum of the displacement of the vessel at 23 feet draught of water.

The following is the description and dimensions of the machinery in detail :

Engines.

There are three horizontal, condensing, direct acting engines, the piston of each cylinder has two piston rods which are secured into lugs on the same crosshead whence the connecting rod extends directly on. The three cylinders are placed on the same side of the keel; their condensers, and air, and feed pumps, are placed directly opposite, and are contained in one casting. The pumps are horizontal, and are worked directly across from the piston rod lugs on the engine crosshead ; the air pump, which is double acting, is worked from one lug in continuation of one piston rod ; and the feed pump, which is single acting, is worked from the other lug in continuation of the other piston rod. The steam valve is worked by the link motion ; it is a three ported equilibrium slide packed on the back and has a lap of 2½ inches which closes the steam port when the piston has performed 2⅓ feet of its stroke. For working the steam more expansively, there is an independent slide cut-off valve actuated by a separate eccentric and cutting off the steam at 11 inches from the commencement of the stroke. The screw shaft is 100 feet long from its junction with the engine shaft, and weighs 50 tons. The engines occupy a space in the vessel 28 feet long by 26 feet athwartship and weigh 290 tons.

The following are the principal dimensions of the engines ; namely :—

Number of cylinders............................	3
Diameter of cylinders...........................	72 inches.
Diameter of the piston rods (two to each cylinder)	6 "

Stroke of pistons	3 feet.
Space displacement of the three pistons per stroke (exclusive of piston rods)	253.877 cubic feet.
Space in cylinder nozzles and clearance at one end of each cylinder	4.978 "
Space between steam and cut-off valves at one end of each cylinder	17.450 "
Clearance at each end	$\frac{11}{16}$ inch.
Area of steam ports, (6 by 39 inches)	234 square inches.
" exhaust ports, (9 by 39 inches)	351 "
" cut-off valve ports	192 "
Travel of the steam valve	13 inches.
Lap of the cut-off valve	3¼ "
Diameter of air pump (double acting)	22 "
Stroke of air pump piston	3 feet.
Area of air pump valves (of india rubber)	380 square inches.
Diameter of feed pump	6½ inches.
Stroke of feed pump piston	3 feet.
Diameter of connecting rod at neck	7¼ inches.
Diameter of cross head journal	10¾ "
Length of cross head journal	14 "
Diameter of engine shaft journals	14, 15¼ and 17 inches.
Length of engine shaft journals	25, 27, and 29 inches.
Diameter of screw shaft journals	16½ inches.
Length of the thrust bearing	48$\frac{1}{16}$ "
Number of collars in ditto	11
Acting surface of collars	1046 square inches.

Boilers.

There are four iron boilers (similar to the Vertical Water-tube boilers of the U. S. S. "San Jacinto") placed in pairs and opposite, with the fire room between in the fore and aft direction of the vessel. The fire room is 10 feet wide, and is ventilated by three large hatches. The area in the vessel occupied by the boilers and fire room is 33 feet in breadth by 44 feet in length. Each pair of opposite boilers has its own smoke-pipe making two for the vessel. These pipes are telescopic for lowering when the ship is under sail alone; the top of the lower or standing part is 12 feet above the spar deck, and the top of the upper or lowering part when at its full elevation is 20 feet higher, making a total distance of 32 feet from the spar deck to the top of the smoke pipe.

The principal heating surface of the boilers is in vertical brass tubes placed, not in straight rows but slightly zig-zag, over the furnaces. The water is in the tubes, and the heated gases pass around them on their way from the furnace to the chimney. The boilers, with the exception of the tubes, are of iron; the shell is double riveted, and of $\frac{3}{8}$ inch plate with the exception of the bottom and ash-pits where the plate is $\frac{7}{16}$ inch thick. The tubes are of brass, drawn instead of being brazed, and composed by weight of 60 parts of copper and 40 parts of zinc. The entire weight of the four boilers is 205$\frac{1}{3}$ tons; and their principal dimensions are as follows; namely:—

Number of boilers	4
Breadth of each boiler, in the fore and aft direction of the vessel	21 feet.
Length of each boiler, athwartship, opposite the fire room	11 feet 6 inches.
Length of each boiler, athwartship, above the fire room	13 " 8 "
Height of each boiler, exclusive of steam chimney	15 "
Number of furnaces in each boiler	6
Width of fire grates in each furnace	2 " 9 "
Length of fire grates	7 " 4 "
Area of grate surface in all the furnaces	484 square feet.
Number of tubes in each boiler	2040.
Internal diameter of the tubes	1$\frac{4}{5}$ inch.
External " "	2 inches.
Length of the tubes (extreme)	37 "
Number of rows of tubes to each furnace in the direction of its breadth	10
Number of rows of tubes to each furnace in the direction of its length	34
Area of heating surface in all the tubes, calculated for the external diameter	12817.73 square feet.
Area of heating surface in the furnaces	1363.20 "
" " " back connexions	665.52 "
" " " tube boxes	1241.26 "
" " " " plates	964.04 "
" " " front connexions	51.03 "

Total area of heating surface in the four boilers.	17102.78	square feet.
Width in clear between tubes, crosswise the boiler.	$1\frac{3}{11}$	inch.
Width of draught opening in direct line, between rows of tubes, crosswise the boiler.........	$\frac{3}{4}$	"
Width in clear between tubes, lengthwise the boiler	$\frac{7}{10}$	"
Number of chimneys	2	
Diameter of each chimney....................	7	feet.
Height of each chimney above the fire grates	60	"
Aggregate area of draught opening in direct line between rows of tubes, for the four boilers..	49.500	square feet.
Aggregate area between tubes, for the four boilers.	84.000	"
Aggregate area of the two chimneys............	76.968	"
Proportion of grate surface to *direct* opening for draught between the tubes................	9.778 to 1.000	
Proportion of grate surface to absolute area between the tubes	5.762 to 1.000	
Proportion of grate surface to area of chimney...	6.288 to 1.000	
" " " heating surface ...	1.000 to 35.336	
Weight of the four boilers	378000	pounds.
" " grate bars.......................	40000	"
" " smoke pipe	31000	"
" " " appendages, &c.......	11000	"
" " water in the boilers..............	230000	"

Screw.

The Screw is of bronze, and made according to the patent of Robert Griffiths with globular hub and blades adjustible to different pitches. The outline of the blades narrow from the hub to the periphery of the screw, so that every portion radially, has a different fraction of the pitch. When the blades are set at the pitch of 24 feet they form a *true* screw; but they were never used at that pitch because it would have required too high a speed of engine. The pitch at which they were originally set, and from which they have never been changed, is 32 feet at the periphery, becoming less and less as the hub is approached. The surface, in fact, is that of a screw whose pitch expands radially, being least at the hub and greatest at the periphery. With the blades set at the pitch of 32 feet at the periphery, the pitch at the hub is 30.40

feet, and the mean pitch of the whole blade in function of surface and of the propelling efficiency of the same is 31¼ feet.

The calculations of the mean pitch, and of the mean fraction used of the pitch, are made on the postulates that the whole blade being decomposed into an infinite number of *helical lines*, their propelling efficiencies are in the direct ratio of their pitches—the ratio of the square of their distances from the axis—and the ratio of an increase of one-seventh in the propelling efficiency for every doubling of the fraction used of the pitch.

The following dimensions of the screw correspond to the position of the blades when their periphery has a pitch of 32 feet:

Diameter of the screw	18 ft. 3 inches.
Diameter of the globular hub	5 ft. 4 "
Mean pitch of the screw, in function of surface and of the propelling efficiency of the same	31.25 feet.
Mean fraction used of the pitch, in function of surface and of the propelling efficiency of the same	0.2114
Number of blades	2.
Length of the screw at the periphery, in the direction of the axis	1.888 feet.
Length of the screw at the longest part (radius 4½ feet), in the direction of the axis	4.994 "
Mean angle of the blade, in function of surface and of the propelling efficiency of the same	34°:29′
Radius of the centre of pressure of the blade	7.38 "
Thickness of the blade above fillet, at the radius of 3 ft.	8 inches.
Thickness of the blade at the periphery	1 "
Diameter of the pivot attaching blade to hub	18¾ "
Helicoidal area of the two blades	72.60 square ft.
Projected area of the two blades on a plane at right angles to axis	53.49 "
Weight of screw	29697 pounds.
Weight of the hoisting apparatus for the screw	21000 "

Maximum Performance in Smooth Water Uninfluenced by Wind or Current.

The following is the maximum performance that, uninfluenced by wind or current, can be permanently sustained in smooth water with the first quality of free-burning steam coal. The different pressures in the cylinder are the mean of a collation of a large number of indicator diagrams.

Vessel's mean draught of water, in feet	22.
Vessel's greatest immersed transverse section, in square feet	856.
Vessel's displacement, in tons	5075.
Vessel's speed per hour in geographical miles of 6086 feet	10.9
Number of double strokes of engine's pistons, and of revolutions of the screw, made per minute	45.
Slip of the screw in per centum of its speed	21.38
Mean distance in inches from commencement of stroke of piston at which the steam is cut off in the cylinders	11.
Steam pressure in the boilers above the atmosphere, in pounds per square inch	19.
Steam pressure in the cylinders at point of cutting off, in pounds per square inch above zero	26.6
Steam pressure in the cylinders at the end of the stroke of piston, in pounds per square inch above zero	13.3
Mean back pressure in the cylinders, in pounds per square inch above zero	3½
Mean vacuum in the condensers, in inches of mercury	26½
Mean gross effective pressure on pistons in pounds per square inch	19.7
Gross horses power developed by the engines	1955.09
Temperature of feed-water in degrees Fahr	100.
Pounds of steam discharged from the cylinders per hour; calculated from the final steam pressure in the cylinder, per Indicator	48281.40
Pounds of steam condensed in the cylinders per hour to produce the power of the engines; calculated according to JOULE'S equivalent	4935.66
Pounds of first quality steam coal consumed per hour	6900.00
Pounds of first quality steam coal consumed per hour per square foot of grates	14.25

Distribution of the Power During the above Performance.

The pressure required to work the engines and shafting *per se* being taken at 1½ pound per square inch of piston, the power thus absorbed is 148.86 horses.

Deducting from the total power of 1955.09 horses developed by the engines this power of 148.86 horses, there remains the power of 1806.23 horses applied to the shaft, of which 7½ per centum or 135.47 horses is absorbed by the friction of the load.

The power expended in overcoming the cohesive resistance of the water by the screw blades, calculated in the ratio of the square of the velocity, and for a value of 0.45 pound avoidupois per square foot of helicoidal surface moving in its helical path with a velocity of 10 feet per second, amounts to 58.82 horses.

The powers (135.47 and 58.82 horses) absorbed by the friction of the load and expended in overcoming the cohesive resistance of the water by the screw blades, being deducted from the power (1806.23 horses) applied to the shaft, there remains 1611.94 horses power expended in the slip of the screw and in the propulsion of the hull. And as the slip of the screw is 21.38 per centum of its speed, the power expended in it is (1611.94×.2138=) 344.63 horses, leaving (1611.94—344.63=) 1267.31 horses expended in the propulsion of the simple hull.

Collecting the foregoing, we have the following distribution of the power, namely:

	Horses Power.		*Per Centum.*
Gross Indicator power developed by the engines	1955.09		
Power required to work the engines and shafting *per se*..................................	148.86		
Net power applied to the shaft...............	1806.23	or	100.00
Power absorbed by the friction of the load......	135.47	"	7.50
Power expended in overcoming the cohesive resistance of the water by the screw blades...	58.82	"	3.26
Power expended in the slip of the screw........	344.63	"	19.08
Power expended in the propulsion of the vessel.	1267.31	"	70.16
Totals............................	1806.23	"	100.00

Thrust of the Screw.

The thrust of the screw during the foregoing maximum performance, can be easily calculated from the data in the above distribution of the power. The power required to propel the simple hull is therein found to be 1267.31 horses, equal to ($1267.31 \times 33000 =$) 41821230 pounds raised one foot high per minute. The speed of the vessel was 10.9 geographical miles of 6086 feet per hour or ($\frac{10.9 \times 6086}{60} =$) 1105.6233 feet per minute; the resistance of the vessel at this speed, or its equivalent the thrust of the screw, was consequently ($\frac{41821230}{1105.6233} =$) 37826 pounds.

Performance at Sea under the Conditions of Ordinary Practice.

In the three following Tables will be found Abstracts of the Steam Log of the "NIAGARA." The first gives the performance under steam alone; the second the performance under steam assisted by the fore and aft sails; the third the performance under steam and the square sails combined. These tables include the whole of the performance up to the present date, during which all the elements are recorded in the vessel's log. They, of course, exclude a considerable amount of steaming for short distances, and also where the log is imperfect or otherwise unreliable and useless.

The number of consecutive hours on each line of the tables, is the time during which the wind, sea, sail, and working of the machinery, continued about uniform. The speed was taken by the common chip log hove hourly by the officer of the deck; and the direction of the vessel and of the wind together with the force of the latter and the state of the sea, are the mean as recorded by him.

The number of revolutions of the screw and double strokes of engine's pistons made per minute, were taken by a self-registering counter and entered in the steam log at the close of each hour by the assistant engineer on watch. He also entered for each hour the mean steam pressure and vacuum, the number of pounds of coal expended and the quantity of refuse in ashes, &c. Opposite the record of each day's steaming there is pasted in the log an Indicator double diagram from all the cylinders, with the necessary particulars noted on it, showing the development of power, &c., at the time taken, and corresponding to the particulars given.

The throttle was always carried partly closed. The principal part of the coal used was Pennsylvania hard anthracite; the remainder was English steam coal, and both were of very good quality. The temperature of the feed-water was very nearly constant at 100° Fahr.

In a log made up in this manner it is not probable that for any particular hour the record was *precisely* the truth. The speed of the vessel cannot, by the chip log, be determined within, say, 5 per centum, and the state of the sea, and the direction and force of the wind are very unreliable, being estimated according to the judgment and sensations of the observer. What would be called a rough sea by one would be considered a moderate sea by another, and the force of the wind would be as variously estimated as there were persons. The direction and force of the wind, too, are the *apparent* ones to an observer on deck, being modified from the true ones by the speed and direction of the vessel. The intensity of the same wind would be estimated very differently when steaming with or against it; and the same remark applies with equal force to estimations of the state of the sea. Still, notwithstanding all these sources of error, the *average* results of a long course of steaming may be depended on as a pretty close approximation to the truth; for the great probability is that the quantities will be as often given too high as too low, and the mean by the correction of errors is quite accurate enough for all practical purposes.

The record of the performance of the machinery is correct for each hour, except in the matter of the coal consumed and its refuse. These are the doubtful elements. The log gives the weight of coal expended per hour, but whether it was consumed in that particular hour and whether the ashes withdrawn belonged to it, it is impossible to ascertain. Also, the quality of the coal, the quantity lost in cleaning the furnaces at irregular intervals, the lessened or increased evaporation due to bad or good firing, and the effect of weather and many other accidental circumstances on combustion, remain, of course, unnoticed.

The slip of the screw is the difference between its speed and that of the vessel expressed in per centum of the former. In the table of the performance under steam and sail combined, there was during May 28th and 29th, 1857; March 9th and 10th and the 14th ; October 20th and 21st ; and November 21st, 1858 ; a *negative* slip, that is to say, the speed of the vessel was greater than the speed of the screw, and this slip is expressed in per centum of the vessel's speed with the minus (—) prefix.

When leaving port with 800 tons of coal on board, 500 men, four months provisions, and 42000 gallons of water (the tanks stow 35000 gallons), but without battery and ammunition, the vessel's draught of water is 21 feet 6 inches forward and 22 feet 10 inches aft, mean 22 feet 2 inches. On arriving at port the mean draught of water was usually 20 feet 6 inches. The average draught for the whole steaming done was about 21 feet 4 inches, the greatest immersed transverse section corresponding to which was 874 square feet, and the displacement 4832 tons.

Abstract of the Steam Log of the UNITED STATES STEAM SLOOP "NIAGARA," embracing all her Performance under Steam alone.

Date.		Number of consecutive Hours.	Course of the Vessel.	Wind. Direction.	Wind. Kind.	State of the Sea.	Speed of the Vessel per Hour in geographical miles of 6,086 feet.	Number of Revolutions of the Screw, and Double Strokes of Engines' Pistons made per minute.	Slip of the Screw in per centum of its speed.	Steam pressure in Boilers in pounds per square inch above atmosphere.	Vacuum in Condensers in inches of mercury, per gauge.	Pounds of Coal consumed per hour.	Ashes, Clinker, and Fine Coal unburnt, in per centum of the Coal.
April 22 & 23,	1857.	14	S. E.	S.	Gentle Breeze.	Smooth.	7.571	30.66	19.85	15.5	25	3,383	18
" 23 & 24,	"	23	N. W. by W.	W. N. W.	Moderate "	"	7.826	34.42	26.19	14.5	24	3,702	"
" 27,	"	8	E.	E. by N.	Light "	"	8.625	34.60	19.09	13.0	24	3,840	"
May 3,	"	11	N. E.	N. E.	Moderate Gale.	Heavy ahead.	2.277	29.71	75.12	13.0	22	4,320	18
" 5 & 6,	"	36	E.	E. by N.	Moderate Breeze.	Moderate swell.	4.639	27.69	45.62	12.5	25	4,160	"
July 27 & 28,	"	31	W. S. W.	W. N. W.	Light "	Smooth.	6.839	30.97	28.32	13.3	24	3,558	19
August 4,	"	11	N. W.	" " "	" "	Moderate swell.	6.273	33.70	39.58	16.5	25	3,718	15
" 11,	"	4	S. E.	W.	Gentle "	" "	6.500	32.10	34.27	16.0	25	4,375	"
" 13,	"	9	S. E.	N. W.	Moderate "	Smooth.	9.200	38.03	21.48	13.0	25	4,645	"
May 29 & 30,	1858.	30	W. ¾ N.	S. W.	" "	"	6.133	31.86	37.52	13.0	27	3,498	20¾
" 31,	"	9	W. ½ N.	W.	Gentle "	"	6.222	33.66	40.00	13.2	26½	3,920	"
July 17 & 18,	"	11	W. N. W.	W.	" "	Moderate.	5.182	30.93	45.62	10.5	26	4,000	9⅔
" 19 & 20,	"	18	N. W. ½ N.	N. W. ½ N.	Moderate "	"	4.833	29.65	47.09	8.0	26½	4,230	"
" 20,	"	12	N. W.	N.	Fresh "	Rough.	3.667	26.75	55.50	7.0	26	3,760	"
" 21, 22 & 23,	"	57	N. W.	N. W.	Gentle "	Moderate.	5.965	31.31	38.16	8.0	26½	4,133	"
August 12, 13 & 14,	"	72	W. N. W.	W.	Light "	Smooth.	8.709	39.38	28.22	10.7	26	5,297	14
" 16 & 17,	"	19	N. W.	W.	" "	"	6.684	31.00	30.01	8.6	26	3,680	"
September 13,	"	12	S.	W.	Light "	"	8.000	32.63	20.42	13.0	26	3,740	16½
" 14,	"	9	S.	E.	Gentle "	"	7.222	29.51	20.57	11.0	26	3,740	"
" 16 & 17,	"	8	W. S. W.	W. N. W.	Moderate "	Rough.	4.125	23.88	43.93	9.0	26	3,655	"
Oct. 15, 16, 17, 18, 19, 20,	"	133	S.	S.	Light "	Smooth.	7.436	32.22	25.09	8.7	26	3,740	18
November 5, 6 & 7,	1858.	55	S. E.	E. by S.	" "	"	7.600	32.25	23.50	8.7	26	3,879	26½
" 8,	"	12	S. S. E.	S.	" "	"	4.583	21.04	29.29	11.0	26	2,338	"
" 17, 18 & 19,	"	54	N. W.	N. N. W.	" "	"	7.500	31.50	22.72	10.1	26	3,714	"
December 5,	"	8	N. W.	N. E.	Light Airs.	"	9.000	36.75	20.50	11.0	26	4,341	19
" 6,	"	24	N. W. by N.	N. W. by W.	" "	"	8.400	34.15	20.16	7.0	26	3,836	"
" 8 & 9,	"	13	N. W.	N. by W.	Strong Breeze.	Moderate swell.	4.153	31.17	56.75	10.0	26	4,633	"
" 10 & 11,	"	28	N. E. by N.	{ 48° from ahead.	Light Airs.	Smooth.	9.643	40.33	22.39	10.3	26	6,137	"
Means.				24° from ahead. {	Gentle breeze.	Gentle swell.	7.003	32.68	30.44	10.4	25½	4,059	18

Abstract of the Steam Log of the UNITED STATES STEAM SLOOP "NIAGARA," embracing all her Performance under Steam and the Fore and Aft Sails.

Date.		Number of consecutive Hours.	Course of the Vessel.	Wind. Direction.	Wind. Kind.	State of the Sea.	Speed of the Vessel per Hour in geographical miles of 6,086 feet.	Number of Revolutions of the Screw, and Double Strokes of Engines' Pistons made per minute.	Slip of the Screw in per centum of its speed.	Steam pressure in Boilers in pounds per square inch above the atmosphere.	Vacuum in the Condensers in inches of mercury.	Pounds of Coal consumed per hour.	Ashes, Clinker, and Fine Coal unburnt, in per centum of the coal.
April 28,	1857.	7	E.	S. E.	Gentle breeze.	Moderate swell.	8.714	34.40	17.78	11.0	23	3,840	18
May 11,	"	4	E. by S.	S. by E.	Strong "	Smooth.	6.000	31.15	37.48	11.0	22	3,840	"
July 12,	"	22	S. E.	W. S. W. by S.	Gentle "	"	7.818	34.95	27.39	14.4	25	4,807	19
March 19,	1858.	18	E. by S.	S.	" "	Moderate.	7.889	37.04	30.87	10.7	26	5,560	20½
June 30,	"	24	E. by S.	S. S. E.	Fresh "	"	6.125	29.42	32.42	11.7	26	3,748	16½
July 24,	"	7	W. by N.	N. N. W.	" "	"	6.714	33.30	34.56	9.0	25¾	4,230	9⅔
August 11,	"	5	S. W. by W.	W.	Light "	Smooth.	7.800	39.60	36.07	14.0	26	5,085	20¾
" 15,	"	22	N. N. W.	S. W.	" "	"	8.455	35.91	23.57	9.7	26	4,718	14
September 15,	"	16	——	On Bow.	Moderate "	Moderate swell.	6.313	30.50	32.81	14.0	26	3,737	16½
" 15 & 16,	"	13	S. E.	S. S. W.	Fresh gale.	Rough.	2.538	22.85	78.37	13.0	26	2,882	"
October 26,	"	4	S. S. E.	E. ½ N.	Moderate breeze.	Smooth.	7.375	25.72	6.93	14.0	26	2,090	18
" 27,	"	17	S. S. E.	E. by N.	" "	"	8.177	31.12	14.72	11.0	26	3,478	"
December 7,	"	24	N. W.	W.	Gentle "	"	8.417	30.57	10.63	7.0	26	3,776	19
" 8,	"	18	N. W.	S. W.	Fresh "	"	9.722	33.32	5.29	7.0	26	3,740	"
" 9,	"	17	W. N. W.	N.	Strong "	Moderate swell.	7.118	34.98	33.95	10.0	26	5,344	"
Means,				78° from ahead.	Moderate breeze.	Gentle swell.	7.425	32.45	25.73	10.8	25¾	4,176	17½

Abstract of the Steam Log of the UNITED STATES STEAM SLOOP "NIAGARA," *embracing all her Performance under Steam and Sail combined.*

Date.	Number of consecutive Hours.	Course of the Vessel.	Wind. Direction.	Wind. Kind.	State of the Sea.	Speed of the Vessel per Hour in geographical miles of 6086 feet.	Number of Revolutions of the Screw, and Double Strokes of Engines' Pistons made per minute.	Slip of the Screw in per centum of its speed.	Steam pressure in Boilers in pounds per square inch above atmosphere.	Vacuum in Condensers in inches of mercury per gauge.	Pounds of Coal consumed per hour.	Ashes, Clinker, and Fine Coal unburnt in per centum of the coal.
April 23, 1857.	11	E. S. E.	W.	Moderate Breeze.	Smooth.	9.818	34.62	7.95	14.0	24	3,360	18
" 24 & 25, "	22	E.	S. W.	Gentle "	"	8.975	37.69	22.71	10.5	24	4,427	"
" 26, "	24	E.	N. N. W.	" "	"	9.062	32.53	9.58	10.7	24	3,570	"
" 27, "	16	E.	S.	Moderate "	"	10.937	35.50	0.00	12.0	24	3,930	"
" 28 & 29, "	41	E. by S.	S.	Strong "	Moderate swell.	11.756	36.24	—5.03	11.2	23	3,494	"
" 30 & May 1, "	36	E. by S.	S. by W.	Gentle "	Smooth.	9.833	34.69	8.00	12.7	23	4,130	"
May 1, "	12	E. by S.	W.	Light "	"	9.500	35.17	12.32	15.5	23	4,800	"
" 2 & 3, "	33	E. by S.	N.	Strong "	Rough.	10.636	36.46	5.31	12.0	23	4,189	"
" 3, "	4	S. by E.	E.	Moderate Gale.	"	7.750	32.25	22.00	12.5	22	3,600	"
" 4, "	12	N.	E. by N.	Strong Breeze.	Moderate swell.	4.833	26.22	40.17	9.0	22	3,360	"
" 10, 11, 12 & 13, "	48	E. by S.	S.	Moderate "	Smooth.	10.792	35.62	1.66	12.2	22	4,550	"
July 13 & 14, "	31	S. E.	N. N. W.	" "	Moderate swell.	9.258	37.67	20.22	15.5	25	4,498	19
March 9 & 10, 1858.	32	E. S. E.	W.	Fresh "	" "	13.500	41.14	—6.11	16.0	25¾	3,567	20½
" 11, 12 & 13, "	59	E. by S.	S.	Strong "	" "	12.593	41.09	0.05	13.8	25½	3,731	"
" 14, "	14	E.	S.	" "	Rough.	8.857	27.64	—3.85	11 8	24½	1,764	"
" 14 & 15, "	40	E. S. E.	N. N. E.	Moderate gale.	Heavy.	9.550	35.54	12.78	13.4	26	3,655	"
" 16, "	11	E. by N.	N. W.	Fresh breeze.	Rough.	12.182	38.50	2.64	13.8	25¾	3,724	"
" 16 & 17, "	36	E. ½ S.	S. S. W.	Moderate "	Moderate.	11.972	41.08	5.40	13.5	25½	4,176	"
" 18, "	24	E. by S.	S.	Fresh "	"	10.875	39.95	11.64	12.1	26	4,522	"
June 2 & 3, "	27	N. E. by E.	S. S. E.	Gentle "	Smooth.	9.333	41.67	27.30	13.9	26	4,602	20¾
July 1 & 2, "	48	E. by S.	S. S. W.	Moderate "	Moderate.	9.000	34.30	14.83	12.0	26	4,050	16½
" 3, "	23	E. by S.	N.	Light "	Smooth.	9.217	34.01	12.03	10.2	26	4,640	"
" 4, "	24	E.	W.	" "	"	9.208	33.16	9.87	10.4	26	4,000	"
" 18 & 19, "	25	N. N. W.	W.	Moderate "	Gentle swell.	8.760	32.11	11.44	9.2	26¾	3,760	9⅔
" 19, "	9	N. W.	Abeam.	Gentle "	" "	7.667	30.54	18.51	8.5	26¼	3,760	"
" 22 & 23, "	15	N. W.	W.	Moderate "	Moderate.	9.733	36.97	14.55	8.2	22¾	4,230	"
August 17 & 18, "	15	W. N. W.	W. S. W.	Light "	Smooth.	8.300	32.80	17.86	8.0	26	3,680	14
September 17 & 18, "	31	W. by S.	N. N. W.	Gentle "	Moderate.	9.290	33.46	9.89	11.7	26	3,728	16½
" 21, "	8	S. S. E.	Abeam.	Moderate "	"	9.250	34.42	12.78	9.0	26	3,788	"
" 22 & 23, "	42	S. S. E.	N. N. E.	Strong "	Heavy swell.	6.238	22.14	8.55	9.7	26	2,087	"
" 24, "	11	S. E.	E. N. E.	Moderate "	Moderate.	7.818	28.53	11.06	9.0	26	1,784	"
October 20 & 21, "	25	S. by W.	S. S. E.	Strong "	Smooth.	12.714	35.63	—13.66	6.4	26	3,793	18
November 20, "	24	N. W.	N. E.	Moderate "	"	9.333	31.80	4.73	7.0	25	3,156	26½
" 21, "	10	N. W.	N. E.	" "	"	9.000	23.46	—22.28	4.0	25	1,840	"
Means.			98° from ahead.	Moderate breeze.	Gentle swell.	9.988	35.08	7.59	11.8	25	3,794	18¼

Results from the Steam Log.

The following Table contains a Synopsis of the Steam Log of the "NIAGARA." The mean of the whole performance at sea "under steam alone," "under steam and fore and aft sails," and "under steam and square sails combined," is arranged in the first three columns ; and in the fourth column will be found the mean of the preceding three.

The mean gross effective steam pressure on the pistons, the pressure in the cylinders at the point of cutting off the steam, and at the end of the stroke of pistons, and the back pressure against the pistons, are the results of a careful analysis of all the Indicator diagrams contained in the log books.

The evaporation is calculated from the steam pressure at the end of the stroke of the pistons ; and to this is added the steam condensed in the cylinders to produce the power developed by the engines, calculated according to JOULE's equivalent of one pound of water raised one degree on Fahrenheit's scale for every 772 foot-pounds developed by the engines. There is furthermore added the evaporation due to the loss of heat by "blowing-off" so much of the boiler water as would maintain its concentration at 1¾ time the density of sea water. There is some uncertainty in this quantity, as in order to obtain it correctly by calculation the *true* evaporation by the boiler must be known, and this the Indicator does not give. It has, however, been assumed, as a reasonably close practical approximation in the present case, that one-fifth of the steam generated by the coal is condensed before being discharged from the cylinders in addition to the condensation for the production of the power, and with this addition of 25 per centum to the weight of steam discharged from the cylinders per Indicator and condensed for the development of the power, the loss by "blowing-off" has been calculated. The feed water entered the boiler at about 100° Fahr. In these calculations the tables of REGNAULT have been used.

It will be observed (referring now and hereafter to the last column of the Table) that the steam was much throttled in passing from the boiler to the cylinder, the initial pressure in the latter being on an average about 7 pounds per square inch less than in the former.

The screw possessed too little propelling efficiency to give the vessel steerage way when steaming with the consumption of 50 tons of coal per 24 hours against a heavy head wind and sea; and its slip, under all circumstances, was too great for economy except when it was employed in conjunction with the square sails.

The speed of the engines' pistons was by no means great, being only 45 double strokes per minute for the maximum, and less than 34 for the average.

Notwithstanding the good quality of the fuel, fair vacuum in the condenser, and unrivalled evaporation given by the boiler, the Indicated horse power cost 4.79 pounds of coal per hour. The steam space between the piston and steam valve was large, while the steam space between the steam and cut-off valves was enormous, and the loss of steam due to these proportions was very considerable. But a still greater loss of effect was due to the low mean effective pressure on the piston, namely 11.2 pounds per square inch, which made the back pressure of 4.8 pounds per square inch, and the pressure of $1\frac{1}{2}$ pound per square inch required to work the engines *per se*, absorb $(\frac{\overline{4.8+1.5} \times 100}{11.1+4.8} =)$ $39\frac{5}{8}$ per centum of the fuel to overcome it. For economy, the cylinders were indeed much too large for the boilers at the speed of piston given by the pitch of the screw; as it reduced the mean effective pressure so low that the back pressure became an enormous loss. The pitch of the screw was too great for the resistance of the vessel and gave too much loss by slip; it could not, therefore, be increased to lessen the revolutions and augment the mean effective pressure on the pistons. If, on the other hand, the pitch had been reduced to lessen the loss from the slip, then the speed of the engines would have been proportionably increased and, using the same weight of steam the mean effective pressure on the pistons would have been greatly reduced while the back pressure remaining the same would have become a much higher per centum of the total pressure and have given an increased loss probably over-balancing the increased gain by the lessened slip due to the lessened pitch.

The disproportionately great capacity of cylinder, therefore, is the great fault of the machinery ; it causes an enormous loss either by the high per centum of the back pressure against the pistons, or by the great slip of the screw, and neither can be lessened without increasing the other. Had only two of the three engines been employed with a better arrangement of the valves, and had the space occupied by the third been appropriated to additional boiler, and had the pitch of the screw been reduced to, say, 22 feet, a far greater power would have been obtained from the same weight of fuel, and of that greater power a much greater per centum would have been usefully applied to the propulsion of the vessel.

As the diameter of the screw was limited by the construction of the vessel, a pitch should have been chosen that would have given the most economical slip, and then the boiler power having been determined for such a consumption of fuel as could be afforded, the smallest engine should have been adopted that would have worked off the steam at as high a boiler pressure as could judiciously be carried at sea with the proper measure of expansion for economy.

With the average consumption of 43 tons of coal per 24 hours, the "NIAGARA" can steam continuously 19 days, and taking the average speed of 8.46 knots per hour for average weather, can perform in that time a voyage of 3857 geographical miles.

SYNOPSIS *of the* STEAM LOG *of the* UNITED STATES SLOOP "NIAGARA."

		Performance under Steam alone.	Performance under Steam and the Fore and Aft sails.	Performance under Steam and square sails combined.	Mean of the three preceding columns.
	Total number of hours	731	218	843	1,792
	Kind of Wind	Gentle breeze.	Moderate breeze.	Moderate breeze.	———
	Angle made from ahead by the wind with the line of the vessel's keel	24°	78°	98°	65°
	State of the sea	Gentle swell.	Gentle swell.	Gentle swell.	Gentle swell.
	Mean speed of the Vessel per hour in geographical miles of 6,086 feet	7.003	7.425	9.988	8.459
	" Number of Revolutions of the Screw and Double Strokes of Engines' Pistons made per minute	32.68	32.45	35.08	33.78
	Slip of the Screw in per Centum of its speed	30.44	25.73	7.59	17.76
	Mean Steam pressure in the Boilers in pounds per square inch above atmosphere	10.4	10.8	11.8	11.1
	" " " " Cylinders at the point of cutting-off, in pounds per square inch above zero.	20.1	19.2	17.4	18.80
	" " " " " " end of the stroke of piston, in pounds per square inch above zero	10.4	10.0	9.0	9.75
	Mean gross effective Pressure on Pistons in pounds per square inch	12.2	11.7	10.0	11.1
	Mean effective Back-Pressure in Cylinders on the Pistons in pounds per square inch	4.5	4.2	5.0	4.8
	Gross Horses power developed by the Engines	879.28	837.31	773.65	824.48
	Steam cut-off at in Cylinders from commencement of stroke of piston	0.305	0.305	0.305	0.305
	Vacuum in Condensers in inches of mercury	25½	25¾	25	25 3/10
	Temperature of the Feed Water entering the Boilers in degrees Fahr.	100	100	100	100
	Number of Pounds of Coal consumed per hour	4,059	4,176	3,794	3,949
	Per Centum of Waste of Coal in Ashes, Clinker, and Dust	18	17½	18¼	18
	Number of Pounds of Combustible consumed per hour	3,328	3,445	3,101	3,238
	Number of Pounds of Coal consumed per hour per square foot of Grate surface.	8.386	8.628	7.839	8.159
	" " Combustible " " " " " "	6.876	7.118	6.407	6.690
	Pounds of Coal consumed per hour per Indicated Horse power	4.617	4.987	4.904	4.790
	" Combustible " " "	3.785	4.114	4.008	3.927
Evaporation from a temperature of Feed Water of 100° Fahr.	Pounds of Steam discharged per hour from the Cylinders	28,051.61	26,978.60	25,336.90	26,644.01
	Pounds of Steam condensed per hour in the Cylinders to produce the power developed by the engines	2,172.02	2,001.40	1,739.90	1,947.98
	Pounds of Steam that would have been evaporated per hour had the heat been so applied that was lost by blowing-off to maintain the sea water in the boilers at 1¾ the natural concentration	6,541.83	6,317.57	5,991.57	6,257.65
	Total number of Pounds of Steam evaporated per hour	36,765.46	3,5297.57	33,068.37	34,849.64
	Number of Pounds of Steam evaporated per pound of Coal	9.058	8.452	8.716	8.597
	" " " " " Combustible	11.047	10.246	10.664	10.763

Performance when Laying the Atlantic Telegraph Cable.

The following Table contains the performance of the "NIAGARA" from mid-ocean to Trinity Bay, when laying the Atlantic Telegraph Cable.

That the paying out of the Cable offered a great resistance to the progress of the vessel, is alike shown by her low speed, by the small number of double strokes made by engines' pistons per minute, and by the great slip of the screw; notwithstanding that the consumption of coal was only about one-eighth less than the sea-going average, and that the weather was very favorable.

At the commencement of this performance, there was 1,100 geographical miles of Cable on board, and the length paid out exceeded the distance run by the vessel by 15 per centum. The average angle made by the Cable with the horizon was 13 degrees, and the depth of water for two-thirds of the distance averaged 2 miles.

Abstract of the Steam Log of the UNITED STATES STEAM SLOOP " NIAGARA," *embracing all her Performance during the laying of the* ATLANTIC TELEGRAPH CABLE.

Date.		Number of consecutive hours.	Course of the Vessel.	Wind.		State of the Sea.	Speed of the vessel per Hour in geographical miles of 6,086 feet, by Patent Log.	Number of Revolutions of the Screw, and Double Strokes of Engines' Pistons made per minute.	Slip of the Screw in per centum of its speed.	Steam pressure in Boilers in pounds per square inch above the atmosphere.	Vacuum in the Condensers in inches of mercury.	Pounds of Cape Breton Coal consumed per hour.	Ashes, Clinker, and Fine Coal unburnt; in per centum of the Coal.
				Direction.	Kind.								
July 29,	1858.	11	N. W.	N. N. W.	Light Airs.	Smooth.	3.545	20.22	43.10	14.6	26	2,820	10¼
" 30,	"	24	"	E. by S.	Gentle breeze.	"	4.388	22.36	36.30	13.8	"	2,742	"
" 31,	"	24	"	N. W.	Light "	"	5.733	28.43	34.58	12.2	"	3,701	"
August 1 & 2,	"	48	"	N. E.	Gentle "	Moderate.	5.896	29.22	34.52	10.6	"	4,024	"
" 3 & 4,	"	36	"	N. by W.	" "	"	5.931	30.47	36.82	12.8	"	3,654	"
Means.				65° from ahead.	Light & Gentle breezes.	Light swell.	5.443	27.56	35.90	12.3	26	3,569	10¼

UNITED STATES STEAMSHIP

"MASSACHUSETTS."

UNITED STATES STEAMSHIP

"MASSACHUSETTS."

The "MASSACHUSETTS" was originally built for a steam packet to ply between New York and Liverpool, which not proving a satisfactory speculation she was next sent to the East Indies, and on her return,—the war between Mexico and the United States being in progress,—was sold to the Army for a transport. After the treaty of peace she was transferred to the Navy and sent to the Pacific on the California coast, whence she returned to Norfolk, Virginia. New boilers and a new screw of different design from the old ones were now placed in the vessel and she sailed in July, 1854, again for the Pacific. The machinery hereinafter described is for the vessel as refitted at Norfolk.

The steam power of the "MASSACHUSETTS" was intended to be purely auxiliary, and to be used only in calms and when the wind was so light as to give the vessel with sails alone a less speed than 4 knots per hour. The original machinery was designed by JOHN ERICSSON and included his screw and hoisting gear.

The following are the dimensions of the hull and refitted machinery; to which is added an abstract of all the performance with the latter that is to be found in the Log books at the Navy Department :

Hull.

Length from forward part of billet-head to after part of taffrail	178 feet.
Length on deck	160 "
Length on water line at 14 feet mean draught,	156 feet 3 inches.
Breadth extreme	32 feet.
Depth of hold	20 "
Depth of keel	1 foot 6 inches.
Deep load draught... Forward	15 feet.
Deep load draught... Mean	15 feet 6 inches.
Deep load draught... Aft	16 feet.
Mean draught of water during the steaming comprised in the Logs	14 "
Depth from rabbet of keel to water line at a draught of 14 feet	12 feet 6 inches.
Displacement at 14 feet draught	1168 tons.
Displacement per inch of draught at 14 feet draught	9.64 tons.
Greatest immersed transverse section at 14 feet draught	352 square feet.
Area of water line at 14 feet draught	4040 "
Immersed surface of hull, exclusive of keel, at 14 feet draught	5370 "
Surface of keel	642 "
Displacement, exclusive of keel, at 14 feet draught	40800.6 cubic feet.
Distance of the greatest transverse section before the centre of the water line at 14 feet draught	13 feet 3 inches.
Angle of entrance of water line at 14 feet draught	76°
Mean angle of entrance for the whole draught of 14 feet	55°
Angle of clearance of water line at 14 feet draught	68°
Mean angle of clearance for the whole draught of 14 feet	32°
Angle of deadrise of the greatest transverse section	6°
Area of water line at 14 feet draught, in proportion to circumscribing parallelogram	0.808
Area of greatest immersed transverse section at 14 feet draught, in proportion to circumscribing parallelogram	0.880

Displacement at 14 feet draught in proportion to circumscribing parallelopipedon	0.653
Displacement at 14 feet draught in proportion to cylinder having for base the greatest immersed transverse section..............	0.742

Sails.

Area of all the plain sails	21082 square feet.
Area of sail in proportion to area of water line at 14 feet draught.....................	5.218 to 1.000
Area of sail in proportion to greatest immersed transverse section at 14 feet draught.....	59.892 to 1.000
Square feet of sail per ton of displacement at 14 feet draught	18.050

Engines.

Two inclined, direct action, condensing engines, connected on one crank pin nearly at right angles to each other. There is but one condenser and air pump for both engines ; the air pump is double acting, horizontal, and fitted with canvass valves. The steam valve is a short three ported slide without lap. The cut-off valve is a simple slide cutting off the steam at exactly one fourth the stroke from the beginning. For starting the engines, and when it is desired to work the steam full stroke, there is a monkey-tail or cock to admit steam to the three ported slide from behind the cut-off valve. The engines are placed in the extreme of the vessel's stern, and the shaft instead of passing through the stern post passes out by the side of it.

Diameter of the cylinders........................	$24\frac{7}{8}$ inches.
Stroke of the pistons...........................	3 feet.
Space displacement of both pistons per stroke	20.250 cubic feet.
Steam space between cut-off and steam slide valves, both cylinders	0.592 "
Steam space between steam slide valves and pistons, at *one* end of *both* cylinders..................	0.642 "
Area of steam port of cylinders ($2\frac{7}{16}$ by 8 inches)..	19.50 square inches.
" " openings through cut-off valve, ($1\frac{7}{16}$ by $7\frac{15}{16}$ inches × 2).........................	22.82 "

Area of steam openings through monkey-tail cock (1¾ by 1¼ inch)	2.19 square inches.
Clearance at each end of cylinders	0.277 inch.
Diameter of air pump	14⅝ inches.
Stroke of air pump piston	2 feet.
Space displacement of air pump piston per stroke	2.254 cubic feet.

Boilers.

The boilers are of iron and two in number, placed side by side with one smoke chimney in common. They are of the single return ascending flue variety, the chimney being immediately over the furnaces. The lower flues, situated behind the furnaces are, for each boiler, eighteen in number, fourteen of which are 9 inches in internal diameter, two 12 inches and two 8 inches ; the length of these flues is 8 feet 9 inches. The upper flues, returned immediately above the lower ones and furnaces, are sixteen in number, 9 inches in diameter and 14 feet 6 inches in length, for each boiler. There are two furnaces to each boiler, each furnace is 4 feet wide, and is fired through two doors. The steam chimney or drum surrounds the smoke chimney and is 5 feet high above the top of the boiler with an area of 34.91 square feet ; the total steam room in it being equal to thirty charges of steam for both cylinders when cutting off at one fourth the stroke of piston from the commencement. The following are the remaining dimensions &c. of the boilers, viz. :

Length of each boiler	19 feet.
Breadth "	9 "
Height " (exclusive of steam chimney)	9 "
Total area of heating surface in both boilers	2475 square feet.
" grate " "	·87 "
Total cross area of lower flues in both boilers	16.902 "
" " upper " "	14.136 "
Cross area of the smoke chimney	15.904 "
Height " " above grates	40 feet.
Total steam room in both boilers	441.2 cubic feet.
Total weight of sea water in both boilers	18.16 tons.

Proportions.

Proportion of heating to grate surface.............	28.449 to 1.000
Proportion of grate surface to cross area of lower flues..	5.148 " "
Proportion of grate surface to cross area of upper flues	6.154 " "
Proportion of grate surface to cross area of smoke chimney..................................	5.470 " "
Proportion of length to diameter of flues..........	31.000 " "
Proportion of steam room to bulk of steam used per stroke of both pistons.....	70.604 " "

Screw.

One expanding pitch screw ; of bronze composed of 9 parts copper, 1 part tin, and ½ part zinc ; weight 5200 pounds. Thickness of blades at hub 2½ inches tapering to ¾ inch at the periphery of the screw. The following are the dimensions &c.:

Diameter of the screw..............................	10 feet 6 inches.
" " hub..............................	14¼ inches.
Length of the screw in the direction of the axis, at the periphery....................................	2 feet.
Length of the screw in the direction of the axis, at $2\frac{7}{12}$ feet radius..................................	2 "
Tapering to the hub where the length in the direction of the axis is..................................	1 foot 6 inches
Number of blades..................................	5
Initial pitch..	15 feet.
Final "	17 "
Mean " (from which the slip is calculated).........	16 "
Mean fraction used of the pitch (16 feet)..............	0.620
Helicoidal area of the screw..........................	67.60 square ft.
Projected area of the screw on a plane at right angles to axis..	50.283
Distance between the surface of the water and axis of the screw at 16 feet mean draught...............	8 feet 1 inch.

Apparatus for Hoisting out the Screw.

The screw can be hoisted out of water either by man power or by a small auxiliary steam cylinder, by means of an arrangement which consists of a shaft on which is a capstan (for lifting the screw by man power) of eight arms measuring 24 inches from the axis of the shaft to the extremity of the arm. This shaft carries an endless screw of $4\frac{1}{8}$ inches diameter working into a wheel of $32\frac{1}{2}$ inches diameter, $2\frac{1}{2}$ inches face and $1\frac{5}{8}$ inch pitch of teeth. The shaft of this wheel carries a pinion of $8\frac{3}{4}$ inches diameter working into a wheel of $42\frac{1}{2}$ inches diameter, 6 inches face and $2\frac{3}{16}$ inches pitch of teeth; the shaft of which in its turn carries a pinion of $9\frac{1}{2}$ inches diameter working into a wheel of $55\frac{3}{4}$ inches diameter, 7 inches face and 3 inches pitch of teeth. The diameters of all the above pinions and wheels are to their pitch circles. On the shaft of the last wheel is keyed the upper end of the bronze lifting arm of the screw, the lower end of which encircles the projecting portion of the screw's hub: the weight of this lifting arm is 1200 pounds. The screw is not keyed to its shaft which merely slips into the hub and is made square in section (with the angles a little taken off) to prevent turning. The outboard section of the screw shaft is of wrought iron and solid; the inboard section is of cast iron and is made hollow to receive the outboard section when the latter is moved inwards in the line of its axis. The solid shaft, after being slipped into the hub of the screw ready for propelling, is connected with the hollow shaft by a strong wrought iron key. When it is desired to hoist out the screw, this key is removed and the outboard section of the shaft is drawn by a screw and yoke directly inwards into the hollow part of the cast iron inboard section sufficiently far to disengage the shaft from the hub of the screw; the capstan being then turned by man power, or its shaft by the small auxiliary steam cylinder, the gearing is set in motion, and the lifting arm making half a revolution hoists the screw out of water and elevates it perpendicularly 14 feet, where it is secured by locking the gearing with a toothed segment and clamp, and by hooking braces to it from the vessel. When it is required to lower the screw, the reverse operation is performed. It required from 10 to 15 minutes with the small steam cylinder, and nearly an hour with the capstan and several men working at their utmost speed, to raise the screw and secure it ready for sailing. To lower and fix the screw ready for steaming required but a few minutes, as it was allowed to descend freely by its gravity.

By the above arrangement it will be perceived that in *backing*, the thrust of the screw is communicated by the collar on the hub to the lifting arm; this arm must, therefore, be made sufficiently strong to hold the thrust of the screw against its leverage of 7 feet. In *going ahead*, the thrust of the screw is communicated by the hub to the after end of the solid shaft; the after extremities of the shaft and of the bore of the hub being tapered to the form of the frustum of a pyramid. From the solid shaft the thrust is communicated to the hollow shaft by a key passing through both, (which key is taken out when the solid shaft is moved forward or back) and from the hollow shaft it is transmitted through a collar to a pillow block bolted to the vessel. The screw is abaft the rudder which being between it and the stern post vibrates past the screw shaft by means of a notch. The shaft being on one side the stern post a small notch in the rudder is sufficient for the purpose.

The advantages of this system of hoisting gear for the screw over the system ordinarily employed are; 1st. That it dispenses with the Well in the stern—a costly, difficult, and weak part of the construction. 2d. That it permits in an armed ship a pivot gun to be mounted on the stern. 3d. That it permits the use of a screw of more than two blades if desired. And 4th. That it permits the use of a screw of greater diameter—a most important dimension in the economical application of the power. The cost and weight of the gear with the two systems are about the same.

In the case of the conversion of a sailing vessel into a steamer with a hoist up screw, the gear of the "Massachu-

SETTS" offers great advantages in the economy of the transformation; as the only alteration needed for the stern is the perforation of two holes, not *through* but by the *side* of the stern-post, one for the screw-shaft and the other for the shaft carrying the lifting arm : not even the rudder need be wasted. With the Well and system of hoisting through the deck, an entirely new stern is required, heavier than the one it replaces and much more overhanging; the whole of the old stern must be destroyed and the remainder of the hull will require additional strengthening for the support of this additional and overhanging weight. The keel must be lengthened too, and a separate rudder-post besides the new and larger stern-post will be required. All these expensive alterations would be avoided by the employment of the hoisting gear of the "MASSACHUSETTS." The objections to it are the unsightly appearance of the screw when up—a matter of no importance, and that it does not offer sufficient guarantee of strength in cases where great power is to be applied. The validity of the latter objection can only be determined by a more enlarged experience. The practical working of the gear on board the "MASSACHUSETTS" during many years was very satisfactory, no trouble of any kind having ever been given by it.

Performance in Smooth Water Uninfluenced by Wind or Current.

During a trial trip of three days duration, the maximum performance that could be permanently sustained by the vessel in smooth water uninfluenced by wind or current was very accurately ascertained. The speed was determined by shore marks in Chesapeake Bay; the number of double strokes made by the engine's pistons was taken by a self-registering counter. The coal was hard Anthracite and both it and its Refuse were carefully weighed. The power was determined by the Indicator. The vessel's draught of water was 16 feet forward and 16½ feet aft, mean 16¼ feet. Greatest immersed transverse section 424 square feet. Displacement 1428 tons.

The following are the results, namely:—

Speed of the vessel per hour in geographical miles of 6086 feet	6.9
Double strokes of engine's pistons and revolutions of the screw per minute	54.
Slip of the screw in per centum of its speed, (calculated for mean pitch of 16 feet)	19.
Mean gross effective pressure on pistons in pounds per square inch by Indicator	25.6
Gross horses power developed by the engines	240.74
Steam pressure in boilers in pounds per square inch above atmosphere	37.
Steam cut off at in cylinders from commencement of stroke of piston	0.25 or 9 inches.
Throttle	Wide open.
Vacuum in condenser per barometer gauge, in inches of mercury	25.
Pounds of Anthracite consumed per hour	970.
Per centum of Refuse in Ashes, etc	24¾.

Distribution of the Power During the above Performance.

The pressure required by Indicator to work the engines and shafting *per se;* that is to say, disengaged from the screw, was 3 pounds per square inch of pistons; consequently the power thus absorbed when the pistons were making 54 double strokes per minute, was $(\frac{478.9 \times 3 \times 324}{33000} \times 2 =)$ 28.21 horses, which deducted from the gross power 240.74 horses developed by the engines, leaves 212.53 horses power applied to the screw shaft.

Of this 212.53 horses power, 7½ per centum or 15.94 horses power were expended in overcoming the friction of the load.

The power expended in overcoming the cohesion of the water by the screw blades, calculated in the ratio of the square of their helical velocity and for a value of 0.45 pound per square foot of helicoidal surface moving in its helical path with a velocity of 10 feet per second, was 15.66 horses.

Deducting the aggregate of $(15.94 + 15.66 =)$ 31.60 horses

expended in overcoming the friction of the load and the cohesive resistance of the water to the screw blades, from the power of 212.53 horses applied to the screw-shaft, there remains 180.93 horses, of which 19 per centum or 34.38 horses were expended in the slip of the screw, leaving 146.55 horses expended in the propulsion of the simple hull of the vessel.

Collecting the foregoing, we have the following distribution of the power, namely:—

	Horses Power.		*Per Centum.*
Gross horses power developed by the engines...	240.74		
Power required to work the engines *per se*......	28.21		
Power applied to the screw shaft..............	212.53	or	100.00
Power expended in overcoming the friction of the load....................................	15.94	"	7.50
Power expended in overcoming the cohesive resistance of the water to the screw blades.......	15.66	"	7.37
Power expended in the slip of the screw.........	34.38	"	16.18
Power expended in the propulsion of the simple hull..................................	146.55	"	68.95
Totals..............................	212.53	"	100.00

Thrust of the Screw.—From the above distribution of the power, the thrust of the screw can be easily ascertained. The number of horses power propelling the simple hull being 146.55, and the speed of the vessel being $\left(\frac{6.9 \times 6086}{60} =\right)$ 699.89 feet per minute, the thrust of the screw will be $\left(\frac{146.55 \times 33000}{699.89} =\right)$ 6910 pounds.

Experiments on the Drag of the Screw when the Vessel is Under Sail Alone.

During the trial trip a number of reliable experiments were made at sea to determine the diminution of the vessel's speed when under sail alone, due to the resistance of the screw both when held stationary on its shaft, and when allowed to revolve freely in the water by the pressure resulting from the forward movement of the vessel.

The experiments were made with the three cases of a light breeze abeam, a light breeze on the quarter, and a moderate breeze on the quarter, and the mean of all the trials in each case was taken for the effect due to its conditions. During every trial it was carefully observed whether the breeze remained steady, and if it changed perceptibly that trial was rejected. The water was smooth throughout and all sail was set from Courses to Royals. Under these circumstances the results for the three cases were as follows, namely:

1*st Experiment: Light Breeze on the Beam.*

Speed of the vessel per hour in geographical miles of 6086 feet, under sail alone, the screw hoisted out of water...........................	4.5
Speed of the vessel per hour in geographical miles of 6086 feet, under sail alone, the screw in water making 15 revolutions per minute......	3.8
Speed of the vessel per hour in geographical miles of 6086 feet, under sail alone, the screw in water held stationary.........................	2.8

From the results of this experiment it appears, that the diminution of the vessel's speed due to the drag of the screw when it was allowed to revolve freely in the water by the reaction of the same, was $(\frac{4.5-3.8 \times 100}{4.5}=)$ 15.55 per centum; also, that the speed of the screw (product of pitch and number of revolutions) was $(\frac{15 \times 16 \times 60}{6086}=2.366$, and $\frac{3.800-2.366 \times 100}{3.800}=)$ 37.73 per centum less than the speed of the vessel. When the screw was held stationary the diminution of the vessel's speed due to its drag, was $(\frac{4.5-2.8 \times 100}{4.5}=)$ 37.77 per centum. In comparing the speeds of the vessel with the screw first revolving in water and then held stationary, it will be seen that the diminution due its drag in the last case was $(\frac{3.8-2.8 \times 100}{3.8}=)$ 26.32 per centum of the speed in the first case.

2d Experiment: Light Breeze on the Quarter.

Speed of the vessel per hour in geographical miles of 6086 feet, under sail alone, the screw hoisted out of water............................ 5.00

Speed of the vessel per hour in geographical miles of 6086 feet, under sail alone, the screw in water making 17 revolutions per minute............ 4.25

Speed of the vessel per hour in geographical miles of 6086 feet, under sail alone, the screw in water held stationary........................... 3.20

From the results of this experiment it appears, that the diminution of the vessel's speed due to the drag of the screw when it was allowed to revolve freely in the water by the reaction of the same, was $\left(\frac{5.00-4.25\times100}{5.00}=\right)$ 15.00 per centum; also that the speed of the screw was $\left(\frac{17\times16\times60}{6086}=2.682\right.$, and $\left.\frac{4.250-2.682\times100}{4.250}=\right)$ 36.90 per centum less than the speed of the vessel. When the screw was held stationary the diminution of the vessel's speed due to its drag, was $\left(\frac{5.00-3.20\times100}{5.00}=\right)$ 36.00 per centum. In comparing the speeds of the vessel with the screw first revolving in water and then held stationary, it will be seen that the diminution due to its drag in the last case was $\left(\frac{4.25-3.20\times100}{4.25}=\right)$ 24.76 per centum of the speed in the first case.

3d Experiment: Moderate Breeze on the Quarter.

Speed of the vessel per hour in geographical miles of 6086 feet, under sail alone, the screw hoisted out of water........................... 7.00

Speed of the vessel per hour in geographical miles of 6086 feet, under sail alone, the screw in water making 25 revolutions per minute........ 6.00

Speed of the vessel per hour in geographical miles of 6086 feet, under sail alone, the screw in water held stationary...................... 4.50

From the results of this experiment it appears, that the diminution of the vessel's speed due to the drag of the screw when it was allowed to revolve freely in the water by the reaction of the same, was $(\frac{7.00-6.00 \times 100}{7.00} =)$ 14.29 per centum; also, that the speed of the screw was $(\frac{25 \times 16 \times 60}{6086} = 3.943$, and $\frac{6.000-3.943 \times 100}{6.000} =)$ 34.28 per centum less than the speed of the vessel. When the screw was held stationary the diminution of the vessel's speed due to its drag, was $(\frac{7.00-4.50 \times 100}{7.00} =)$ 35.10 per centum. In comparing the speeds of the vessel with the screw first revolving in water and then held stationary, it will be seen that the diminution due to its drag in the last case was $(\frac{6.00-4.50 \times 100}{6.00} =)$ 25.00 per centum of the speed in the first case.

The mean of the foregoing three experiments gives for the diminution of the vessel's speed under sail alone with the screw hoisted out of water, due to the drag of the screw when it was in water and revolving freely by the pressure of the same on the forward face of the blades $(\frac{15.55+15.00+14.29}{3} =)$ 14.95 per centum. When the screw is in water dragging and revolving it makes for a mean $(\frac{3.95+4.00+4.17}{3} =)$ 4.04 revolutions per minute to each geographical mile per hour of the vessel's speed; and the longitudinal speed of the screw is $(\frac{6086-4.04 \times 16 \times 60 \times 100}{6086} =)$ 36.27 per centum less than the speed of the vessel. Between the speed of the vessel under sail alone when the screw is in the water and revolves freely by the pressure on its forward surface, and when the screw is held stationary and dragged through the water, there is a difference of $(\frac{\frac{3.80+4.25+6.00}{3} - \frac{2.80+3.20+4.50}{3} \times 100}{\frac{3.80+4.25+6.00}{3}} =)$ 25.27 per centum of the speed of the first case in favor of the revolving screw.

An examination of these experiments shows, that the Drag

15

of the Screw when revolving caused a slightly less diminution of the vessel's speed at the higher than at the lower velocities. The diminution when the vessel made 4.50 miles per hour with the screw hoisted out of water, was 15.55 per centum; when the speed was increased to 5.00 miles per hour, it became 15.00 per centum; and finally, when the speed rose to 7.00 miles per hour, it fell to 14.29 per centum. This change of proportion is evidently in the right direction and indicates that at the higher speeds of 9 and 10 miles per hour the decrease would become important. It doubtless arises from the fact that as the vessel's velocity increases, the resistance of the dragging screw is lessened by a decrease of solidity in the water at the stern owing to its inability for want of time to flow in and fill solidly the vacuity left by the forward movement of the vessel. The fuller, then, the stern, the more strongly should this effect be marked, and contrasted with screw steamer models of the present day, the stern of the "MASSACHUSETTS" had full water lines.

It will be observed, that the number of revolutions made by the dragging screw per minute per mile of vessel's speed is about the same in the three experiments; as is also the reduction caused in the speed of the vessel when the screw is revolving and dragging, by holding it stationary and dragging it.

The above determination of the diminution of the vessel's speed due to the Drag of the Screw, is for sailing in perfectly smooth water when the vessel opposes only its normal resistance; but just in proportion as the water becomes rough and thereby increases that resistance, will the diminution of the speed due to the drag of the screw become less and less. The truth of this will appear if we consider, that for equal speeds of vessel—be the condition of the water what it may—the resistance of the drag of the screw, and consequently the amount of power required to overcome it, will remain the same, because the screw will make the same number of revolutions in equal times; not so, however, the power required to propel the simple hull, which, at equal speeds will vary according to the roughness of the water, becoming greater as the roughness increases. Now as the power expended in dragging the screw is a portion of the gross power propelling the vessel, it is evident that as the former increases, the latter—being constant absolutely—decreases *relatively* and becomes a less per centum of it. Hence we perceive that the diminution of the vessel's speed due to the Drag of the Screw, is greatest when sailing in perfectly smooth water, and least when sailing in the roughest water, being governed inversely by the gross power required to propel the vessel at the given speed.

To illustrate this proposition, we will determine from the foregoing data, what will be the diminution of the speed of the "MASSACHUSETTS" in water of a roughness to increase the resistance of the hull one third; a common fact in practice. Let us take the speed of the vessel at 6.9 knots per hour in *smooth* water when dragging the revolving screw; then as this drag operated a diminution of, say, 15 per centum of the speed when the screw is hoisted out of water, the vessel's speed, *ceteris paribus*, with the screw hoisted out, would be (100—15=85; and 85 : 6.9 : : 100 :) 8.118 knots per hour. On referring back to the "Distribution of the Power," we find that to propel the simple hull at a speed of 6.9 knots per hour requires 146.55 horses power; consequently, to propel it at the speed of 8.118 knots per hour would require (6.9^3 : 146.55 : : 8.118^3 :) 238.88 horses power. The difference of these powers, namely, (238.88—146.55=) 92.33 horses measures the resistance opposed by the drag of the screw at the speed of vessel 6.9 knots per hour.

If now, the vessel being under sail alone and dragging the screw revolving, the speed being the same as before, namely 6.9 knots per hour, but the water instead of being smooth as before, were so rough as to increase the normal resistance of the vessel one-third; then the power to obtain this speed will also be increased one-third, and will become instead of 146.55 horses, ($146.55\times1\frac{1}{3}=$) 195.40 horses, while the power opposed by the drag of the screw will continue the same

92.33 horses as before, because it is uninfluenced by roughness of water and depends only on speed of vessel. Now if the screw were hoisted out of water, the vessel would evidently receive an acceleration of speed equal to what would be produced by the application of an additional power of 92.33 horses; and as the speeds are in the ratio of the cube roots of the powers, the speeds would be in the ratio of $\sqrt[3]{195.40}$ to $\sqrt[3]{195.40.+92.33}$; and the speed 6.9 knots would become 7.85 knots per hour; the difference between these speeds is 0.95 knot which is $(\frac{7.85-6.9\times100}{7.85}=)$ 12 per centum of the speed of the vessel with the screw hoisted out of water, instead of 15 per centum as in smooth water.

We may then consider it established, that the diminution of the speed of the "MASSACHUSETTS" due to the drag of the screw, would be in smooth water 15 per centum; and in water of such roughness as is usually found at sea with wind sufficient to sail the vessel, 12 per centum of the speed that would have been obtained by the vessel had the screw been hoisted out of water.

Performance at Sea under the Conditions of Ordinary Practice.

The following Tables contain all that is recorded in the Log Books at the Navy Department of the performance of the vessel at sea under the conditions of ordinary practice, and with the hereinbefore described machinery. The average mean draught of water was 15 feet 8 inches. Area of greatest immersed transverse section 405 feet. Displacement 1361 tons. The average vacuum in the condenser was 25 inches of mercury per gauge. The steam was cut off at one-fourth the stroke from the commencement. In the column of "Slip of the Screw" in the Table of the "Performance under Steam and Sail," the minus mark (—) prefixed to the figures shows the per centum that the longitudinal speed of the screw is less than the speed of the vessel.

Performance of the " MASSACHUSETTS " under Steam alone.

Date.		Number of consecutive hours.	Course of the Vessel.	Wind. Direction.	Wind. Kind.	State of the Sea.	Speed of the Vessel per hour in knots of 6,086 feet.	Slip of the Screw in per Centum of its speed.	Number of double strokes of engines' pistons, and of revolutions of the screw, made per minute.	Steam pressure in boilers in pounds per square inch above the atmosphere.	Proportion of Throttle valve open.	Pounds of Anthracite consumed per Hour.
July 8 & 9,	1854.	18	E.	S. E.	Moderate breeze.	Moderate swell.	4.222	35.61	41.56	36.0	1.00	930
August 12,	"	8	S. by W.	S. W. by W.	Light "	Ordinary "	5.000	29.57	45.00	31.5	0.50	750
September 22, 23 & 24,	"	31	N. E.	On Bow.	Fresh "	Moderate "	4.057	41.73	44 13	34.1	0.50	782
November 15,	"	7	S.	S.	Light "	" "	4.429	33.83	42.43	29.0	1.00	850
December 4,	"	4	S.	S. W.	Strong "	Rough.	3.900	44.07	44.20	33.5	1.00	850
" 7 & 8,	"	20	S. W.	W.	" "	"	3.612	45.88	42.30	34.8	1.00	820
" 11,	"	10	——	On Bow.	Moderate "	Light swell.	5.206	25.00	44.00	30.2	1.00	842
" 12 & 13,	"	18	——	"	" "	" "	5.118	27.56	44.78	32.7	1.00	930
" 17,	"	11	W.	——	Calm.	Smooth.	6.000	16.60	45.60	26.0	1.00	720
January 7,	1855.	12	N. by W.	N. W. by W.	Gentle breeze.	"	5.417	23.12	44.67	25.5	0.50	771
March 9,	"	6	N. E.	——	Calm.	"	6.000	17.31	46.00	25.0	1.00	563
" 30,	"	17	W. by N.	S. W.	Gentle breeze.	Moderate swell.	5.000	32.19	46.82	25.3	0.75	559
July 16,	"	4	S. S. W.	W.	" "	Light "	6.000	27.54	52.50	32.5	1.00	600
August 26,	"	5	S.	S. W.	Light "	Smooth.	6.000	20.75	48.00	32.5	1.00	810
September 5,	"	10	E. by N.	S. W.	Light airs.	"	5.800	16.05	43.80	29.0	1.00	662
" 6,	"	12	E. by N.	W.	Light breeze.	"	5.750	21.32	46.33	32.0	1.00	745
" 6,	"	12	E. by N.	W.	" "	"	3.357	20.00	26.60	30.0	0.14	350
" 8,	"	10	S. by W.	S. S. W.	" "	"	5.800	18.29	45.00	32.0	1.00	696
" 10,	"	12	S. E.	S. W.	" "	"	5.583	23.22	46.10	27.0	1.00	648
Means,				{ 60° from ahead.	Moderate breeze.	Gentle swell.	4.859	29.05	43.42	30.8	0.82	743

Performance of the "MASSACHUSETTS" under Steam and Sail.

Date.		Number of Consecutive hours.	Course of the Vessel.	Wind.		State of the Sea.	Speed of the Vessel per hour in knots of 6,086 feet.	Slip of the Screw in per Centum of its speed.	Number of double strokes of engines' pistons, and of revolutions of the screw, made per minute.	Steam pressure in Boilers in pounds per square inch above the atmosphere.	Proportion of Throttle valve open.	Pounds of Anthracite consumed per Hour.
				Direction.	Kind.							
July 22 & 23,	1854.	15	S. E.	S. W.	Light breeze.	Moderate swell.	6.250	7.80	43.33	30.5	0.30	634
" 23 & 24,	"	19	"	"	Fresh "	" "	8.658	—13.46	48.37	27.3	0.25	634
December 11,	"	5	"	"	" "	Smooth.	9.000	—14.09	50.00	34.0	0.50	840
" 16,	"	9	S.	"	Moderate "	"	7.000	—2.85	43.14	25.0	0.33	625
January 4,	1855.	16	S. W.	S. by E.	Fresh "	Moderate swell.	8.125	—3.33	49.80	25.5	1.00	890
" 15,	"	11	N. N. E.	N. N. W.	Light "	Smooth.	6.614	13.79	48.64	26.0	0.75	675
February 10,	"	10	N.	S. E.	" "	"	5.200	15.25	38.90	22.5	0.50	440
March 31,	"	8	W. N. W.	S. W. by S.	Moderate "	Moderate swell.	6.813	0.00	43.13	26.5	0.75	595
July 22,	"	5	E. ½ S.	N. W.	" "	" "	8.000	7.79	55.00	32.5	1.00	750
September 11,	"	12	S. E.	S. W.	Light "	" "	6.167	15.37	46.20	28.0	1.00	663
Means,				Abeam.	Moderate breeze.	Moderate swell.	7.177	1.91	46.39	27.3	0.61	672

Summary of the Steam Log.

The following Summary exhibits the performance of the vessel under steam alone, under steam and sail combined, and the means of the whole, both under steam alone, and combined with sail. The piston pressures are by Indicator.

	Under Steam alone.	Under Steam and sail combined.	Mean of Under Steam alone, and combined with sail.
OBSERVED.			
Total number of hours	227	110	337
Speed of the Vessel per hour in geographical miles of 6,086 feet	4.859	7.177	5.616
Number of double strokes of engines' pistons and revolutions of the Screw made per minute	43.42	46.39	44.39
Steam pressure in boilers in pounds per square inch above atmosphere	30.8	27.3	29.7
Proportion of throttle valve open	0.82	0.61	0.75
Vacuum in Condenser in inches of mercury per gauge	25	25	25
Tons of Pennsylvania Anthracite consumed per hour	7.96	7.20	7.71
Pounds of Pennsylvania Anthracite consumed per hour	743	672	720
Pounds of Refuse in Ashes, Clinkers, and Fine Coal, per hour	176	148	167
Per Centum of the Anthracite in Refuse	$23\frac{7}{10}$	22	$23\frac{2}{10}$
State of the Sea	Gentle swell.	Moderate swell.	
State of the Wind	Moderate breeze.	Moderate breeze.	
CALCULATED.			
Slip of the Screw in per centum of its speed	29.05	1.91	19.79
Mean gross effective pressure on pistons in pounds per square inch	22.00	18.25	20.77
Gross horses power developed by the engines, by Indicator.	168.81	149.61	162.54
Pounds of Anthracite burned per hour per square foot of grate surface	8.54	7.73	8.28
Pounds of Anthracite burned per hour per square foot of heating surface	0.300	0.272	0.291
Pounds of Anthracite burned per hour per Indicated horse power	4.401	4.492	4.430
Pounds of Combustible burned per hour per Indicated horse-power.	3.359	3.502	3.402

www.ingramcontent.com/pod-product-compliance
Lightning Source LLC
LaVergne TN
LVHW020104110826
845151LV00001B/54

9781425544614